KENOSIS

KENOSIS

The Self-Emptying of Christ in Scripture and Theology

EDITED BY

Paul T. Nimmo and Keith L. Johnson

WILLIAM B. EERDMANS PUBLISHING COMPANY
GRAND RAPIDS, MICHIGAN

Wm. B. Eerdmans Publishing Co.
4035 Park East Court SE, Grand Rapids, Michigan 49546
www.eerdmans.com

28 27 26 25 24 23 22   1 2 3 4 5 6 7

ISBN 978-0-8028-7920-2

Library of Congress Cataloging-in-Publication Data

A catalog record for this book is available from the Library of Congress.

Unless otherwise noted, quotations of Scripture are from the New Revised Standard Version of the Bible.

For Bruce L. McCormack—
scholar, teacher, colleague, friend

Contents

Acknowledgments

It takes a community to publish a book, and we are fortunate to be surrounded by a supportive community of scholars, editors, family, and friends who have helped make this volume possible.

Each of the scholars who contributed to this volume made sacrifices to compose their chapters within a short time frame during a vicious global pandemic. We are deeply thankful for their scholarship and collegiality. We would also like to express our warm appreciation of our colleagues at our respective institutions, the University of Aberdeen and Wheaton College, for their friendship and encouragement throughout the disruptions of recent seasons.

We would like especially to acknowledge the contribution by Christoph Schwöbel, who submitted his chapter to us only a few weeks before his tragic passing. We remember him for the keenness of his insight, the range of his knowledge, and the charity he consistently displayed in his work. But even more, we treasure the memories of his generosity of spirit, his warm laugh, and the deep joy he displayed as he faithfully went about the task of theology.

The wonderful team at Eerdmans worked diligently to shepherd this volume through the publication process on a rather compressed schedule. We are particularly grateful to our editor, James Ernest, who believed in this project from the beginning, offered critical insights at key moments, and guided the volume through to completion. But we are also indebted to the manifold labors of Amy Kent, Laurel Draper, and J. Andrew Edwards behind the scenes.

A volume of this sort requires a significant amount of work on the part of its editors, and in our case, many of these hours were made possible by the grace and kindness of our families, who at times adjusted their lives and plans to create space for our labors. Paul Nimmo would like to thank his wife, Jill, for her patience and presence; and his children, Samuel, Daniel, Rebekah, and James, for the distraction, laughter, and hugs they provided en route. Keith Johnson would like to thank his wife, Julie, for her love and support; his children, Everett and Blake, for reminding him that there are far more important things in life than work; and his dog, Josie, who always stands ready for a frisbee break during long days of writing.

This volume is dedicated to Bruce L. McCormack, a remarkable systematic theologian and profound Christian witness, who in 2022 retired from teaching at Princeton Theological Seminary. At different times, he has been a colleague, teacher, or friend to all of the contributors to this volume. In various ways, and at diverse points, he has connected with and impacted upon their life and work—in several cases, with remarkable and transformative effect. As editors, we are hopeful that the dedication of this modest collection of essays, on a theme close to his own constructive work, offers him a small but tangible indication of the high esteem, warm appreciation, and great affection in which he is held by those around him.

Paul T. Nimmo and Keith L. Johnson
All Saints' Day, 2021

Abbreviations

BBR	*Bulletin for Biblical Research*
BDAG	Danker, Frederick W., Walter Bauer, William F. Arndt, and F. Wilbur Gingrich. *Greek-English Lexicon of the New Testament and Other Early Christian Literature.* 3rd ed. Chicago: University of Chicago Press, 2000
EC	*Early Christianity*
EKKNT	Evangelisch-katholischer Kommentar zum Neuen Testament
ICC	International Critical Commentary
IJST	*International Journal of Systematic Theology*
JBL	*Journal of Biblical Literature*
JTI	*Journal of Theological Interpretation*
MT	*Modern Theology*
NICNT	New International Commentary on the New Testament
NIGTC	New International Greek Testament Commentary
NTL	New Testament Library
SJT	*Scottish Journal of Theology*
TDNT	*Theological Dictionary of the New Testament*
VC	*Vigiliae Christianae*
WUNT	Wissenschaftliche Untersuchungen zum Neuen Testament
ZTK	*Zeitschrift für Theologie und Kirche*

Introduction

The Canvas of Kenosis

Paul T. Nimmo and Keith L. Johnson

The doctrine of kenosis concerns the biblical claim that Christ Jesus emptied and humbled himself in obedience on his way to death upon the cross. While the doctrine traditionally has been conceived as a locus in relation to Christology, its substance also bears upon the doctrine of the Trinity, the doctrines of creation and providence, the doctrine of the church, and the discipline of theological ethics. Debates about Christ's kenosis played an important role in the development of the Nicene tradition, and a line of careful consideration of the teaching by the church's most significant theologians can be traced down through the following centuries. However, the doctrine of kenosis has received more sustained treatment over the past two hundred years than at any other point in its history. A range of constructive proposals have been advanced within several different traditions, with the result that the doctrine has been firmly in the foreground of theological attention. A similar dynamic has played out in contemporary biblical studies. While much attention related to the doctrine has been focused on the so-called "Christ-hymn" of Philippians 2:5–11, biblical consideration of the theme has ranged far and wide—not only across the immediately surrounding epistolary material but also into the Gospel sources and even into the Old Testament. These developments mean that attending to the doctrine of kenosis today requires a simultaneous engagement with the complexities of biblical interpretation, historical theology, and constructive dogmatic theology. This volume is designed to guide readers into this complexity in order to achieve greater clarity and to encourage further reflection.

***

The word kenosis has its origins in Paul's description of Christ Jesus in Philippians 2. A careful consideration of the doctrine of kenosis will both begin with and remain connected to this passage, which reads:

> Let the same mind be in you that was in Christ Jesus,
>   who, though he was in the form of God,
>   did not regard equality with God
>   as something to be exploited,
>   but emptied himself,
>   taking the form of a slave,
>   being born in human likeness.
> And being found in human form,
>   he humbled himself
>   and became obedient to the point of death—
>   even death on a cross.
> Therefore God also highly exalted him
>   and gave him the name
>   that is above every name,
> so that at the name of Jesus
>   every knee should bend,
>   in heaven and on earth and under the earth,
> and every tongue should confess
>   that Jesus Christ is Lord,
>   to the glory of God the Father. (Phil 2:5–11, NRSV)

In these verses, Paul narrates a series of events that occur before, during, and after this very particular human life on earth. The narrative takes the form of a "V" pattern, in that it begins from the heights, descends to the depths, and then ascends again to the heights. The turning point occurs with the word "Therefore" (*dio*) in verse 9, when the active agent changes from Christ Jesus (vv. 6–8) to God (v. 9), and thereafter to creatures (vv. 10–11).

Remarkably, Paul depicts Christ Jesus as in some way the agent of his own human birth. While he does not explain directly *how* this is the case, he implies that Christ Jesus possesses this agency because he exists in the "form of God" (*morphē theou*) and has "equality" with God (v. 6). He gives no indication that this equality is something to which Christ Jesus has aspired, nor does he signal that Christ Jesus has been granted this status at some point. He simply depicts this equality as a mode of existence in which Christ Jesus is "subsisting" (*hyparchōn*, translated as "was" in v. 6) before the incarnation. From this divine position, Christ Jesus exercised his agency in two correlated actions. First, he "emptied" (*ekenōsen*) himself in order to be born as a human and take the "form of a slave" (*morphē doulou*). Then, second, he "humbled" (*etapeinōsen*) himself during his human life by obediently submitting his will to God, even to the point of embracing a degrading and shameful death on a cross.

The contrast between Christ Jesus's preincarnate life in the *morphē* of God and his incarnate life in the *morphē* of a slave is turned on its head when viewed in light of the fact that the direction of movement is the same in both cases: *downward*. Both before and after his human birth, there is a clear movement toward a lower status in order to fulfill the divine will. This self-humbling and self-giving movement prompts a corresponding upward movement effected by God, signaled by the "therefore" (v. 9). God vindicates Christ Jesus by exalting him to the highest possible status by giving him "the name that is above every name" (v. 9), which can be none other than the divine name. Paul immediately links this divine name to the "name of Jesus," drawing them together. He emphasizes this connection by referencing a text drawn from Isaiah, in which God says: "There is no other god besides me, a righteous God and a Savior; there is none besides me. Turn to me and be saved, all the ends of the earth! For I am God, and there is no other. By myself I have sworn, from my mouth has gone forth in righteousness a word that shall not return: 'To me every knee shall bow, every tongue shall swear'" (Isa 45:21–23). In the original context, the text from Isaiah emphasizes God's singularity and the challenge it poses to every false idol. Paul's use of this passage drives home his own point: Christ Jesus, the one who emptied himself and acted with humility and obedience, is one and the same as the God of Israel. And this is the point at which the agency of creatures enters the picture, so that they may worship Christ as Lord—and not simply any particular group of creatures, but *all* creatures.

***

In the many centuries that have followed Paul's letter, this brief narrative about Christ's descent and ascent has played an outsized role in the Christian tradition, and at times provoked raging controversy, in part because of the way in which it gestures so simply and so serenely toward so many complex metaphysical issues. Thus questions have arisen concerning the relationship between the preincarnate and the incarnate Jesus Christ—in other words, between his existence in the form of God and his existence in the form of a slave—and concerning the kind of continuity and distinction that is to be claimed on either side. Questions have also emerged regarding the way in which Christ Jesus—in the form of God and in the form of a slave—relates to God, both in terms of being and in terms of agency, and again regarding the continuity and distinction that are in view. In this connection, particular pressure on Christian thinking has arisen at the point where the narrative of kenosis reaches its critical turning point—where the relation between the depths of the incarnate one's suffering on the cross and the depths of the eternal divine being is considered. And finally, questions have also been posed regarding the appropriate ethical directives and dispositions to formulate and follow in light of the example of Jesus Christ, and regarding what it might mean to "have the same mind" that was in him (v. 5).

It is clear that a broad consensus quickly emerged in the Christian tradition in terms of how to approach this difficult text and its attendant implications. Thus, in the patristic era, there was a general willingness to subscribe to the view that the being of God in Jesus Christ was not subject to change or suffering, and that the assumption of flesh at the incarnation represented a kenosis by way of addition and concealment: the addition of human being to the Son of God and a consequent concealment of the divine glory during his life on earth. This view, or views closely related, dominated the theological scene in east and west through the medieval period and into the Reformation. At this point, however, a development in Lutheran Christology led to a new question arising in respect of kenosis. Under the assumption that in the hypostatic union, the attributes of the divine nature were communicated to the human nature, the question arose as to what the human nature did with its possession of these divine attributes in the course of his earthly history. Two possible answers arose—(1) that the incarnate Jesus Christ refrained entirely from using these communicated attributes or (2) that these communicated attributes were used, but only in secret. Caught between two equally awkward doctrinal formulations, the Lutherans finally decided broadly in favor of the former.

A rather different controversy in theological accounts of kenosis was to arise three centuries later, and again had its roots in Lutheran theology. At this point, under the influence of increasing attention to the history, humanity, and personhood of Jesus, a number of German theologians began to advance the view that in the incarnation, there was a kenosis of the divine attributes on the part of the Son of God. This allowed for the depiction of a more human Jesus Christ without the metaphysical difficulty of trying to account for two natures within one person, but at the cost of engendering major theological controversy. Nevertheless, such kenotic views remained popular for some time, transferring with lasting effect into English-speaking circles in the late nineteenth century. Indeed, the idea of an ontological kenosis of the divine being in the incarnation—and even outwith the incarnation—once again became prominent in the second half of the twentieth century. Such reinvigorated interest was spurred by various factors: the ongoing appeal of a very historical, personal account of the life of Jesus; the influence following two terrible world wars of questions of theodicy on consideration of the identity of God; and the liberationist rise in concern regarding the deleterious consequences of the ethics of self-denial usually associated with traditional accounts of kenosis. And interest in kenosis has remained strong in the opening decades of the twenty-first century as well: not only because it is a theme bequeathed by Scripture for the ongoing consideration of Christian exegetes and theologians, but also because of its capacity to invoke many of the central metaphysical claims of the Christian faith. This last feature has ensured that kenosis has remained at the forefront of theological attention and significance at a point in time when the exploration, defense, and revision of such claims represent a prominent focus of theological endeavor.

***

The present collection of essays seeks to offer a timely orientation to some of the most important historical consideration of and current research on this compelling theme. By offering soundings along an interdisciplinary trajectory, from the biblical through the historical to the constructive, this book seeks to offer an extensive overview of a wide range of exegetical and theological material, yet without any sacrifice of scholarly rigor or intensity. In this way, it seeks both to inform readers and to provoke them to consider further for themselves the complexity yet also the fruitfulness of contemplating the kenosis of Christ Jesus.

1

Kenosis and the Drama of Salvation in Philippians 2

John M. G. Barclay

The theological term kenosis derives from the phrase "he emptied himself" (*ekenōsen heauton*) in Philippians 2:7, which occurs within an evocative narrative running from 2:6 to 2:11. This is a story that, by common consent, falls into two halves: a "downward" movement expressed in three short clauses (2:6–8), followed by an "upward" trajectory also structured in three three-line sections (2:9–11). In the first half, Christ, depicted as "being in the form of God" (2:6), emptied himself (2:7) and humbled himself, becoming obedient all the way to death, even death by crucifixion (2:8). In the second half, the subject changes to "God," who "super-exalted" Jesus and gave him "the name above every name" (2:9), evoking universal worship and acknowledgment that "Jesus Christ is Lord" to the glory of God the Father (2:10–11). In contrast to the verbless articulations of divine realities found elsewhere (e.g., 1 Cor 8:6; Rom 11:36), this paragraph has at its heart a sequence of past-tense verbs whose *telos* is eschatological (2:10–11). As a sequenced narrative of actions, with named agents and shifts in agency and momentum, one may reasonably dub this story a "drama," in which every act has its place in a narrative line.[1]

---

1. For analysis of this text as drama, including comment on its theatrical language, see Susan G. Eastman, "Philippians 2:7–11: Incarnation as Mimetic Participation," *Journal for the Study of Paul and His Interpreters* 1, no. 1 (2010): 1–22; Susan G. Eastman, *Paul and the*

The compressed, poetic style of Philippians 2:6–11, its crafted design, and its use of terms unparalleled in the Pauline corpus have convinced many that the origins of this text lie before and outside Paul's letter to the Philippians, perhaps in an early Christian faith-summary or "hymn."[2] Nowadays there is less confidence in judgments concerning the historical, cultural, and liturgical origins of this text. Whatever its source, it reaches us already contextualized and interpreted by Paul, and this fact should be decisive for our own interpretation. Rather than speculate on its "original meaning," we should ask what sense can be made of this drama within the frame of Paul's theology, as articulated in this letter to the Philippians and within the corpus of Pauline letters.[3] In other words, rather than isolating this paragraph, I will ask how its allusive poetry acquires meaning within its wider literary and theological context. There is a place for the historical self-discipline that examines each text or text-segment on its own. But when a text such as this could "mean" many different things, it seems reasonable to ask what understanding is gained by placing it within the literary frame generated by its first known user, or author, Paul.[4]

I will argue that Philippians 2:6–11 is first and foremost about soteriology: kenosis (like its other motifs) is located within a drama that climaxes in a depiction of eschatological salvation, in acclamation of Jesus as Lord (2:10–11). Without this soteriological frame, neither the Christology expressed in this text nor the ethics that derive from it can be properly understood. Within God's determination of all things toward the saving Lordship of Christ, the kenosis that descends to crucifixion enables the obedience that draws all reality (even death) into the compass of God's transformative love. Because

---

Person (Grand Rapids: Eerdmans, 2017), 126–50. I gratefully acknowledge Eastman's influence on my analysis. In what follows, all translations of the New Testament are my own.

2. The pioneering analysis was Ernst Lohmeyer, *Kyrios Jesus: Eine Untersuchung zu Phil. 2,5–11* (Heidelberg: Winter, 1961; originally 1928). There is a comprehensive survey of scholarship in Ralph P. Martin, *Carmen Christi: Philippians ii.5–11 in Recent Interpretation and in the Setting of Early Christian Worship* (Cambridge: Cambridge University Press, 1967; rev. ed., Grand Rapids: Eerdmans, 1983). Subsequent debates are collected in *Where Christology Began: Essays on Philippians 2*, ed. Ralph P. Martin and Brian J. Dodd (Louisville: Westminster John Knox, 1998).

3. Because the echoes of this text reach into Colossians and Ephesians, I will occasionally include those letters within the horizon of Pauline theology, whatever their original authorship.

4. The scholarly shift in this direction was apparent and developed in Morna D. Hooker, *From Adam to Christ* (Cambridge: Cambridge University Press, 1990), 88–100 (an essay first published in 1975).

humility is not an end in itself, the Philippians' conformity to this good news entails not the imitation of "selfless" sacrifice, but a "self-with" solidarity that participates in the reconciling work of God.

Philippians 2:6–11 as a Drama of Salvation

If Philippians 2:6–11 is a narrative drama, what is it a narrative about? It is clearly a *christological* narrative, but it would be completely unparalleled for Paul to tell a story about Christ that made no difference to the condition of the world. Especially since the nineteenth century, the drama has been read in *ethical* terms, with Christ exemplifying the heroic self-humiliation that the Philippians are to imitate. As we shall see, Paul does draw out social and ethical implications, and it would be a mistake to pit soteriology *against* ethics: Paul has no interest in relating the Christ-event if it makes no difference to the way that believers behave. But both the Christology and the ethics can be understood aright only if our text is read first as a *soteriological* drama, as a depiction of how "God was in Christ reconciling the world to himself" (2 Cor 5:19).[5]

This claim may surprise New Testament scholars, who have been known to insist that "Philippians 2 makes no direct soteriological statement."[6] It is true that we find within Philippians 2:6–11 no "for us" statements and no references to sin, faith, or the church. Nonetheless, there are at least two reasons to read this text as outlining the saving movement of God toward the cosmos. First, the characteristically Pauline "even death on a cross" (2:8) evokes numerous associations in the letters of Paul, for whom "the cross" is never a bare fact, but the site of God's saving power (e.g., 1 Cor 1:18–25; Gal 3:13–14; 6:14–15). Secondly, one should read 2:9–11, the *telos* of this drama, as the installation of Jesus as *saving* Lord of the cosmos. For Paul, the acclamation "Jesus Christ is Lord" does not merely recognize the authority of Christ (as if his Lordship was an objective fact with no subjective implications);

---

5. My reading supports the main thrust of a famous article by Käsemann, while resisting his either/or between soteriology and ethics directed against Lohmeyer's ethical reading; see Ernst Käsemann, "Kritische Analyse von Phil. 2,5–11," *ZTK* 47 (1950): 313–60; English translation in *Journal for Theology and the Church* 5 (1968): 45–88. For assessment, see Robert Morgan, "Incarnation, Myth, and Theology: Ernst Käsemann's Interpretation of Philippians 2:5–11," in Martin and Dodd, *Where Christology Began*, 43–73.

6. Stephen E. Fowl, *The Story of Christ in the Ethics of Paul* (Sheffield: Sheffield Academic Press, 1990), 72. Michael J. Gorman finds it "implicitly soteriological" only if one hears intertextual echoes of Isaiah's servant songs, *Inhabiting the Cruciform God* (Grand Rapids: Eerdmans, 2009), 32n80.

it affirms allegiance to and alignment with his purposes. The (baptismal?) confession "Jesus is Lord" (1 Cor 12:3) is a self-involving declaration of faith, and Paul makes plain that "if you confess (*homologeō*) with your mouth that Jesus is Lord and believe in your heart that God raised him from the dead, you will be saved" (Rom 10:9). Those in our text who "confess" (*exomologeō*) with their tongues that Jesus Christ is Lord have recognized that God has "super-exalted" him (Phil 2:9—an act that at least includes the resurrection). As Lord of all, he is rich to all who call upon him, for "everyone who calls on the name of the Lord will be saved" (Rom 10:13, citing LXX Joel 3:5). In other words, the bending of "every knee" and the acclamation of "every tongue" in Philippians 2:10–11 is not just submission but *saving* submission, since it is through reordered alignment to the lordship of Christ that the world is rescued from its "enemies" (1 Cor 15:20–28).[7] As Paul puts it later in Philippians, those who await the "Lord Jesus Christ" (an echo of 2:11) await him as *Savior*, whose power to submit all things to himself redeems created beings from their humiliating subjection to decay (Phil 3:20–21). That submission is depicted in Philippians 2:9–11, and Jesus's eschatological power is, for Paul, not an overpowering, but a salvific reordering of creation toward its *telos*.[8] The things in heaven, on earth, and under the earth that will confess the Lordship of Christ may include nonhuman powers, but they do not *exclude* human beings, since Paul traces a close connection between the redemption of humanity and the liberation of the cosmos (Rom 8:19–23; cf. Col 1:15–23). Thus the climax of our Philippian drama is a scene in which Christ determines the destiny of the cosmos, which is restored to worship and thereby to its proper share in the glory of God.

If Philippians 2:9–11 depicts the goal of the Christ-event, how does it follow from the first half of this passage (2:6–8)?[9] The *dio kai* ("that is why," 2:9) that serves as the hinge between the two halves suggests a logical connection. Those who offer an *ethical* reading of the passage sometimes

7. The text from Isaiah 45 echoed in Phil 2:10–11 is prefaced by "Turn to me and be saved, all the ends of the earth" (Isa 45:22).

8. For the "liberation" of all creation, see Rom 8:19–21. The themes and vocabulary of Phil 2:8–11 and 3:21 are developed in Col 1:18–20 and Eph 1:19–23. I leave to one side what Phil 2:10–11 might or might not suggest regarding "universal" salvation.

9. One of the weaknesses of the purely (or primarily) "ethical" reading of Philippians 2:6–11 is its failure to account for the second half of the passage (2:9–11). This was hardly included only because it formed part of Paul's source (as if he had no option but to cite it all). But readings like mine that start with the *telos* in 2:9–11 are required to give an adequate account for what comes before.

take 2:9–11 to vindicate or validate the example of Jesus: God's exaltation of Jesus authorizes his life of humility, which provides a "Lordly example."[10] Or the reversal of Jesus's fortunes is the "reward" for his exemplary behavior, a demonstration of the "divine law" (Lohmeyer) that God lifts up the humble and delivers the oppressed. But to be installed as Lord of the cosmos is no ordinary reward or paradigmatic deliverance: Christ's Lordship is completely incommensurate with anything that humble believers could expect for themselves, even if it is the *source* of their hope (3:20–21). Those whose reading of our text is primarily *christological* find in 2:9–11 God's manifestation of the status of the one who emptied himself: God here demonstrates who the humble Jesus really is. But 2:9 depicts a substantial *change* in conditions (with the change in subject, from Christ to God): what happens in 2:9–11 does not simply *reveal* what was true in 2:6–8; it follows on from it as a *result*. So our question becomes sharper: How does the downward Christ-movement of 2:6–8 lead toward God's action in 2:9–11?

After the description of Christ "in the form of God," the downward movement in 2:7–8 is described in two sets of three clauses, each with one main verb. First, Christ "emptied himself, taking the form of a slave, coming to be in the likeness of humans" (2:7); then, "being found in form as a human being, he humbled himself, becoming obedient all the way to death, even death on a cross" (2:7–8). Leaving aside for now what it means for Christ to "empty himself" (see the next section), we may examine the explanatory clauses that follow. The "form of a slave" indicates a radical lack of power and honor. Slaves, who had no rights over property, their children, or even their own bodies were legally and socially the most powerless members of ancient society, even if a fortunate few derived influence from the power of their owners.[11] In what sense did Jesus take the form of a slave? Some suggest that Jesus is here the "slave of God" (echoing the Servant of Isaiah) whose life is lived in "obedience" (2:8). But Paul nowhere else uses that title of Jesus, whose status is that of a Son not a slave. Others find a forward reference to the cross (which was often but not only used for slaves), although Paul never himself associates the cross with slavery.[12] Since "the form of a slave" is

---

10. L. W. Hurtado, "Jesus as Lordly Example in Philippians 2:5–11," in *From Jesus to Paul: Studies in Honour of Francis Wright Beare*, ed. Peter Richardson and John C. Hurd (Waterloo, ON: Wilfrid Laurier University Press, 1984), 113–26.

11. For the conditions of Roman slaves, see Keith Bradley, *Slavery and Society at Rome* (Cambridge: Cambridge University Press, 1998).

12. For these options, see, e.g., Markus Bockmuehl, *The Epistle to the Philippians*, Black's New Testament Commentaries (London: A & C Black, 1997), 136–37; Stephen E.

immediately followed by "coming to be in the likeness of humans," it seems more likely that Jesus's slavery is part of his human condition, "under" the constraints that have befallen the whole created order. In a parallel text, Jesus is described as "born of a woman, born under the law" (Gal 4:4), the latter state described as "slavery" (Gal 4:1; 5:1) and correlated with a general condition of slavery "under the elements of the cosmos" (Gal 4:3, 9). Elsewhere the whole creation is subject to "the slavery of decay" (Rom 8:21). If death "no longer rules" (*kyrieuei*) over the risen Christ (Rom 6:9), it appears that once it did, when he died (what is subject to a *kyrios* is a *doulos*, a slave). In sharing the human lot, Christ became subject to the limiting conditions, including mortality, that rule our current created life.

In the second set of clauses (2:7–8) Jesus's self-humbling takes him all the way to death, indeed, most shamefully, death on a cross. As we know from 1 Corinthians, the term "cross" (*stauros*) evokes for Paul utter incapacity and degrading foolishness (1 Cor 1:18–25). Death—and Jesus's "cursed" death, in particular (Gal 3:13)—is as far removed from God as a human can be, the nadir in human alienation from the life of God. And that seems to be the point. Jesus goes all the way to the furthest point of human misery, in full solidarity with a broken world. Elsewhere, Paul links the dead Jesus with the "abyss" (a bottomless depth) to which one might think of "descending" to bring Jesus up (Rom 10:7). As described in Ephesians 4, he descended to the "lower parts of the earth" (Eph 4:9), probably when he joined the dead. There may be hint of this solidarity in Philippians 2:10, when the knees that bow to the exalted Lord belong to entities that are heavenly, earthly, and "beneath the earth" (*katachthonia/oi*). That last term was widely associated with death (both the dead themselves and the powers that rule the "underworld"), and Jesus's presence *even there* is integral to his capacity to be Lord of *every part* of the cosmos.[13] The logic seems to be spelled out in Romans 14:9: "For this reason Christ died and lived again, that he might be the Lord both of the dead and of the living" (Rom 14:9). That suggests that Jesus's participation in death entails not just his acceptance of human mortality or

---

Fowl, *Philippians*, The Two Horizons New Testament Commentary (Grand Rapids: Eerdmans, 2005), 97–98.

13. For *katachthonioi* as "the dead," see Otfried Hofius, *Der Christushymnus Philipper 2,6–11* (Tübingen: Mohr Siebeck, 1976), 53, with reference to the Psalms' depiction of those who "go down" to Sheol (e.g., LXX Pss. 21:30; 27:1; 29:3–4, 10; 54:16; 113:25). The language of Phil 2:10 is echoed in Ignatius, *Trall* 9.1 in the context of Jesus's death. Other early Christian texts reflect on the impact of Jesus's death on those already dead: cf. Matt 27:52–53; 1 Pet 3:19; 4:6; Gospel of Peter 10:39.

his complete self-devotion. It is his self-extension into the world of the dead, normally regarded as lost to God.[14]

Now we begin to sense why God's exaltation of Christ to universal Lordship *follows from* his kenosis and self-humbling in 2:6–8. Throughout Jesus's path of descent, even to death, he operated in "obedience" (2:8), that is, in obedience to God: this is, for Paul, Jesus's singular mark that no human being had displayed since Adam (Rom 5:12–21). Obedience indicates that there is a divine purpose in this descent, and that in his solidarity with the limitations and horrors of human life Jesus maintained an unfailing "link" with the Father. His obedience tethers the whole human experience to the life of God, holding it within God's purpose and "reach." Why? So that God's redemptive power might work from *within* the alienated world, and might absorb, enclose, and thereby *transform* what is lost. It was *because* Jesus reached to these depths but still, in obedience, was joined to the saving purposes of God, that therefore (*dio*, 2:9) God installed him as universal Lord, as the *fulfilment* of the plan to which Jesus was obedient. What is depicted in 2:9–11 is not the reward for Jesus's self-humbling obedience, but the completion of its purpose. Although the exaltation of Jesus was a reversal of his previous condition, it fulfilled the purpose of the kenosis. Jesus went to those depths not to display an ethical ideal but to envelop the full gamut of human life within the renewing love of God—a purpose that reaches its goal in the saving Lordship of Christ.

What is envisaged here is what Paul calls the "swallowing" of death by life (1 Cor 15:54; 2 Cor 5:4), the absorption and enclosure of all that is alienated from God *within* a larger, re-creative power. Jesus enters *into* the human condition in all its vulnerability in order that God may assume it and enfold it within a transformative grace. By raising the dead Jesus, God "owns" the world that Jesus has entered and transforms it by taking it up within the superior power of life, the mortal "clothed" with immortality (1 Cor 15:53–54; 2 Cor 5:2, 4).

The soteriological logic is what Morna Hooker has called "interchange" and what Susan Eastman labels "double participation": Christ participates in our condition in order that we might participate in his.[15] In order to reconcile

14. For the theological ramifications, see Edward T. Oakes, SJ, "'He Descended into Hell': The Depths of God's Self-Emptying Love on Holy Saturday in the Thought of Hans Urs von Balthasar," in *Exploring Kenotic Christology: The Self-Emptying of God*, ed. C. Stephen Evans (Oxford: Oxford University Press, 2006), 218–45.

15. Hooker, *From Adam to Christ*, 13–69; Eastman, *Paul and the Person*, 126–65. Both

the world, God made Christ "sin" so that we might become the righteousness of God in him (2 Cor 5:19–21); Christ became a curse so that we might receive the blessing of Abraham in him (Gal 3:13–14); he became poor so that by his poverty we might become rich (2 Cor 8:9). Within Philippians 2:6–11, Christ's participation in the fallen world is given significant attention, while "our" participation is depicted only within the universal acclamation of the exalted Lord (2:10–11). But it *is* depicted there, and it is not long before Paul spells it out. Just as Christ "was found" in human form (2:7), salvation consists in "being found" in Christ (3:9), and just as Christ took the "form" (*morphē*) of a slave (2:7) all the way to death, so Paul is "conformed" (*symmorphizomenos*) to his death (3:10) "in order that I might attain somehow to the resurrection of the dead" (3:11). Just as Jesus humbled (*etapeinōsen*) himself (2:8) but was exalted within the glory of God (2:11), so believers expect that their bodies of humiliation (*tapeinōsis*) will be transformed and conformed (*symmorphon*) to Jesus's glorious body, thanks to his power as Lord (3:21). Thus, the drama of the incarnation is oriented toward the incorporation of every being into the transformed cosmos under the power of Christ (or in Paul's shorthand, "in Christ").[16] That theme will be developed in Colossians (Col 1:15–20; 2:9–10) and Ephesians (Eph 1:7–10, 19–23; 2:11–22; 4:1–16), but it is already adumbrated in Paul's earliest letter: "For God has determined us not for wrath but to obtain salvation through our Lord Jesus Christ, who died for us so that whether we are awake or asleep [that is, alive or dead when he comes] we might live together with him" (1 Thess 5:9–10). Christ is "for us" (and with us) into death, that we might be "with him" in life: that is precisely the shape of the drama in Philippians 2:6–11.

"He Emptied Himself"

The Philippians 2 drama is from first to last the drama of God: at its opening Jesus is "in the form of God" (2:6), and at its close, his lordship (echoing Isa 45:23) includes him within the identity of God, "to the glory of God the Father."[17] As the opening makes clear, this is not the story of a divinized human being, raised from human status to divine: whatever the echoes of

---

reflect Irenaeus's famous tag: *factus est quod sumus nos, uti nos perficeret esse quod est ipse* (*Adv. Haer.* V praef.).

16. For "in Christ" meaning "in the hands of Christ," see Teresa Morgan, *Being 'in Christ' in the Letters of Paul* (Tübingen: Mohr Siebeck, 2020).

17. For the christological implications of Phil 2:9–11, see Richard Bauckham, *Jesus and the God of Israel* (Grand Rapids: Eerdmans, 2008), 182–232.

Adam in this narrative, this figure who *became* a human being (2:7) is "the man from heaven" (1 Cor 15:47), truly human but not what any other human has been since creation.[18] In fact, the drama of salvation sketched above requires that the human life and death of Jesus is *God's* radical self-involvement within the created world, so that the figure who is center-stage in this drama is integral to the identity of God, in origin and destiny, even if distinguished from "God" (2:9) in the sense of "the Father" (2:11).[19] The complexity here (as in 1 Cor 8:6 and Col 1:15–20) will take a long time for the church to unravel, but it is not the main focus of our text, which is concerned with Christ's action for and with humanity.

That this person "in the form of God" acts *for* the world seems to be the point of the puzzling language of Philippians 2:7. Both the rare noun *harpagmos* and the odd expression *to einai isa theō* continue to elicit hefty scholarly dispute. Although I cannot here provide the necessary philological detail, I consider that the best reading is somewhat at odds with the prevailing consensus. The phrase *to einai isa theō*, which is normally translated "equality with God," is best taken as a statement not of status but of mode or quality of being: the Greek word *isa* is an adverb ("equally/equivalently"), not an adjective ("equal"). The meaning is: he did not consider *harpagmos* to be a manner of existence equal/equivalent to God.[20] When we understand this phrase aright, it opens anew the possibility to read *harpagmos* in its most common meaning, as an act of seizing/taking. In the last fifty years, New Testament scholarship has been unduly influenced by a single article that interpreted *harpagmos* as "something to take advantage of," or "something to use for his own advantage."[21] That fitted a primarily ethical reading of this text (in effect, Christ decided not to be selfish) and was safely orthodox, since it had Christ consider how to use an equality he securely possessed (not how

18. With the vast majority of scholars, I disagree with James D. G. Dunn, *Christology in the Making* (London: SCM, 1989), 107–21, who overemphasizes Adamic themes and denies that our text contains any notion of "preexistence."

19. See the careful analysis by Wesley Hill, *Paul and the Trinity: Persons, Relations, and the Pauline Letters* (Grand Rapids: Eerdmans, 2015), 77–110.

20. The adverb *isa* can mean simply "like" (e.g., in metaphors, LXX Job 5:14; 10:10; 13:28, etc.), but the equivalence may be of different kinds, including some form of equality. For recent analysis, challenging the normal translation, see Crispin Fletcher-Louis, "The Being That Is in a Manner Equal with God (Phil 2:6c): A Self-Transforming, Incarnational Divine Ontology," *JTS* 71, no. 2 (2020): 581–627.

21. R. W. Hoover, "The *Harpagmos* Enigma: A Philological Solution," *HTR* 64 (1971): 95–119. This forms the basis for the influential treatment by N. T. Wright, *The Climax of the Covenant* (Edinburgh: T&T Clark, 1991), 56–98.

to grasp it). But this is an almost unparalleled meaning for the term, which is more naturally translated as a verbal noun, "seizing/snatching." Thus, as I read the verse, "being in the form of God, Christ did not consider seizing to be a manner of existence equivalent/equal to God."[22]

The implied contrast here may be the normal behavior of rulers (who expropriate what is not their own in conquest or exploitation) or the classic myths of Greek and Roman deities (whose sexual "conquests" and general abuses of power are often described with this vocabulary). Paul uses the cognate verb ("to seize") elsewhere (1 Thess 4:17; 2 Cor 12:2, 4), as well as the concrete noun ("thief" or "exploiter," 1 Cor 5:10, 11; 6:10), and the implied contrast is gift. Christ "gave himself for our sins" (Gal 1:4); he "loved me and gave himself for me" (Gal 2:20); "because (or though) he was rich, he made himself poor, so that by his poverty you might become rich" (2 Cor 8:9, a metaphor close to Phil 2:6). Christ reckoned the divine nature to be not taking but giving, not using creation but giving himself for it. As Paul makes clear elsewhere, it is the Christ-event that establishes this truth about God: "If God is for us, who is against us? He who did not spare his only Son but gave him up for us all, will he not also give us all things with him?" (Rom 8:31–32). Philippians 2:6–11 is the story of this gift.

"He emptied himself" indicates how this came about, but what does this "emptying" mean?[23] Once again, Paul indicates how this language is best received. Elsewhere he uses the verb *kenoō* four times, twice in relation to a boast ("emptied" in the sense of having no impact; 1 Cor 9:15; 2 Cor 9:3), once with reference to faith (Rom 4:14), and once in relation to "the cross of Christ" (1 Cor 1:17). In this last, to "empty" the cross means to render it powerless, without effect, and that sense predominates in Paul's use of the adjective *kenos* and the adverbial clause *eis kenon*: to say that God's grace to Paul was not *kenē* is to insist that it was not ineffective (1 Cor 15:10), while to assert that Paul has not labored or run *eis kenon* is to claim that his

22. This reading of *harpagmos* as "the act of snatching" was ably defended by C. F. D. Moule, "Further Reflections on Philippians 2:5–11," in *Apostolic History and the Gospel*, ed. W. Ward Gasque and Ralph P. Martin (Exeter: Paternoster Press, 1970), 264–76. It is further defended and explained (as a contrast to the normal "robbery" of rulers) in Samuel Vollenweider, *Horizonte neutestamentliche Christologie* (Tübingen: Mohr Siebeck, 2002), 263–84.

23. If there are echoes of Isaiah 53 in this text, we may note that the servant is described (in the Hebrew text) as "pouring himself out to death" (53:12). The LXX text departs from the Hebrew at this point, but the Hebrew verb used in Isa 53:12 (*'rh*) is elsewhere translated with the verb *kenoō* (Gen 24:20; 2 Chron 24:11; Ps 136:7).

efforts were not fruitless.[24] This gives good grounds for understanding "he emptied himself" as meaning "he deprived himself of power." That would fit the following clause "taking the form of a slave" (2:7), since, as we have seen, the slave is paradigmatic of the person without social, legal, or personal power. For Christ to "empty" himself as a human being would mean that he renounced the capacity to exercise power as humanly understood, humbling himself to the epitome of powerlessness, "even death on a cross" (2:8). Something here is given up, such that the human Christ is not isolated from, or immune to, human weakness, but is fully present "with" the human condition at its most vulnerable.

But now everything depends on how one understands the relationship between divine and human power, and here again Paul helps us out. In 1 Corinthians 1–2, where "death on a cross" is the central theme, Paul explores the paradox that a scene of abject human weakness (a naked man pinned helpless in agony in public view) is, humanly conceived, weakness and folly, "but for those who are called, both Jews and Greeks, Christ the power of God and the wisdom of God; for the foolishness of God is wiser than human beings, and the weakness of God is stronger than human beings" (1 Cor 1:24–25).[25] It is clear from this text that "stronger" does not mean "stronger on the same scale as humans measure strength," because in human terms there is no power on the cross, only total incapacity. The crucified Jesus can be "the power of God" only if God's power is *qualitatively different* from human power—not greater on the same scale, but operating on a different plane. Nor is it the case that God's power can be equated with human weakness or can be expressed only there: that would again place God's power on the scale of human power, only at its opposite pole. Rather, God's power is radically transcendent, such that it can be expressed *both* in humanly measured weakness *and* in humanly measured power. Because it is a different *kind* of power, it is not limited in expression to any point on the spectrum of human power. It can take effect in phenomena that humans recognize as "powerful" (e.g., the "signs and wonders" that Paul calls acts of power, Rom 15:18–19; Gal 3:5; 1 Cor 12:10). But it can *also* be expressed in

24. Adjective: 1 Thess 2:1; 1 Cor 15:10, 14, 58; adverbial clause *eis kenon*: Phil 2:16 (*bis*); 1 Thess 3:5; Gal 2:2; 2 Cor 6:1.

25. See John M. G. Barclay, "Crucifixion as Wisdom: Exploring the Ideology of a Disreputable Social Movement," in *The Wisdom and Foolishness of God: First Corinthians 1–2 in Theological Exploration*, ed. Christophe Chalamet and Hans-Christoph Askani (Minneapolis: Fortress, 2015), 1–20.

phenomena that humans experience and can categorize only as weakness (1 Cor 1:24–25; 2 Cor 12:9–10).

Divine power and human power are thus profoundly *incommensurable* kinds of power, even if we use the same term for both. We have seen that Jesus "emptied himself" in the sense that he renounced the capacity to exercise power as humanly understood. He determined that his divine life would be expressed not in the form of human power but as a "slave," subject to humiliation and death. He renounced, in other words, *one possible expression of divine power* (that is, as humanly recognizable power), but that does not mean that he renounced divine power as such. The crucified Christ is still (viewed from a perspective freed from human measurement) "the power of God" (1 Cor 1:24), and the humiliated Christ is still (when viewed aright) "the Lord of glory" (1 Cor 2:8). Thus, this kenosis is not the loss of divine power as such, nor its diminution. There is genuine loss, the loss of the capacity to express divine power in humanly powerful forms, but that does not entail that divine power is no longer at work and no longer fully powerful. Nor is this the concealment of divine power; it is the choice to exercise it only in humanly powerless forms. Divine power is here limited neither in extent nor in visibility but in its mode of expression, a limitation necessary for Christ to enter the human condition, in humble (but powerful) obedience, all the way to death. Only so could the divine self-giving enter the depths, but without losing its divine, salvific effect.

The "Kenotic" Life of the Church in Christ

The linguistic links between Philippians 2:6–11 and its surrounding context indicate that Paul expected this narrative to shape the Philippian church. We have noted how being "conformed with the death" of Christ in the hope of resurrection (Phil 3:10–11) echoes the christological drama, and how the saving effects of the lordship of Christ (2:10–11) are reflected in the eschatological hope of 3:20–21.[26] Closer to home, what immediately follows our paragraph is a conclusion (*hōste*, "therefore") urging the Philippians to "obey" (like Christ, 2:8) and to "put into effect your own salvation, for God is at work in you to effect both your desire and your action, for the sake of his good will" (2:12–13). Paul expects the Philippians to become embedded in and

---

26. For a careful analysis of Phil 3:1–11 and where kenosis is (and is not) reflected there, see Dorothea Bertschmann, "Is There a Kenosis in This Text? Reading Philippians 3:2–11 in Light of the Christ-Hymn," *JBL* 137, no. 1 (2018): 235–54.

aligned with the divine drama that leads to salvation (cf. 1:28), because "I am confident that he who began a good work in you will bring it to completion up to the day of Christ Jesus" (1:6). That "day," the eschatological *telos* of God's action, will include the universal acclamation of the lordship of Christ, as described in 2:10-11. The "downward" momentum of Christ's entry into the human condition has seized hold of the Philippians and drawn them into the reconciling momentum of the salvific drama.[27] What is asked of them is not primarily that they "imitate" Christ, or that they draw analogies from his exemplary action, but that they take their place under his lordship and participate in the drama that is heading toward its eschatological climax.[28]

If that goal is the unification of all things (*every* knee and *every* tongue) under the lordship of Christ, the momentum toward that end necessitates the unity of the community in its solidarity with Christ. Believers await the Savior (3:20) because their hope is to be "with" him (1:23). They are conformed (*symmorphizomenos*) to his death, in "solidarity" (*koinōnia*) with his sufferings (3:10), and they anticipate resurrection in a body shaped to (*symmorphon*) his glorious body: it is their union with Christ that constitutes the salvific trajectory. As a community, they are copartners in his grace (*synkoinōnoi tēs charitos*, 1:7) and in partnership with the Spirit (*koinōnia pneumatos*, 2:1), and Paul puts notable emphasis on the co-operation and common purpose of the community "in the Lord." Striving and rejoicing with Paul and with one another (1:27, 30; 2:2, 17-18, 25; 3:5; 4:2-3, 14), they should have the same mind, share the same love, and be in full accord, with a single purpose and focus (2:2; cf. 4:2). Just as every (*pan*) knee and every (*pasa*) tongue will confess Jesus as Lord (2:10-11), *all* the Philippians (*pantes hymeis*) make a single entity (1:4, 7, 8; 2:17, 26; 4:21) as they make common cause for the sake of the good news (1:5; 4:14-15).[29] The unity of the com-

---

27. As 2:12-13 makes clear, there is no zero-sum competition between divine and human agency, since God's agency both enables and energizes their strenuous activity. If they press on to grasp the "prize" of the upward calling (3:12-16), it is because they have already been grasped by Christ (3:12).

28. I take the "obedience" in 2:12 (echoing 2:8) as directed first and foremost to God (or Christ), not to Paul—or if to Paul, only because he directs their primary allegiance to Christ. Käsemann's reaction against a purely ethical reading of 2:6-11 led him to reduce its practical implications to the one demand, "obey," and in response most interpreters of 2:6-11 have sought to retrieve imitation of Christ (or better, conformity to Christ) as at least the implication of 2:6-11. For nuanced discussion, see David G. Horrell, *Solidarity and Difference: A Contemporary Reading of Paul's Ethics* (London: T&T Clark, 2005), 206-14. But it is crucial to place this conformity within its soteriological matrix, not as a moral end in itself.

29. The disunity mentioned in 4:2-3 draws out from Paul a flood of "with" (*syn-*)

munity is not just a political ambition; it is integral to the reunification of the cosmos in Christ.

This is the frame in which to read the instructions on humility (2:3–4) that are the immediate precursor to the drama of 2:6–11: "Do nothing from rivalry or hollow conceit, but in humility consider one another of higher status than yourself, each one looking not to their own interests, but also/especially to the interests of others" (2:3–4).[30] It is common among scholars to use these verses as the lens through which to read the following Christ-narrative: be humble and serve one another, as Christ became a servant and humbled himself. That makes the Christ-story primarily an *ethical* drama (an example of humility), whose ending (2:9–11) then becomes difficult to explain.[31] On my reading, this gets everything the wrong way around. Philippians 2:6–11 is first and foremost a *soteriological* narrative, the story of Christ's entry into a stricken cosmos in order to enfold it within the lifegiving and reordering power of God. Christ's humility is the means to that end, not an end in itself, and when the Philippians are called to humility in their treatment of one another that is also not an end in itself, but a necessary means toward the solidarity of the community (2:1–2), which is a central element in the salvific momentum of the Christ-event.

The instruction to look out for the interests of others (2:2–3) is importantly *reciprocal*—a command to *each* and *every* person, as they "consider *one another*" of higher status than themselves. There is no possibility that one member (or one type of member) should be subject to a one-sided exercise of power, because *everyone* is at the same time looking out for the superior interests of *everyone* else. In paradoxical but characteristic fashion, Paul's

---

terminology. It is not necessary to posit that communal disunity is the main target of this letter, but it is clear that solidarity with one another (and with Paul) is given unusual emphasis throughout. Even if suffering is the context for this appeal (1:27–30), it should not be seen as the only motivating fact.

30. The equivocation in the translation reflects a textual and linguistic uncertainty: if *kai* is to be read (some MSS omit it), how should it be construed? For discussion, see John M. G. Barclay, "Benefitting Others and Benefit to Oneself: Seneca and Paul on 'Altruism'," in *Paul and Seneca in Dialogue*, ed. Joseph R. Dodson and David E. Briones (Leiden: Brill, 2017), 109–26.

31. Recent political readings of Phil 2:6–11, which place it in contrast to the Roman quest for honor as an upside-down *cursus honorum* or a subtle dig at the Roman emperor, likewise say too little about the cosmic dimensions of 2:6–11; see, e.g., Peter Oakes, *Philippians: From People to Letter* (Cambridge: Cambridge University Press, 2001); Joseph H. Hellerman, *Reconstructing Honor in Roman Philippi: Carmen Christi as Cursus Pudorum* (Cambridge: Cambridge University Press, 2005).

path to equalization runs through not a static equality but reciprocal asymmetry (cf. Gal 5:13: "through love be slaves of one another"). This mutual service "for" one another is a necessary antidote to rivalry (the stance of the self "against" another), but its purpose is not an individualized virtue but the construction of a harmonious community: such instructions serve the vision of 2:2, that the Philippians be of the same mind and share the same love. Solidarity arises through mutual commitment, putting the self in service "for" one another in order to be fully "with" each other.

This is how the Philippians are to "conduct your social relations in a way that is worthy of the good news" (1:27). The good news is what Paul spells out in Philippians 2:6–11: Christ has entered fully into the powerlessness of the human condition, in order that through his obedience and by the lifegiving power of God all of creation might be reconciled to God under the lordship of Christ. The Philippian church sits in the middle of this drama, God operating among them with the same lifegiving power as he has enacted in the Christ-event (2:12–13). Their solidarity with one another is part of the reconciliation effected by Christ, and the means to that solidarity is the same as that of Christ. Through the humility that works *for* and *with* the other, they participate in and help bring to fruition the saving drama of Christ. In other words, in Paul's overly compressed terms, they are to adopt in their communal relations the mindset that they have "in Christ" (2:5).[32]

As we have seen, the "kenotic" movement of Christ, which grounds the resulting, parallel humility of believers, is not an end in itself. Nor is its *telos* the loss of the self. One of the reasons for the popularity of "kenotic" Christology among nineteenth- and twentieth-century British theologians was that it exemplified a "heroic" ethical ideal, matching the nineteenth-century invention of "altruism."[33] Comte's moral alternatives, "altruism" or "egoism,"

32. This verse is famously ambiguous as its second clause lacks a verb: "Think this among yourselves which also in Christ" (2:5). Many interpreters supply "was" (or "is"), with Paul pointing to the mindset of Christ—a reading that supports the ethical interpretation of what follows. But the ellipsis in Greek, with otherwise matching clauses (this/which; in/in), is best read as implying the same verb: "think this among yourselves as you think in Christ" (cf. 4:2: think the same "in the Lord"). That is, let the Philippians' social practice be moulded by their participation in the saving dynamic of the Christ-event (Morgan, *Being 'In Christ'*, 73–75). The instruction therefore parallels 1:27 where they are told to conduct their social lives in a manner worthy of the good news.

33. See Hugh Ross Mackintosh, *The Doctrine of the Person of Jesus Christ*, 2nd ed. (Edinburgh: T&T Clark, 1913), 265: "This I believe to be the profoundest motive operating in the Kenotic theories—this sense of sacrifice on the part of a pre-existent One." Such "moralising of Dogma" (P. T. Forsyth) is explicit in A. B. Bruce, *The Humiliation of Christ in Its*

created a polarity between disinterest and self-interest, selflessness and self-ishness, such that serving others' interests rather than your own became a self-standing moral ideal, the ultimate expression of love.[34] But this polarity is neither necessary nor helpful. The Pauline opposite to selfishness (that is, the "self-apart" or the "self-against") is not the loss of self, but the "self-for" that is also the "self-with," the self whose commitment to the other is not ultimately at the expense of the self (properly configured) but aims at shared benefit and conjoint flourishing. If we read the story of 2:6–11 in the wrong way, as an exemplary ethic of selflessness and self-loss, its final verses (2:9–11) are not just an excess, but a contradiction: Christ ends up not lost, but Lord of the cosmos!

As we have seen, there is true cost in Christ's kenosis, the commitment to refrain from power as humanly understood; and the acme of that kenotic path is death. But the acme is not the *telos*. Christ commits himself to be *for* and *with* humanity so that humanity may share *with him* in the telos of the story. By the same token, where believers commit themselves to be *for* and *with* each other, their goal is not to annihilate themselves, but to share together in the grace of God. Paul makes difficult choices for the sake of the Philippians (Phil 1:22–24), as do Timothy (2:19–24) and Epaphroditus (2:25–30). He is prepared to be "poured out as a libation on the sacrifice of your faith" (2:17), just as Epaphroditus risks his life because of the work of Christ (2:30). Their deaths would be the acme of their commitment to the Philippians and to Christ, but not its end. Their goal is to rejoice *together* (2:17–18) and to be "with Christ" (1:23); their names are written in the book of *life* (4:3) not death. The eschatological *telos* of their story, as of Christ's in 2:6–11, will not allow the sacrifice of the self to be the ultimate goal.[35] The goal and pattern of

---

Physical, Ethical and Official Aspects (Edinburgh: T&T Clark, 1895), 12: "I am desirous to have ground for believing that the apostle speaks here [in Philippians 2] not only of the exemplary humility of the man Jesus, but of the more wonderful, sublime self-humiliation of the pre-existent personal Son of God. For then I should have Scripture warrant for believing that *moral heroism* has a place within the sphere of the divine nature" (italics original). For Bruce, Jesus is the "Great Exemplar of self-renunciation" (*Humiliation*, 15).

34. Andrew Wernick, *Auguste Comte and the Religion of Humanity* (Cambridge: Cambridge University Press, 2008). John Stuart Mill popularized Comte's notion of disinterest, which "carries the thoughts and feelings out of the self, and fixes them on an unselfish object, loved and pursued as an end for its own sake." John Stuart Mill, *Three Essays on Religion* (London: Longmans, Green, Reader, and Dyer, 1874), 110.

35. Cf. Oliver O'Donovan, *Resurrection and Moral Order* (Leicester: Inter-Varsity Press, 1986), 249: "No account of the Christian moral life can be adequate unless it is allowed to point forward to the resurrection."

the Christ-narrative, for all its renunciation of "taking" (2:6) and of power, is to be not self-less but self-with. Wrapped within this christological narrative and moving toward its same end, believers are called to renounce whatever turns the self into a self-apart or a self-against, but that involves not the loss of the self but the relocation of the self in solidarity with the other, in shared solidarity with Christ.

Kenosis in Philippians 2 is not to be taken in isolation. It is part of a drama whose goal is the reordering and reconciliation of the cosmos under the lordship of Christ. God's movement in Christ toward humanity (and all creation) is a movement for and with what is alienated and subject to death. It involves a genuine loss (of the capacity to exercise humanly construed power)—a loss that led to the horror of crucifixion. But this is a story of salvation, not of ethical heroism, and its *telos* is not kenosis itself, but the saving lordship of Christ. The kenosis of Christ is the necessary means for God's saving presence with creation, and it stands as the preeminent work and permanent sign of God's self-giving love. But to extract kenosis from the drama, and to turn self-humiliation into an ethical end, is not only morally dangerous but a failure to appreciate its place within the whole. If what is at work in the humanly powerless Christ is "the power of God" (1 Cor 1:24), this costly kenosis has as its goal not the loss of the Savior but his reconciling rule and, together with him, not the loss of the self-giving believer, but her fulfilment in solidarity with other believers under the lifegiving sovereignty of Christ.

2

Power and Kenosis in Paul's Letter to the Romans

Beverly Roberts Gaventa

The language of kenosis is absent from Paul's letter to the Romans. By contrast with Philippians, where he writes that Christ "emptied" himself (*ekenōsen*, 2:7),[1] Romans opens with a statement about Christ and power (1:4).[2] That phrase, "Son of God in power," anticipates a major concern with power that runs through the letter. From beginning to end, Romans announces God's power for salvation, God's power in creation, and God's redemption of the disempowered. A close examination of references to power in Romans reveals that it is displayed largely in God's conflict with suprahuman powers, and the climactic point in their struggle is the death and resurrection of Jesus Christ. Yet the working of God's power often does not conform to customary notions of power, since it is displayed kenotically, especially in the handing over of God's son.

As is well known, the opening lines of Romans contain a compact summary of "the gospel of God," one that has attracted immense exegetical

1. Only in Phil 2:7 does Paul use the verb *kenoō* of Christ. In Rom 4:14; 1 Cor 1:17; 9:15; and 2 Cor 9:3, he applies it to the emptying out or vacating of something of crucial importance, such as faith, or the cross, or Paul's own apostolic boast. In addition, the verb appears in no other New Testament writing.

2. To be sure, the first thing said about Christ is that he is David's offspring *kata sarka*, also a crucial thread in the letter. Below I will examine specifically the way Christ's fleshliness functions in the working of divine power in Romans.

industry.[3] Martin Hengel once observed, "In recent years, more has been written about Romans 1:3-4 than about any other New Testament text."[4] Whether that was the case in 1976, when the sentence was published, whether it is the case decades later, or even how such a statement could be tested, this passage has received extensive scholarly attention. The exegetical tradition is replete with investigations into the origin of these lines, Paul's possible modification of them, their connection to early developments in Christology, and the relationship between flesh and spirit in Paul's thought, to name only the most obvious.

For the purposes of this chapter, I will put aside most of those questions, as my interests lie elsewhere. I will stipulate, however, that I remain skeptical about the widespread scholarly agreement that Paul is drawing on a creed or creed-like formulation already in use.[5] Even if he employs a formulation he inherited, he does so because he agrees with it. It was not forced upon him, and it is no longer possible to distinguish the pre-Pauline formula from any modifications Paul might have made.[6] I assume, therefore, that Paul is not adapting lines foreign to his own thinking, and they must be taken seriously as part of any inquiry into the substance of the letter.

As my title indicates, the focus at present is the phrase "in power" (*en dynamei*), which may be the least contested phrase in these two verses. To be sure, there is some debate about whether "in power" functions as an adverb or an adjective; that is, does it modify the participle *horisthentos*, producing "designated with power" or "powerfully designated"? Or does it modify *huiou theou*, yielding "Son of God in power"? Although Robert Jewett takes

3. An earlier short version of this paper was delivered at a 2019 session of the Institute for Biblical Research chaired by Nijay Gupta and John Goodrich, and I am grateful to them for their invitation and for the conversation on that occasion. I am also indebted to Keith Johnson and Paul Nimmo for their numerous constructive suggestions.

4. Martin Hengel, *The Son of God: The Origin of Christology and the History of Jewish-Hellenistic Religion* (Philadelphia: Fortress, 1976), 59.

5. Robert Jewett provides an extensive discussion of the factors prompting the identification of the passage as a pre-existing formulation in his "The Redaction and Use of an Early Christian Confession in Romans 1:3-4," in *The Living Text: Essays in Honor of Ernest W. Saunders*, ed. Dennis E. Groh and Robert Jewett (Lanham, MD: University Press of America, 1985), 99-122. A summary of this same argument appears in his *Romans*, Hermeneia (Minneapolis: Fortress, 2007), 97-98, 103-4. For a recent response concluding that Paul himself wrote these lines, see Robert Matthew Calhoun, *Paul's Definitions of the Gospel in Romans 1*, WUNT 2/316 (Tübingen: Mohr Siebeck, 2011), 92-106.

6. So also Michael Wolter, *Der Brief an die Römer*, EKKNT, 2 vols. (Neukirchen-Vluyn: Neukirchener, 2011), 2:78.

the phrase adverbially, as a reference to the means of Christ's designation, the tendency among other recent commentators is to take it adjectivally.[7] I concur with the adjectival reading because the issue at hand seems to be that of Jesus Christ's own power or even his powerful location at God's right hand (as in 8:32) rather than the nature of the identifying act.[8]

This distinction between adjectival and adverbial readings is important, but it also may distract from giving full attention to the possible significance of the phrase "in power." It is worth observing that every other phrase in these two verses is connected with the body of the letter in substance even if not in precise expression. Paul does not elsewhere refer to Jesus Christ as seed of David, but he does identify him with the flesh of Israel in 9:5. More specifically, in 15:12, Paul quotes Isaiah 11:10 by way of identifying Christ as the "root of Jesse," connecting Jesus with the Davidic line. The verb *horizō* ("designate") does not recur, but the compound form *proorizō* appears in 8:29–30, in reference to those God has identified in advance as siblings of Jesus Christ.[9] That Jesus is God's son recurs with some frequency (1:9, 5:10; 8:3, 29, 32), to say nothing of the multiple other expressions of their relationship. The activity of the Spirit/spirit, here expressed as a "spirit of holiness," dominates much of chapter 8, with its treatment of life in the Spirit and the Spirit's advocacy for believers. Finally, Christ's own resurrection and its consequences dominate the discussion in chapter 6. In other words, however much these expressions are distinctive, the realities to which they refer are also deeply enmeshed in the fabric of the letter.

That survey leaves aside "in power," the only remaining phrase in this summary of the gospel. Douglas Moo concludes that it means Jesus occupies "a new and more powerful position in relation to the world"; similarly, Arland Hultgren explains that it has to do with "an act of investiture of the Son with power."[10] Such claims are not wrong, although they can under-

---

7. Jewett, *Romans*, 107. Those who take it adjectivally include Wolter, *Römer*, 2:90; Arland Hultgren, *Paul's Letter to the Romans: A Commentary* (Grand Rapids: Eerdmans, 2011), 48; Richard Longenecker, *The Epistle to the Romans: A Commentary on the Greek Text*, NIGTC (Grand Rapids: Eerdmans, 2016), 68–69; Douglas Moo, *The Epistle to the Romans* (NICNT; 2nd ed.; Grand Rapids: Eerdmans, 2018), 46.

8. In addition, C. E. B. Cranfield cites the adjectival use of "in power" in 1 Cor 15:43 and 1 Thess 1:5 (*A Critical and Exegetical Commentary on the Epistle to the Romans*, 2 vols. ICC [Edinburgh: T&T Clark, 1975], 1:62).

9. As noted also in J. D. Kirk, "Appointed Son(s): An Exegetical Note on Romans 1:4 and 8:29," *BBR* 14, no. 2 (2004): 241–42.

10. Moo, *Epistle to the Romans*, 47; Hultgren, *Paul's Letter*, 48.

write the problematic denigration of the Davidic flesh of Jesus. They also overlook the extent to which preoccupation with power runs throughout Paul's letter. What I contend in this chapter is that, along with the rest of verses 3–4, the phrase "in power" also anticipates the argument of the letter; in other words, power is crucial to understanding Paul's letter to the Romans. More specifically, the divine power on display in Romans is at work for the purpose of rescuing humanity from cosmic powers that go by the name of Sin and Death, powers humanity is unable to escape or overcome. That divine power particular to the God of Jesus Christ becomes salvific in his Jewish flesh in a move consistent with a notion of kenosis. In what follows I begin with a review of power language in Romans, then take up the perils associated with such language before examining the content and contexts of power language in Romans.

The Language of Power in Romans

A good starting point is a brief review of the explicit references to the noun *dynamis* ("power"), together with the related verb and adjective. Shortly following the announcement of the "son of God in power," Paul opens the body of the letter with the claim that the gospel *is* God's power bringing about salvation. Interpretive attention to 1:16–17 focuses on salvation, the relationship between Jew and Greek, and righteousness, to say nothing of the Habakkuk citation, and those major concerns detract from the initial statement: "the gospel is God's power."[11] Yet there may well be a connection between the phrase "Son of God in power" in verse 4 and the assertion in verse 16 that "the gospel is God's power."[12] Desta Heliso has in fact suggested that the "power of God" in 1:16 is "something that is embodied in Jesus."[13] It might be better to say that the "power of God" in 1:16 is enacted in and through Jesus, but the salient point at present is that both formulations evidence the fact that the letter opens with claims about power.[14]

11. All translations of New Testament texts are mine unless otherwise indicated.

12. Jewett briefly notes this connection (*Romans*, 107) as do Calhoun (*Paul's Definitions*, 149–50) and Joshua Jipp (*Christ Is King: Paul's Royal Ideology* [Minneapolis: Fortress, 2015], 248).

13. Desta Heliso, Pistis *and the Righteous One: A Study of Romans 1:17 against the Background of Scripture and Second Temple Jewish Literature*, WUNT 2/235 (Tübingen: Mohr Siebeck, 2007), 81.

14. See also Calhoun, who identifies 1:3–4 and 1:16–17 as "definitions" of the gospel, based on ancient philosophical and rhetorical texts (*Paul's Definitions*, passim).

Immediately following this statement about God's power, verse 18 intro-duces the theme of divine wrath, which is being apocalyptically revealed against humans who suppress the truth about God. Debate persists as to the identity of the persons whom Paul invokes here, to say nothing of the func-tion of the passage itself. What is pertinent at present is Paul's comment that divine wrath comes as the result of human suppression of the truth about, among other things, God's power (1:20). Unpacking that initial assertion, Paul finds that "they" refused to worship God and reverenced objects of their own crafting, serving the "created rather than the creator" (v. 25). That is, crucial to the human refusal to acknowledge God is the rejection of, even the rebellion against, God's power as creator of all that exists.

This scenario finds a counterpart in the discussion of God's dealings with Abraham. Recalling the promise God made to Abraham concerning not just Isaac but "the world," Paul writes that Abraham "trusted God who makes the dead live and who calls into being things that do not exist" (4:17). Elab-orating on Abraham's role in 4:20–21, Paul claims that Abraham "gave glory to God" (by contrast with 1:21) and that Abraham was convinced that "what God has promised he is powerful (*dynatos*) also to do."

Paul again employs the language of power (specifically, *dynamis* and re-lated words) in relationship to God in chapter 9, when he narrates a short but rather peculiar history of Israel that resolutely emphasizes God's unilateral intervention to create and sustain Israel.[15] After recounting the birth—the calling into being—of Isaac, and the choice of Jacob rather than Esau even before the twins were born, Paul raises the obvious question of God's fair-ness: Is there injustice with God? By way of reiterating God's prerogatives, he introduces Pharaoh. Here Paul explicitly quotes Scripture: "I have raised you up for this reason, that I might demonstrate in you my power and that my name might be spread throughout all the earth." Paul is quoting the LXX of Exodus 9:16, although in the LXX the word for power is *ischys*; in Romans, the word is *dynamis*. The alteration is small, to be sure, and it is uncertain whether it is Paul's. Further, if Paul himself made the change, it is unclear whether he did so intentionally. In any case, the citation as it stands under-scores his claim that God acts upon Pharaoh in a particular way for God's own purposes, specifically, to demonstrate God's own power. Reinforcing

---

15. See Beverly Roberts Gaventa, "On the Calling-Into-Being of Israel: Romans 9:6–29," in *Between Gospel and Election: Explorations in the Interpretation of Romans 9–11*, ed. Florian Wilk and J. Ross Wagner with the assistance of Frank Schleritt, WUNT 257 (Tübingen: Mohr Siebeck, 2010), 255–69.

and generalizing this point a few lines further on, Paul writes in 9:22–23 that God may choose to make God's power known through "vessels of wrath."

Toward the end of Romans 11, while confronting gentile arrogance with respect to the "rest" of Israel whom God has hardened for the time being, Paul writes that "God is able [is powerful] to put them in again" (11:23). And in 14:4, confronting what is at least competition between those who believe they can eat anything and those who continue to observe kosher law, Paul advises both sides to cease judging one another, explaining that "the Lord" is able [is powerful] to make them stand.[16]

By contrast with this repeated attribution of *dynamis* to God, Romans has little to say about the power of humans. In fact, what Leander Keck aptly referred to as the "spiral" argument of 1:18–8:4 culminates with the declaration that humanity is *dis*empowered by virtue of its captivity to sin.[17] I refer specifically to 8:7–8: "So then, the thinking of mere flesh is at enmity with God, it does not submit to God's law, since it is not able to do that. Those who are in the flesh are not able to please God." In both sentences the expression "not able" translates *oude/ou dynamai*: humanity simply lacks the power to live according to the law, to please God. The stunning result of God's intervention in Jesus Christ is that "we" are "powerful," powerful enough to bear with the weaknesses of those who are not powerful. Contrary to our customary reference to Romans 14 as a discussion of "the weak and the strong," Paul never identifies anyone as "the strong" until 15:1, where the strong—the powerful—are strong in that they emulate Jesus.[18] And they do so, to the extent that they do, by the power (the *dynamis*) of the Holy Spirit (15:13; and see also 15:14, 19).[19]

One additional use of *dynamis* proves important, and that pertains neither to God nor to humanity. At the end of chapter 8, as Paul dramatically imagines the impossibility of anyone or anything challenging God for God's

16. Given that Paul has just recalled that "God has received him" in v. 3, the "Lord" of v. 4 would appear to be God the father, even if later in v. 9 he identifies Christ as the one who "lords it over" the dead and the living by virtue of his resurrection.

17. On the "spiral" of Romans, see Leander Keck, "What Makes Romans Tick?," in *Romans*, ed. David M. Hay and E. Elizabeth Johnson, vol. 3 of *Pauline Theology* (Minneapolis: Fortress, 1995), 3–29.

18. See Beverly Roberts Gaventa, "The Paradox of Power: Reading for the Subject in Romans 14:1–15:6," *JTI* 5, no. 1 (2011): 1–12. This appeal to unity based on Christ's action of course calls to mind the similar move in Philippians 2, from Christ's kenosis to the mindset of believers.

19. The verb *dynamai* also appears in 12:18, when Paul urges being at peace with all people, "if that is possible for you."

people, he calls out the agents who might attempt to separate "us" from God's love. Included in the list is the word "powers" (*dynameis*). The list consists of paired opposites:

death		life
angels		rulers
things present		things to come
	powers	
height		depth

Inserted between the last two pairs, as a stand-alone item, and the only such stand-alone item in the list, is "powers." This single term in turn sets up the play on words in Paul's triumphant declaration that none of these created things has the power (*dynatai*) to break God's claim on redeemed humanity (v. 39). The implications of this reference run well beyond the use of the single word, however, as will become clear below.

This survey is restricted to the appearance of *dynamis* and related words without taking into account other expressions of power. In 6:4, for example, Paul writes that Christ was raised from the dead by "the glory of the father," employing an expression that elsewhere is closely identified with the active power of God's presence.[20] The long treatment of the relationship between God and Israel (and the gentiles) in chapters 9–11 culminates in the declaration of 11:32, "God confined all to disobedience that God might have mercy on all." Paul follows that declaration by extolling God's unsearchable ways and judgments, which at least implies power to bring those about. The notorious counsel to respect authority and pay taxes in 13:1–7 is anchored in the notion that God has put governing authorities in place, that there is no authority apart from God. Closing the letter is the dramatic assurance that "the God of peace will quickly crush Satan under your feet" (16:20).

It is not too much to say that Romans constitutes one long exposition of the power of God as that power has been and is and will be at work for God's own people, which turns out to include all people. When Paul opens the letter with the declaration that Christ is "son of God in power," the phrase has clear and consequential association with this dominant concern.

---

20. See Beverly Roberts Gaventa, "The 'Glory of God' in Paul's Letter to the Romans," in *Interpretation and the Claims of the Text: Resourcing New Testament Theology; Essays in Honor of Charles H. Talbert*, ed. Jason A. Whitlark, Bruce W. Longenecker, Lidija Nova-kovic, and Mikeal C. Parsons (Waco, TX: Baylor University Press, 2014), 29–40.

Power and Its Consequences

Drawing attention to this thread in Romans is illuminating, particularly because little attention has been focused on the attribution of power to Christ in 1:4. It also raises a problem, however, since the dangers of power are all too well known. The notion that God's power is at work to save "us" can be used to license manipulation of divine power for personal gain, to fund exclusion of the "other," or to authorize human claims to power in imitation of divine power.

One specific form of this problem, and one tied closely to Romans 1:3–4, takes center stage in Anthony Umoren's dissertation, *Paul and Power Christology*. Umoren puts Paul, specifically what he refers to as Paul's power Christology in Rom 1:3–4, in conversation with popular power Christology in his own context of Nigeria. In the territory of Abuja, where he conducted his survey, he found the interpretation of that power Christology in utilitarian, materialist terms. It is Christ's power "miraculously [to] transform a negative situation to a positive one, on behalf of the one who believes."[21] Umoren finds evidence of this power Christology in "prosperity preaching, popular literature, songs and prayer," in the names given to churches, in advertising, and in testimonies.[22]

Nothing about this desire to access divine power for one's own advantage is new. Robert Matthew Calhoun investigates early Christian employment of miniature Gospels (in the form of fragments or individual statements), in some cases worn around the neck, and in others displayed within residences. At least some patristic writers regard them as whole Gospels and appear to understand them to serve protective functions. Calhoun suggests that this reasoning reflects the influence of Romans 1:16 and that Paul's identification of the gospel (event) with God's saving power was connected with the Gospel (book), so that the miniature or abbreviated form of the Gospel is itself understood to be salvific, which in this sense means it is protective of the wearer or householder.[23] In a related vein, Jennifer Strawbridge has studied the curious appearance of Romans 8:31 ("If God is for us, who is against us?") in epigraphic evidence before 604 CE, particularly on door lintels. She

---

21. Anthony Umoren, *Paul and Power Christology: Exegesis and Theology of Romans 1:3–4 in Relation to Popular Power Christology in an African Context* (Frankfurt: Peter Lang, 2008), 2 and often elsewhere.

22. Umoren, *Paul and Power Christology*, 50.

23. "The Gospel(-Amulet) as God's Power for Salvation," *EC* 10, no. 1 (2019): 21–55.

suggests that the verse may have been understood as an invocation of the whole of the passage and of that whole interpreted apotropaically; that is, God's power is being invoked at the thresholds of Christian homes to protect the inhabitants from evil.[24]

By introducing ancient technologies and practices in contemporary Nigeria, I do not intend to suggest that the power on display in Romans constitutes a problem only for "other" people and other historical eras.[25] The prosperity gospel is alive and well in North America, to say nothing of the myriad avenues toward misperceiving the implications of divine power for theological, cultural, and political ends.[26] The particular value of the investigations of Calhoun and Strawbridge lies in their demonstration of the early domestication of Paul's interpretation of divine power. And Umoren's study is especially helpful because he does not allow interpreters to persist in extolling divine power without coming to grips with the possibility of unintended consequences.

Yet rightful concern about power's abuse and its corrosive effects should not render interpretation timid when discussing divine power and empowerment. Instead, it may encourage us to examine biblical claims about divine power more carefully for indications of its ways and its means. In the *Göttingen Dogmatics* Karl Barth puts the matter with uncharacteristic brevity: "the statement 'God is power,' like the statement 'God is life,' is not reversible." To say that God is power is not to say that power is God. Further, Barth writes, "in the case of a conflict between the subject and the predicate, between God and power, it is the predicate power that fundamentally has to yield, or rather, we have to see the inadequacy of all our views or concepts of power."[27]

---

24. "Early Christian Epigraphy, Evil, and the Apotropaic Function of Romans 8.31," *VC* 71, no. 3 (2017): 315–29.

25. This discussion reflects my own value judgment about such actions and would not be satisfying to those for whom any religious conviction or practice is manipulative and delusional. As it happens, I rather appreciate the notion of marking the threshold with Romans 8:31, not unlike the Jewish mezuzah. There is a fine line between trusting in divine power and instrumentalizing or commodifying it, however, and we do well to examine our own consciences even as—or before—we examine the motives of others.

26. See, for example, Kate Bowler, *Blessed: A History of the American Prosperity Gospel* (Oxford: Oxford University Press, 2013); Kristin Kobes Du Mez, *Jesus and John Wayne: How Christian Evangelicals Corrupted a Faith and Fractured a Nation* (London: W. W. Norton, 2020). The most pervasive distortion of power lies in the claims of white supremacy, especially as those remain unexamined by white Christians, on which see James Cone, *The Cross and the Lynching Tree* (Maryknoll, NY: Orbis Books, 2011).

27. Karl Barth, *The Göttingen Dogmatics: Instruction in the Christian Religion*, trans.

Barth does not invoke Romans in that discussion, but he might well have done so. Several key moments in Romans witness to powerful acts of God that scarcely conform to standard notions of power, if power is understood only as force or coercion or violence. The first of these moments comes in the lengthy discussion in chapter 1 of gentile refusal to acknowledge God, a refusal later disclosed to be shared by Jews as well (3:9–18). In response to gentile suppression of the truth about God, refusal to acknowledge God, and idolatry, Paul writes that God "handed them over" (1:24). The same expression recurs in 1:26 and 28: "God handed them over." The verb *paradidōmi* has strong associations with the act of surrender in conflict situations.[28] Below I will suggest that the conflict here involves a third power, but at present it suffices to notice that the disclosure of God's rectifying power (*dikaiosynē*; 1:16–17) and God's wrath (1:18) takes place because God has surrendered.

Further troubling customary notions of power is 3:21–26. In that passage, Paul brings his analysis of the human problem to a close with an announcement about the "now" event, which is identified as God's righteousness through the death of Jesus Christ. Pivotal to the announcement is the claim that God "put forward" Christ as *hilastērion*, "the cover of the Ark of the Covenant."[29] Among the many other things that may (or may not) be conveyed by this term, it is at least worth observing that in Exodus 25:10–22, it is Israel that builds the cover at God's instruction. Exodus lavishes considerable detail on the instructions God gives Moses about the materials and dimension of this place where God meets Israel. But when Paul introduces the term, it is God who puts Jesus forward as the "cover of the Ark of the Covenant," not Israel. At least in a limited sense, God has taken on what had earlier been a human role. Instead of directing humans to build this cover (often referred to as the "mercy seat"), God "builds" it by putting Jesus forward.

A third instance that undermines conventional notions of power comes at the end of chapter 8. As Paul contemplates the disturbing present of be-

---

Geoffrey W. Bromiley (Grand Rapids: Eerdmans, 1991), 1:405, 408. Elsewhere Barth comments that "the power of God, real power, is opposed to 'power in itself'" (*Dogmatics in Outline*, trans. G. T. Thomson [New York: Harper & Row, 1959], 48).

28. Evidence for this assertion may be found in Beverly Roberts Gaventa, *Our Mother Saint Paul* (Louisville: Westminster John Knox, 2007), 113–24, 194–97.

29. The complex debate about translating *hilastērion* cannot be rehearsed here. It must suffice to note that the LXX regularly translates *kapporet* with *hilastērion* (e.g., Exod 25:18–22; Lev 16:2; Num 7:89). While 4 Macc 17:22 is adduced as an instance of the use of *hilastērion* as an abstract noun (propitiation), even there it appears to be a figurative use of the thing itself rather than an abstract concept.

lievers ("the sufferings of the 'now' time" in 8:18), even with the assistance of the Spirit, he epitomizes God's action in Christ by identifying God as "the one who did not withhold his own son but handed him over on behalf of all of us." In addition to the repetition of "handed over" from 1:24, 26, and 28, he adds the statement that "God did not withhold" (8:32). Although often collapsed into God's love of the son, "spare" or "withhold," like *paradidōmi*, also occurs in situations of conflict.[30] Power itself is here emptied, or at least it is emptied of association with control in service of the self, control for self-aggrandizement. God is imaged in the role of the defeated, someone forced to concede his "own son."

Other passages might be adduced to reinforce this point. The Isaiah quotation that concludes chapter 10 places God in the role of supplicant: "The whole day I have stretched out my hands" (10:21). In 15:1–3, Paul connects real power with those who bear the weaknesses of others and do not please themselves, invoking Christ, "who did not please himself." Returning to Barth's proposal that power should be learned from God rather than God from conventional notions of power, power here looks very little like coercion or destruction or force. Instead, it looks like forbearance, steadfastness, lovingkindness, even weakness. Again, power—at least in the sense of sheer strength for its own sake—is emptied out.

Divine Power in Cosmic Context

The kenotic power God exercises in Romans runs against the grain of widespread notions of power, but more can be said about that power. In this letter the question is not simply what power does but in what context it is at work. It is not simply that God's power is counterintuitive in its expressions, as explored above, but that God's power is at work in a context that includes suprahuman powers. Indeed, God's power is exercised primarily as a consequence of conflict with suprahuman powers.[31]

---

30. On *pheidomai*, see Beverly Roberts Gaventa, "Interpreting the Death of Jesus Apocalyptically," in *Jesus and Paul Reconnected: Fresh Pathways into an Old Debate*, ed. Todd D. Still (Grand Rapids: Eerdmans, 2007), 125–45.

31. The exegetical observations in this section build on my earlier work in "Neither Height nor Depth: Discerning the Cosmology of Romans," *SJT* 64, no. 3 (2011): 265–78; and "The Rhetoric of Violence and the God of Peace in Paul's Letter to the Romans," in *Paul, John, and Apocalyptic Eschatology: Studies in Honor of Martinus C. de Boer*, ed. Jan Krans, Bert Jan Lietaert Peerbolte, Peter-Ben Smit, and Arie Zwiep (Leiden: Brill, 2013), 61–75.

Romans 8:31–39 provides a vantage point from which to illumine this context. As noted earlier, in the closing lines of this passage, Paul includes "powers" (*dynameis*) among those agents that are aligned against "us." Although the list itself is varied, it features agents that are larger than human life, such as "angels" and "rulers." The passage imagines a situation in which there are agents that seek to do harm to God's people. They are "against us," they "accuse" us, they "condemn" us (vv. 31, 33, 34). That all of these actions are attempts to separate "us" from God's love is raised as a rhetorical question in verse 35, before the possibility is adamantly rejected in verses 38–39. The entirety of the paragraph assumes that God's people are under assault and that the agents who attack are such that humanity cannot resist on its own, not even that portion of humanity that now lives by the Spirit (8:9–11) and has the firstfruits of the Spirit (8:23).

The passage stands at a crucial juncture in the letter, in that it concludes the exploration of the consequences of Christ's death (begun in 5:1) and anticipates Paul's prolonged consideration of God's relationship with Israel (and the gentiles) in chapters 9–11. If Paul is not assuming both the existence and the existential threat of these powers, understanding the function of this lengthy and powerful passage becomes exceedingly difficult.[32]

Central to Paul's response to the threat posed by the powers is the comment in verse 39, which the NRSV translates as "For I am convinced that . . . nor anything else in all creation, will be able to separate us." As noted above, the Greek verb here is again *dynamai*: nothing will have the power. Nothing within the list of agents, and presumably nothing outside that list, exists that has the accusing, condemning, separating power that is able to overcome God's love in Christ Jesus. Further, that last phrase is not "anything else in all creation" but the more specific phrase *tis ktisis hetera*: "some other creature." The addition of the indefinite *tis hetera* puts these agents in their place. They are all merely creatures. This is as close as Paul comes to an ontological description of the agents, but it does seem clear that for Paul they are real, whatever their origin and ontological status.

Further, this discussion of opposing agents is not an alien intrusion in the middle of the letter. The opposing agents are glimpsed already in 1:18–32, when God hands humanity over to impurity, dishonorable passions, and an

---

32. One way of framing the problem of chapters 9–11 is as a response to 8:31–39. If nothing in all creation can separate God from God's people, what is to be said about Israel? Put bluntly, can disobedience (10:21) accomplish what the powers cannot achieve? The answer provided by 11:26 and 32 is resoundingly negative.

unperceiving mind, metonyms for the antigod powers.[33] They come into full view in chapter 5, as a result of Adam's disobedience, when Sin and Death are said to rule like kings over the entire human population (5:14, 17, 21; 6:9, 12, 14). They make slaves of humanity (6:18). They rule even over the one who attempts to keep God's holy and right and good law, in that they enslave the person through the law itself (7:12–14).[34]

As a result of their enslaving force, Adamic humanity is held captive. It exists "under Sin" (3:9), enslaved to Sin and earning Sin's wages, namely, death itself (6:23). Humanity is unable to redeem itself. The power of God intercedes, but God's conflict is not with them, not with or against any human. God intercedes to rescue humanity from its plight in a conflict that resolves the question, "Who is in charge? Who is in control of the world and humanity?"[35]

Locating this conflict between God and God's suprahuman enemies (Sin, Death, and other agents named in 8:38–39) helps us to appreciate Paul's sharp invocation of divine power. It also may help us to distinguish this working of divine power from distorted, abusive, exercise of human power. The conflict is not between God (or God's people) and humans but between God and other powers, with God acting on behalf of human beings. God's redemptive action in Romans does not authorize human power, except as that power—gifted by the Spirit—is at work for upbuilding (as in 12:3–8; 14:1–23). At the very end of the letter, Paul writes that "the God of peace will quickly crush Satan under your feet," providing an apt summary of this conflict. It is God's battle, for which "you" are the victors (or the "supervictors,"[36] in the terminology of 8:37).

This necessarily compact survey will have to suffice for now. A more extended exploration would take account of the antecedents for this conflict in the divine warrior traditions of Israel's Scripture and other Jewish liter-

---

33. For argumentation on this point, see Gaventa, *Our Mother Saint Paul*, 113–24, 194–97.

34. The classic argument for this understanding of Romans 7 appears in Paul Meyer, "The Worm at the Core of the Apple: Exegetical Reflections on Romans 7," in *The Word in This World: Essays in New Testament Exegesis and Theology*, ed. John T. Carroll, NTL (Louisville: Westminster John Knox, 2004), 57–77.

35. Eugene M. Boring, "The Language of Universal Salvation in Paul," *JBL* 105, no. 2 (1986): 283. In the same vein, Ernst Käsemann identifies the central question of apocalyptic as "Who owns the earth?" in "On Paul's Anthropology," in *Perspectives on Paul*, trans. Margaret Kohl (Philadelphia: Fortress, 1971), 25.

36. Jewett, *Romans*, 531.

ature.[37] In addition, there would need to be investigation of connections to biblical accounts of God as "almighty," according to which God's power is exercised on behalf of those on the margins.[38] Understanding power requires understanding the context(s) in which it operates, and that is especially true of God's power.

God's Kenotic Power in Christ's Kenosis

Divine power, as that power is represented in Romans, is at work in a context of conflict between God and suprahuman powers, conflict that necessitates what can reasonably be termed a rescue operation (*apolytrōsis*, 3:24). When we ask how it is that God defeats these powers, we find the answer comes in the person of Jesus Christ. God's power rescues humanity from its enslavement through Jesus Christ, whose own role is one of weakness rather than strength. Paul never says in Romans that Christ had power and put it aside, that he "emptied" himself (as he does in Phil 2:7), but among his pivotal comments about Christ are those that cohere with and reinforce the logic of kenosis.

References to Christ directly locate him within the portrait of God's power exposed in the letter, all of which identify him in terms of his death and resurrection. In 3:25, he is the "cover of the Ark of the covenant" (*hilastērion*) that God puts forward for God's own right-making purposes. In 4:25 and 8:32, God is said to hand him over, surrendering him to the powers of Sin and Death. He is raised from the dead (4:24; 6:4; 8:34) and sits at God's right hand, where he intercedes with God (8:34), a statement that assumes both the power of Christ to intercede (an act that is other-centered) and that of God to act in response to Christ's intervention. By virtue of that resurrection, he is lord of the dead and the living (14:9).

These statements reflect Paul's understanding of the relationship between God and Christ and establish their roles. They are glimpses of the kerygma Paul assumes is shared by all who are "called to be saints" (1:7). Two additional statements, however, take us further into the logic of Paul's Christology.

37. See now the extensive work of Scott Ryan in *Divine Conflict and the Divine Warrior: Listening to Romans and Other Jewish Voices*, WUNT 2/507 (Tübingen: Mohr Siebeck, 2020).

38. As in Reinhard Feldmeier and Hermann Spieckermann, *God of the Living: A Biblical Theology*, trans. Mark E. Biddle (Waco, TX: Baylor University Press, 2011), 147–99.

The first comes in 6:9–10. Paul has already introduced Christ's death as the point at which God makes things right (3:21–26), but that is only part of what he has to say about that death, not the full explication of it, as seems clear from its placement in the letter. Paul returns to the death of Christ in chapter 5, first to its reconciling achievement (5:1–11), then to its character as the central act of obedience that overturns the entire history of Adam, most crucially the reign of Sin and Death (5:12–21).

As chapter 6 takes up the implications of Christ's death and resurrection for the death and new life of believers, Paul epitomizes the event: "Christ, having been raised from the dead, no longer dies. Death no longer rules over him. For the Death he died, he died to Sin one time only,[39] and the life he lives, he lives to God" (vv. 9–10). Here Paul is emphasizing the singular character of Christ's death and life in order to prompt the Romans to understand their own death and new life, but the language used of Christ is revealing. It assumes that Death did rule over Christ and that he too was under the power of Sin. Given the partnership between Sin and Death in 5:12–21, the two cannot be separated.

There is little room here for mistaking the implication. Death ruled over Christ, just as it did over every human since the time of Adam. Christ was subject not only to Death itself but also to Sin. This statement is easily overlooked, perhaps under pressure from 2 Cor 5:21, but it rather plainly implies that Christ was under Sin's power. To be sure, 5:12–21 depicts his obedience, but it is the single act of obedience in death that is contrasted with the single act of Adam's disobedience.

The second glimpse into Paul's Christology comes in 8:3. Following on the contrast in chapter 6 between the old and the new life of believers, Paul takes up in chapter 7 the implications of his argument for understanding the Mosaic law. The problem, as he demonstrates, is not with the law itself, which is holy and right and good (v. 12), but with Sin, which has taken the law as its captive and used it to enslave the "I."[40] This is the final, the deepest point in the spiral that begins with 1:18, and it culminates in the cry for deliverance (7:24) and the declaration of that deliverance in 8:2. In 8:3 Paul sums up the situation: "God, by sending his son in the likeness of the flesh controlled by Sin and to deal with Sin, condemned Sin in the flesh [of Jesus]."

---

39. The NRSV's "once for all" suggests Paul intends "once for all people," but *ephapax* is simply a time reference, as in "once and never again" (BDAG s.v.).

40. Meyer, "The Worm at the Core of the Apple," 69–71.

Much could be said by way of explicating this translation, but at present my concern is with the assertion about God and the son.

God dealt with Sin by sending his own son in the likeness of "flesh controlled by Sin." The translation "sinful flesh," found in the NRSV, NIV, and often elsewhere, suggests a phrase composed of noun (flesh) and adjective (sinful), but what Paul writes is, more literally, "flesh of sin" (noun combined with noun). "Sinful flesh" is misleading if it is construed to mean that flesh itself is inherently sinful. In addition, "sinful flesh" ignores much of what Paul has written since 5:12 about Sin's enslaving power. The problem is not flesh but Sin. But on either translation, this statement reinforces 6:9–10: the Son whom God sent was subject to Sin and Death.

With the claim that God sent his own Son, the relationship between father and son comes into view, implying the uniqueness of this sonship. Christ is not any son, but God's own, the first, among many siblings (8:29). In addition, he comes "in the likeness" of flesh. Two things are conveyed at once by *homoiōma*: Christ both is and is not like humans.[41] He is subject to Sin and Death, along with all flesh, and yet he remains the Son whom God sent.

Paul does not here write that Christ emptied himself. He does not stipulate that the Son was something else before being sent, something that he then put off or aside. And the actor here is God, who sends "his own" son. Yet the implication of what he has written is that Christ's existence in flesh is distinct from another existence. More to the point, Christ's existence in likeness with humanity reveals that God's power in Christ is a far cry from typical human notions of power, subject as those notions are to Sin and Death. It is at this point that the language of kenosis in relation to divine power becomes appropriate.

To put it another way, something other than the fact of incarnation alone is being conveyed here. A comparison with Gal 4:4 may be instructive. There Paul writes that Christ was "born of a woman, born under the law." He is a human, born as all humans are born, born particularly a Jew (under the law). In Romans 8 the inflection is somewhat different. Here he is not simply identifying the particulars of Christ's birth as a Jew (as in 1:3; 9:4) or his taking on flesh, but his taking on of flesh that is subject to the powers of Sin and Death.

---

41. Susan G. Eastman, "Imitating Christ Imitating Us: Paul's Educational Project in Philippians," in *The Word Leaps the Gap: Essays on Scripture and Theology in Honor of Richard B. Hays*, ed. J. Ross Wagner, C. Kavin Rowe, and A. Katherine Grieb (Grand Rapids: Eerdmans, 2008), 438.

What is "emptied," not explicitly but by implication, is Christ's exemption from these powers. It is in his very weakness, his willing vulnerability to these forces, that he arrives in human life and is handed over to death. And it is precisely *this* Christ, the one who displayed weakness, who is "declared to be the Son of God in power" by his resurrection from the dead.

The Kenosis of Power

The language of kenosis is absent from Romans, but the idea of emptying is not absent. In Romans Paul anticipates the gospel he will preach at Rome (1:15), a gospel of God's son in power (1:4), of God's own power for salvation (1:16). The working of divine power pervades the whole of the letter, perhaps because Paul is also aware of the vastness of the disempowering forces of Sin and Death. Examined closely, however, the power God exercises is peculiar, so peculiar as to constitute a threat to any understanding of human power as coercive, destructive, or oppressive. By contrast, this power, emptied of its usual associations, is the power to redeem. It is, at the end, the "God of peace" who will triumph.

3

The Vocation of the Son in Colossians and Hebrews

Grant Macaskill

This essay will consider the representation of the creating, sustaining, and redeeming Son in Colossians and Hebrews, with particular attention to how the one who creates and sustains is identified with the one who redeems. These texts—which may well incorporate earlier Christian liturgical material and hence represent widespread early beliefs about Jesus—enact a seemingly deliberate strategy to associate the real humanity of Jesus with cosmic mediatorial roles which predate his life within earthly history. The authors seek to exclude understandings of the eternal Son that involve "antinomies" or "fissures"[1] between his identification as the one who mediates the existence of the cosmos and his identification as the one who mediates redemption. For them, the "mystery" that has been revealed in Christ is that the creation itself is *evangelically* conditioned, along with everything that occurs within it. Correspondingly, the Creator is *evangelically* identified; for God to create, God must be the God of the Gospel.

I have made some of these observations previously,[2] but I develop them here in critical reflection on the recent work of Bruce McCormack, who has

---

1. This language is used by Harold Attridge, *The Epistle to the Hebrews: A Commentary on the Epistle to the Hebrews*, Hermeneia (Philadelphia: Fortress, 1989), 25.
2. See Grant Macaskill, "Union(s) with Christ: Colossians 1:15–20," *Ex Auditu* 33 (2017): 93–107.

sought to develop an account of Christology that is carefully resourced and constrained by Scripture and that takes these elements seriously.[3] McCormack has been particularly attentive to the "eternal humility" of the Son and has drawn upon and reframed some of the language used in kenotic Christologies to articulate this concept, which he considers to be necessitated by Scripture. Against a certain tendency to distinguish the preincarnate, eternal Son from the incarnate Jesus, and to use the language of kenosis and humiliation only of the latter, McCormack asserts that the eternal Son must be regarded as a "composite person," that is, in ways that understand *both* his divine and human natures to constitute his eternal being.

While he draws the language of "composite person" from Chrysostom, McCormack's approach leans most heavily on Barth's "cautious affirmation of the *genus tapeinoticum*,"[4] the "predication of human attributes to the divine nature"[5] that is "the logical contrary to the *genus majestaticum*,"[6] the ascription of divine attributes to the human nature of Christ. The *genus tapeinoticum* was conceived and then rejected by both Lutheran and Reformed theologians as incompatible with the notion of divine impassibility. Barth cautiously reappropriated the concept as a means of speaking about the willed "receptivity" of the Son of God to the acts and experience of the man Jesus, such that those things are properly identified as belonging to the eternal Son. This receptivity entails not a confusion of substances, but the kind of *actualism* that is characteristic of Barth's account of being and central to his christological theology.[7] This allows a modified affirmation of divine immutability that necessitates the eternity of the elect condition of the Son within the unchanging life of God.

> If this receptivity is not to effect a change in being in the eternal Son, then it must be grounded in the sovereign and free decision by which God

3. See Bruce L. McCormack, "'With Loud Cries and Tears': The Humanity of the Son in the Epistle to the Hebrews," in *Epistle to the Hebrews and Christian Theology*, ed. Richard Bauckham et al. (Grand Rapids: Eerdmans, 2009), 37–68; Bruce L. McCormack, *The Humility of the Eternal Son: Kenotic Christology in Reformed and Ecumenical Perspective* (Cambridge: Cambridge University Press, 2021).

4. McCormack, "With Loud Cries," 48.

5. McCormack, "With Loud Cries," 48.

6. McCormack, "With Loud Cries," 49.

7. On Barth's "actualistic ontology," see Paul T. Nimmo, *Being in Action: The Theological Shape of Barth's Ethical Vision* (London: T&T Clark, 2007); an overview is provided on 4–12.

makes himself to be a God "for us" in the covenant of grace. There must be, in other words, an eternal humility of the Son which makes the second mode of being of the one God to be what it is, as distinct from the first and the third modes. To say this much is completely commensurate with saying that the Logos is already in eternity, as a consequence of eternal election, a "composite person."[8]

McCormack is careful to guard against any confusion of the natures in his representation of this "composite person" and does so by drawing upon John Owen's pneumatological Christology, which emphasizes the role of the Spirit in the acting of God upon and through the human nature of Jesus. The humanity of Jesus does not lose its essential creatureliness through amalgamation with the Logos, but it participates in the divine work and in the very identity of the Son through the Spirit's work. In drawing upon Barth's reappropriation of the *genus tapeinoticum*, read in conjunction with Owen's arguments, McCormack's account is thus a particularly Reformed species of Spirit Christology. The human nature of Jesus remains distinct from the divine, such that it is not itself eternal but temporal and finite, with particular points of conception and termination within time. The divine nature of the Son is understood to be united to this one, in all of his being and works, through the willed act of divine election internal to the unchanging God, so that the Son is never identifiable as anything other than the composite person of the mediator.

While McCormack's work takes the biblical material seriously, his interaction with exegetical discussion is understandably selective. In the essay that follows, I will seek to supplement this discussion in targeted ways that reinforce some of his core claims and that should, I think, prompt any who take Scripture seriously to recognize that something of the sort proposed by McCormack is required. I will briefly discuss the association of Jesus with mediatorial roles in 1 Corinthians 8:5–6 and will consider how this association might relate to the rhetoric of Jewish thought about the uniqueness of God. Early Christian language and imagery about the incarnation drew upon Jewish rhetoric around divine eternality and was sensitive to the intersection of the eternal and the temporal in the Christ-event; even within the New Testament period, authors were beginning to "lean in" to the challenges associated with speaking of such an intersectional reality, to reflect fruitfully

---

8. McCormack, "With Loud Cries," 50. He takes the language of "composite person" from John of Damascus.

on its implications for both creation and salvation. I will then rehearse what I have argued elsewhere about how such tendencies are visible in Colossians 1:15–29.[9] Thirdly, I will consider the Epistle to the Hebrews and note some similar elements emerging in the development of its christological account. Here, I want to be particularly attentive to the way that divine speech functions within the rendering of Christology, which I consider to be significant for how we understand the being of God in Jesus Christ.

The Name of God, Time, and Mediation: Emergent Christological Appropriations of Divine Identity in the New Testament

1 Corinthians 8:5–6 is widely understood to be an appropriation of the Shema (Deut 6:4), extended to incorporate the figure of Jesus into the identity of God.[10]

> Indeed, even though there may be so-called gods in heaven or on earth— as in fact there are many gods and many lords—yet for us there is one God, the Father, from whom are all things and for whom we exist, and one Lord, Jesus Christ, through whom are all things and through whom we exist. (1 Cor 8:5–6, NRSV)

Several points are noted as standard in commentary on these verses. First, 8:5 reflects standard rhetoric concerning the uniqueness of God in relation to the things "called" (*legomenoi*) gods and lords, building on the assertion that there is no God but One (8:4). Rhetoric of this kind is often particularly associated with the imagery of Deutero-Isaiah, where the unique relation of Israel's God to time and cosmos is repeatedly cited as the difference between this one and the idols.[11] Second, the identification of Israel's deity as "the Lord our God" (Deut 6:4) is here parsed out in such a way as to individuate God

9. Macaskill, "Union(s) with Christ."

10. I use the word "identity" here principally because the Shema is about divine self-identification. Broadly, I think the strategy visible is in line with the argument developed in Richard Bauckham, *God Crucified: Monotheism and Christology in the New Testament* (Grand Rapids: Eerdmans, 1998), though as will be clear from what follows, I think the authors are more interested in *how* Jesus is to be identified with God than Bauckham here allows.

11. See Richard Bauckham, "The Divinity of Jesus Christ in the Epistle to the Hebrews," in *The Epistle to the Hebrews and Christian Theology*, 16–17; Grant Macaskill,

the Father, "*from* whom are all things and *for* whom we are" (*ex hou ta panta kai hēmeis eis auton*), and the Lord Jesus Christ "*through* whom are all things and *through* whom we are" (*di' hou ta panta kai hēmeis di'autou*). The two are hence individuated by title, but also by the prepositions governing their relationship to "all things"; Jesus is characteristically the mediator "through" whom all things are. Third, however, while individuated, both are identified with the term "one," and hence associated with the "oneness" of God that is central to the Shema. Within the wider context, this oneness serves as the premise for the non-division of the church, which shares in the oneness of God through the one mediator and the one spirit whom all have been given to drink (12:13). Here, though, it primarily serves to summon believers to abandon any plurality of service by which they participate not just in the worship of the One God, but also of the idols. Crucially, it does this by identifying Jesus as the mediator of all creaturely existence: all things are, and exist, "through" him.

Two further points need to be noted. First, it is, specifically, "Jesus Christ" who is identified as this mediator. This may not reflect a deliberate identification of the human being, *qua* human, with the mediation of all existence, but it provides the ingredients for such an identification to be developed. Second, the saying is marked by poetical structuring (e.g., in the symmetry of the "all things" clauses) that suggests it may have been an independent saying or a component of liturgy. So, the identification of the human Jesus with cosmic, creational, and providential mediation—i.e., not only with redemption—is likely to have been early and widespread.

It is interesting that later in the same epistle, in an account that extends the central concern of this text to challenge idolatry on the basis of commitment to the one God, Paul identifies the spiritual rock from which "our fathers" (*hoi pateres hēmōn*) drank during their time in the wilderness as Christ (10:4). We may not wish to stretch the significance of this too far: Paul speaks of these events as *typoi* and it is possible that what he does here is "typological" in the sense that many would recognize today, drawing an analogy that has significance for the understanding of later events. His logic, however, seems to require that there is a genuine correspondence between the wilderness generation's experience of deliverance and that of the Corinthians to whom he writes: despite the real, Spirit-constituted[12] presence of

---

"Name Christology, Divine Aseity, and the I Am Sayings in the Fourth Gospel," *Journal of Theological Interpretation* 12 (2018): 217–41, esp. 220–30.

12. The repetition of *pneumatikos* suggests this, rather than necessarily something non-somatic.

Christ with both, they remain vulnerable to the risk of idolatry.[13] While this may be read in ways that stop short of identifying the man Jesus as present through the Spirit with *hoi pateres* in the wilderness, it reflects at minimum a willingness to coordinate the intratemporal reality of the incarnation—the life the Son of God lived within the temporal and spatial confinements of true humanity—with the eternality of God.

There is plenty of evidence to suggest that Jewish thinkers of the period understood God's relationship to time to be distinct from that of created beings, with this reflected in the divine name itself, which was understood to point toward eternality.[14] Targum Ps. Jonathan, for example, expands the divine self-identification in Deuteronomy 32:39 in temporally interesting ways: "I am he who is, and was, and I am he who will be, and there is no other God beside me: I, in my Word, kill and make alive."[15] God's unique eternality also lies at the core of the Isaianic claims to monotheism that are generally understood to resource the "I am" sayings of the Fourth Gospel: the One who identifies himself with the words *egō eimi/'anī hū* (e.g., in Isaiah 41:4, 43:10, 45:18) was before and will be after any other god, and is the only one who can claim the status of Creator. Jesus's appropriation of these sayings in the Fourth Gospel is a radical self-identification with the eternal God himself, and there is an explicitly temporal aspect to that radicality: "Before Abraham was, I am" (John 8:58).

I note this in order to highlight that in various New Testament writings there is an observable interest in how the incarnate identity of the Son as Jesus Christ relates to the history of the cosmos and his mediatorial function within it, and that this is resourced by Jewish rhetoric about the unique eternality of the one God, in which he participates. The human Jesus exists within the demarcated reality of created time, within which he is conceived and dies, but his temporal reality is *unchangeably* united to the uncreated and eternal Logos. If the authors ascribed preexistence to the Son and associated him with cosmic roles, their particular identification of the mediator of *all things* as "Jesus" at least opens the door for further association of these

---

13. Grant Macaskill, "Participation and the Ontology of the Incarnation in the Pauline Literature," in *'In Christ' in Paul: Explorations in Paul's Theology of Union and Participation*, ed. Kevin J. Vanhoozer, Constantine Campbell, and Michael Thate (Tübingen: Mohr Siebeck, 2014), 87–101.

14. See Grant Macaskill, "Name Christology, Divine Aseity, and the I Am Sayings in the Fourth Gospel," *Journal of Theological Interpretation* 12 (2018): 217–41, esp. 220–30.

15. My translation. Cf. Rev 1:8.

mediatorial roles with his status and nature as creature and human. This association, as we will see, is made explicit in Colossians and Hebrews.

The Image of the Invisible God and Firstborn of Creation: Colossians 1:15–29

Colossians 1:15–23 has often been regarded as a prior unit of tradition, perhaps a hymn, incorporated into the epistle with some modification to fit its context.[16] Modern biblical scholarship has widely questioned whether the author of the epistle is the apostle Paul himself, often preferring to ascribe it (along with Ephesians) to a later author or school, though support for the identification of the author as Paul himself has grown among critical scholarship in recent years and is no longer dismissed as a traditionalist position.[17] One of the arguments *against* Pauline authorship has centered on the relative scarcity of the pneuma within the discourse, given that this is a conspicuous theme in the indisputably Pauline material. The word occurs only twice, and only once clearly of the Holy Spirit.[18] Why this is the case is a matter of debate, but part of the explanation might be that the author is distinctively concerned to affirm the primacy of Christ within the work of God, and to avoid anything that might compromise such beliefs with a defective pneumatology, one that ascribes significance to the *pneuma* apart from Christ.[19]

A growing body of recent scholarship has been attentive to the "Jewishness" of this particular unit of text.[20] I use this word to indicate that what

16. For overview and discussion, see especially Matthew E. Gordley, *The Colossian Hymn in Context: An Exegesis in Light of Jewish and Greco-Roman Hymnic and Epistolary Conventions,* WUNT 2/228 (Tübingen: Mohr Siebeck, 2007).

17. As an interesting illustration of this, see the appendix to Paul Foster, "Who Wrote 2 Thessalonians: A Fresh Look at an Old Problem," *Journal for the Study of the New Testament* 35 (2012): 150–75. Foster's essay, as a whole, considers a range of issues on the disputed authorship of Pauline epistles and its scope is wider than just 2 Thessalonians. The appendix contains the results of a survey of opinions on the matter among attendees at the British New Testament Conference in 2011. Perhaps surprisingly, a slight majority of 51.4 percent supported Pauline authorship for Colossians and only 15.6 percent were decisively against it. Thirty-three percent were uncertain, because of the ambiguity of the evidence. See also Foster's table, listing the position taken by commentators, in his own commentary: Paul Foster, *Colossians* (London: Bloomsbury, 2016), 73–78.

18. See Foster, *Colossians,* 35–38, esp. the table on 36.

19. Foster, *Colossians,* 28–35.

20. See Christopher Rowland and Christopher R. A. Morray-Jones, *The Mystery of God: Early Jewish Mysticism and the New Testament* (Leiden: Brill, 2009), 156–64.

scholars note is not simply the presence of certain ideas or tropes from Jewish tradition and culture, but particular ways of combining and associating Scriptures.[21] Most importantly these tropes and combinations draw upon the imagery classically associated with Wisdom's role in creation and providence (particularly as found in Proverbs 8), which is commonly *figured* with Torah or with "the Word," the Memra of the Targums. The Genesis Rabbah, for example, reads Genesis 1:1 and Proverbs 8 together, quoting the latter and identifying Wisdom with the Torah, which provides the schematic plans for the cosmos. The Targums, meanwhile, will often add the phrase "by (or 'in') the/his/my Word" to references to God's act of creation. The representation of Christ as the firstborn by whom and through whom all things were made and all things are sustained quite obviously belongs within this pattern of figuration.[22]

There are four points that I think need to be noted specifically. First, the core identification of the one here described is "the Son" or, more fully, "the Son of his love"/"the beloved Son." This can be overlooked because most modern translations will observe the obviously poetic structure of the material by setting this section of the text apart from that which precedes it and beginning with a new independent clause and pronoun (e.g., NIV or NRSV: "He is the image of the invisible God," etc.). Actually, however, verse 15 begins with the relative pronoun *hos* ("who"), which makes it dependent upon the previous verses and specifically "the Son of his love," into whose kingdom God has transferred those he has rescued. So, the primary identification of the one described in these words is the Son, and his significance is itself presented within the terms of the work and the love of the Father. The beloved Son mediates the Father's work (1:12–14).

Second, while "the Son" is the primary identification of this figure, the unpacking of this identification is made in specifically "creaturely" terms. It is as "the firstborn (*prōtotokos*) of all creation" that the Son makes "all things."[23] While this term has connotations of superiority,[24] it cannot be overlooked that it identifies the creating Son precisely in terms of his status

21. For some of us, this is a good reason to be cautious about rejecting Pauline authorship, which might make better sense of these phenomena than the ascription of authorship to a later Christian writer who is not steeped in Jewish interpretative tradition.

22. See Macaskill, "Union(s) with Christ," 94.

23. The merisms—"in heaven and on earth, visible and invisible"—serve to emphasize the inclusivity of the imagery.

24. See Constantine R. Campbell, "Response to Macaskill," *Ex Auditu* 33 (2017): 109–10.

as a creature. This need not lead to an Arian interpretation; rather, it understands the creaturely nature of Jesus to be a property of the eternal Son, necessary to his work as creator and providential agent. If we are to speak of the Son as "preexistent," then, the language of the text would seem to press back on any notion that preexistence is synonymous with preembodiment. This is further reflected in the core term *eikōn*, "image," since it identifies the Son precisely in terms of his visibility and substance. In fact, as Christopher Rowland notes, the word may carry the significance that is associated with it as a loanword in the Aramaic targums, where it is used specifically of human embodiment of divine glory.[25]

Third, the text systematically coordinates the terms with which the Son's creative and providential roles are described with those describing his salvific work. He is the firstborn of all creation, and he is the firstborn of the dead; his "firstness" in both of these capacities is linked to his "firstness," his preeminence, in all things (*en pasin autos prōteuōn*, v. 18). Compounds of "first" (*prōt-*) and variants of "all" (*pas, panta*) recur and are expanded. As the "first," he is also the "head," *kephalē*, of the church, a word that stands in parallel with *archē*, "beginning." *Kephalē* indicates supremacy and reign, but it can equally have the connotation of a "source," an observation that helps to draw out further the parallelism with *archē*. The language of "all things," meanwhile, is applied inclusively to the cosmos, expanded in the merisms of visible/invisible and in heaven/on earth; but the term is also used, with a parallel inclusivity, of the work of reconciliation. At every point, then, the language used of creation and providence mirrors that used of redemption, and all such language is associated with the Son, as a participant in the creation and as the one in whom all creation participates. Interestingly, and quite conspicuously, some of the prepositional differentiation between Father and Son that we noted in 1 Corinthians 8:6 is removed or reworked here: "all things" are not only made "through him" but now, also, "for him" (1:16), a *telos* associated exclusively with the Father in the Corinthian text.

Fourth, once all of this has been done, the author speaks of Christ as "the mystery hidden from the ages and the generations, but now revealed to his holy ones (*hagioi*)" (1:26). The concept of a "mystery" here is quite clearly of a previously hidden truth that has now been disclosed, and not of something essentially or perennially "mysterious" (as we might use the word today). This association of mystery with revealed truth is common in Jewish literature from antiquity, with the Aramaic word *raz* often functioning with

25. See Rowland and Morray-Jones, *Mystery of God*, 164.

this technical sense. In the Dead Sea Scrolls, for example, the word is encountered quite commonly and typically associated with a body of truth or interpretation known to the community and seen as an eschatological gift. In the work known as 4QInstruction, the *raz nihyeh* is associated with both cosmic order and eschatological judgment, so that knowledge of it facilitates righteous living; it absorbs some of the significance associated with Wisdom or Torah but also expresses a more developed eschatological overtone.[26] There, as here, it is important that the word "mystery" does not designate a new truth, a new set of conditions, but the disclosure of an old or eternal truth that has always been operative. The analogy that I commonly use for this is the disclosure of the truth about Keyser Söze at the end of the movie *The Usual Suspects*; that truth has actually shaped the whole film, as its underlying mystery, but once the viewer knows it and rewatches the film, every scene is understood differently.

What is radical in this observation is the deliberate and strategic identification of the "mystery" with the physical body of Jesus and its biography, accomplished through the explicit parallels of language that we noted above. The eschatological, providential, and creational elements are coordinated, especially through the repetition of "all things," and their intersection runs through the "blood of the cross," by which God makes peace (1:20), and "his body of flesh" (1:22, cf. 1:24), in which reconciliation is located. The author, or the tradition that the author appropriates, seems intent on refusing any belief that the creative and providential works associated with the fullness (*plērōma*) that dwells in this one (1:19) can be separated from the physical identity of Jesus Christ.[27] This imagery of the indwelling fullness is expanded in 2:9: *hoti en autō katoikei pan to plērōma tēs theotētos sōmatikōs*. As well as using the distinctive word *theotēs*—"deity"—the expansion is interesting for its emphasis on the *sōmatikōs*, "bodily," character of the dwelling. The present tense of *katoikei* ("dwells") in 2:9 requires that the Son's present heavenly state is embodied, but the coordination with past activities in the Christ-hymn suggests that this embodiment defines all of the Son's activity.

---

26. In general, see Samuel I. Thomas, *The "Mysteries" of Qumran: Mystery, Secrecy, and Esotericism in the Dead Sea Scrolls* (Atlanta: Society of Biblical Literature, 2009). On the eschatological dimension, and the specific details of 4QInstruction, see my *Revealed Wisdom and Inaugurated Eschatology in Ancient Judaism and Early Christianity* (Leiden: Brill, 2007), 72–114.

27. Translations often add "of God" to this word, but it is simply *to plērōma*. This is accusative in form, and the verb (*eudokēsen*, 3rd singular aorist: "was pleased") lacks an obvious subject, occasioning much discussion among commentators.

The Son mediates creation as the creaturely firstborn, just as he mediates resurrection; his mediation of creation and providence parallel, at each and every point, his mediation of redemption. He does all of these as the Son; he does all of them as Jesus.

Made Lower than the Angels, Upholding All Things: Hebrews 1–2

As with Colossians 1, we begin our discussion of Hebrews by identifying the subject and finite verb that governs all that follows: "God . . . spoke" (*ho theos . . . elalēsen*). Translations tend to mask the grammar of the Greek text by using the finite verb "spoke" in both verses 1 and 2, as if the flow of the text contrasts two events of speech, but the author uses the aorist participle *lalēsas* of God's diverse acts of communication through the prophets (1:1) and reserves the aorist indicative *elalēsan* for the distinct disclosure that is made *en huiō* (1:2). While this is clearly intended to establish the unique significance of his speech *en huiō*, the arrangement actually coordinates the acts of speech with respect to God's subjecthood and identity: the very God who had variously spoken of old through prophets in these last times spoke in a Son.[28] The concern to identify properly "the Son," then, is itself located theologically, i.e., with respect to the identity of God as communicating agent.

The temporal interest of the opening sentences is conspicuous. The epistle opens with the adverbial construction *polymerōs kai polytropōs palai* ("at many times and in many ways in the past"), which is paired somewhat contrastively with *ep' eschatou tōn hēmerōn toutōn* ("in these last days").[29] The language of "the last days" or "the last things" evokes the anticipations found in a range of prophetic texts, but the addition of *toutōn* ("these") is significant: the fulfillment of hopes is not represented as an event of the future, but of the present, defined by a recent speech-act of God. The temporal quality in the imagery is developed still further by the language of "to our fathers" and "to us," which must also be seen as establishing continuity and kinship even as it articulates contrast.

Given this temporal interest, with its concern to both distinguish and connect past and present, it is striking that the second finite verb (*ethēken*)

28. There is, in fact, no article attached to Son. It is legitimate and appropriate to see the construction *en huiō* as having qualitative significance: the "Sonly" speaking of God is qualitatively different from his prophetic speaking. Cf. John Webster, "One Who Is Son: Theological Reflections on the Exordium to the Epistle to the Hebrews," in *The Epistle to the Hebrews and Christian Theology*, 78.

29. The sharply contrastive "but" found in most translations is an insertion; the Greek lacks any such word.

indicates that God "appointed" the Son to be the heir of "all things," and the third finite verb (*epoiēsen*) indicates that God "made" the world(s) through him.[30] Translations tend to mask the coordination of the three aorist verbs—all of which have God as subject—with the identity of the Son: God *spoke* in a Son, "whom" (*hon*) God *appointed* the heir of all things and "through whom" (*di' hou*) God *made* all things.

There are numerous similarities here with Colossians 1:15–23, particularly in the inclusivity or totality of the image. Again, echoes of Wisdom traditions or perhaps those of the Memra have been identified, and it is reasonable to believe that there may have been some common patterns of appropriation visible within early Christian traditions.[31] As we will see below, however, it is also clear that the author seeks to disambiguate the significance of the Son as revealer and mediator from that of other figures, resisting tendencies to identify him fully by means of these categories.

The description of the Son in 1:3 is linked into this chain by its parallel use of the relative pronoun *hos*. The pronoun here occurs in the nominative, however, which cues us to expect another finite verb of which, this time, the Son will be the subject. That verb occurs near the end of verse 3: *ekathisen*, "he sat."

Where the Son sits is clearly important—"at the right hand of the majesty in the heights"—since this location will play a key part in the various ways in which he is represented as superior to the angels. *That* he sits is also important: by sitting, he adopts not simply a position of enthronement, but a posture of rest associated with the completion of his work, his accomplishment of purification.[32] Of greatest importance, however, is *who* he is as he sits: he sits *as* the Son, and this is represented in terms precisely of his embodied disclosure of God. He sits, "being (*ōn*) the effulgence of his glory and the imprint (*charaktēr*) of his person (*hypostasis*)" and "having made (*poiēsamenos*) purification."

30. The Greek is actually *aiōnas*, the plural of *aiōn*. This could also be rendered as "ages," but the word has certain cosmic associations that are generally maintained in translations; KJV, NRSV both use "worlds," while NIV uses "universe" as the equivalent.

31. See, for example, Ben Witherington III, *Jesus the Sage: The Pilgrimage of Wisdom* (Edinburgh: T&T Clark, 1995), who notes the range of points where the New Testament preserves apparently hymnic material drawing upon Wisdom motifs in relation to the figure of Jesus (pp. 249–94), including the Colossian "hymn" (266–72) and the opening verses of Hebrews (275–82).

32. See David Moffitt, *Atonement and the Logic of Resurrection in the Epistle to the Hebrews* (Leiden: Brill, 2011), *in toto*.

This description utilizes various participles to identify the Son in terms of the conditions of his enthronement. It is interesting that while one of those participles is aorist in form (*poiēsamenos*), pointing back to his completed work of purification, the others are present (*ōn* and *pherōn*), pointing to what the Son is and what he does at the level of the cosmos presently upholding all things. Note, too, that visibility and tangibility are essential characteristics of the Son who creates, sustains, and saves: he is the "radiance/effulgence" and the "imprint" of God's being.

The author is clearly interested in the real experience of time for the human Jesus. In the next verse, the superiority of the Son to the angels is articulated using the aorist participle *genomenos*, "having become," which should be understood to indicate a change of status that is most obviously the counterpart of humiliation and is hence associated with the human Jesus. The exaltation here, then, is particularly that of the human being who has now been raised, a thread that runs through the following chapters.

This is important, because the rest of the opening chapter is particularly concerned to distinguish the status of the exalted one from that of the angels *precisely* on the basis of his humanity.[33] This is accomplished through a set of quotations from the Scriptures in which God addresses a human figure as his Son and, in doing so, associates an exalted status with that figure that is not available to the angels.

> For to which of the angels did God ever say,
> > "You are my Son;
> > > today I have begotten you"?
> > Or again,
> > > "I will be his Father,
> > > > and he will be my Son"? (1:5, NRSV)[34]

The author appears to be aware that the category of the angelic constitutes one of the options for how their readers might have understood the status

---

33. Amy Peeler, "The Son Like No Other: Comparing the Son of God to the Angelic 'Sons of God' in the Epistle to the Hebrews," in *Son, Sacrifice and Great Shepherd*, ed. David M. Moffitt and Eric F. Mason (Tübingen: Mohr Siebeck, 2020), 1–12.

34. The section weaves together Psalm 2:7, Psalm 110 (109 LXX), and 2 Sam 7:14. The texts are clearly coordinated or even conflated, something that Jewish interpretation is comfortable doing. In fact, these are commonly combined texts in Jewish messianic discourse. See Matthew Novenson, *Christ among the Messiahs: Christ Language in Paul and Messiah Language in Ancient Judaism* (Oxford: Oxford University Press, 2012).

of the exalted Jesus and seeks to close that option to them. Angels are splendid beings (1:7), but they are not enthroned as the Son is (1:8–9); they are, indeed, commanded to worship the firstborn (*prōtotokos*, 1:6)[35] when he is brought into the world,[36] so that even in his humiliation, he is treated as deserving of worship.

The communicative quality of this set of quotations is important and is part of the reason that I have used the word "vocation" in the title of this essay (the other part being simply the concern with mediatorial roles): the status of the Son *as Son* is grounded in acts of divine address and summons, and these are specifically directed toward a human being. I do not wish to be misunderstood on this point: it is not that the divinity and associated status of this human being is a consequence of a divine appointing, but that his identification as Son is rendered in communicative terms that cannot be temporally isolated from his humanity within the text. When the Father addresses the Son, he addresses "today" a human being who experiences time.

Some recent scholarship, most notably that of David Moffitt, has drawn attention to the central importance of "embodiment" within the atonement theology of Hebrews.[37] Against a trajectory of scholarship that considered the epistle to be characterized by a form of Platonism similar to that seen in Philo and that, further, understood this thought to ascribe little value to bodies, Moffitt and others have shown that the soteriology of Hebrews demands an affirmation of the "full-blooded" embodiment of Jesus as high priest and sacrifice. Atonement turns on the application of blood to the heavenly reality and to the worshipper, and on the status of the high priest as a human being. As well as affirming the physicality of both offering and offerer, this approach affirms the particularly human identity of the high priest, a theme that is developed through the emphasis on the kinship of Jesus with those whom he represents. This is exemplified in 2:10–18, where Jesus is identified as "brother" to those whom he makes holy (2:11) and is associated with those "children" (2:13–14). As in Hebrews 1, the Scriptures that are quoted center on the communicative activity between Father and Son, now shifting to the perspective of the latter, who responds "I will declare your name to my brothers" (2:12). The incorporation of these brothers into the

35. Note the use of this word, which we also saw in Colossians; both passages have been understood to incorporate earlier liturgical material, which might suggest that this word had quite widespread usage in early Christian contexts.

36. On the significance of the word *oikoumenē*, see the detailed discussion in Moffitt, *Atonement and the Logic of Resurrection*, 45–144.

37. Moffitt, *Atonement and the Logic of Resurrection*.

congregation of the holy is itself, then, a matter of communication, as the Son who communicates with the Father now shares that communication with his brethren. The identification is again directed toward distinguishing Jesus, as human, from the angels: "for it is surely not angels that he helps, but the seed of Abraham; for this reason, he had to be made like his brothers in all ways, so that he might become a merciful and faithful high priest before God, to make atonement for the sins of the people" (2:16–17). Finitude and dependency are necessary qualities of human being, defining the shape of creaturely faithfulness to God; so, the Son, in "the days of his flesh," engages in supplication "with loud cries and tears" (5:7). Suffering and service are necessary to his being made perfect (2:10; 5:9).

My own key observation is that this emphasis on the embodied humanity of the sanctifier—the *hagiazōn* (2:11)—is discernible also in the representation of the creative and providential Son in chapter 1. The embodied humanity of the Son is necessary to the logic of atonement—he "participated" (*meteschen*, 2:14) in flesh and blood, and necessarily within time, "for a little while" (2:9)—but because this participation is an act of the eternal Son, it cannot be isolated from his eternal reality.

This emerges further in the application of Melchizedek imagery to Jesus. The use of this imagery may be partly intended as a further rejection of an angel Christology: the Qumran text 11QMelkizedek is often read as a description of the angel Michael, treated as an exalted figure, and the uptake of similar imagery here, applied to a human being, can be seen as a subversion of such angel veneration. The story also, of course, provides the author with a figure who is both priest and king (7:1–2).[38] But alongside both of these, the use of Melchizedek imagery in Hebrews allows the author to consider the implications of the mediator's divine identity, particularly in relation to time:

> Without father, without mother, without genealogy, having neither beginning of days nor end of life, but resembling (*aphōmoiōmenos*: being like) the Son of God he remains a priest forever (*diēnekes*). (7:3)

The string of privatives with which this description opens has been seen to mirror the terminology of Hellenistic god-language.[39] What is particularly

38. Jewish figuration is more complex than notions of typology often allow. See my forthcoming essay "Israel's Scripture in Early Jewish Literature," in Matthias Henze and David Lincicum, *The Old Testament in the New* (Grand Rapids: Eerdmans, forthcoming).

39. Jerome H. Neyrey, "'Without Beginning of Days or End of Life' (Heb 7:3): Topos for a True Divinity," *Catholic Biblical Quarterly* 33 (1991): 439–55.

interesting is that the true basis of the figuration is in the identity of the Son of God, rather than in Melchizedek: the significance of the Son's eternal priesthood conditions the significance of Melchizedek's, rather than vice versa. Melchizedek is "like the Son."

The distinctive relevance to our study lies in the use of the word "forever," focusing as it does the description of these figures as being "without beginning of days or end of life" upon their status as "priest." The logic of Hebrews, as we have noted already, demands that a priest is truly human and truly embodied; to "remain" a "priest forever" is to inhabit this condition without beginning of days or end of life. The perfected humanity of Jesus, then, is represented in eternal terms, with its eternity not just stretching forward (having no "end of life") but also backward (having no "beginning of days"). That his blood effects "the eternal covenant" (13:20) is striking, as is the fact that he offers it through the "eternal Spirit" (9:14).

This casts into somewhat different light the language of 2:9: "we do see Jesus, who for a little while (*brachu*) was made lower than the angels, now crowned with glory and honor because of the suffering of death." The author affirms the real experience of created time by the mediator, but maps this onto his eternal status as priest. This is intelligible if we understand it to be a function of the eternal union between the Son and the human history of Jesus: the wording calls attention to the temporal particularity of humiliation that is contained within the eternal being of the Son.

Conclusions: Synthesis and Implications for a "Kenotic" Christology

I remain nervous about any attempts to use the noun "kenosis" or the adjective "kenotic," since transforming the verb used in Philippians 2:7 into nominal and adjectival forms will potentially determine it in ways that move beyond its native verbal significance. This caution aside, the representation of the eternal Son that we have considered in these texts provides much to give further support and detail to McCormack's core claims.

First, in speaking of the Son's mediatorial work in creation and providence, all the texts we have considered use language proper to "the composite person." That is, when these texts describe the eternal Son in his eternal roles, they identify him either as Jesus (1 Cor 8:6) or as a creature (Col 1:15), placing an emphasis on his visibility and materiality (Heb 1:3). There is no willingness to speak of the Son in terms that suggest he was ever identifiable as something other than this. Even though some of the language is indicative of change, of the Son's becoming something that he was not previously, there are other elements within the texts that balance this language, pressing the reader to consider how the temporality necessary to the human nature of Jesus, with its proper contingency, relates to the eternal reality of the Son, with its proper aseity. In representing this "composite person," they draw upon the Wisdom traditions, since these provide resources by which a personal entity might be understood as an embodiment of divine will, and thus identified in divine terms. Hence, these traditions provide some of the resources by which a personal individuation can be introduced to discourse about the One God and his agency within the world. But the New Testament writings move into distinctive territory by identifying this Wisdom with a specific human individual and incorporating the narrative of his life and death into the imagery.

Second, Hebrews and Colossians associate the creaturely and temporal identifiers proper to the human nature of Jesus with the Son, *qua* Son. That is to say that the elements of exaltation and humiliation are coordinated with respect to this particular person, identified with this particular title. The Son cannot be identified apart from Jesus.

Third, the texts strategically coordinate the creational, providential, and redemptive work of the Son by establishing terminological links between them that resist any attempts to compartmentalize them. The humility and finitude of Jesus are properties of the creative and providential Son, as they are properties of the redeeming Son, the eternal high priest; and, of course, the "beloved" Son is by definition identified in relation to the Father. The effect is to ensure that the Father's Son is "characterized" by his humility and finitude, even in his identification as the mediator of cosmic roles.

Fourth, specifically in the case of Hebrews, it is noteworthy that the identity of the Son, again *qua* Son, is specifically represented in communicative terms and that the acts of communication are between God and a human being. The "being" of the Son *as* Son is represented in relational and vocational terms, constituted in communicative dialogue with the Father. While this may not provide decisive support for McCormack's development of two-natures Christology, which he roots in an account of being as act, it at least points in the direction of such an approach: the Son eternally relates to the Father with the humility constituted in the incarnation.

Whether McCormack's actualist and pneumatological account of the divine and human natures can be maintained as a reading of the New Testament, or whether it does adequate justice to the development of patristic thought, will require a good deal more theologically sensitive work by biblical scholars. I hope, though, that this essay has shown that such ways of speaking about the relationship of the temporal and eternal in the incarnation are traceable to the New Testament writings themselves—where they determinedly coordinate creation, providence, and redemption—and should not be regarded as alien developments within speculative theologies.

4

The Divine Name as a Form of Kenosis in Both Biblical Testaments

Rinse H. Reeling Brouwer

The *Synopsis Purioris Theologiae* contains a series of Disputations held at Leiden University, and it appeared in 1625 because of the need for clarification of Reformed doctrine after the troubles that had led to the Synod of Dort of 1618–19. In the Third Disputation, "Concerning the Canonical and Apocryphal Books," its president Antonius Thysius drafted the following, twentieth thesis:[1] "The canonical books, and thus the canon, at first comprised the Books of Moses."[2] To this initial canon other texts—namely, historical, didactic, and prophetic books and the New Testament—were then added for various reasons. And thus, the thesis concludes:

1. *Synopsis Purioris Theologiae—Synopsis of a Purer Theology*, Latin Text with English Translation, Studies in Medieval and Reformation Traditions, ed. Dolf te Velde (Leiden: Brill, 2015), 1:86–87. Previously, the *disputatio* that was held on March 21, 1620, had been published separately. See D. Sinnema and H. van den Belt, "The *Synopsis Purioris Theologiae* as a Disputation Cycle," *Church History and Religious Culture* 92 (2012): 505–37.

2. Reference is to Deut 4:2 (the "canonical formula") and Rom 2:17–20. Despite the apostle's irony, for Thysius what Paul said of the Jews is apparently true, namely that they have "a corrector of the foolish, a teacher of children, having in the law the embodiment (*morphōsis*) of knowledge and truth" (v. 20).

As the Old Testament is the foundation of the New, so the New Testament is the fulfilment of the Old. And so the canon was not made complete by means of these books insofar as the universal doctrines of salvation are concerned, but insofar as their unique qualities, clarity and evidence are concerned.[3]

This last sentence assumes some premises that are questionable for our modern consciousness, such as the historical premise that the Pentateuch, with Moses himself as its author, contains the oldest parts of the biblical canon, and the philosophical premises that the perfection of the whole should also be essentially present in all its parts and that universal truth cannot include any development. Nevertheless, Karl Barth, who refers to the thesis from the Leiden Synopsis (as well as to a similar sentence of William Bucanus[4])—and who undoubtedly did not subscribe to the premises I mentioned—could write: "We can say that this is too bold a view. In any case, it is gratuitous, for we do not have to do now only with the Pentateuch. But I cannot see where it is wrong. If all scripture does in fact attest one thing, it cannot be denied that if we only know one part of it, it attests it perfectly even in that part."[5]

Barth's approbation concerns the presence of the whole doctrine of salvation in all the parts of Scripture, not specifically its presence in the "Books of Moses." In my valedictory lecture as professor of biblical hermeneutics on May 7, 2019, I announced a project in which, starting from the theses of orthodox Reformed theologians such as Thysius and Bucanus, I aim to explore the possibilities of developing *quaestiones* in Christian doctrine from within the Torah, albeit self-evidently not from the Torah as a collection of texts in isolation from the canon as a whole.[6] The present chapter—in which

3. "Adeoque hisce libris Canon non est factus perfectior, quoad universalia salutis dogmata, sed quoad eorum singularitatem, claritatem et evidentiam."

4. Guielmi Bucanus, *Institutiones Theologiae, seu Locorum communium christianae religionis* etc. (Bern: Iohannes & Isaïas le Preux, 1605), Locus IV, xi. Quaestio, 40–41: "Quando tantum quinque libri Mosis fuerunt, sufficientes fuerunt. His autem accesserunt Prophetae tamquam interpretes. Erat ergo Vetus Testamentum integrum et sufficiens quoad sensum, etsi quod non quod ad verba: accessione igitur Novi, non perfectius, sed clarius factum est."

5. Karl Barth, *Church Dogmatics* I/2, ed. G. W. Bromiley and T. F. Torrance, trans. G. T. Thomson and Harold Knight (Edinburgh: T&T Clark, 1956), 485.

6. Rinse Reeling Brouwer, "Het onderwijs van Mozes en het onderwijs van de ek-

I explore the possible presence of the concept of kenosis in the Torah—is meant as an example of the quest that I intend to undertake. However, in our correspondence following the above lecture, Bruce McCormack expressed some hesitations with regard to my program and its presupposition that the Torah is basic to the structure of the biblical witness.[7] He wrote: "I remain convinced that Von Campenhausen was right to say that Irenaeus made the Hebrew Scriptures to be the Christian Old Testament through his suggestion that the New Testament itself had effected a shift from a center of gravity in Torah to a centre of gravity in the prophetic literature in its reading(s) of Old Testament texts."[8]

In the following, I will first examine the presupposition that was questioned by McCormack and ask whether and to what extent the Torah (as "teaching," "instruction," which in Latin would be *doctrina*) can function as a source and authority in unfolding Christian doctrine. In that context, I will also consider a possible falsification of this presupposition in conversation with Katherine Sonderegger. Thereafter, given (as Calvin would say[9]) the similarity as well as the difference between the relationship of YHWH, Moses, and the people of Israel on the one hand, and of divinity and humanity in Jesus Christ on the other hand, I will explore four particular aspects of proto-christological patterns in the former relationship, with a particular focus on the presence of possible kenotic tendencies. These aspects will be (1) the humility of God and of his servant; (2) the speaking and the writing of the Word; (3) the authority, the sin, and the death of Moses; and (4) the Mosaic mediation of the covenant. And finally I will draw two lines from the Torah to the *locus classicus* of kenoticism, the hymn in Philippians 2:5–11. These lines will trace, first, the child of Adam, resisting temptation and ready to share in the human condition, and, second, the Name that is above every name.

---

klesia," https://www.rinsereelingbrouwer.nl/wp-content/uploads/2019/08/oratie-tekst -rinse-reeling-brouwer.pdf, accessed June 1, 2021.

7. This was also the conviction of the Dutch theologian K. H. Miskotte, one of the eponyms of my chair, especially in *Edda en Thora*, his major pamphlet against the neo-paganism of Nazism from 1939 (3rd ed. 1983). Now see the German translation: K. H. Miskotte, *Edda und Thora: Ein Vergleich germanischer und israelitischer Religion* (Berlin: Lit Verlag, 2015).

8. Private correspondence, March 4, 2020.

9. Cf. John Calvin, *Institutes of Christian Religion*, ed. John T. McNeill, trans. Ford Lewis Battles, Library of Christian Classics (Philadelphia: Westminster, 1960), 2.10–11.

The Instruction of Moses and the Doctrine of the Church

In the epoch-making view of Wellhausen, the prophets were initially the founders of the law, but prophecy lost its critical force in its postexilic elaboration, suffocating in legalistic regulations and bringing living history to an end through a dead literalism until Jesus, in his conflict with the aristocracy of the temple and the lawyers, revitalised the original prophetic spirit.[10] Wellhausen was accused of anti-Judaism for this line of thought, and although others did use it in that way, it is more likely that his own motives within the Protestant world were primarily anticlerical. At the same time, however, for Wellhausen the slogan *lex post prophetas* did not include the process of canonization. On that level, the closure of the redaction of the Pentateuch came slightly earlier than that of the books of the prophets. This classical thesis has been contested in the more recent literature, e.g., by Stephen Chapman.[11] He shows that Deuteronomy 34:10–12 explicitly links Moses at the end of his "books" to the prophets—"There has not arisen since in Israel a prophet quite like Moses" is meant in a superlative degree—and that Malachi 4:4–6, as the last words of the books of the prophets and corresponding to those last words of the Torah, insists on remembering the law of Moses. In addition, Chapman traces how in the later parts of the Scriptures, such as Chronicles and Daniel, the twofold nature of the law and the prophets is emphatically underlined.[12] An alternative to Wellhausen's classical thesis has thus been developed.[13]

Nevertheless, although the law and the prophets are canonically linked and there are many cross-references between these major parts of the canon,[14] at the same time each of them represents its own literary genre and a specific theological purpose. Ever since the second century BCE, the

10. Julius Wellhausen, *Israelitische und Jüdische Geschichte* (Berlin: Riemer, 1914).

11. Stephan B. Chapman, *The Law and the Prophets: A Study in Old Testament Canon Formation*, extended ed. (Grand Rapids: Baker Academic, [2000] 2020).

12. This is also the case in the New Testament; Chapman, *Law and Prophets*, 266, 276–79.

13. Chapman, *Law and Prophets*, 20n22, mentions that even in Von Campenhausen, *The Formation of the Christian Bible* (Philadelphia: Fortress, 1972), "the standard model," although "magisterially expressed," "remained the consensus view."

14. Examples of such cross-references include: the covenant of releasing slaves in Gen 15 and Jer 34; the tension between Judah and Joseph in Gen 37–50 and the tensions between Judah (the South), and Ephraim (the North) in the "early prophets" and many later texts; the "calf (calves) of gold" in Exod 32 and 1 Kings 12 (Jeroboam), as well as the connection between the appeal of Moses in the same chapter of Exod 32 (v. 26) and that of Elijah in confrontation with Baal in 1 Kings 18 (v. 21).

Torah has stood as a category on its own.[15] One can say: "the river Jordan flows between Deuteronomy and Joshua."[16] Intentionally, the Torah concludes at the border of the promised land: it remains, to express it in Kantian categories, a "regulative principle" that never legitimizes the actual practice of habitation and, for exactly that reason, can survive any experience of exile. In terms of systematic theology, I would say that the Torah contains teaching and instruction, or "doctrine"—albeit not in the categorical mode to which we are accustomed—while the prophets contain "contextual theology," as it is always related to an (at least alleged) particular time: "It came to pass in the days of . . . , that the Word of the Lord came to. . . ." Both modes are important, but they must not be confused or divided. In my project, I will explore the Books of Moses as "doctrinal" dogmatics and ethics, but not without considering their *perichoreses* with the prophets as the other main part of the Old Testament canon.

Now it is undeniable that no easy continuity exists between those portions of Scripture and the New Testament. For Paul, the law had become an obstacle for the relationship of Jews and Gentiles and an oppressive, even deadly, institution. In his eyes, the law could no longer indicate a way of life unless the Spirit—that is, the Spirit of Jesus Christ—functioned as its forceful presupposition (Rom 8:2). But at the same time, a careful reading of his letters by Jewish and Christian scholars together has also found that, as the disciple of Gamaliel, his instructions for the *ekklēsiai* show remarkably halakhic traits.[17] And for John, the aim of the law, i.e. "grace and truth"—the translation of *hesed we-'emet*, "abounding in steadfast love and faithfulness" in God's self-proclamation of Exodus 34:6—was fulfilled only in the coming of Jesus Christ (John 1:17).[18] At the same time, in the Fourth Gospel the story of Jesus is told on the basis of the Jewish festivals (*heortai*, feasts, 17 times in

15. Cf. Acts 15:21: "For in every city, for generations past, Moses has had those who proclaim him, for he has been read aloud every sabbath in the synagogues" (Acts 13:15 speaks about the reading of Moses and the Prophets).

16. Karel Deurloo, *Exodus en Exil: Kleine Bijbelse Theologie Deel 1* (Utrecht: Kok, 2003), 63–66.

17. Peter J. Tomson, *Paul and the Jewish Law: Halakha in the Letters of the Apostle to the Gentiles* (Assen: Van Gorcum; Minneapolis: Fortress, 1990). Campenhausen, *The Formation*, 24–37, was not yet acquainted with such insights.

18. Campenhausen, *Formation*, 52, referring to the similar view of Bultmann: "'The Law was given through Moses, grace and truth came through Jesus Christ,' meaning only through Christ, who truly knew the Father, and absolutely never at any time through Moses and the Law." That is an extremely strong wording.

the Gospel).[19] However, John's calendar is different from that of Matthew. In one such difference the crucifixion coincides with the slaughtering of the paschal lamb on 14 Nisan (John 19:36). This corresponds with the tradition of the Quartodecimans of Asia Minor, who (perhaps for reasons of delimitation from Judaism) would be condemned at the First Council of Nicaea. The christological preaching on the text of Exodus 12 in Melito of Sardis's *Peri Pascha* (around 165 CE) also evidences the same tradition. Von Campenhausen observes that Melito, almost a contemporary of Irenaeus, still kept the same "old method" of reading the Old Testament that the young Irenaeus had practiced.[20] For him, Christ himself was speaking in the Torah, also in some of its halakhic aspects. In my view, the key for this development that we can trace in the texts of John and Melito is to be found in the loss of the second temple in 70 CE. For the rabbinic tradition, the way out of this predicament was as follows: when the priestly parts of the Torah could not be practiced in the temple anymore, they could nevertheless be transformed and "democratized" in the daily halakhic practice of the Jewish household.[21] At the same time, for the messianic groups, they were fulfilled in the crucifixion of the Lord and to be retained in remembrance of him. Therefore, in both traditions, the Torah had to be reread.

At this point in my argument, having claimed that early Christianity heard Christ himself speaking in the Torah, I must halt. For another view has been presented by a Christian theologian, whom I greatly admire for many reasons, which stresses that Torah is the "form" and "pattern" of biblical teaching but at the same time refuses to appropriate its text by way of a christological reading. I am referring to the fascinating first volume of Katherine Sonderegger's *Systematic Theology*.[22] Her starting point is the Shema: "Hear, O Israel" (Deut 6:4). This is taken as indicating the oneness of God, a "metaphysical predicate" of the godhead that in systematic theology must be treated prior to the reflections on the Trinitarian-christological dogma of the church and must "govern and conform and set forth" those reflections.

19. Aileen Guilding, *The Fourth Gospel and Jewish Worship* (Oxford: Clarendon, 1960), had already appeared before the German original text of Campenhausen's *Formation* in 1968. Her proposals are critically revised in the posthumous edition of Dirk Monshouwer, *The Gospels and Jewish Worship* (Vught: Skandalon, 2010), 253–84.

20. Campenhausen, *Formation*, 184.

21. Jonathan Sachs, *Leviticus: The Book of Holiness*, Covenant & Conversation 3 (Jerusalem: Toby Press, 2015).

22. Katherine Sonderegger, *The Doctrine of God*, vol. 1 of *Systematic Theology* (Minneapolis: Fortress, 2015); "form and pattern" appears at 10.

She does not hesitate to call monotheism the conviction that "aligns the Christian God with the faiths of Abraham, Judaism and Islam."[23]

"Hear Israel, YHWH our God, YHWH is One." The meaning of the Hebrew sentence is not fully transparent, and one can combine and translate the words differently. But it is certainly clear that the Name YHWH here determines what can be said about *'elohim*, godhead. In contrast with the view of Sonderegger that divine *quiddity* should not be compressed into divine *identity*, the "Who?" of God is not in His "what?"[24] I read this wording precisely the other way around: although YHWH is always veiling himself in his unveiling, the revelation of the Name, i.e., the identity, predicates the nature (*'elohim*, as the general designator for divine entities). In contrast with the Torah, we read in the Qur'an, Surah Al Ikhlas, 112:1: *Qoel: Allahu ahad*, "Say: He is God (Allah), the One." A personal name as a subject of the sentence is missing here, and the generic name takes over its function. Therefore, the Torah (and Jesus in the Gospel, Mark 12:29) and the Qur'an differ in their phrasing and therewith in their witness.[25] For precisely that reason, the Shema can function as an indication of the covenant of this specific name with this specific people, the people of Israel in the whole of the book of Deuteronomy. Certainly, Sonderegger refers to the covenant,[26] but what are the implications for the One Himself that He is willing to be the God of this covenant? Surely my Reformed mind is to blame, but I cannot imagine speaking of divine Oneness in this context without reflecting on the meaning of election and covenant for the One God. But that is not the way Sonderegger proceeds; see also her rejection of the concept of the will of God in favor of the divine nature in §4 of this first volume of her *Systematic Theology*.

At the very beginning, Sonderegger points to references in the Gospel and in James to the Shema, but she is silent about Paul's reference to it in Galatians 3:19–20. I can imagine why this is the case, for verse 19 in particular is a notorious *crux interpretum*, if only because of the divergent manuscripts.[27] In the preceding verses, Paul has stressed the provisional character of the Torah: it was not yet there in the days of God's promises to

---

23. Sonderegger, *Doctrine of God*, quotes on 15, xv, xiv, respectively.

24. Sonderegger, *Doctrine of God*, 11.

25. This observation is made against one of the main theses of Miroslav Volf, *Allah: A Christian Response* (New York: HarperCollins, 2011), 143.

26. Sonderegger, *Doctrine of God*, e.g., 12, 20.

27. For the following, cf. Rochus Zuurmond, *God noch gebod: Bijbels-theologische notities over de brief van Paulus aan de Galaten* (Baarn: Ten Have, 1990), 154–59.

Abraham, and it is no longer there in the days of the Messiah, and now he poses the question, "Why then the law?" He responds (according to P46): "[the law] of works?—[that functions as an interim] until the seed would come to whom the promise had been made." Perhaps because this sounds too enigmatic, most manuscripts write instead: "It was added because of transgressions, until. . . ." This assertion seems to be an allusion to the later explanation in the letter to the Romans.[28] However, in the explanation of early Christian commentators on Exodus, the verb "to transgress" refers to the apostasy in the story of the calf (Exod 32:8): because of this sin, Moses (and not the Lord himself, as was the case the first time) is supposed to have written the Ten Commandments on two tablets again (see some variants of Exod 34:28 and 34:1). It may be for that reason that the following verses speak of a mediator: the first two tablets were written "with the finger of God" (Exod 31:18); the second tablets, on a lower level, "by the hand of Moses" (for this expression see Lev 26:46 [KJV]), the mediator. Galatians 3:19b states: "(and it was) ordained by angels in the hand of a mediator" (KJV). The theophany at Sinai gives the impression that angels are present at the divine revelation and organize it. But for Paul, in this context, that is a minor aspect. At the center is Moses being called a mediator. This can be related to Moses's writing the law, but even more, in accordance with the tradition of Philo and the rabbinic figure of a *sirsur* (broker), to his intercession after the history of the calf (Exod 32:31–33:17)—I will return to both aspects below. Then, in verse 20, Paul sketches a clear antithesis: "however, a mediator is not *a mediator* of one, but God is one" (KJV). As a middleman, Moses (the intercessor) mediates between two parties, God (represented by his angels) and sinful Israel. Therefore, the Torah reflects an antagonism, a compromise, an interim. And now, strikingly, Paul confronts this defect in respect of the involvement of the mediator with the Shema: for God is not two, but one! In his Septuagint, the apostle would have read: *Akoue, Israel, kyrios ho theos hēmōn kyrios heis estin.* Kyrios! I presume that Paul is seeing Jesus here as *kyrios*, a translation of the tetragrammaton YHWH. Appealing to the Shema, he is provocatively saying: "in Christ, more than Moses is here, not the mediator,[29] but the divine Name, the divine Name that is one!"

---

28. E.g., Rom. 5:20, although Gal. 3:19 uses *parabasis* and Rom. 5:20 *paraptōma* for "transgression." For the argument, cf. also Rom. 7:13.

29. Because of Gal 3:20, H. J. Iwand in his 1953/54 lectures in Bonn questioned the title "mediator" for Jesus Christ in theology, in particular since Schleiermacher and Hegel. See Hans Joachim Iwand, *Christologie*, Nachgelassene Werke. Neue Folge Band 2 (Gütersloh: Gütersloher Verlagshaus, 1999), 111. He especially judged the way Emil Brunner used the

In my view, this text must be brought into conversation with Sonderegger's argument that the interpretation of the Shema should not be confused with christological reflection, and furthermore it should be a motif for examining the mediatorship of Moses in the Torah.

Kenotic Aspects of the Speaking and Acting of YHWH and of Moses

There are four aspects of the relationship between YHWH, Moses, and the people of Israel that evidence proto-christological patterns, and possible kenotic tendencies in particular. These are the humility of God and of his servant; the speaking and the writing of the Word; the authority, the sin and the death of Moses; and the Mosaic mediation of the covenant. Each of these aspects will be explored in turn in what follows.

First, in his revelation to Moses in the burning bush, YHWH says: "I have come down (*'ered*) to deliver [my people] from the hand of the Egyptians, and to bring them up (*ha'alot*) out of that land to a good and broad land" (Exod 3:8). The divine Name is coming down, and the people will be brought up. This twofold movement is comparable with the twofold movement in Karl Barth's doctrine of reconciliation—"the humiliation and obedience of the Son of God" and "the exaltation of the Son of Man" (*Church Dogmatics* IV/1–IV/2)[30]—although Barth, as far as I know, never refers to this verse from Exodus to clarify this twofold movement so fundamental to his understanding of Jesus Christ.[31] The metaphor of the "coming down" of YHWH

---

category in his book *Der Mittler* (Tübingen: Mohr, 1927) to be incorrect. Jesus is not to be seen as a "middleman" between God and human beings. Jesus Christ is not the "third" person, who as a man represents me before God, but God was in him reconciling the world to himself. That does not mean that it would be inadmissible to use the term at all. As Zuurmond, *God noch gebod*, 159, argues, 1 Tim 2:5 can be read as a "christological midrash" on the *shema'* (and perhaps on Gal 3:19–20). See also Karl Barth, *Church Dogmatics* IV/3, ed. G. W. Bromiley and T. F. Torrance, trans. G. W. Bromiley (Edinburgh: T&T Clark, 1961), 51: "The prophecy of Jesus Christ is that of the Mediator. It is not, then, the prophecy of a partisan. Nor is it that of a negotiator running to and fro between two parties and now speaking for the one, now for the other. It is that of the One who is both Yahweh and the Israelite, both the Lord and His Servant and the Servant and His Lord, in one and the same person. He does not need to look or point beyond Himself to attest the fulfilment of the covenant."

30. Karl Barth, *Church Dogmatics* IV/1, ed. G. W. Bromiley and T. F. Torrance, trans. G. W. Bromiley (Edinburgh: T&T Clark, 1956), and IV/2, ed. G. W. Bromiley and T. F. Torrance, trans. G. W. Bromiley (Edinburgh: T&T Clark, 1958).

31. The objection could be made that Barth is speaking of reconciliation and the book

(cf. Gen 11:5; Exod 19:11; Num 11:17; etc.) is significant for understanding who he is in his revelation to his people. In this context, I would say that it makes sense to speak of the "humility of God," linking the Torah to a motif of kenosis in the New Testament. However, I am aware that this is not quite the same meaning of the divine attribute as it finds in Sonderegger's study. She speaks of God's omnipotence as the Lord's "holy humility," and therewith she primarily means the divine hiddenness in the world he has created—a "holy and gracious freedom exercised by the One for others"—such that God can be near to creation without overwhelming it.[32] If I understand this correctly, the concept expressed in this way approximates to the Jewish-kabbalistic conviction of divine self-limitation, in which YHWH makes room for his creatures to be and to act of their own accord. This element, in my perception, is not absent in the Torah: particularly after the great catastrophe of the golden calf, YHWH attentively issues commands so as to provide means for his covenant partners to express themselves: the priestly parts on the tabernacle, the sacrifices, and the feasts all point in that direction. But there is a divine humility in the central drama of the story, too, and that is what interests me in the present context: the divine coming down, with the intent of causing the ascent of his enslaved people.

The figure of Moses reflects this descent of his Lord. When Origen, at the very beginning of his work *On First Principles*, wants to illustrate that Christ had already spoken before his incarnation, he simply quotes Hebrews 11:24–26: "By faith Moses, when he was grown up, refused to be called a son of Pharaoh's daughter, choosing rather to share ill-treatment with the people of God than to enjoy the fleeting pleasures of sin. He considered abuse suffered for the Christ to be greater wealth than the treasures of Egypt."[33] From here, we can certainly draw a line to the *etapeinōsen*, "he humbled himself," that is said of Jesus Christ in Philippians 2:8. The same can be said of the characterization of Moses in Numbers 12:3—said in the context of several challenges to his authority here and in the following chapters—that Moses

---

of Exodus of liberation (*hatsil*, to deliver). However, in that respect it is remarkable that the Gospel of John—as already occurs in Ezek 45—combines imagery of the Passover and the Day of Atonement, i.e., of the feasts of the first and of the seventh month. Cf. Monshouwer, *Gospels and Jewish Worship*, 273–74. In the Christian calendar, the triduum of Easter includes characteristics of both main theological themes, to at times quite confusing effect.

32. Sonderegger, *Doctrine of God*, e.g., xii, 140, 151 (title §4).

33. Origen, *De Principiis*, I praef. 1; "abuse suffered for the Christ" ("the reproach of Christ," KJV): *inproperium Christi*.

was "very humble, more so than anyone else on the face of the earth." He did not try to become powerful or rich at the expense of his solidarity with this people of former slaves.

Second, the authority of Moses is clearly connected with his office of speaking and writing the Word of the Lord. The book of Deuteronomy offers an explicit and subtle theological reflection on this office.[34] Chapters 9 and 10 reflect on the story of the great rupture in the covenant that each new generation must appropriate again for itself. The focus here is not on the image of the calf, but on the second set of tablets that Moses receives from the Lord and stores in the Ark of the Covenant (Deut 10:5). The importance of this action becomes clear at the end of Deuteronomy. Moses writes down in the "book of the Torah" the words that he has spoken and places the book *at the side* of the ark (Deut 31:24–26). Anybody who wants to pay attention to the words that YHWH himself wrote down must turn to Moses's book. At the same time, the authors of Deuteronomy have managed, in a sophisticated way, to identify the "book of the Torah" with their own book without explicitly saying so. With regard to the Lord, this means that he had laid his own words "in the hands of Moses" (as a text in its canonical shape) and made himself dependent on his servant for their handing on, which is itself a kenotic expression of confidence.

We have already noted that Paul in Galatians 3:19 was overly critical of the mediatorship of Moses in this respect. The literary unit of 2 Corinthians 3:1–4:15 likewise has frequently been interpreted as displaying a similarly critical approach. Nevertheless, here too the method of interpretation is strongly influenced by rabbinic practice. The (liturgical) combination of Exodus 34:30–35, on the shining face of Moses coming down from mount Sinai, and Jeremiah 31:31–34, on the renewal of the covenant that shall be written in the hearts of the people, may be venerable. And the quibble between *cherōt* (engraved; Exod 32:16) and the Aramaic *cherut* (freedom; 2 Cor 3:17) can be found in the Mishna as well.[35] There thus may be a consensus that what Paul is stressing here is how only our turning to the Messiah in his Spirit can make the understanding of the text of Moses effective. Paul, formulating this hermeneutical rule, did not know about a "New Testament" *as a text*. For us, therefore, the rule is not so much a reproach in the direction of the synagogue, as it implies a challenge to us in our reading of *all* the Scriptures.

---

34. G. J. Venema, *Schriftuurlijke Verhalen in het Oude Testament* (Delft: Eburon, 2000).
35. mAbot 6.2.

The Lord has laid the books of Moses as well as the epistles of Paul in our hands, and he has taken a great risk in doing so.

Third, from the day YHWH called Moses (Exod 3:4), the voice of Moses (Exod 3:18)—through his own mouth and through the mouth of Aaron (Exod 4:15)—would speak the Word of the Lord to the king of Egypt and to the people. This *gratia unionis* between Word and word, however, does not have an anhypostatic character. For there existed a separate human being, Moses, before it. His fury about injustice led to a murder that harmed his reputation (Exod 2:11–15), and his flight and afterward his marriage led to inactivity with regard to the liberation of Israel (Exod 2:15–22). Only then did YHWH intervene, coming down and calling his servant. And again, also after his calling, Moses existed as a separate human being. Although the Lord protects him against the many complaints and insurrections of the people (between the Sea of Reeds and Mount Sinai, Exod 15–19; between Sinai and Kadesh, Num 10–20; and from Kadesh to the plains of Moab, Num 20–26), at one point the old fury and revolutionary impatience turn up again, when Moses at Meribah prematurely smites the rock with his rod for water, not trusting sufficiently in God's promises (Num 20:2–13).[36] The response is immediate: "But the LORD said to Moses and Aaron, 'Because you did not trust in me, to show my holiness before the eyes of the Israelites, therefore you shall not bring this assembly into the land that I have given them'" (v. 12).

However, when in Deuteronomy Moses tells the people that he asked the Lord to let him cross the Jordan, he continues: "But the LORD was angry with me on your account and would not heed me" (Deut 3:26). "[O]n your account"—what can that mean? I suggest that it has to do with the function of the Jordan flowing between the Law and the Prophets mentioned above. Had Moses settled with the people in the land, he would inevitably have become the legitimizing instance of the practices of settling. But because Torah is a "regulative principle," that kind of legitimizing function of the Torah must be avoided. In this way, "on your account" is said as an act of *preparing the place* for the people. Moses must sacrifice himself to avoid idolatry with his name (and with his unknown grave, across from Peor in Moab that shall not become a place of pilgrimage; Deut. 34:6). He sinned, but in a particular sense you can say he did so *for our sake*: for Moses as well, God "made him to be sin" (cf. 2 Cor 5:21).

36. Mary Douglas, *In the Wilderness: The Doctrine of Defilement in the Book of Numbers* (Oxford: Oxford University Press, [1993] 2004), 58, 190, sees an earlier parallel in the story of Moses asking Hobab to be their guide in the wilderness, insufficiently trusting the guidance of the divine cloud (Num 10:29–32).

The Torah does not often connect Moses with the experience of death. It preaches a witness of life, and for Israel to be holy means to stay away from cadavers (e.g., Lev 21:11–12, Num 19:11–22, and connected halakhic provisions). Therefore, it is not easy to link the "learned obedience" of Moses with "what he suffered" (Heb 5:8) in an unambiguous way. Nevertheless, this element is not missing in the Torah. We can recall in particular the moment when, after a most intense insurrection of the people, it was not Moses but his brother, the priest Aaron, who "put on the incense, and made atonement for the people. He stood between the dead and the living; and the plague was stopped" (Num 16:47–48).[37] The death of Moses himself at the end of Deuteronomy has a more peaceful connotation. The Rabbis explain the expression *'al phy YHWH* (at the mouth of the Lord) as his being taken away with a kiss. This makes possible the presence of Moses with Elijah as companions of Jesus and voices of the Word eternal. Sonderegger dares to speak of the "deification" of Moses.[38] While I am not sure whether I would adopt this wording, it is remarkable that the last verse of the Torah speaks of "all the mighty deeds and all the terrifying displays of power that *Moses* performed in the sight of all Israel" (Deut 34:12). Did he do them, or did his Lord?

Finally, as we saw, Paul in Galatians 3 downgraded the standing of Moses (in comparison to Jesus Christ) to that of a middleman negotiating between two parties. Nevertheless, one can doubt whether the apostle's understanding of mediatorship is the only possible one. Therefore, let us look at the story of Moses as a mediator after the catastrophe of the adoration of the calf more closely.[39] K. H. Miskotte drafted a reflection on Exodus 33:10–16, meant for meditation in connection with the kerygmatic and didactic work of interpretation and witness. In what follows, I quote some sentences from this study. First, considering verse 10:

> The people confess, by their falling down to worship, that the encounter with them takes place *in* the encounter with Moses. But one could also say—in view of what is inherent in the "Name"—that God defers to the

---

37. Sonderegger, *Doctrine of God*, 271–94, treats the wilderness experiences in Numbers under the heading of the divine perfection of Omnipotence. At the end of this discussion, 293–94, she notices christological patterns in Moses's prophetic "hypostatic union with the Word," as well as in this priestly intercession of Aaron.

38. Sonderegger, *Doctrine of God*, 288, 293.

39. A parallel narrative can be found in the meeting of YHWH and Moses after the murmuring of the people because of the false reports of the promised land spread by scouts, Num 14:10b–35. Verse 20, where YHWH says: "I have pardoned, according to thy word" (KJV), became part of the synagogal liturgy on the Day of Atonement.

approach of the mediator. Thus, the whole of the Old Testament (though the origin of the covenant can be called "monopleuric") is concerned with the relation between divine and human yearning and waiting, the mutual suffering and patience of God and his people. They stand over against each other and become "as enemies," and then they come together and find each other. There is a divine suffering on account of men, but also a suffering *with* men, and there is a human suffering on account of God, but also a suffering *with* God. Nowhere in the Old Testament is there a trace of an absolute, unchangeable God; nowhere is he presented as "almighty" in the abstract sense; nowhere is there a conflict between his honour and the honour of the creature.[40]

Then, in verses 11–13, "the speech in which the Lord[41] and Moses engage here" is "an independent, antecedent secret, a friendship, as it were, a relationship that possesses a far higher degree of immediacy than the relationship to the people." Miskotte writes: "How tremendous is this Moses who can rise up and boldly accuse YHWH of dealing equivocally with his servant." He continues: "This prayer, this 'demand' of the mediator, is pitched exceedingly high. We stand aghast at the temerity with which Moses insists that the apostasies which occurred so recently shall be accepted and transformed into a knowledge (*yadaʿ*) of God's nearness." And he observes: "How 'superhuman' all this is, and how 'subdivine.'"[42] This last sentence shows that, for Miskotte, Moses is far from being a particular specimen of the general category "mediator" in religious history. He is intimate with the intentions of the Lord to such a degree that, as his servant, he must remind YHWH to prove who he is in his Name. Although the categories of "superhuman" and "subdivine" exceed the boundaries of the definition of Chalcedon, one could paraphrase that here the Lord is humiliating himself, listening to and following the demand of his servant, whereas, in the same movement, the human servant is exalted to the highest stage of intimacy, reaching the heart of the Lord. While this is not a direct Christology, I dare to call it proto-christological. And it can help transform Chalcedon in a much more vivid,

---

40. Kornelis H. Miskotte, *When the Gods Are Silent*, trans. John W. Doberstein (London: Collins, 1967), 388–97, here at 392; translation revised.

41. Miskotte writes "Here" in Dutch, which is the functional title for "Lord" that became an intimate name in Dutch Reformed piety.

42. Miskotte, *When the Gods Are Silent*, 392, 393, 395, and 393, respectively.

dialogical, and moving direction. Perhaps Paul, writing to the Galatians at the beginning of his apostleship, struggling with the Law, and enthusiastic regarding the appearance of *YHWH ʿěkhād* in Christ, underestimated these specific proto-christological traits of the mediatorship of Moses.

Lines Leading from the Torah to the Kenotic Hymn in Philippians 2

By way of conclusion, two lines might be drawn from the Torah to the text of the kenotic hymn in Philippians 2. These lines follow, first, the child of Adam who resists temptation and is ready to share in the human condition and, second, the Name that is above every name.

First, whoever is used to hearing the Torah in the circular form of the sabbatical lectures of the liturgical years can experience how the narratives of Genesis 1–4 follow the books of Numbers and Deuteronomy. In the wilderness, Israel became acquainted with temptations, the desire in its heart to be as gods, and the desire to be tested in its ability to obey and to be humbled (Deut 8:1–10). However, in the garden of Eden man and woman showed they could not manage the test and were not willing "to live by every word that comes from the mouth of the Lord." By contrast, early Judaism (and not only in its Hellenistic circles) developed a tradition of the original Adam, made in God's image (Gen 1:27), resisting temptation. There are grounds for recognizing such a first and true Adam in the person that is described in the first stanza of the song that Paul quotes in Philippians 2:6–11.[43] In that sense, the words *en morphē theou hyparchōn* can be translated as "existing in God's image."[44] When the son of Adam, of whom the hymn sings, "thought it not robbery" to be as God, he is characterized as the one who resisted the temptation to which the Adam of Genesis 3 succumbed. In this connection, it is less important whether we must interpret this figure as a "heavenly Adam" or as the person Jesus in his earthly appearance. In a *haggadic* sense, both at

---

43. Rinse Reeling Brouwer, "Kenosis in Philippians 2:5–11 and in the History of Christian Doctrine," in *Letting Go: Rethinking Kenosis*, ed. O. Zijlstra (Bern: Peter Lang, 2002), 69–109. For arguments on the heavenly Adam (Lohmeyer), see 73.

44. This translation has been defended in Oscar Cullmann, *The Christology of the New Testament*, trans. Shirley C. Guthrie and Charles A. M. Hall (Philadelphia: Westminster, 1959). See the chapters on the "Servant of the Lord" and the "Son of Man." One objection might be that the usual translation of *demut* in Gen 1:26 is *eikōn*, as in 1 Cor 15:49, and that of its synonym *tselem* rather *homoiōma*, as in Rom 5:14. However, see the lemma *morphē* in *TDNT* 4:751n53 (Behm).

the same time can be true. In the same way, the narratives of the temptations in the Synoptic Gospels (Mark 1:13 par.) are written in a "mythic" tonality yet without lacking reference to the history of Jesus Christ as a whole.

The second stanza starts: *all' heauton ekenōsen, morphēn doulou labōn*. While the image of God is associated with dominion, now the child of Adam in question realizes this image in accepting the existence of a slave. Regarding this motif, a *midrash* that is handed down in several variants in the Babylonian Talmud may be instructive:

> When Moses ascended on high to receive the Torah [Exod 19:20ff.], the ministering angels [cf. the angels in Gal 3:19] said before the Holy One, blessed be He: Master of the Universe, what is one born of a woman doing here among us? He said to them: he came to receive the Torah. The angels said before Him: The Torah is a hidden treasure that was concealed by you 974 generations before the creation of the world [i.e., 1000 generations, Ps 105:8, minus 26 generations between Adam and Moses], and you seek to give it to flesh and blood? "What is the man that You are mindful of him, and the son of man that You think of him?" (Ps 8:4 [here, distinguished from its original meaning, quoted in a disdainful sense]). . . . The rightful place of God's majesty, the Torah, is in the heavens. The Holy One, blessed be He, said to Moses: Provide them with an answer as to why the Torah should be given to the people. . . . Moses said before Him: master of the Universe, the Torah that you are giving me, what is written in it? God said to him: 'I am the Lord your God, who brought you out of Egypt from the house of bondage' [Exod 20:2]. Moses said to the angels: did you descend to Egypt? Were you enslaved to Pharaoh? Why should the Torah be yours?[45]

The Torah was not written for the glorious essences in heaven, but for that man who—in his kenotic existence—shares the burden of being tempted, is bewildered by the mysteries of earthly existence, and has been imprisoned in slavery. And the Son of Man on earth who lives in obedience to this Torah, he will experience his glory (Phil 2:11) precisely because he resists temptation, because he shares the fate of a condemned slave on the cross (v. 8).

---

45. bShabbat 88b (quotation of r. Jehoshua ben Levi, around 250 CE); cf. bSanhedrin 38b.

Second, the hymn can be compared with the musical form of a fugue.[46] In such a reading, the "prologue in heaven" about the true Adam who resisted temptation figures as the first voice, and the portrait of the human being in his solidarity with the fate of slavery as the second. The fugue-like *development* (starting with the *dio*, "therefore" in v. 9) does not introduce a new phrase, but it offers a perspective on both themes or voices sounding together: this servant is qualified as "the name above every name," and therefore, he is *kyrios*, Lord (v. 11). No other person deserves the designation Lord than he who went the way of a servant to his bitter end.

Is it permissible to identify this name *kyrios* with the tetragrammaton, the name of the God of Israel?[47] In my eyes, it is too simplistic to pose the question in this way. To begin with, *kyrios* is a translation not of YHWH but of *'ādon*, lord. And lord is not a name, but a title, a functional designator. Consequently, when it functions as an indication of the name YHWH, it does so in the shape of a specification. God (the subject, that does not appear in the hymn before v. 9!) is the one who is "handing over the Name to Jesus"[48]—as God did to Moses in Deuteronomy 34:12, as we saw above. But God does this without enclosing his Name in him, because it happens to "the glory of God the Father" (v. 11). R. Kendall Soulen praises Karl Barth for reflecting the roots of the ecclesial doctrine of the Trinity when he identifies the "revealed" divine Name, characterizing it as *Yahweh-Kyrios*.[49] But Soulen regrets that, at the same time, Barth speaks of a "dissolution" (*Aufhebung*) of the Tetragrammaton in its actualization by the incarnation of the Son in Jesus Christ.[50] In this way, the divine Name of the Old Testament is eclipsed,[51] and in the end the notorious threat of Christian supersessionism has by no

---

46. G. H. ter Schegget, *Het lied van de mensenzoon: Studie over de Christuspsalm in Filippenzen 2:6–11* (Baarn: Wereldvenster, 1975).

47. Rinse Reeling Brouwer, "Wel 'JHWH is de drie-ene God', en niet 'De naam is Jezus Christus?' In gesprek met Jan Muis over de ene Naam," *Kerk en Theologie* 68, no. 3 (2017): 237–48.

48. C. R. Seitz, *Figured Out: Typology and Providence in Christian Scripture* (Louisville: Westminster John Knox, 2001), 141–44.

49. R. Kendall Soulen, "YHWH the Triune God," *Modern Theology* 15, no. 1 (1999): 36–41; R. K. Soulen, *Distinguishing the Voices*, vol. 1 of *The Divine Name(s) and the Holy Trinity* (Louisville: Westminster John Knox, 2011), 93–104; Karl Barth, *Church Dogmatics* I/1, 2nd ed., ed. G. W. Bromiley and T. F. Torrance, trans. G. W. Bromiley (Edinburgh: T&T Clark, 1975), 348.

50. Barth, *Church Dogmatics* I/1, 316–19.

51. Heinrich Assel, "Gottes Namen nennen—Karl Barth oder Franz Rosenzweig?,"

means been overcome.[52] To prevent the continuation of this tendency, I have tried to show in this chapter that the story of YHWH "behind" the story of *Iēsous Kyrios* has its own power and its own contribution to make to the ongoing reflection of the Christian church on divine humility—on the kenosis of the Lord, the kenosis of his servant, and more particularly the kenosis of the Lord as servant—as well as of the servant as Lord. Moses's witness must not be dissolved in our reading of the New Testament's witness but can be thought through on its own terms. This witness has a certain surplus, one that deserves further elaboration.

Zeitschrift für dialektische Theologie 22, no. 1 (2006): 8–33, speaking here of "Die Emergenz des Namens."

    52. Soulen, "YHWH the Triune God," 29–30, quotes the abovementioned Melito of Sardis as a classical example of this supersessionism.

5

Origen of Alexandria on the Kenosis of the Lord

John A. McGuckin

Origen of Alexandria (ca. 186–255) was, by turns, a classical grammarian, rhetorician, and commentator (in the style of the Great Library at Alexandria).[1] In short, he was a master of semantics and leader (as well as founder) of a new school in the Sophistic sense of that concept, one that outlasted him for several centuries until, by the fifth century, a great deal of his original vision had become common currency in the church. Origen excelled in a wide range of semantic and expositional skills to such an extent that no less than the most educated Christian of antiquity, that most consummate rhetorician Gregory of Nazianzus, called him the "whetstone that keeps us sharp."[2] Moderns tend to call him a theologian and exegete, thus fitting him

---

1. Further see J. A. McGuckin, "Origen as Literary Critic in the Alexandrian Tradition," in *Origeniana Octava* 1, ed. L. Perrone (Leuven: Peeters, 2003), 121–35; J. A. McGuckin, "Structural Design & Apologetic Intent in Origen's Commentary on John," in *Origeniana Sexta* [*Origen and the Bible*], ed. G. Dorival and A. Le Boulluec, Bibliotheca Ephemeridum Theologicarum Lovaniensium 118 (Leuven: Leuven University Press/ Peeters, 1995), 441–57; also J. A. McGuckin, "The Life of Origen" and "The Scholarly Works of Origen," in *The Westminster Handbook to Origen*, ed. J. A. McGuckin (Louisville: Westminster John Knox, 2004), 1–44. See also G. Bostock, "Origen's Exegesis of the Kenosis Hymn," in *Origeniana Sexta*, 531–47.

2. Alluding to Prov 27:17. The citation is recorded in the *Suidae Lexicon*, ed. A. Adler (Berlin: Teubner, 1928–38), 3:691.

more understandably (from our point of view) into the post-fourth-century ecclesiastical world, to which he certainly did not belong. While he unquestionably was a major foundational force in the making of that later Christian intellectuality, it had many aspects that would have puzzled him. In turn, the later Christian ages adopted a great deal of his insights, but they did so in a way that more or less dismantled several of the fundamental structures of his intellectual architecture, leaving him piecemeal as a theorist, and then often criticizing the supposed incoherence of his views.

Certainly, by the later sixth century, Christianity had so far departed from Origen's own native environment of late antique Hellenistic Paideia, that the church itself could barely understand (or tolerate) him, and he himself might well have been appalled at the "closure of the mind" he would have witnessed in regard to theological reflection and dogmatic teaching. It was, in fact, against his own intellectual legacy, that of a man who had adopted as his axiom *Opou Logos Agei*,[3] that the forces of those who wished for much more "closure" in Christian intellectual horizons mustered themselves.[4]

New Approaches in Origenian Studies

In studies composed before the great revival of close interest in Origen's writings (a new feature of scholarship beginning at the turn of the twentieth century and assuming an increased pace from the 1960s onward), he had often been caricatured both as suffering from a massive "Platonizing" habit and as taking little care for the literal and obvious meaning of the biblical text on which he was commenting. Both presuppositions have been shown to be so removed from the facts of what he has to say that they raise the suspicion that such observations were made on the basis of something other than an attentive reading of his text. The problem here, of course, was not simply a tired reliance on textbooks to supply clichés of judgment, but more so the great *lacunae* in our knowledge about what was really going on in the world

---

3. "[Let us go] wheresoever the Logos leads." The pun is deliberate—Logos as signifying both "Divine Word" and also the scholarly spur of "inquiring reason."

4. The controversy against his speculation began in his own lifetime with the issuing of the treatise *Peri Archōn* (ca. 225) and came to a second pitch in what is now known as the First Origenistic Controversy in the time of Theophilus of Alexandria (ca. 385–412). It reached a third pitch in the mid-sixth century, the so-called Second Origenistic controversy, culminating in Justinian's court securing synodical condemnations (553) against aspects of his teaching and that of Evagrius of Pontus (ca. 345–399), one of his most ardent disciples.

of late antique philosophical schools: the precise extent of eclecticism in the philosophical hermeneutics of the age; and the degrees of, and rhythms within, the principle of "fidelity to the school" of the various *Diadochoi*; and the work of those Sophists from the age of Numenius, Ammonius, Plotinus, and Origen to the time of Proclus—an age of immense creativity and adaptation as well as hermeneutical "school rules" that were observed with allegiance, but only within certain prescribed ranges.

This *terra incognita* in relation to the traditions of antique philosophy in the later Hellenistic period has also yielded to great advances in modern times because of detailed work by many classicists now turning their attention to the late antique period and, as a result, much more is now known about Origen and the living intellectual context of his times. Origen's scholarly agenda, then, is certainly not to use a Platonic lens woodenly when scrutinizing the scriptural text. It is now clear, as Mark Edwards has ably shown (and as Plotinus's own disciple Porphyry argued at the time), that Origen is one of the dedicated opponents of Platonism.[5]

Though he has been caricatured by some as one who simply imposes his imagination on top of a text regardless,[6] Origen consistently and carefully approaches the body of Scripture as a set of sacred oracles that contain secret knowledge set within them in various levels of hiddenness, as appropriate to the degree of spiritual advancement in virtue and wisdom on the part of the commentator.[7] For him, the biblical corpus is one coherent totality, not to be interpreted in terms of atomistic linear historical developments (various books emanating from different authors and various historical conditions), but as one overarching schema delivered to Jewish and Christian seers[8] of varying levels of acuity, for the sake of the enlightenment, and thus salvation, of a people (all the souls on earth) who had fallen away from the truth of their metaphysical origins and goals to the extent that they had departed from the integral knowledge of God.

5. M. J. Edwards, *Origen against Plato* (Farnworth: Ashgate, 2002; reprint: London: Routledge, 2017).

6. R. P. C. Hanson's treatment of him in *Allegory and Event* (Richmond: John Knox Press, 1959; reprint, 2002) was typical of this old-school approach, but it has been overshadowed by Karen Torjesen's seminal and very exact study of his exegetical process: *Hermeneutical Procedure and Theological Method in Origen's Exegesis* (Berlin: de Gruyter, 1986).

7. The issue is that as one advances in virtue one gains in the capacity of wisdom.

8. He does not rule out that the Greek philosophers were sometimes possessed of wisdom, which he sees as a divine permeation of truth in the cosmos.

Origen's Exegetical System

For Origen, the single author of the "revelatory text" (the mystery embedded in the historical words) was the divine Word or Logos of God.[9] The earthly author was by definition the saintly prophetic figure—chief among them the apostles, King David, the great prophets and so on—who all served as significant media of the divine message in so far as they were "inspired" by the illumination the Logos afforded them. There is, therefore, a profoundly varied set of valances across the Scriptures, with some of the texts being clearer and more important vehicles of the revelation of the Logos and others more obscure and of lesser portent.

The dynamic of Scripture is a chief element in the overall greater scheme of creation and restoration. Origen understands the Logos as the active agent of creation, which was fundamentally a hierarchical process of communion of life[10] that was willed by the Supreme and Transcendent Father, but effected through the agency of the Logos who, because of this, was given the salvific mission of returning all the lapsed souls to union with God the Father through his own high priestly work.[11] The creation of the corpus of Scripture is only one factor (albeit an important one) in a broad plan of salvific work that begins in the creation of spiritual intelligences (*noes*),[12] reaches its midpoint in the incarnation of the divine Logos who embodies himself for a salvific ministry to (fallen) souls (*psychai*) on earth, and will finally attain its apex in the return of the universe to divine harmony, when God will once more be "all in all" (the *apokatastasis*).[13]

9. For a fuller exposition of Origen's sophisticated exegetical theory and praxis see Torjesen, *Origen's Exegesis*, and also E. A. Dively-Lauro, *The Soul and Spirit of Scripture within Origen's Exegesis* (Leiden: Brill, 2005); J. A. McGuckin, "The Exegetical Metaphysic of Origen of Alexandria," in *What Is the Bible? The Patristic Doctrine of Scripture*, ed. M. Baker and M. Mourachian (Minneapolis: Fortress, 2016), 3–20; J. A. McGuckin, "Exegesis and Metaphysics in Origen's Biblical Philosophy," in *Seeing the Glory*, Collected Studies 2 (New York: St. Vladimir's Seminary Press, 2017), 159–74.

10. This too had multiple valences, but the apex of this sharing of life flowed out from the Trinity to the angels and the noetic consciousness rooted in humanity.

11. This work took place in prehistory, within history, and in posthistory. Origen is ultimately a profoundly eschatological thinker in the antique Christian sense of eschatology. See J. A. McGuckin, "Origen's Eschatology," in *The Oxford Companion to Origen*, ed. R. Heine and K. Torjesen (Oxford: Oxford University Press, 2021).

12. The angels are the remnants of this order of being.

13. 1 Cor 15:28; Origen, *Peri Archōn* 3.5.7 and 2.3.7; *Commentary on Romans* 8.9; *Homilies on Joshua* 1.16.91.

While many parts of Scripture have a simpler moral-instructional purpose, or can serve to give guidance on prayer, it is this overarching story of eschatological salvation that is the deep narrative, as it were, a mystery that is not available or immediately apparent to all. For Origen, it is a pattern and an explicatory key to the totality of Scripture,[14] and it is characterized constantly by the quality of being wholly logocentric. The passion of the Logos for the salvation of the world that he made in his own image is, therefore, the inner dynamic not only of history, but of all being. This "movement" or *kinēsis* is why Origen posits mystical union as the flow-direction of all Christian theology, as in his *Commentary on the Song of Songs* where he brings this schema openly to the fore, and why he is rightly known as the "father of Christian mysticism." I have begun with this rapid summation of Origen's macro-arguments because his doctrine of the Word's kenosis is entirely set within this matrix of ideas, and it is typical of all his approach to exegesis.

The hymnal unit in which the reference to the kenosis appears[15] is one of those deep ocean trenches of Scripture that no simple swimmer can hope to exhaust. But it has been widely agreed that it is a pre-Pauline hymnic unit that the apostle quotes as a familiar confession to his audience of believers, possibly in 61 CE, one that he uses to sketch out a theology of the passion and glorification of the Lord. In Philippians 2:5, he tells us it is to illustrate a *phronēma* that he uses it.

Origen's Approach to the Idea of Kenosis

Kenos, throughout the New Testament, signifies an empty or useless thing.[16] The shorthand calque "kenosis" is the Anglicized summation of the idea we find at a cardinal point in the hymn that uses juxtaposed antitheses to project its stresses. The noun is not used in the New Testament text, for the concept there is decidedly an action, a *dynamis*, not a state (*stasis*). Similarly, there is no reference to the word "kenosis" anywhere in the writings of Origen. The phrase at issue really is the verbal form used in Philippians 2:7—*heauton ekenōsen*—and it derives from the verb *kenoō*, namely, "to deprive of pos-

---

14. It also indicates the very "why" of the Church's adoption of the "Old Covenant" to illuminate the "New" (terms Origen first introduced to Christianity as part of his explication of the totality argument, refuting Marcion in the process).

15. Phil 2:5–11. All biblical translations are the author's own.

16. See 1 Cor 15:14.

session or content." As Oepke has demonstrated,[17] in this sense it appears only once in the whole of the New Testament—a striking *hapax legomenon* at this juncture.

The verbal form of the "deprivation/dispossession" should not, Oepke argues, be taken (as is often the case) as a referent simply to the personal subject (*heauton*, himself) stated earlier (namely, "He who was in the form of God," Phil 2:6), but (in order to sustain the clear parallelism operative here of loss and gain, honor and shame) should be received rather as a referent to the "omitted object," namely, *tou einai isa theō*, "the [state of] being equal to God." It is this that the subject deprives himself of—and not "himself" as such, which would do violence to the sense of the verb. In short, "dispossession" would be a better rendering than "emptying."

Origen makes an exegetical reference to this passage no less than two hundred and eleven times in his extant works.[18] This number would probably have been a lot higher if we had all the works surviving. Even for Origen, voluminous commentator that he was, this is a very high incidence and shows that the text was important to him.

As part of his general theory of relative degrees of revelation contained in Scripture, Origen posits that some of the inspired writers were better than others in conveying the secrets the Logos of God communicated to them. The "prime" seers of God whose writings open up the deepest revelations within Scripture are listed in this order: John the evangelist and Paul the Apostle, then the Psalms of David and the (Apostolic) Synoptic Gospels, and then the rest of the Scriptures, especially Isaiah, the other apostolic writings, the Song of Songs and the remaining prophets. Pauline and Johannine theology are, therefore, the primary highways of Origen's entry into scriptural meaning and form the lenses through which he tends to approach most other questions. For Origen, Paul is not merely an insightful theologian, but the inspired seer who was lifted into the heavens to receive secret initiation from the divine Word.[19] This initiation makes him privy to mysteries beyond the capacity of an earthly mind to know otherwise (just as the Beloved Disciple was privy to secrets since he reclined on the breast of the Logos incarnate).[20]

17. A. Oepke, "*Kenoō*," in *Theological Dictionary of the New Testament*, ed. G. Kittel et al., trans. G. W. Bromiley (Grand Rapids: Eerdmans, 1965), 661–62.

18. See *Biblia Patristica*, ed. J. Allenbach et al. (Paris: Editions du Centre National de la Recherche Scientifique, 1980), 3:432–33.

19. 2 Cor 12:3–4.

20. John 13:23.

It follows then, that Origen does not accept the Philippians hymn as an extraneous element that Paul quotes, but rather as a mystery that Paul has witnessed and conveys to the church on his own apostolic authority. The massive number of references to the hymn suggest from the outset that Origen actually sees the text as a quintessence of the Pauline theology. Let us see, as briefly as we can, the import of his general remarks about the passage. I shall here restrict myself to consideration of Origen's *Commentary on Matthew's Gospel*, and his references in *On First Principles*—a dossier of texts that more or less gives us his habitual usage of the kenotic hymn.

Kenotic Thought in Origen's Matthew Commentary

While *On First Principles* is a relatively early work, concerned with setting out the parameters of the Apostolic Tradition and where it requires clarification, Origen's *Commentary on Matthew* is one of his later and most mature works. Sadly, a great deal of the latter has been lost, not least the first nine books, up to Matthew 13:36. However Pamphilus of Caesarea's *Apology for Origen* preserves an early fragment, and other pieces are found in the *Series of Commentaries on Matthew* (*Mat. Com. Ser.*) as collated from other ancient authorial sources.[21]

Pamphilus wrote to defend Origen against later accusations that he underestimated the divine honor and eternity of the Son of God. That argument would reach a crescendo during the Nicene crisis and was the core issue in the controversy surrounding Origen's reputation in the later fourth-century church. Pamphilus insisted that Origen did not teach the creaturely status of the Son of God and never inferred that he was non-eternal.[22] Later, leading Nicenes such as Athanasius, Gregory Nazianzen, Basil, and Gregory of Nyssa would concur, although Arius seems to have leaned on Origen to deduce the contrary in his own dogmatics. In any case, long before the Nicene crisis,[23] this is how Origen approaches the Philippian kenotic hymn when he discusses the genealogy in the very opening of Matthew's Gospel:

---

21. Pamphilus (ca. 240–309) was a leading theologian of Origen's *schola* and library in Caesarea Maritima and mentor of Eusebius who, after his teacher's martyrdom, himself became bishop and head of the Origenian school there.

22. His several references to the subordination of the Word to the Supreme Father were, by the end of the third century, suggestive of being read in that way.

23. This can be read in many ways as a crisis about the reception of Origen's dogmatic synthesis.

If, when Christ Jesus "was in the form of God He did not think it robbery to be equal to God, but dispossessed Himself, taking the form of a servant, made in the likeness of a human being, found as a human being, humbling Himself He became obedient to death even the death of a cross," then there is no doubt that His birth was not that of one who did not previously exist commencing to exist, as is taken to be the case of the birth of human beings. Rather, He who existed previously and "was in the form of God" came that He might also receive the "form of a servant." Therefore, as He said: "What is born of the flesh is flesh"; meaning, what is born of her who said "Behold the handmaid of the Lord. May it be done to me in accordance with your word," this is the "form of a servant," which is certainly flesh.[24]

In this instance Philippians 2:6–8 (used to elucidate Matthew's genealogy passage) is itself commented on by means of John 1:1; 3:6; and Luke 1:38. The creedal element in 1 Timothy 3:16 also bears on the same sense as Origen reads here.

This practice of the citation of the New Testament text along with para-phrastic forms of it, and a creative *mélange* of associated passages,[25] is typical of Origen and thereby becomes constitutive of a very long chain of pre-modern Christian commentators. Here the Johannine prologue is not cited explicitly but allusively. As here, the eternal or divine *archē* of the Logos becomes a very common "associated text" in many other Origenian passages dealing with the Philippians hymn. We can sense the Johannine echo, as it were, because of the way that Origen is dealing with the question of Jesus's "origins" (*archē/archai*), while Matthew also deals with them in his genealogy text. It is Origen's constant habit to answer one biblical question

24. Pamphilus, *Apology for Origen* 5, in *The Commentary of Origen on the Gospel of Matthew*, ed. R. Heine (Oxford: Oxford University Press, 2018), 1:320–21 (henceforth "Heine").

25. As with the procedure of the Commentators of the Great Library of Alexandria (on the classical canon) this issue of elucidation of the text "by reference to the canonical text" was established hermeneutical procedure. The rules of association (which texts ought to be considered together) was determined by common thematic treatment or shared word usage. A more superficial example is the way Origen deals with Jesus's entry to Jerusalem (where the foal of an ass plays a cardinal role) with other examples in the Bible where that animal also appears. Dragging in Balaam's ass has often appeared risible to modern historicist critics (although it overlooks the way the original evangelist proceeds the same way, in principle, by associating Jesus's donkey with that of the peaceful messiah of Zech 9:9). Here there is a thematical allusion suggested to John 1 (the *archē* of the divine Logos) because of the evangelist Matthew's reference to "origins" in his genealogy.

by reference to another biblical answer (in the tradition of the rabbis), and nowhere, for him, is more significant to illustrate the true "origin" of the Son of God than the Johannine prologue, which deals with ultimate beginning ("Within the beginning [*archē*] was the Word").

In the *Catena* fragments of the *Commentary on Matthew*, another of Origen's remarks on Matthew's genealogy (Matt 1:18) has been preserved. Here he begins by noting the distinction in what Matthew says about the "book of generation" and the "birth of Jesus Christ," and asks: What is the difference between birth and generation? An idea is intangible and invisible, he argues, but once it is written in a book and given tangible form, it can be both seen and touched:

> And in the same way, the Logos of God who is devoid of flesh and body, being neither seen nor describable in his deity, is both seen and described when He is made flesh. It is because He was made flesh, therefore, that there is also a "book of his generation."[26]

This time he clearly reads the beginning of Matthew through the lens of the beginning (*initium*) of both the Gospel of John ("And the Word became flesh"[27]) and the First Epistle of John ("That which was from the beginning, which we have heard, which we have seen with our eyes, which we have looked upon, and our hands have handled, concerning the Word of life— the life was manifested, and we have seen, and bear witness, and declare to you that eternal life which was with the Father and was manifested to us.").[28] Having set the Johannine context by the reading of these three apostolic *Initia*, Origen then goes on, as in our previous fragment, to take up the Pauline apostolic witness by means of the Philippians hymn. This time we note how he also correlates it with Paul's remarks about the first Adam. He certainly notices the very heavy "Adamic" inferences present in the Philippians hymn—how the First Adam arrogated to himself a divine honor not his own and fell from grace because of it, while the Second Adam humbly did not arrogate a false honor and was exalted for it. Paul clearly held the idea of the Adamic antitheses very dear. If this has not escaped Origen, it often seems to have done so for many later commentators. Origen says:

26. Heine 1:325.
27. John 1:14.
28. 1 John 1:1–2.

Generation and birth are different things.[29] Generation refers to the initial formation by God, while birth is the taking up of the sentence of death by virtue of the passage from the one to the other. Moreover, generation is possessed of incorruptibility and blamelessness, while birth is liable to death and is prone to sin. Accordingly, He who had received the sinlessness of generation by His nature as Lord, did not [need to] assume incorruptibility in addition. And although He had assumed birth's liability to death He did not additionally assume its sinfulness as well, but bore the First Adam without diminution, with the attributes relative to both [states]. In the case of Christ, therefore, generation was not an advance from non-existence to existence, but rather the movement from being "in the form of God" to taking up the "form of a slave."[30]

Origen understands the entire motive of the advent of the Word to history as pedagogical. I have avoided using the term "incarnation of the Word" at this instance, for his own christological explanation of the advent of the Word to earth involved the mediating role of the Great Soul Jesus, who, being one in spirit with the eternal and divine Word, himself assumed flesh in order to live on earth as Jesus of Nazareth, and thereby served as the subjective medium for the Divine Word's personal advent to history. In such a way Origen carefully avoided the concept that the Eternal Word "personally" (that is, hypostatically) "changed into" a fleshly condition or "personally became flesh." It was a nicety in respect of which the following generation of patristic theologians (that is, Dionysios, Alexander, and—most famously—Athanasius of Alexandria) all corrected him, rendering the Logos the personal (hypostatic) subject of the incarnate experience and eliminating Origen's theory of the mediating Great Soul Jesus. Even so, Origen sees the whole purpose of the advent of the Word to Earth as a re-education of fallen souls: a consistent attempt to raise them up from ignorance and darkness, so as to enlighten them morally and mystically (especially about their own psychic origins) and prepare them for their destiny of ascent to union with God. This is the heart and soul of the dynamic of salvation instigated by the Logos of God, prepared from ancient times by the Word's own creation of

---

29. This had been a hot question among the Gnostic commentators, as Origen well knew. See R. Heine, "Origen's Alexandrian Commentary on Genesis," in *Origeniana Octava* 1:68.

30. Heine 1:325.

the body of sacred Scripture that will set out and chart this process of return that culminates in his own advent to his chosen people.

Three times in the Matthew Commentary, Origen uses the Philippians hymn of kenosis to illustrate this humble descent of the Word to save fallen souls. The first instance is in book 11, chapter 17.[31] Here Origen is commenting on the approach of the Canaanite woman who asked Jesus for help in liberating her possessed daughter.[32] He writes: "Now someone may well ask the meaning of this phrase—'It is not possible to take the loaf of the children and throw it to the little dogs'." So he begins with the literal meaning and agrees that in a normal household there would be no desire to feed dogs bread since (a) loaves were beautiful things unfit for such a use and (b) they were expensive and thus too rare to be so used. But, he goes on, why is Jesus giving such an answer to the woman's *spiritual* request? Could it be that his own spiritual power, like the rare loaves, was limited in capacity in his earthly state and had to be given only parsimoniously? Was this because, he asks out loud: "He who had emptied himself out to assume the form of a slave, had brought with him a limited power related to the capacity of earthly things?" Origen refers the reader at this point to the incident of the hemorrhagic woman who touched Jesus, causing him to say: "I know that power has gone out from me."[33] From this Origen concludes that there is clearly a sense that this power (*dynamis*) is related to particular events in the ministry—what a later theological era would describe as "economic" *dynamis*.

But he then presses on (as he habitually does after introducing what is basically an *aporia*, an open "seminar question" in the text: "Was the power limited?") to what he himself considers the deeper and more correct answer: the real question is not whether the power of the Lord was limited but rather why do children and little dogs receive different economies (of salvation)? And his response to this is that salvation and illumination are given according to the human being's spiritual receptivity. This is his overarching pedagogic theory of salvation. Children of God can receive the grace of God, but those who are dogs (a symbol of irrational recklessness) have hindered their own receptivity to the life God offers. However, when the Syrophoenician woman (presumed to be a "dog" by not being an Israelite) demonstrates her immense inherent spiritual faith, she thereby proves her capacity to receive

31. Heine 1:84–85.
32. Matt 15:25–26.
33. Luke 8:46.

the bread of children. In this, Origen concludes, she is the model for those who are like her, who "will obtain the kind reply of Jesus, who says to such a person: Great is your faith."

The second time Origen refers to the kenosis hymn as a symbol of humble soteriology in the Matthew Commentary is in book 13, chapter 10.[34] Here he is commenting on the incident where Jesus's disciples have been asked whether they are going to pay the poll tax.[35] This gives rise to the *aporia* set before the disciples by Jesus: Who pays taxes to the "kings of the land": sons or foreigners? Origen moves on to consider how foreigners in a strange land are not only not admitted to sonship, but are often even reduced to slavery, as was the case for the Israelites in Egypt, who were "forcibly reduced to slavery."[36] This triggers his use of Philippians:

> It was for the sake of those who are slaves (like the slavery of those He-brews) that the Son of God assumed only "the form of a slave"[37] since He performed no servile work of clay. But because He had that "form of a slave" He paid the customs duty and the poll tax no differently than that paid by His disciples, for the same stater sufficed, namely a single coin given for Jesus as well as his disciples.

His point here is a precise one: namely that assuming the "form of a slave" does not mean that the Son of God, as Lord of all, *actually became* a slave. Again, in a later generation, as is evidenced in the way Gregory of Nazianzus deals with the issues in the *Theological Orations*,[38] the language of *oikono-mia*[39] would be fitted to this question: namely, that in the earthly ministry the assumption of human life and its limitations was an economy of one who was the Lord, assuming the status of a slave, in order to work for the freedom of slaves so as to make them sons.

In Origen's mind, the importation of extraneous systematic terms (such as "soteriological economy") is not as preferable as making the point by a paralleled scriptural allusion; and in this case he concludes his argument by noting that

34. Heine 1:138–39.
35. Matt 17.24.
36. Exod 1:13.
37. Phil 2:7.
38. Gregory Nazianzen, *Orations* 27–31, composed in 379–380, with close awareness of the need to update Origen's christological terms.
39. The distinction of what was *kat' ousian* or *kat' oikonomian*: ontologically intrinsic or utilitarianly appropriate (essential or contingent characteristics).

the overall point of the passage is an ironic one (just as it began with an ironic *aporia* question): although Jesus does decide to pay the tax to Caesar (which Origen takes as a symbol of the "Ruler of this Aeon" who "has nothing in the Son of God")[40] he makes it clear that Christ does not "indebt himself" by using or touching anything that bears Caesar's image—and so instructs Peter to retrieve a coin from a fish in the sea. Origen ends by saying: "He did not assume a coin, or procure it, or obtain it, or ever make it his own possession, so that never might the image of Caesar exist alongside the 'image of the invisible God'."[41]

The third reference to Philippians' kenosis humility in the Matthew Commentary is given at book 15, chapter 7, where Origen is discussing why Jesus allowed children to approach him despite the harsher attitude of the disciples.[42] He wished to teach his adult followers, Origen says, "to condescend for the benefit of children, so that they might become children to the children in order to gain the children."[43] He then lifts out the *logion* of Jesus, "For to such as these belongs the Kingdom of Heaven,"[44] and connects this to the Philippians text, "Although He was in the form of God, He did not count equality with God a thing to exploit, but became a child." At this point Origen reminds his readers how Herod had ordered for a search to be made for this child and how the Nativity angel also referred to him as a child.[45] He concludes: "Jesus, therefore, not only in the historical sense, but also in the figurative, 'humbled himself as a child'." This switches the narrative of the children coming to Jesus back to the more potent text about the children in the earlier section of Matthew's Gospel where Jesus says that the "greatest in the Kingdom" is the one who is like the humble child.[46] For Origen this, of course, is the reference to Jesus himself, who in his very humility (the form of a slave) is revealed as the Lord. The rapid switching of symbols in the text might obscure for us moderns what was for Origen a definite and obvious textual link between the various "child passages" and the Philippians' symbol of the servant. In Greek the term for child (*pais*) is, we remind ourselves, the same cipher as for "servant" (*morphē doulou*).

These three episodes set what is for Origen a typical account of the humility of the Lord in his earthly ministry: his divinely pedagogic approach,

---

40. John 14:30.
41. Col 1:15; Heine 1:139.
42. Heine 1:197; Matt 19:13.
43. 1 Cor 9:22.
44. Matt 19:14.
45. Matt 2:8–9, 13.
46. Matt 18:4.

stooping down to the weakness of those he wishes to teach and save. This is what would be called in a later, more systematic, age the christological language of the incarnate economy, but in Origen (writing before the Arian controversy has raised the question to a high pitch) it is resolved, by preference, out of the whole cloth of a web of scriptural allusions tied together by shared referents.

On two occasions in his Matthew Commentary, Origen refers to the transfiguration narrative as one of his scriptural contexts for illuminating the Philippians' Christology.[47] The first is a long and reflective passage in book 12, chapter 37, which opens:

> Here is a point to investigate: When He was transfigured in front of those He took up into the high mountain did He appear to them "in the form of God" in which He existed long ago, just as He appeared to those who stood below in the "form of a slave." For those who had followed Him "into the high mountain" "after six days had passed,"[48] He certainly did not have this servile form, but rather the form of God.[49]

Origen makes, in this whole passage, the basic point that God appears only to those who have the spiritual receptivity to see, and to them in accordance with the degree of their "elevation," that is, spiritual initiation. The three chosen disciples are the symbols of advanced believers, whom Jesus is able to lead up on high to a better Sinai than that known by Moses, one in which the form of God does not pass by behind but is revealed to them face to face. This revelation makes their faces also shine with light (for which Sinaitic reference he prefers to use the reference of the Pauline theme as at Eph 5:8) to show that it is moral purity which makes the believer radiant in the sight of God and men: "When He is made manifest He will shine on these [sons of the day] not simply as the sun shines, but rather as revealing Himself to them as the Sun of Righteousness." Here, at the very end of the passage Origen brings out into the open the deeply eschatological nature of his thinking on the kenosis hymn in relation to the transfiguration event. He has explicitly noted the manner in which the evangelists preface the gospel narrative with the phrase "after six days." In Matthew the word "later" refers back to the occasion of the two *logia*: "For the Son of Man is to come with his angels in the

47. Mark 9:1–8; Matt 17:1–8; Luke 9:28–36; 2 Pet 1:16–18.
48. Matt 17:1.
49. Heine 1:120.

glory of his Father, and then he will repay everyone for what has been done. Truly I tell you, there are some standing here who will not taste death before they see the Son of Man coming in his kingdom."[50] So Origen takes as his cue that the eschatological motif of the glorious coming of the Lord inspires both the kenosis hymn (outlining the cosmic scheme of the Lord's salvation, and his *katabasis* and *anabasis* in the process of achieving it), and also the transfiguration narrative, which he interprets as an anticipation (before the purified disciples) of the final manifestation of the glory—that *Apokatastasis* when all creation will be pulled into the glory of the redeemer.[51] The "After six days" has thus suggested not only that the event happened, historically, a week after he had spoken about the coming of the Son of Man, but that he had symbolically manifested this (the radiance of the Glorious Son) as an eschatological event of the "seventh," namely, as the symbol of that last aeon of the seven-staged creation.

When Origen is commenting on the approach to Jesus by the father of the epileptic demoniac[52] in the Matthew Commentary at book 13, chapter 3, he returns to the parallelism of the kenosis hymn and the Transfiguration narrative to underline that the *katabasis* and *anabasis* is fundamentally a movement of the divine Logos to the world for the sake of a sacrificial pedagogy which demands that the incarnate teacher adopt the humility of those to whom he wishes to communicate salvation.[53] It is by virtue of this parallelism that Origen, perhaps more than any other writer of the early period, nails into the history of exegesis the interpretation that the "form of a slave" and the "form of God" refer to the humanity and divinity of the Logos:

> A man approached Him, falling on his knees before Him and saying: "Lord, be merciful to my son for he is epileptic and suffers badly." . . . Well, people who are suffering, or are the family of those suffering are not "on the mountain," but are part of "the crowd." Just so, for the sake of the people He himself descended to His human ministry from the high mountain of divinity, as it were, just as He had climbed the high mountain and had there transformed Himself into his glory, for the sake of his chosen disciples who knew Him. He had previously descended to the lowliness of His humanity for the sake of those who did not know Him. Once He became known to

---

50. Matt 16:27–28.
51. See also the similar approach in *Series Com. Mt.* 50, cited in Heine 2:625–26.
52. Matt 17:14–15
53. Heine 2:402.

them He led them up to the knowledge of His divinity so that they might say, along with the Apostle, "And if we have known Christ according to the flesh, we do not know Him in this way now."[54] This is why He descended to the crowd so that He might be of benefit to those who were unable to ascend on high because of their infirmities. If He had not come to the crowd with his chosen disciples, the man could not have approached Him, falling on his knees and saying: "Lord, be merciful to my son."

Kenotic Thought in Origen's On First Principles

Allowing for very obvious differences in the meaning of the term today, the *Peri Archōn* of Origen, or *On First Principles*, is, compared to his gospel commentaries, predominantly a work of systematic theology. It is also an early work (begun ca. 220). In it Origen sets out to expound the structure of the apostolic tradition that undergirds the early catholic faith. He does this for three reasons; first to underline the boundaries that separate catholicity from the gnostic traditions which were making claims to speak for educated Christian attitudes in the Alexandria of his day;[55] secondly, to demonstrate what were those areas of faith that had not yet been clarified by the wider Christian culture, and could thus stand some expert commentary and enquiry (often by means of *aporia* or open questions); and thirdly, to show the Christian intellectual tradition to good effect in the character of a school of philosophy (with himself as the *Magister Scholae*) deserving of serious student attention.[56] There are about half a dozen times Origen refers to the Philippians kenosis hymn in this seminal work.

Coming at the question of the relationship of the Word (*theos Logos*) to the Father (*autotheos*), Origen rivets the hymn's slavery–glory antitheses to the *katabasis* and *anabasis* themes of the Fourth Gospel to render them into ontological markers of being. As usual he approaches major questions of exegetical enquiry by going to the two primary carriers of the Apostolic tradition: John and Paul. Here the opening phrases of the Johannine prologue are very much behind his mind, but he explicitly begins by referring to

54. 2 Cor 5:16.
55. Origen would turn his attention next to making a magisterial corrective commentary on the Gospel of John, that takes Heracleon's example into account.
56. The text has been ably redacted and retranslated recently by John Behr: Origen, *Origen on First Principles*, ed. J. Behr, 2 vols., Oxford Early Christian Texts (Oxford: Oxford University Press, 2017) (henceforth Behr).

Paul's resolution of the problem he wishes to illustrate. Specifically, he notes how Paul describes the Son as the figure of the substance of God (*figura est substantiae vel subsistentiae dei*), equating this with the "splendour of glory"[57] and "the fullness of deity"[58]:

> In order that we may more fully understand how the Son is the "figure of the substance" or subsistence of God, let us use an example[59] ... so that we can see that when the Son, "who was in the form of God, emptied Himself," He intended to demonstrate by this very emptying "the fullness of deity."[60]

This paradox of emptying to demonstrate fullness reaches its explication at the end of section 1.2.8 when he explicitly returns to the Johannine text:

> By emptying Himself of equality with the Father and showing us the way we might know Him, He thus becomes the "express figure of His substance"[61] and we who were unable to look upon the glory of the Pure Light while it dwelt in the magnitude of His divinity, might now (since for our sake he becomes "the splendour")[62] find the way to look upon the divine light by gazing upon the splendour. . . . The Son of God, though placed in the very small confines of the human body, demonstrated that the immense and invisible greatness of God the Father was in Him through the similarity of His works and power. It is, as He said to his disciples: "Whoever has seen Me has seen the Father," and "I and the Father are One"; alongside which we should understand the similar saying[63]: "The Father is in Me and I in the Father."[64]

This equation of the humility and glory with the Incarnational descent is stated even more abruptly in the *Praefatio* 4 to the *Peri Archōn*: "In these

---

57. *Peri Archōn* 1.2.7–1.2.8. Behr 1:50–52 (*in loco* citing Heb 1:3).
58. Col 2:9.
59. He applies, with reservations, the example of a person unable to appreciate the significance of a monumental sculpture because of its vast size, but who can appreciate its beauty when a smaller model is shown to him.
60. *Peri Archōn* 1.2.8. Behr 1:52.
61. Heb 1:3b.
62. Heb 1:3a.
63. John 14:9; 10:30; 10:38; cf. Origen, *Commentary on John* 20.153–159.
64. *Peri Archōn* 1.2.8. Behr 1:52–54.

last times emptying Himself out He became human, and was incarnate; though being God, when He was made human He remained what He was, namely God."[65]

The poetic beauty of the antitheses of glory and humility, captured by the Philippians hymn, is not lost on Origen, as can be seen later in the *Peri Archōn* 2.6.1, when he sketches out the significance of the Incarnation for cosmic redemption:

> After considering such great things as these concerning the nature of the Son of God, we stand in the stupefaction of most exalted amazement that such a being, pre-eminent above all others should have "emptied Himself out" of His state of majesty so as to be made man and dwell among human beings,[66] as it is witnessed by that "grace poured out upon His lips,"[67] and just as the heavenly Father bore witness to Him,[68] and as is confirmed by the various signs and wonders and mighty deeds that He accomplished.[69]

Later in the *Peri Archōn*, when Origen is speaking about the final consummation of things when God will be all in all, he returns to the text of the Philippians hymn to again underscore his vision of the entirety of the salvific order as being a movement of the pedagogue Logos, teaching creation to ascend to its lost vision of God. The humility of the Pedagogue who stoops down to meet his ignorant charges is, Origen explains, the manner in which the Logos ontologically and morally exemplified total obedience in his own person, by his humble kenosis:

> The Only Begotten Son of God, who was the Word and Wisdom of the Father, even when He was with the Father "in that glory He had before the world was,"[70] "emptied Himself, and taking the form of a slave became obedient even to death"[71] in order that He might teach obedience to those who could not obtain salvation other than through obedience. . . . And since He had come to restore the discipline not only of ruling and reigning, but also that of obeying, as we have said, He first fulfilled in Himself what He desired to be fulfilled in others and became obedient to the Fa-

---

65. *Peri Archōn, Praef.* 4. Behr 1:14.
66. John 1:14.
67. LXX Ps 44:3; cf. Origen, *Selecta in Psalmos* 44.3 (PG 12.1428–29).
68. Matt 3:17.
69. *Peri Archōn* 2.6.1. Behr 2:202.
70. John 17:5.
71. Phil 2:7–8.

ther, not only to the point of death on the cross, but also in the consummation of the age, by means of embracing within Himself all those whom He subjects to the Father, and who thus come to salvation through Him.[72]

As was Origen's custom generally, he often considers many possible avenues of thought—not all of which he is willing to adopt. It is in the course of his reflections on the pedagogic force of the kenosis that at one time he reflects on the opinions of "some" of his predecessors. He does not stipulate who they were, but one suspects some unnamed gnostic sages from Alexandria. The passage has been preserved at the end of the *Peri Archōn* in the context of his thoughts on the *anakephalaiōsis*, or the recapitulation that is implicit in the final restitutory age (*apokatastasis*):[73]

> Some indeed want even that statement of the Apostle's (that is, "Who was in the form of God did not think it robbery to be equal to God but emptied Himself taking the form of a slave") to be referred to the soul itself, when it first assumed a body from Mary: since He most certainly restored to it the form of God by means of better examples [of behavior] and better teachings and recalled it to that fullness of which He had emptied Himself.[74]

After his death this was one of those "controversial statements" that were stored up by his enemies as proof that he was a heretic. Jerome quotes this passage in the most damaging (and careless) way he can manage:

> I reckon among the many bad things Origen said these to be especially heretical . . . that the soul of the Saviour existed before it was born of Mary, and it was this which was "in the form of God and did not think it robbery to be equal to God but emptied itself taking the form of a slave."[75]

And in this guise, it became one of the anathemata aimed against the Origenists (though largely attacking the teachings of Evagrius of Pontus) of the Council of 553.[76]

---

72. *Peri Archōn* 3.5.6. Behr 2:434.

73. Further see F. W. Norris, "Apokatastasis," in McGuckin, *Westminster Handbook to Origen*, 59–62; also H. Ramelli, *A Larger Hope: Christian Universalism from Christian Beginnings to Julian of Norwich* (Eugene, OR: Cascade, 2019), 41–63.

74. *Peri Archōn* 4.4.5. Behr 2:570.

75. Jerome, *Against Rufinus* 46.6–7; cf. Behr 2:619.

76. *Anathemata* 7 of the Council of Constantinople II (553); cf. Behr 2:618.

Conclusion

In conclusion, therefore, from Origen's exegetical use of the Philippians hymn we can see something of the richly imaginative mindset of one of the early church's greatest theologians. Two macro ideas undergird it all: his belief that Scripture is a mystical totality within which John and Paul are the deepest interpreters; and his vision that all the Logos's works are *dynameis/* powers of a humble pedagogy of salvation. By so riveting together the vision of Paul and John, Origen is the commentator *par excellence* who makes the Christian tradition read the kenosis hymn as primarily a tale of the incarnation of the divine involving a change of *staseis*: what in a later generation would soon be nuanced as stages in a doctrine of two natures.

6

Augustine, Kenosis, and the Person of Christ

Han-luen Kantzer Komline

Some doctrines appear to be late bloomers, rising from the seedbed of Christian thought only centuries or more after Christ. Kenosis, at least in its well-known forms, may seem a prime candidate for membership in this unhurried company. But while "kenoticism" did not emerge until the nineteenth century, "kenosis," the concept enshrined in Paul's statement in Philippians 2 that Christ *emptied himself* (*ekenōsen*), had already attracted attention, even in the earliest centuries of the church.[1] Since the term is scriptural, this attention should hardly be surprising. For these earlier thinkers, kenosis was as unavoidable as it was perplexing. Yet Augustine seems to have given it significantly more than the passing acknowledgment mandated by the re-

1. For a brief overview in English of early Christian approaches to the doctrine of kenosis, see Friedrich Loofs, "Kenōsis," in *Encyclopedia of Religion and Ethics*, ed. James Hastings (Edinburgh: T&T Clark, 1914), 7:680b–87. Michel-Yves Perrin, "Variations tardo-antiques sur Philippiens 2,5–11. 'La loi de l'humilité,'" in *Philippiens 2, 5–11. La kénose du Christ*, ed. Matthieu Arnold et al. (Paris: Les Éditions du Cerf, 2013), 41–73, provides a useful recent entry point into the secondary literature on the patristic reception of Phil 2:5–11. The most extensive published summary of early Christian treatments of kenosis, however, remains P. Henry, "Kénose," in *Dictionnaire de la Bible, Supplément V* (Paris: Letouzey et Ané, 1928), 7–161. On kenosis in Origen and subsequent Greek figures, see Michael C. Magree, "'Shaped to the Measure of the Kenōsis': The Theological Interpretation of Philippians 2:7 from Origen to Cyril of Alexandria" (PhD diss, University of Notre Dame, 2019).

quirements of biblical fidelity. The idea receives extensive, if piecemeal, consideration in his writings. This chapter analyzes Augustine's interpretation of the significance of kenosis for the person of Christ.[2]

Though Augustine cites Philippians 2:7 more frequently than any other verse within the Christ hymn,[3] his use of the phrase "he emptied himself" has eluded intensive scrutiny.[4] There are a number of possible explanations for this fact. First, Augustine never addresses kenosis programmatically in a single work. He does not have a commentary on Philippians, and only rarely do his discussions of the phrase extend beyond a few paragraphs. His treat-

2. In Augustine's Latin terminology the relevant terms, which together occur around two hundred times in Augustine's corpus, are *exinaniuit*, from the verb *exinanio*, and the nominal form *exinanitio*. Though rare, the latter form is attested twice at *Io. eu. tr.* 26.19, where Augustine states, "his sending, you see, is his *kenōsis*" and then puts the word *kenōsis* in Christ's mouth: "my *kenōsis*, in which he sent me" (my translations; CCL 36:269) and at *s.* 265E.2: "His *kenōsis* was to receive what is lowly, not to lose what is lofty" (my translation; PLS 2:806). In this note and subsequently, I use the standard abbreviations for Augustine's works and their critical editions employed in the *Corpus Augustinianum Gissense*. Unless otherwise indicated, English translations are taken from *The Works of Saint Augustine: A Translation for the 21st Century*, ed. J. Rotelle (New York: New City Press, 1990–).

3. See Albert Verwilghen, *Christologie et Spiritualité selon Saint Augustin: l'hymne aux Philippiens*, Théologie historique 72 (Paris: Beauchesne, 1985), 205. On the significance of Phil 2:6–7 for Augustine, see also Lewis Ayres, *Augustine and the Trinity* (Cambridge: Cambridge University Press, 2010), 146–47, 155–59.

4. P. Henry's extended treatment of kenosis in the early church accords but one part of one column to Augustine, and most of this is a pastiche of quotations preceded by a paragraph that begins: "Saint Augustine, who often cites Phil 2:5–11 but without ever tarrying there very long, does not teach us anything new." See Henry, "Kénose," 127. Though the topic of kenosis in Augustine, understood as his reception of the biblical term *exinaniuit*, has not received serious programmatic treatment, the theme does come up obliquely in studies of related topics in his oeuvre. Kenosis surfaces in discussions of Phil 2. Verwilghen, for example, treats the kenosis of Christ in *Christologie et Spiritualité*, 206–9, 488–90. See also his "Le Christ Médiateur selon Ph 2, 6–7 dans l'oeuvre de Saint Augustin," *Augustiniana* 41, no. 1 (1991): 469–82, and "Jesus Christ: Source of Christian Humility," in *Augustine and the Bible*, ed. Pamela Bright, The Bible through the Ages 2 (Notre Dame, IN: University of Notre Dame Press, 1999), 301–12. Kenosis also appears in treatments of humility in Augustine's thought. See, for example, Joseph J. McInerney, *The Greatness of Humility: St. Augustine on Moral Excellence* (Eugene, OR: Pickwick, 2016), 107–11. Treatments of Augustine's Christology have also touched on kenosis. See, for example, Volker Drecoll, "Der Christus Humilis," in *Augustin Handbuch*, ed. Volker Drecoll (Tübingen: Mohr Siebeck, 2007), 438–45, and Frances Stefano, "Lordship over Weakness: Christ's Graced Humanity as Locus of Divine Power in Augustine's Tractates on the Gospel of John," *Augustinian Studies* 16 (1985): 1–19.

ment of it is copious but diffuse. Second is the undertreatment of Augustine's Christology more generally. Less attention to Augustine's Christology has meant less attention to kenosis. Third, Augustine's treatment of kenosis toes what came to be regarded as the orthodox line when it comes to the significance of kenosis for the divine being and attributes. Its very "correctness" may have prematurely quenched scholarly curiosity.[5] Finally, the specific matter of kenosis has been eclipsed by its own immediate biblical context. So largely do the Christ hymn and the theme of humility loom in Augustine's thought and the interpretations of his commentators that kenosis easily collapses into more general considerations of the surrounding material.[6] Kenosis is a star lost in the dazzle of its own constellation.[7]

If anything about Augustine and kenosis is generally known, or at least familiar, it is his trenchant diagnosis in *Confessions*. In the Platonists, he writes, he "found expressed in different words, and in a variety of ways, that the Son, 'being in the form of the Father did not think it theft to be equal with God', because by nature he is that very thing." Yet something was missing: "But that 'he took on himself the form of a servant and emptied himself (*semet ipsum exinaniuit*), was made in the likeness of men and found to behave as a man, and humbled himself being made obedient to death' . . . that these [Platonist] books do not have."[8] However much other wisdom they contained, in the final analysis the absence of the self-emptying Christ from these learned books left Augustine himself empty. They did "not have [*non habent*]" the heart of the gospel, the good news of a God who descends.

Augustine's writings, in contrast to these Platonist books, abound with references to kenosis. He treats it in programmatic theological tomes; po-

---

5. In this respect, too, the fate of Augustine's account of kenosis serves as a microcosm of the reception of his Christology. See Brian E. Daley, "A Humble Mediator: The Distinctive Elements in Saint Augustine's Christology," *Word and Spirit* 9 (1987): 101.

6. Consider, for example, Stephen Pardue, "Kenōsis and Its Discontents: Towards an Augustinian Account of Divine Humility," *Scottish Journal of Theology* 65, no. 3 (2012): 271–88. Pardue acknowledges a distinction between kenosis and humility, but his analysis of Augustine focuses mainly on Augustine's treatment of the latter as a means of addressing concerns about kenosis in contemporary theology.

7. It is lost in terms of direct, programmatic analysis, not in terms of ad hoc retrieval or allusion. For recent constructive appropriations of Augustine's treatment of kenosis, see, in addition to Pardue, Jason Byassee, *Praise Seeking Understanding: Reading the Psalms with Augustine* (Grand Rapids: Eerdmans, 2007), 74; Matthew Drever, *Image, Identity, and the Forming of the Augustinian Soul* (Oxford: Oxford University Press, 2013), 163.

8. *Conf.* 7.14 (CCL 27:102). Augustine, *Confessions*, trans. Henry Chadwick (Oxford: Oxford University Press, 1991), 121–22.

lemical texts, including his anti-Manichean and anti-Arian writings; and in many of his pastoral works. These various contexts overlap: he takes on the Arians in discussing kenosis in *De Trinitate*; ponders the implications of kenosis for the mysteries of the intratrinitarian relations in his *Debate with Maximinus*, a homoian Arian Christian; and, with his congregation, considers kenosis in relation to both the Trinity and the dangers of subordinationism in his preaching. In each of these contexts, his overarching approach is consistent: kenosis happened, not by giving up the form of God, but by taking up the form of a servant.

With each of these interlocutors, Augustine's strategy is to situate kenosis in a more expansive hermeneutic than his polemical opponents can imagine. The incarnation scandalizes Faustus the Manichee almost as much as it would any good Platonist: "as if we believe that the divine nature itself came into existence from the womb of a woman," he scoffs.[9] Kenosis is not so much the presenting problem as it is Augustine's chosen solution. If Faustus would only understand how the Word emptied himself, a way would open for him to affirm the humiliation of the Lord.[10] But Augustine does not expend much energy warding off attacks on kenosis from this quarter; the natural sense of the relevant biblical text already flies in the face of such critiques.

Ultimately, Augustine is far more concerned to articulate the meaning of kenosis in conversation with varieties of Arian theology.[11] For, when it comes to kenosis, such perspectives can seem to take the Bible even more seriously than does Augustine. Indeed, Augustine's Arian opponent Maximinus seems to have believed not only that Philippians 2:7 was on his side but also that it expressed the heart of Maximinus's Christology.[12] In an Easter

9. The Manichees regarded Jesus as one of the "gods of salvation" emanating from God the Father. Use of Phil 2:5–11 in Manichean psalmody indicates their belief that Jesus took up human form but they did not believe that he underwent human birth or that a "divine incarnation" had occurred. See Michael Cameron, *Christ Meets Me Everywhere: Augustine's Early Figurative Exegesis* (Oxford: Oxford University Press, 2012), 103–5. On the Manichean use of Phil 2:5–8, see also 107–8, 124–25, 147.

10. Augustine writes: "After all, he was said to have emptied himself for no other reason than because he took the form of a servant, not because he lost the form of God" (*c. Faust.* 3.6).

11. On the use of Phil 2:6–7 in Latin Nicene writers and the anticipation of Augustine's anti-Homoian use of the term in Hilary and Ambrose, see Ayres, *Augustine and the Trinity*, 156–57.

12. See *conl. Max.* 15.2, 15.14, 15.15, where his guilelessness gets the best of him in live debate: "The words of the apostle are certain: *Since he was in the form of God* . . . but we preach with all our might that *he emptied himself.*"

sermon Augustine interprets Jesus's famous *noli me tangere* ("don't touch me!") statement as a caution to those of "Arian" persuasions. The Arians want to do what Jesus warned Mary about: in their eagerness to touch his human nature, they risk letting his divinity slip through their fingers. Augustine urges, "Don't touch, don't believe like that."[13] In other words, in Augustine's view, by seizing on subordinationist texts, these misguided interpreters are regarding the apparent inequality with the Father of the "self-emptied" Christ as itself something to be grasped. By fixating upon that and trying to wrest it from its context in the larger hymn, they have failed to touch God in Jesus. Augustine understands the exegetical attractions of this temptation. And perhaps this is why he so vigorously defends the notion of self-emptying against possible Arian interpretation: their tendency is as natural as was Mary's to cling to the body of the Lord.

Augustine does, in a limited number of texts, focus on the ethical implications of kenosis.[14] For Augustine, kenosis is an outworking of divine mercy[15] that models love,[16] humility,[17] obedience,[18] and accommodation to the spiritually weak.[19] On occasion he counters Arian interpretations of self-emptying by emphasizing the hortatory context for Paul's comments about kenosis: the self-emptying, far from signifying any deficiency in the Son's own nature as God, stems from humanity's deficiencies and its need for an example.[20]

Yet the concept of self-emptying in particular does not, for Augustine, primarily signal something we should do, offering a model for human action more generally.[21] Augustine sees kenosis as more than just an example

---

13. *S.* 244.3.

14. See *spec.* 35, *trin.* 7.5. On the imitation of Christ, see also Verwilghen, *Christologie et Spiritualité*, 285–94.

15. In his view, kenosis not only illustrates the divine mercy but also defines what "affection [*affectus*]," "compassion [*compassio*, though he uses the verb]," and "mercy [*misericordia*]" mean. To discover the significance of these terms, Augustine claims, we need look no further than Christ's self-emptying, which unites them in one act. See *en. Ps.* 33.1.9 (CLL 38:280). See also *s.* 361.17 and *s. Lambot* 25.1 = 265F.1.

16. See *diu. qu.* 71.3, *s.* 144.4 and *s.* 264.3.

17. See *en. Ps.* 126.5, *Io. eu. tr.* 55.7, *uirg.* 31, *s.* 30.9, *s.* 68.11, and *s.* 292.3.

18. See *Dolbeau* 2.8 = *s.* 359B.8. For a recent interpretation of this sermon, including a diagnosis of some of its more problematic aspects, see Matthew Elia, "Slave Christologies: Augustine and the Enduring Trouble with the 'Form of a Slave' (Phil 2:5–7)," *Interpretation* 75, no. 1 (2021): 19–32. Kenosis does not figure in Elia's essay.

19. See *en. Ps.* 30.2.1.2 and *cat. rud.* 15.

20. See *c. Max.* 1.5, 2.15.1 and *c. s. Arrian.* 6.

21. In this sense, then, some characteristics of the Christ hymn as a whole in Augus-

of humility. It is *the* "unequalled" example, which is also a remedy: "*But he emptied himself.* . . . What unequalled humility! Christ humbled himself [*humiliauit se Christus*]; you have something, Christian, to latch on to [*quod teneas*]. . . . Such is the example we have of humility, such the remedy for pride."[22] The God of the Platonists and the Manichees, a perfect being devoid of humility—the God who never emptied himself—was unreachable. The "God" of the Arian Christians, "God junior,"[23] as Augustine once quipped, was not worth reaching. But this God—this humble Jesus, this God who had emptied himself—was a God to which a Christian might cling, in both imitation and worship.

Augustine ventures to touch upon the mystery of kenosis without transgressing the Lord's command to Mary, while holding together Christ's perfect divinity and genuine humanity as neither the Arians nor the Manichees could. The resulting account of the implications of kenosis for Christ's person involves seven major theses: (1) kenosis signifies incarnation; (2) the subject of kenosis is the Son in his divine nature; (3) kenosis ushers in a new epoch ending in the cross; (4) kenosis is a matter of addition; (5) kenosis implies both equality and inequality; (6) kenosis has a varied but often paradoxical effect on the divine attributes; and (7) kenosis entails revelation in hiddenness. In and, to some extent, despite his efforts to articulate kenosis along the lines of these basic axioms, Augustine's quest, as always in his thought, was a return from the far country to the homeland found in the person of Jesus Christ—to go to Christ by way of this same self-emptying Son.[24]

Kenosis Signifies Incarnation

Augustine can be abstemious with his speculation on the meaning of kenosis. But he says enough for patterns to emerge. In sermon 341, for exam-

---

tine's thought, or even of smaller parts of the hymn including but not limited to the "self-emptying," do not necessarily apply to kenosis in particular. According to Verwilghen, for example, "the normative and figurative value of Phil 2.6–8 was principally deployed from the theme of humility." See Verwilghen, "Jesus Christ: Source of Christian Humility," 302. This statement does not hold true with respect to the self-emptying in particular.

22. *S.* 304.3 (PL 38:1396).

23. The inimitable translation of Edmund Hill. Augustine pronounces, "Let the Arian step forward. 'I,' he says, 'believe that Christ is God, but God junior'": *ego, inquit, deum credo Christum, sed minorem.* See *s.* 244.4 (PL 38:1150).

24. On the theme of Christ as both homeland and the way that leads there, see Goulven Madec, *Le Christ de Saint Augustin: la patrie et la voie* (Paris: Desclée, 2001).

ple, he quickly deflects attention from the "how" question about kenosis—Augustine's answer: "By his becoming man . . . he thereby *emptied himself, taking the form of a servant*"—and turns to the wherefore: "Why, in fact, did he empty himself?" The bishop's reply: "Not in order to lose divinity but in order to put on humanity." Only with this clarification does Augustine comment further on how kenosis occurred: "It was by appearing visibly in this way that he emptied himself, keeping back, that is to say, the majestic greatness of divinity, and presenting us with the fleshly garment of humanity."[25] This approach serves as a microcosm of his larger method of approaching kenosis. He starts with the economy of God's saving purposes, and then reasons back to the "how" within those parameters. When he does broach the "how" question it nearly suffices him to say: by taking on flesh. But his whole theology testifies to the beauty of the "why," and here too a convenient shorthand is available: love.

In an Athanasian mood, Augustine preaches that out of love God willed to save from death the human race he had made: "So *he emptied himself, taking the form of a servant, being made in the likeness of men*—because in the form of God he was not made . . . so the one who made all things was made himself, in case what he made should perish."[26] Though it required the making of the Maker, kenosis was, in a deeper sense, not inconsistent with God's nature at all, but perfectly in tune with his faithful love as Creator. Elsewhere Augustine emphasizes an intervening step. To save us from death, a mediator was required.[27] And to become the mediator, the Son had to empty himself.[28] Augustine famously describes Christ as at once our home and the road leading to it. But perhaps it is not so well known that, for Augustine, the paving was in kenosis:

> You have a home country, you have a way to it. You have a home country: *In the beginning was the Word* (Jn 1:1); you have a home country: *Since he was in the form of God, he did not consider it robbery to be equal to God* (Phil 2:6). You have a way to it: *The Word became flesh* (Jn 1:14); you have a way to it: *He emptied himself, taking the form of a servant* (Phil 2:7). He is the home country (*patria*) we are going to, he is the way (*uia*) we are going by.[29]

25. *S. Dolbeau* 22.11 = *s.* 341.11.

26. *S. Lambot* 16.2 = *s.* 265E.2.

27. On the connection of the themes of Christ's self-emptying (from Phil 2:7) and Christ's mediation, see Verwilghen, "Le Christ Médiateur."

28. See *en. Ps.* 103.4.8 and *exp. Gal.* 24.

29. *S.* 92.3 (PL 38:573).

Why did the Son of God empty himself? To become our way home.

As his parallel appeals to John 1:14 and Philippians 2:7 suggest, for Augustine kenosis signifies the incarnation. In some cases, Augustine explicitly identifies kenosis with incarnation.[30] In others, he places Christ's self-emptying and the incarnation in apposition.[31] He even cites Philippians 2:7 as evidence of the incarnation: "If the one who is always the Son of God did not himself become the son of man, how can the apostle say about him . . . *he emptied himself.*"[32] For Augustine, kenosis is not only, or even primarily, about the humility of Jesus Christ as a man but about the movement from God to humanity.

The Subject of Kenosis

Indeed, Augustine underlines that the subject of kenosis is, properly speaking, God the Son in his divine nature.[33] Augustine makes a pithy statement to this effect in a Christmas sermon: "It wasn't, after all, someone else, but he himself, equal to the Father in the form of God, who is of course the only-begotten Son of God, that *emptied himself, being made in the likeness of men.*"[34] Augustine's point here is that God truly did become incarnate, but he does attribute the self-emptying to the Son of God in the form of God in particular. In his *Homilies on the Gospel of John*, we find the same affirmation embedded in a more complex argument. Here, in the context of proving that the whole Christ includes both soul and flesh, Augustine draws on Philippians 2:6–7 to demonstrate that both the form of God and the form of a slave coexist in Jesus Christ. In the process, he specifies that it was "the Word in the form of God" who "took the form of a slave" by emptying himself.[35]

---

30. See *s.* 183.5, *trin.* 2.20, and *s.* 380.4.

31. See *s.* 214.6, *s.* 196.1, and *en. Ps.* 44.12.

32. *S.* 186.3.

33. In Verwilghen's words, Augustine "does not leave any room for doubt that the Son is the grammatical subject of the phrase" *exinaniuit semetipsum.* See Verwilghen, *Christologie et Spiritualité*, 207. Verwilghen devotes his section discussing the phrase *exinaniuit semetipsum* to showing that Augustine thought the subject of the self-emptying was the Son, not the Father or the Spirit, a point of significance in relation to the Arian argument that the pre-incarnate Son emptied himself out of obedience to the Father, indicating subordination in his divine nature. To counter this view, Augustine emphasized the Son's voluntary self-emptying. Cf. *c. s. Arrian.* 34 and *s.* 361.17. He emptied *himself*; he was not coerced into the incarnation.

34. *S.* 186.3.

35. See *Io. eu. tr.* 47.13, which Verwilghen identifies as the only text in which Augus-

Augustine also attributes the self-emptying to the Son in the context of emphasizing that the self-emptying and birth are his work, as well as the work of the Father, while actually being born is something the Son alone does.[36]

In regarding the Son as the subject of kenosis, is Augustine ruling out a concomitant identification of the subject with the historical Jesus Christ? Technically speaking, the answer seems to be yes. In his view, the moment of self-emptying marks the time when it begins to be appropriate to refer to the Son as Christ: "Before he assumed the form of the servant, he was not yet the Son of Man, but the Son of God. . . . He was not then Christ; he began to be Christ, when *he emptied himself.*"[37] Yet Augustine prefaces this statement by observing, "It said, nonetheless, of this same Christ, *Since he was in the form of God. . . .*" Technicalities are one thing; actual practice, even of the biblical authors themselves, is another.

Kenosis Inaugurates a New Epoch

However the agent of the event is described, kenosis indicates an epochal change. Before kenosis, the Son is "equal to the Father in the form of God" simpliciter. After he empties himself, taking on the form of a servant, he does and suffers things appropriate to this newly assumed form.[38] Kenosis inaugurates a kind of change *in re* that is expressed in how the Word acts. Kenosis is also a pivot point in terms of what kinds of christological statements pertain, as exemplified in Christ's own statements: "After emptying himself, he said, *The Father is greater than I* (Jn 14:28)."[39] In this descriptive sense too, the self-emptying is a kind of chronological dividing line. Because an ontological change has occurred, statements subordinating the Son to the Father hold with respect to his humanity (though of course without detracting from the simultaneous truth of statements of equality). Augustine describes the transformation effected in relational terms as well. Because of his self-emptying, our God has become our brother: "So the one who

---

tine explicitly poses the question of the subject of Phil. 2:7 in particular. Verwilghen also reasons that "if the subject of Phil 2:7 is essentially that of Phil. 2:6, one can" conclude that Augustine places certain nouns in apposition to the subject of *exinaniuit*, such as "our healer, our Lord and God, truth, head of humanity, savior of the body, etc." See Verwilghen, *Christologie et Spiritualité*, 208–9.

36. *S.* 52.11.
37. *C. s. Arrian.* 6.
38. See *trin.* 1.29.
39. *Ep.* 170.9.

was our Lord was prepared to be our brother; Lord always, brother from a point in time." How does Augustine mark or label the time when this transformation occurred? The answer is kenosis: "So where brother? *He emptied himself, taking the form of a servant* (Phil 2:6–7)."[40]

For Augustine, kenosis is not just one of many human acts of modesty. It is a divine-human turning point. As Augustine observes:

> There [*ibi*], where he clothed himself in the form of a servant, he took on our poverty. He emptied himself, lest you be frightened away by his wealth and not dare to approach him with your beggarly needs. There, I tell you, there [*ibi*] did he take the form of a servant, there [*ibi*] he arrayed himself in the rags of our poverty, there [*ibi*] he impoverished himself, and there [*ibi*] he enriched us.[41]

A quintuple emphasis does not exaggerate the kind or measure of change that occurs in the event of kenosis.

Yet to emphasize that what occurs precisely "there" brings about a transformation is not to divide the incarnation from the rest of Christ's life, or to separate it from the subsequent actions of Christ. Augustine sets the moment of kenosis apart, not in opposition to what follows, but because Christ's subsequent actions flow from it. Discussing the washing of the disciples' feet at the Last Supper, Augustine emphasizes in a series of rhetorical questions how the humble acts of this drama—each of which would be almost shocking on its own—are not so unbelievable given the radical self-humbling that has already occurred in kenosis; they are of a piece with this more basic divine act of service. He begins by asking, for example, "What is so surprising, though, about his rising from the supper and laying aside his garments, seeing that although he was in the form of God, he emptied himself?"[42] Augustine sees kenosis as a paradigmatic instance of God's humility, from which all subsequent acts of divine humility in the economy follow. This initial kenosis is so basic, profound, and radical, that, in one sense, these subsequent acts of humility cannot really exceed it or add anything to it to elicit greater surprise.

In another sense, kenosis is but the beginning of a crescendo that ends with the cross. As the resurrection marks the starting point of glorification, so kenosis marks the starting point of a path of humiliation: "His humility begins at the place where he says, *He humbled himself, taking the form of a slave,*

---

40. *S. Lambot* 25.1 = 265F1.
41. *En. Ps.* 101.1.1 (CCL 40:1425–1426).
42. *Io. eu. tr.* 55.7.

and goes as far as to *death on a cross."*[43] The Word's self-emptying begins the dynamic of humiliation whose most extreme point is the cross, the absolute pit of lowliness.[44] Kenosis marks both a dramatic change in itself and the beginning of a longer trajectory of humility that leads to Golgotha.

Kenosis as Addition

How does this radical act of humility occur? Judging by the frequency of his own statements, the single most important thing to say about Augustine's view of kenosis is that it involves the addition of humanity rather than the subtraction of divinity. He typically expresses this idea relying on Paul's own form of God/form of a servant phraseology, insisting that *"he emptied himself,* not losing the form of God, but *taking the form of a servant."*[45] Augustine's explanations presuppose repeated interrogation, whether coming from members of his congregation, his own inquisitive exegetical mind, Arian interlocutors, or—most likely—all three. In one sermon, he explains: "That's how he emptied himself, taking the form of a servant, not losing the form of God. The form of a servant was added, not the form of God subtracted. That is to confess that Christ has come in the flesh." And then he reiterates, lest there be any misunderstanding: "The form of a servant was added, not the form of God subtracted."[46] Elsewhere, Augustine indicates that the question of how the self-emptying happened was one that Paul himself had anticipated and immediately answered in the ensuing phrase of the Christ hymn: "It was by taking on the form of a servant that he emptied himself."[47] Augustine's response to the question of what self-emptying means is to repeat what Paul has already said: taking the form of a servant.[48]

Preaching on the Gospel of John, he restates the additive principle three times in a row: "not, therefore, losing the one but rather taking on the other"; "the form of a slave was added, in fact; the form of God was not subtracted"; and "the one was assumed; the other was not annihilated."[49] Augustine never

43. *Io. eu. tr.* 99.1.
44. *S. Dolbeau* 13.5 = *s.* 159A.5.
45. *C. Max.* 1.5. See also *c. Max.* 2.14.7, 2.15.1; *trin.* 1.14; *Io. eu. tr.* 67.1; *ep.* 140.4.12; *ep.* 170.9; *c. s. Arrian.* 6; *s.* 279.8; *s. Lambot* 16 = *s.* 265E.2; *s. Dolbeau* 22.11 = *s.* 341.11.
46. *S.* 183.5.
47. *S. Lambot* 16 = *s.* 265E.2.
48. *S. Dolbeau* 2.8 = 359B.8.
49. *Io. eu. tr.* 78.1 (CCL 36:523): *non ergo amittens illam, sed accipiens istam . . . forma quippe serui accesit, non forma dei recessit . . . haec est assumta, non illa consumta.*

saw kenosis as a metamorphosis whereby one form replaces the other, no matter how many times he reconsidered it. The repetition in these sermons well represents his rhetorical strategy in other individual works and across his broader corpus: this is a point worth hammering home.

Augustine also commonly underlines the additive character of kenosis by stating that the Son emptied himself by taking what he was not rather than by giving up what he was.[50] "Listen to how he emptied himself, hear how he didn't empty himself by losing what he was, but by taking on what he was not," Augustine urges, in one typical example.[51] In another sermon, he again takes the tack of triple repetition, at one point phrasing the principle in these terms: "So the emptying consisted of taking on a lowly state, not of losing a sublime one."[52] Elsewhere he makes the same point in slightly different language: in emptying himself "he both became man and remained God."[53] Whatever the wording, the logical structure is the same: kenosis is a matter of humanity gained not divinity lost.

Not content to leave this explanation in general terms, Augustine emphasizes that kenosis could never involve even a partial loss of divinity, whatever such a notion might mean. Augustine rejects two major forms of this, to his mind, objectionable approach to kenosis. First, kenosis does not diminish or downgrade the divine nature in any way. Perhaps Augustine's clearest repudiation of this idea occurs in his *Expositions of the Psalms*:

> *He emptied himself.* . . . Was he changed thereby? Was he diminished? Was he left the poorer? Did he fall or decline by accepting it? Far be it from us to think so. What does the text mean, then—*he emptied himself, and took on the form of a slave*? He is said to have emptied himself because he took to himself what was lower, not because he degenerated from his equality with God.

Not only, then, was divinity not lost in an absolute, final, or totalizing sense; rather, as Augustine suggests here using a variety of terms, the "godhead was in no way degraded."[54]

---

50. See *c. Max.* 1.5; *s.* 186.3; *s. Lambot* 16 = *s.* 265E.2, *s.* 292.3, *en. Ps.* 58.1.10; *ep.* 140.4.10–12.

51. *S. Dolbeau* 2.8 = 359B.8.

52. *S. Lambot* 16.2 = 265E.2.

53. See *ep.* 170.9. See also *ep.* 219.3.

54. *En. Ps.* 74.5.

Two of Augustine's letters echo this rejection. In one, he develops an analogy between the Son's self-emptying in the incarnation and the spiritual adoption of believers. Just as in becoming children of God, we remain human children, so in becoming human, the Word remains God. Augustine also points out some of the limits of such a comparison: "His participation in our nature did not make him worse, but our participation in his nature makes us better."[55] In another letter, as a part of his argument that the "form of God" is not lost in the self-emptying, Augustine offers a pithy rejection of the idea that kenosis diminishes the divine nature: "The man was assumed by God, but God was not consumed in the man" (*Ep.* 170.9). The divinity of Christ does not in any way fall prey to, or become exhausted by an encounter with, his humanity.[56]

Second, Augustine rejects the idea that the Word's divinity undergoes any change in kenosis. This is the mode in which he most frequently repudiates a partial loss of divinity. We find consistent statements of this variety in a wide array of texts, from *On Genesis against the Manichees* to *On the Trinity*. In the former he writes: "This again [John 1:14] doesn't signify any change in the nature of God (*commutationem naturae dei*), but the taking on of the nature of a lower, that is, of a human, person. That is also the force of the statement, *he emptied himself*." In the latter text we find the statement, "*he emptied himself* (Phil 2:6), not by changing his divinity [*non mutant diuinitatem suam*] but by taking on our changeability."[57] Across a number of different genres and contexts, Augustine unchangingly rejects any kenotic change to divinity.

There are certain prices Augustine is not willing to pay for this rejection. Docetism will not do: being clothed in humanity (being "found in *habitus* as a man"—Phil 2:7) did not mean "transformation into a man" but neither did it mean Christ's humanity was a deceptive appearance; instead, "he somehow united and conformed to himself and joined [humanity] to his own immortality and eternity."[58] Moreover, this union and conformity and conjoining involved more than the acceptance of an extraneous, alien appendage: by kenosis the Word became "one thing with that which he

55. *Ep.* 140, 4.10.

56. In *ep.* 219, Augustine also denies any "impairment" of divinity from the sufferings that *followed* upon the self-emptying of Christ.

57. See *Gn. adu. Man.* 2.24.37 and *trin.* 7.5. See also *trin.* 1.14, *ep.* 219.3, *f. et symb.* 18, *s.* 186.2; *s.* 187.4.

58. *Diu. qu.* 73.2.

had taken."[59] At the same time, Augustine unknowingly addresses what would later be called Nestorianism: "The form of the servant had to be distinguished, not separated and distanced and set up as another person."[60] As concerned as Augustine is to avoid any sort of compromise of, or alteration to, divinity, he also makes clear in his *Enchiridion* that kenosis results in but "one Christ from both natures" who is "one and the same" and "both." Indeed, Augustine at one point not only insists that such a union is compatible with kenosis but also that Paul's reference to self-emptying itself indicates the unity of the person of Christ: "He, one and the same, is both, one Christ from both natures since (*quia*), though he was in the form of God, he did not regard what he was by nature, that is, being equal to God, as something to be grasped. But he emptied himself, taking the form of a servant, not losing or diminishing the form of God."[61] There can be no diminution of divinity in kenosis, but neither can the import of kenosis itself be diminished so as to imply that humanity was taken on artificially, or in such a way as to be separable from Christ's divinity.

In the end, there is a kind of analogical echo, chiasmus, and even symmetry between the faithfulness of the Word to his divine identity in becoming human and his faithfulness to his human identity, even after departure from this world. Augustine says, addressing Christ, "I know of course that you emptied yourself, but because you took the form of a slave you didn't abandon the form of God, to which you would return, nor did you leave behind what you took."[62] In him is all the fullness of the Godhead. He is the one who fills all in all. But even when he ascends to fill all things and the whole earth is full of his glory, he will remain "empty" in the Augustinian kenotic sense, that is: human.

Kenosis and Equality

What are the implications of this paradoxical understanding of kenosis by addition? The threat of Arianism, which is for him live, not just historical,[63]

---

59. *S.* 361.16.
60. *S.* 47.20.
61. *Ench.* 35.
62. *Io. eu. tr.* 69.3. Later in the same section he repeats this idea: "You came through [flesh], while remaining where you were; you returned through it, while not abandoning where you had come to." Augustine also notes in *Io. eu. tr.* 99.1 that the form of Christ "presented at the judgment" will be "that which he took on when he emptied himself, for *he emptied himself, taking on the form of a slave.*"
63. He emphasizes this point in *s. Dolbeau* 22.13.

pressures Augustine to address one issue in particular: the question of what this self-emptying entails for the equality, or lack thereof, between the Father and the Son. Augustine devotes intensive and extensive attention to this matter, drawing repeatedly on his additive conception of kenosis.

Augustine's first step in responding to the question of the implications for the relationship between the Father and the Son is to admit that kenosis entails becoming inferior. Explaining the apparently subordinationist statement "I came forth from the Father" in John 16:28, for example, Augustine describes what Jesus meant as follows: "'It was not in the form in which I am equal to the Father that I was manifested, but in another guise, namely as less than he in the creature I took on'; and *I have come into this world*, that is, 'I have shown the form of a servant, which I emptied myself to take (Phil 2:7).'" For Augustine, the form of a servant entails being "less than" the Father and it is this form that is the result of self-emptying.[64] In *On the Trinity*, Augustine characterizes the self-emptying as basically synonymous with becoming inferior to God, stating that the Holy Spirit "was never an inferior, because he never *emptied* himself, *taking the form of a servant* (Phil 2:7), like the Son."[65] In his *Homilies on the Gospel of John*, too, Augustine takes Jesus to have indicated that by virtue of his self-emptying he is less than the Father.[66] Augustine's initial step in countering the idea of an absolute inferiority of the Son to the Father is to concede inferiority as a legitimate part of the story, namely, the part inaugurated and entailed in the self-emptying.

Augustine's Arian interlocutors take self-emptying as the whole story, such that Jesus Christ is inherently lesser.[67] But, as we have seen, for Augustine self-emptying is a change that happens insofar as humanity is added, without depleting the fullness of the godhead;[68] he is committed to embracing and qualifying the distinctions this change entails. Hence, Augustine speaks about the biblical testimonies to the equality of the Son with the Father just as forcefully as he does about biblical testimonies to his inferiority. By virtue of the Word's self-emptying, Christ is (in his humanity) less than the Father, but only "in the form of a servant," not without qualification. The self-emptying happened in such a way that "he remained equal to the

---

64. See *trin.* 1.21.

65. *Trin.* 1.18.

66. *Io. eu. tr.* 26.19: Augustine takes Jesus to be saying in John 6:57: "'That I might live because of the Father, that is, that I might attribute my life to him as greater, was the effect of my self-emptying, into which he sent me.'"

67. *S.* 244.3–4.

68. *S.* 293E.

Father in the form of God."[69] For Augustine, Philippians 2:7, paired with the preceding verse, supports the idea that the Son is "unequal to the Father" with respect to his humanity but at the same time "equal to the Begetter . . . in the equality of the divinity."[70] In that Paul directly juxtaposes, relates, and therefore upholds these two ideas simultaneously, the context of Philippians 2:7 constitutes an unmistakable indication of the compatibility of self-emptying with equality to the Father. This interpretation not only defangs the concept of kenosis as a potential indicator of absolute inferiority to the Father, but also helps to demonstrate that other texts, such as Jesus's statement in John 14:28 that "the Father is greater than I," can be compatible with the fundamental equality between Father and Son.

Augustine turns the paradoxical screw a few twists further with a counterintuitive idea: Christ is not only less than the Father in one sense and not in another, he is also less than himself in one sense and not in another. One might be inclined to dismiss this strange notion as an ill-considered christological slip.[71] But Augustine employs this unusual expression on multiple occasions, in both homiletical and dogmatic contexts.[72] Not one to suffer an attack lying down, he uses the phrase to offer a riposte, not by avoiding but by pressing even further into the validity of his opponents' claims. He revels in the paradox. Augustine wants to outdo the Arians at their own game: his perspective on self-emptying not only better accounts for the equality of Father and Son, but it also justifies a more full-throated affirmation of the Son's inferiority.

Augustine does not regard himself as venturing onto a constructive limb in stating the Son's inferiority in such bald terms. He sees the point as an inevitable entailment of the biblical text. Paul had already done the deed grammatically by using a reflexive verb:

> They say that the Son is less than the Father because it is written in the Lord's own words, *The Father is greater than I* (Jn 14:28); the truth, however, shows that as far as that goes the Son is less even than himself (*se*

---

69. See *c. Max.* 2.14.7. See also *Io. eu. tr.* 26.19 and *s.* 359B.

70. *Io. eu. tr.* 78.1.

71. Thomas Aquinas explains the proper interpretation of Augustine's affirmation that "the Son is less than Himself," noting how the phrase might be misunderstood, in *Summa Theologiae*, trans. English Dominican Province (New York: Benziger Bros., 1947), IIIa, q. 20, art. 2. Thomas does not attribute the phrase to any other authorities.

72. See *s.* 229G.4 = *s. Guelf.* 11.4, *Io. eu. tr.* 78.2 and *ep.* 170.9 in addition to the texts treated in the following paragraph of the main text.

ipso minorem). How could it be otherwise with him who *emptied himself, taking the form of a servant* (Phil 2:7)?[73]

Augustine literally deduces the slogan "he is less than himself" directly from the "he emptied himself" phrase of Philippians 2:7.[74]

At the same time of course, Augustine affirms the opposite point: the self-emptying makes Christ greater than himself too: "Christ himself, then, the Son of God, equal to the Father in the form of God, is also greater than himself because he emptied himself."[75] Insofar as the Son emptied himself, taking on a human nature in addition to his divine nature, and insofar as these two natures themselves entailed a kind of disparity of greatness, it naturally followed that the Son could be described as relating to himself in this way. Augustine's view was not so much proto-Nestorian as precisely proto-anti-Nestorian, proto-anti-monophysite, and anti-Arian in one stroke: the ontological distinction internal to Christ's person implied in the incarnation could not be resolved through segregation or by reducing the divine or human element to the other. Augustine's response to this Pauline paradox was simply not to resolve it at all. Christ was greater than himself and he was less than himself simultaneously as one unified person.

Augustine's tolerance for unvarnished paradox, while virtually unrecognized in this form and widely underestimated as a general characteristic of his thought,[76] anticipates the work of Cyril of Alexandria, whose insistence that the impassible God suffered in the flesh is well known. Augustine's claim that "the Son is less than himself" can be viewed as a way of articulating the ontological bedrock of Cyrilline-type formulations, even while acknowledging the distinctions that pertain between the different ways in which these two thinkers understand the person of Christ. Paradoxical affirmations about christological attributes are derivative upon the more primal reality Augustine describes, that of the coincidence without compromise of humanity and divinity in Christ. It is unsurprising in principle, then, to see that this parallel between Cyril and Augustine finds an echo internal to Augustine's thought as

---

73. *Trin.* 1.14 (CCL 50:45).

74. He offers the same biblical justification for the move a little later in *On the Trinity*. See *trin.* 1.22.

75. *Io. eu. tr.* 78.2. See also *trin.* 1.14.

76. Despite efforts to overcome the stereotyped opposition between Augustine the western father allergic to mystery and the associative, open-minded, and imaginative Greeks, such caricatures regrettably persist.

he speaks of "God crucified."[77] Augustine's willingness to use christological language that at first blush seems overtly contradictory finds a basis in the grammar of his ontological axiom that Christ is at once less than himself and greater than himself.[78]

Augustine devotes significant attention to the implications of kenosis for the Son's equality with the Father and even, as we have seen, to its implications for the unlikely notion of the Son's lack of equality with himself. In one place in his corpus, Augustine addresses a third kind of implication for relative status that kenosis entails, namely, subordination to other human beings. En route to making the point that Mary and Joseph were considered Jesus's parents, in his treatise *On Marriage and Concupiscence* Augustine discusses the sense in which Jesus was "subject to them" (Luke 2:50–51). His explanation: "Why then was he subject to those people who were far beneath the form of God, if not because he emptied himself, taking the form of a servant (Phil 2:7), the form of which they were the parents?"[79] This subordination by virtue of self-emptying to persons who would otherwise not only be inferior but on a categorically different ontological plane represents the extreme endpoint of a trajectory. Christ's kenosis is so complete as to extend from inferiority in relation to God the Father, to inferiority to his own self by divine nature, and even to inferiority to the very creatures of whom he is Maker.

It is striking that Augustine only makes the latter point in a single text, whereas his corpus is replete with comments about the implications of kenosis for the Son's equality (and inequality) with the Father and even with himself. This distribution signals the focus of Augustine's interest when it comes to the Word's self-emptying: the most pressing matter is not how the divine nature might impinge upon or unduly dominate Christ's humanity given kenosis but rather the possibility that this pattern might reverse.

A question Augustine raises in a sermon on behalf of his listeners points to his own key concern about kenosis. Augustine says: "he emptied himself." He imagines an interlocutor replying: "In what way, emptied? I'm afraid he must have lost his equality." Augustine responds: "Don't get that idea; listen to what follows, listen to how he emptied himself, hear how he didn't

---

77. *Trin.* 1.28.

78. In explaining a number of apparent contradictions in John, Augustine can write, "Thus you can have it both ways: both 'the Son of man will judge,' and 'the Son of man will not judge.'" See *trin.* 1.29.

79. *Nupt. et conc.* 1.12.

empty himself by losing what he was, but by taking on what he was not." The interlocutor is unsatisfied: "In what way? I implore you, tell me at once."[80] The bishop of Hippo's manifold efforts to grapple with the topic befit the urgency of the question.

Kenosis and the Divine Attributes

One gains further insight into Augustine's approach to the concrete character of the self-emptying by considering *ad hoc* comments he makes throughout his corpus. Christ was emptied, he explicitly states, of "majesty," of "what he possessed,"[81] of "nobility,"[82] and of "beauty and seemliness."[83] In the first of these passages, we find the closest thing in Augustine to a suggestion of an actual change or transformation of the divine nature involved in the self-emptying, rather than just the addition of humanity. Augustine writes:

> And so God's only Son became the *mediator between God and human beings* when the Word of God, God with God, both laid down his own majesty to the level of the human [*maiestatem suam usque ad humana deposuit*] and exalted human lowliness to the level of the divine, in order that he—a human being who through God was beyond human beings—might be the *mediator between God and human beings*.[84]

If this excerpt were the only statement Augustine made about kenosis, the notion of "laying aside" (*depono*) might be taken as indicating that the Son's majesty was temporarily relinquished. If indeed Augustine does mean to suggest actual relinquishment, developments in his theology over time may help to explain the incompatibility of this statement with his usual approach to kenosis.[85] Yet it would be hard to make a strong argument for such a

80. *S. Dolbeau* 2.8 = *s.* 359B.8. Augustine's starting point is to reply: "taking the form of a slave," but the conversation continues.
81. *En. Ps.* 68.1.9.
82. *En. Ps.* 28.6.
83. *En. Ps.* 103.1.5.
84. *Exp. Gal.* 24 (CSEL 84:87).
85. Augustine's commentary on Galatians was written early in his career, between 394 and 396. See Eric Plumer, *Augustine's Commentary on Galatians: Introduction, Text, Translation, and Notes* (Oxford: Oxford University Press, 2006), 3–4. Augustine's Christology developed significantly over the course of his career. For an overview of some key changes, see Daley, "A Humble Mediator." Over time, however, Augustine tended to take Christ's humanity with more, rather than less, seriousness, at least if the issue of Christ's

reading. An interpretation along the lines of veiling or concealment is more plausible in light of Augustine's statements elsewhere.

Christ's beauty provides a case study in how Augustine thinks through what it means for Christ to lack an attribute one would expect to belong to him by virtue of his divine nature. Augustine does in one place indicate that Christ "was devoid of beauty (*speciem*) and majesty (*decorem*), because *he emptied himself*," observing that on a basic empirical level, Christ simply had no comeliness to commend him: "most assuredly did people see him stripped of beauty and majesty."[86] At the same time, however, Augustine affirms what he takes to be said of Christ in Psalm 44:3 (LXX): that he is fair beyond all the children of human beings. How could this be since he was human? Augustine explains that Christ's beauty consisted precisely in his willingness to become "ugly himself" in order to come "to the ugly one [i.e., the church] to make her beautiful." His beauty was a matter of spiritual humility and generosity. From a physical standpoint, "he became ugly [*foedus*], he was himself deformed [*deformis*]."[87] Augustine sees Paul as uniting both of these testimonies with his reference in Philippians 2:6–7 to the form of God and the form of a servant.[88]

Augustine also comments briefly on the implications of kenosis for some of the classical divine attributes. Whatever omnipotence may mean, it must be compatible with genuine physical weakness and needs. In interpreting the story of the Samaritan woman, Augustine therefore observes:

> The weariness he suffered was the Lord's weakness, the weakness of strength itself, the weakness of wisdom, and this weakness is his humility. Thus, when weakness obliges him to sit down, his very posture betokens humility. Moreover, his need to sit down, this humility on his part, was our salvation, for *the weakness of God is stronger than mortals* (1 Cor 1:25).

---

human will is any indication. See Han-luen Kantzer Komline, "The Second Adam in Gethsemane: Augustine on the Human Will of Christ," *Revue d'études Augustiniennes et Patristiques* 58 (2012): 41–56; *Augustine on the Will: A Theological Account* (Oxford: Oxford University Press, 2020), 277–330. So if the early date of the *Commentary on Galatians* is a factor in explaining Augustine's unusual statement, this may have to do more with the experimental and unsettled nature of his thinking as a whole in this time than with particular developments in his Christology.

86. Augustine is quoting Isaiah 53:2. See *en. Ps.* 103.1.5 (CCL 40:1477).

87. *En. Ps.* 103.1.5.

88. Augustine offers similar interpretations of Christ's beauty and comeliness in *adu. Iud.* 5 and *s.* 95.4.

Here we find a common theme in Augustine: the idea that weakness and humility are, from the vantage point of God's kingdom, power and greatness.[89] Christ did not feign physical needs: he was "obliged" by weakness to sit down. He really did take on genuine weakness in a physical sense yet, in an absolute sense, he remained omnipotent precisely in and through this bodily frailty, even if he did not look so.

Augustine comments briefly on other attributes in relation to kenosis as well. When it comes to omnipresence, Augustine articulates a view compatible with the *extra Calvinisticum*. Because of kenosis, the Son as "unequal to the Father" can go from place to place and will come to judge the living and the dead. But as the Father's equal, "he never leaves the Father, but with him he is everywhere in his totality and in the equality of the divinity that no place contains. For, *although he was in the form of God . . . he emptied himself.*"[90] Augustine makes clear that the immortality of the Word is not abrogated in the self-emptying with respect to divinity,[91] even as kenosis did entail his becoming "subject to death . . . in the flesh. . . . For *he emptied himself.*"[92] Augustine's treatment of the Word's omniscience falls short of his usual nuance. Augustine takes Jesus's statement in Mark 13:32, "of that hour and day no one knows, neither the angels in heaven nor the Son, except the Father," as an indication that "what he does not know is what he makes others not know, that is, what he did not know in such a way as to disclose there and then to the disciples."[93] In essence, Augustine pins the lack of knowledge on the disciples to avoid attributing it to Jesus himself. In his defense, his reasons for this reading are other passages that he takes to establish omniscience as a given; canonical exegetical considerations come into play. On the issue of immutability, Augustine maintains a more balanced view typical of his treatment of other attributes: in his divine nature he "remained immutable," but taking on a human nature entailed assuming "our mutable nature."[94] Repeatedly,

89. On this point, see McInerney, *The Greatness of Humility*; Pardue, "Kenōsis and Its Discontents." This paradoxical character of humility is the focus of Pardue's interpretation of Augustine on kenosis and humility. On Christ's weakness, cf. also *s. Liver* 8.7 = *s.* 265A.7.

90. *Io. eu. tr.* 78.1. Loofs notes that the view later known as the *extra Calvinisticum* represented "the settled belief of all the theologians of the early Church" both east and west. See "Kenōsis," 684.

91. *Conl. Max.* 14 and *s.* 187.4.

92. *S. Dolbeau* 26.40.

93. *Trin.* 1.22–23.

94. *C. Faust.* 3.6.

Augustine appeals to kenosis as explaining why we may conclude that certain attributes do not apply to Christ in his human nature.

Augustine's approach to interpreting these attributes in relation to kenosis yields a few overarching observations. First, the Bible often influences Augustine's treatment of the attributes, or at least this is how he presents things. He does not have one rigid paradigm that he imposes woodenly on all the attributes but, to a certain degree, takes things case by case in light of biblical evidence. This tendency makes sense given that Augustine lacks a programmatic treatment of kenosis and ends up reflecting on these attributes as they arise organically in exegetical considerations of various passages. Nonetheless, it is also the case that Augustine operates under certain assumptions. One of these is that Christ does not just have attributes but is them.[95] A second follows logically from the first: as a rule, the divine attributes cannot be relinquished: "When he emptied himself, he did not lay aside what he had but he took on what he didn't have."[96] Yet Augustine is also committed to a real unity of the human and divine natures in a single person. The single most important illustration of how Augustine's discussion of the divine attributes in light of kenosis balances these various commitments appears in *s.* 212.1. Here we find on display Augustine's highly paradoxical view whereby Christ retains the classic attributes of divinity while at the same time becoming their opposite:

> But since *he emptied himself,* not losing the form of God, but *taking the form of a servant* (Phil 2:7), through this form of a servant the invisible one was seen, because *he was born of the Holy Spirit and from Mary the virgin.* In this form of a servant the almighty became weak, because *he suffered under Pontius Pilate;* through this form of a servant the immortal one died, because *he was crucified and buried.*

He is invisible while seen, almighty in weakness, immortal but dies.

Kenosis and Revelation

Lurking in the crannies of Augustine's writings, never too far from daring paradox, is language of concealment. Kenosis makes the invisible God seen,

---

95. *Trin.* 1.26: "The Son of God, the only-begotten *through whom all things were made* (Jn 1:3), is not like a creature (not at least before his incarnation and his taking on of a creature) in that what he is differs from what he has; what he is is the very same as what he has."

96. *Io. eu. tr.* 55.7 (CCL 36:466): *non quod habebat deposuit, sed quod non habebat accepit.* Note the verbatim contradiction of *exp. Gal.* 4, discussed above.

the Son perceptible. Even as he "passed by" the literally blind men in Matthew's Gospel, so, because of kenosis, he passes by us, entering our time, making himself available to be known.[97] And yet there is also a stream in Augustine's thinking that emphasizes the hiddenness of God in the self-emptied form of Christ. The whole purpose of kenosis is God's self-revelation, but kenosis also involves an element of obscurity.

At one point, Augustine uses neutral language to describe this shadow side: by virtue of having emptied himself, the Son does not "appear [*apparuit*] ... in the form in which he is equal to the Father."[98] The Word empties himself without ever "forsaking" or "withdrawing" from the Father, Augustine explains in his christological reading of Ephesians 5:31, but at the same time he does not manifest himself in the "form of God" that is his by nature. This is the sense in which he does "leave the Father." Even in and through kenosis, the Word is with God and the Word is God, but he does not always appear in this light, Augustine observes.

For Augustine, this appearance is not so much wrong as incomplete. The Father *appears* greater because he is so with respect to the fact that the Word "*emptied himself and took on the form of a slave* (Phil 2:6–7)." But this is only part of the picture. Though "the Jews assumed that what met their eyes was all there was to him," this part did not exhaust the whole.[99] For Augustine, the Son's condescension to be known in this small way shows in what kenosis consisted: "In what sense, then, did he empty himself? By appearing to you in such a way, by not revealing to you the dignity he had with the Father, by offering to you now only his weakness, and reserving the sight of his glory for you later, when you are purified."[100] Augustine makes this same kind of quantitative thinking even more explicit just a little later when commenting on the perplexing *noli me tangere* passage: "Do not think that what you see is all there is of me, or your eyes will be as restricted as your sense of touch. I appear lowly to you, for *I have not yet ascended to the Father*."[101] In other words, kenosis is a matter of a restricted, or limited—not necessarily false—perspective on who Christ is.

---

97. *S.* 88.11: "if he had always remained equal to God in the form of God, he would not have emptied himself, taking the form of a servant; nor would the blind men have perceived him, so as to be able to cry out."

98. *Io. eu. tr.* 9.10.

99. *En. Ps.* 63.13.

100. *En. Ps.* 58.1.10 (CCL 39:737). I have modified Maria Boulding's translation, replacing the phrase "appearing to you in that humble guise" with "appearing to you in such a way [*tibi talis apparuit*]." The term "guise" is not in Augustine's Latin.

101. *En. Ps.* 58.1.10. See also *Gn. adu. Man.* 2.24.37.

In a number of texts, Augustine uses stronger language. It is not simply that kenosis discloses a partial picture of who Christ is, a picture in which only one aspect of his dual identity appears. Kenosis also involves hiddenness, or even concealment. In one sermon Augustine pronounces, "For *he emptied himself.* . . . This was not said in such a way that we should conclude he had been changed, but because he wished to be manifested in a humble and servile [way], while remaining secretly [*manens in secreto*] Lord and God with God."[102] He likewise urges in one of his expositions of the Psalms that contemplating the vision of Christ of Philippians 2:7, a vision of Christ as "poor man," we ought to "understand that where weakness is displayed before your eyes, there godhead lies hidden."[103] On the surface, one sees the poverty he assumed to give us wealth; the secret beneath is that the son is "rich, because that is what he is."[104] Augustine can describe this hiddenness as active and intentional: "So he emptied himself among us, not by becoming what he was not in such a way that he would no longer be what he had been; but by concealing what he was [*occultans quod erat*] and openly displaying what he had become."[105] In these more extreme statements, self-emptying, for Augustine, involves a kind of self-concealing.

Reconsidering Augustinian Kenosis

Augustine's discussion of the concealment involved in kenosis is another instance in which his treatment of self-emptying tends toward an emphasis upon the divinity of Christ. Eager to counter subordinationist interpretations of kenosis, he sought to restrict the attribution of self-emptying to Christ in his human nature. An implied distinction in Paul supported him in this move. A self-emptying entailed some kind of differential in Christ's person. As Augustine capitalized on this and other features of the biblical text to counter subordinationist readings, he threw the divine nature of Christ into relief.

Despite the heavy layer of theological and exegetical explanations with which he wraps the divine nature of the Son, kenosis is not, for Augustine, cold christological doctrine—an oxymoron if ever there was one. Kenosis is,

---

102. *S. Dolbeau* 26.40 (Dolbeau, Vingt-six, 397/961). To avoid overstating things, I have tweaked Hill's translation, replacing the word "guise" with "way." Augustine's Latin reads *quia humiliter et seruiliter uoluit apparere.*

103. *En. Ps.* 40.1. See also *s.* 244.304.

104. *En. Ps.* 40.1.

105. *S.* 187.4 (PL 38:1003). See also *s. Lambot* 16 = 265E.2 (PLS 2 805:51) for a passive construction: "Inside, God was concealed in the man [*intus in homine deus latebat*]."

for the bishop of Hippo, a powerful testimony to the ardent love of God. In his early dialogue *On Order*, probably recorded on a heady philosophical retreat shortly before his baptism, Augustine had compared God's providence to a beautiful tapestry woven according to a pattern whose appreciation required a view of the whole. But in a sermon on providence from the thick of his pastoral career, Augustine ends with an entirely different sort of appeal. The single most important reason to believe that God cares what happens to us, he writes, is not the orderly courses of the stars in the heavens, the beauty of the earth, or even the marvelous workings of the human body, though all of these do, Augustine believes, point to the benevolent providence of the Creator. The single most important reason to believe in God's goodness is not a persuasive image or a general class of creaturely beings. The single most important reason to believe that God cares for us is particular—and personal. Indeed, it is a particular person: the self-emptying Savior. Kenosis is the best proof we have of God's love.[106]

106. *S. Dolbeau* 29.11 (= *prou. Dei*): "As for us, however, besides these obvious signs of order to be perceived in heaven and earth, we have in faith the surest possible indication to prove to us that human affairs fall under God's care, such that it would be unlawful for us not just to deny this, but even to doubt it: namely our Lord Jesus Christ himself, *who though he was in the form of God, did not reckon it robbery to be equal to God, but emptied himself* (Phil 2:6–8)."

7

Cyril of Alexandria and the Sacrifice of Gethsemane[1]

Katherine Sonderegger

In his lecture series, *Incarnation and Atonement*, T. F. Torrance speaks eloquently of the saving condescension and descent of the true Son of God:

> We have to think of this [Incarnation] as the condescension of the Word, to enter into our humanity and within our humanity to accommodate himself to us in reconciling revelation. Thus the eternal Word or Son of God veiled his effulgence of glory that our weak eyes might behold him in the meek and lowly Jesus, and in communion with him be raised from seeing him in the form of a servant to seeing him in the glory of the one whose name is above every name. As his poverty means that he stooped down to enter our flesh, that he brought divine omnipotence within the compass of our littleness, frailty and weakness, that he the holy one entered our bondage and curse under the law, so it means that the eternal Word and truth of God entered into the darkness of our ignorance in order to redeem us

---

1. This essay, which began life as a Costan Lecture in Patristic Theology, owes two happy debts: one to the Costan family which graciously endowed the lecture series at Virginia Seminary, and the other to Bruce McCormack who has been a lifelong friend, colleague, and exemplar of Barth interpretation and of dogmatic passion. His profound fidelity of Jesus Christ as sum and foundation of any proper theology, of any proper Christian life, is a testimony I deeply admire and am grateful for.

from the power of darkness and ignorance, in order to deliver us from the untruth and to make us free for and in the truth of God.[2]

Augustine and Barth speak boldly in this passage. Torrance does not make use of the transliterated term *kenosis* in this section, but the semantic field of the whole is redolent with it. Lowliness, veiling of glory, stooping down, entering into the compass of our littleness: all the fundamental idioms of kenosis. Perhaps in this particular form of Scottish Reformed dogmatics, the notion has entered deep into the marrow of the Christology of Bruce McCormack. Torrance's Scriptural and dogmatic idiom allows for Barth's hesitation to embrace the divine self-abdication of later nineteenth-century German and English kenoticists, yet does not shy away from the profound movement of descent that animated Augustine's treatment of the *forma servi* in *De Trinitate*. As Augustine knew, the "form of a servant" is tried in the cauldron of Gethsemane. Any Christology that affirms the deity of the Son is challenged by Christ's passion, but it poses a special riddle for Cyrillian Christology, a "single subject" Christology, as the irrepressible Cyril scholar John McGuckin expresses it.[3] In my reading of McCormack's Christology, he combines a commitment both to Cyril and to the singular self-emptying of the Son in his passion, a Cyrillian kenosis, we might say. The history of patristic furor over the form of union in the one Christ between his humanity and deity makes Gethsemane the trial and the limit of a proper doctrine of the incarnation. To bring kenosis and Cyril into one firm, conceptual whole is the special province of McCormack's Christology, and in a much more modest compass, this essay. But to do so with proper reverence for the biblical text and for the supreme personal union of the God made flesh is no simple matter. For how can the one, eternal Son of God undergo suffering in his own flesh, and die on a Roman cross? It is no straightforward answer a Cyrillian can give to this axial question of the faith; yet without it, no true Christology of the one who took that cup of suffering for his own can be imagined. The winding path must be pursued to its end. So, we begin with Cyril and his own special encounter with Gethsemane.

---

2. T. F. Torrance, *Atonement: The Person and Work of Christ*, ed. R. T. Walker (Downers Grove: IVP Academic, 2009), 162–63.

3. See, for example, his unreserved defense of Cyrillianism in John McGuckin, *St. Cyril of Alexandria and the Christological Controversy* (Crestwood, NY: St Vladimir's Seminary Press, 2004).

The Unity of Jesus Christ

Here is Cyril on Gethsemane and the cry of dereliction, as expressed in his late essay, *On the Unity of Christ*:

> And so the Word of God became an example for us in the days of his flesh, but not nakedly or outside the limits of the self-emptying. This was why he was quite properly able to employ the limitations of the manhood. This was why he extended his prayer, and shed a tear, at times even seemed to need a savior himself [an amazing thing for Cyril to say!], and learned obedience, while all the while he was the Son. It was as if the Spirit-bearer in this passage was almost astonished at the mystery, that he who was truly and naturally the Son, and eminent in the glories of the Godhead, should bring himself to such abasement as to undergo the abject poverty of the human state. Yet the beautiful and helpful example of this action was for our sake, as I have said. . . . For he did not sin, but the nature of man was made rich in all blamelessness and innocence in him, so that it could now cry out with boldness: My God, My God, why have you forsaken me? Understand that in becoming man, the Only Begotten spoke these words as one of us and on behalf of all our nature.[4]

The passion of Jesus Christ strains the very limits of Cyril's Christology; indeed of every attempt to properly consider the incarnate life of the Son of God. Time and again, Cyril will point to the utter mystery, the ineffability of this self-giving descent of the Son to us and in our kind. He knows—far better, I would say, than his opponent Nestorius—that theological language must find itself at the very edge of sense and rationality when it speaks of the suffering death of the eternal God. Cyril did not however allow his confidence to give way. He did not attempt to resolve this pathos by crudely dividing up the natures: God does these things, in these passages; the human does these other things, in these other passages. No, that was to "divide the person," to borrow Chalcedonian language here for a moment, and to exalt a slender section of Pope Leo's letter—the Tome of Leo, as it's called—to a central christological teaching. That troubling phrase from the Latin magisterium seemed all too Nestorian for Cyril's comfort. Embedded in much that sounded familiar to Cyril and orthodox to the council was this from Leo's

---

4. Cyril of Alexandria, *On the Unity of Christ*, trans. John A. McGuckin (Crestwood, NY: St Vladimir's Seminary Press, 1995), 103, 105.

Tome: "Each nature of Christ doing what was proper to it."[5] We can spot the danger right away: the sole acting subject of the incarnate life, the eternal Son, seems now to be replaced by two agencies, two natures, each acting it seems on its own, One radiant with life and immortality, the other suffering and weighed down with grief, possible and passionate, even unto death. Of course, it seems to solve many of our worries—hence its popularity down to our own day—but at a terrible cost! We cannot vindicate one unitary life out of divisions of this kind. The vital term, unity, or in the more expressive Greek, *henōsis*, making one, must mean that the Word of God becomes one with its flesh; one Christ, one Son, one Lord.

I want for a moment to distinguish Cyril's position from some other modern contenders for the ineffable unity of deity and humanity in Christ. For Cyril this ineffable unity that just is Christ does not take the form of *contradiction* or, in more modern idiom, of *paradox*. Cyril is not a Hegelian; that is, he does not see the death of the Son of God as the utter negation of the immutable God, becoming in a dynamic contradiction the higher unity of the God who is Absolute Spirit. Nor does Cyril entertain the language that Søren Kierkegaard and later Paul Tillich make stylish in modern Christologies: that Christ is himself "paradox," a unity of two irreconcilable realities, God and mortal humanity. No, Cyril aims for something higher here; or perhaps better, something more scriptural, more spiritual and mysterious. He seeks what many commentators call a *theandric* reality, a God-Man who is utterly One, the Word incarnate as a single, unique, unrivalled saving life. And that life must make the dark passage through death: it must become sacrifice.

Let me add one final citation from Cyril's treatise here to complete our stage setting, before we enter deeply into this final mystery of the incarnate one's earthly life. Cyril's interlocutor asks the question we have all longed to raise:

> But they [Cyril's Nestorian critics] say, how can the same one both suffer and not suffer?

And here is Cyril's answer—of a kind:

> He suffers in his own flesh, and not in the nature of the Godhead. The method of these things is altogether ineffable, and there is no mind that can attain to such subtle and transcendent ideas. . . . The force of any

---

5. The Tome of Leo, as translated by William Bright, can be found in *Christology of the Later Fathers*, ed. Edward Hardy (Philadelphia: Westminster, 1954), 359–70.

comparison falters here and falls short of the truth, although I can bring to mind a feeble image of this reality which might lead us from something tangible, as it were, to the very heights and to what is beyond all speech. It is like iron, or other such material, when it is put in contact with a raging fire. It receives fire into itself, and when it is in the very heart of the fire, if someone should beat it [here the analogy takes up the Passion], then the material itself takes the battering but the nature of the fire is in no way injured by the one who strikes.[6]

Notice here the analogy that will become vital in eucharistic as well as christological debates, the iron, heated red-hot in the roaring fire. In that molten bar there is fire and there is iron, the two distinct natures even in their joining, the fire not identical to iron, nor the iron reduced to the fire; yet they are one, one fiery, metallic reality. Far more potent than the other analogy many of the Fathers reach for, that of the soul as the life of the body, this likeness allows us to consider something well beyond the notion of *parts*. Altogether and through and through, the iron bar is fiery hot; and altogether and without reserve, the fire is ironclad. They penetrate one another, that is, and although the fire is the *sole efficient cause*—important for Cyril and later for Thomas Aquinas—the iron receives the fire wholly, and indeed becomes a molten mass. The direction is right here: God as acting subject—the fire; the humanity, the iron bar, made whole and wholly by God; and just so is the mystery of the incarnate Word, human flesh suffused utterly by the Son who bears and makes our lot.

Now the reader may find him or herself unimpressed by this analogy. You would not be alone! Sergei Bulgakov, the great twentieth-century Russian Orthodox theologian, despised this likeness.[7] How can similes drawn from inanimate things ever disclose the reality of the living God? Of course, he daringly took Cyril to task over many, many things, and he allowed him into the canon of proper dogmatic authorities only on the recognition that Cyril was a saint, and the Holy Spirit—despite all Cyril's confusions and wooly-headedness—kept him from fatal error. So you can see I'm not likely to follow Bulgakov on these matters! But let me cite another modern analogy, this one from Rowan Williams, that is drawn decidedly from human life rather than the cool warehouse of inanimate things. In *Tokens of Trust*, Williams proposes the likeness of Christ to a performer and her piece of mu-

6. Cyril of Alexandria, *On the Unity of Christ*, 130–31.

7. Sergius Bulgakov, *The Lamb of God*, trans. B. Jakim (Grand Rapids: Eerdmans, 2008).

sic. Thinking of the meteoric and calamitous figure of the cellist Jacqueline du Pré, and the film made by EMI of her performance, Williams writes:

> When you see a great performer, a singer or instrumentalist, at work re-
> alizing a piece of music, you are looking at one human being at the limit
> of their skill and concentration. All their strength, their freedom and you
> could even say their love is focused on bringing to life the work and vision
> of another person. . . . The vision and imagination of another person, the
> composer, has to come through—not displacing the human particularity
> of the performer but 'saturating' that performer's being for the time of
> the performance. . . . In the fullness of their skill and their joy, another is
> made present. So with Jesus; this is a human life and a human will whose
> power and joy is the performance of who God is and what God wants, the
> performance of the Word of God.[8]

Now, of course this is a deeply attractive and suggestive likeness! The film Williams mentions in passing is haunting, mesmerizing: here is Du Pré at the height of her powers, her health, and her fame; conducting her and the starchly formal orchestra is her young, richly talented husband Daniel Barenboim, both of them performing their art without score, and in a bravura move, for Barenboim, without podium or lectern or railing of any kind. The cinematographer knows the passion of this piece: Elgar is said to have composed the rudiments of it as artillery shelled the fields of Flanders into a wasteland of brutality and death. The film twins the Romantic longing of the concerto with the passion of the cellist, and the oddly abstract and rootless stage on which the musicians perform only serves to heighten the intimacy of Du Pré with the elegiac outpouring of Edward Elgar.

This analogy captivates us, I think, because most of us can think of an example of this kind. To hear Leontyne Price hold a five-tiered Metropolitan Opera House in thrall as the doomed Aida, for example, or to see the ageless Satchell Paige humiliate an opposing batter, or to read James Baldwin, pen in hand, take up analysis of social crises, theological blindness, his own remarkable life, or in truth anything at all is to witness a performer one with the instrument and the art, an intellect and body utterly given over to the truth of the word. We can see, then, why Rowan Williams's analogy tells us so much about Christology: it gives us a glimpse of how two can be one, one living eternal Son.

8. Rowan Williams, *Tokens of Trust* (Louisville: Westminster John Knox, 2007), 72–74.

But we can see the weakness right away as well. The direction of agency is reversed here, and thus all wrong, in the analogy of the artist, her instrument, and her inspiration. The little word "realization" gives the whole away—a "great performer realizing a piece of music." Now I should be quick to say there are weaknesses in any analogy: that's why they are only an image, not a definition! On the whole, with a likeness, we strive to screen out what is useless and hold on to the good, elevating it as we hand it over to its new use: this is the "way of remotion," as the scholastics called this traditional path of knowing and naming God. But here it is difficult to pare away and elevate what remains, for at its very core we have a human life, giving itself over to a higher art form, to an idea, or to the elixir of subtlety, grace, wit, and skill that is a human sport. In Williams's telling phrase, a "human being [is] at the limit of their skill and concentration." The one acting, that is, is human, and in Du Pré's case, she at once performs—realizes—and delivers herself over to Elgar and his sweeping, demanding Cello Concerto in E minor. But it cannot be so with Christ! The sole acting subject of the life of Jesus Christ must be the eternal Son, the deity, and not the humanity: this is Cyril's central teaching, the axiom of his entire christological system.

So I think there's a second reason—a much less elevated or salutary reason—that Rowan Williams's analogy captures our imagination. And that is this: in the modern era we have developed Christologies in which the *human* life of Jesus Christ is the sole acting subject. It is hard, in truth, to overemphasize the revolution this makes over the theology of the past. When our ancestors examined the Gospels, and also the Old Testament, Israel's Scriptures, they saw *God* acting. It may not have been as bold as the celebrated perhaps apocryphal saying of Luther's, that in the Gospel we see "God walking down the street," but it was most assuredly the deity that is the controlling genius of the life of Jesus Christ. Maximus the Confessor, the late Byzantine admirer and exponent of Cyril's Christology, said that the human will of Jesus Christ always "followed" the divine, and this axiom finds its way into Thomas Aquinas's treatise on the person and work of Christ in the *Summa*. On the whole, it seems to me, this proper directional flow, from divine to human, was followed, or perhaps only quietly assumed, in monastic and university dogmatics through the Catholic and Protestant Reformations.

But something happened in European letters in the Enlightenment, in France and in England and above all in Germany, that did not happen under the impress of the Vetruvian Man, however humanistic Leonardo and the Italian renaissance appeared to be to Romantic historians such as Burkhardt.

This revolution is more than the philosophical "turn to the human subject" that we associate with the great name of Immanuel Kant. It is rather a lowering and fixing of the European gaze to its own kind, an originary focus, in which the human being, most especially the European man, becomes *the agent*, the dynamism, the center point of all culture, knowledge, and especially theology. Little wonder that Barbara Fields and Cornel West have looked to this era as the cruel furnace out of which race and a racialized society are forged. It's the fully humanized scenario of worldly events in which the central, causal power is carried, like Promethean fire, in human arms.

Now, I do not want to make a jeremiad against modernity! Were it not for the emancipatory impulses rising up like sparks from the French Revolution, a woman such as I am would not be writing this essay, nor holding an academic post, nor wearing a collar; for all this was unthinkable to our forebears in the faith. It is all too easy for those who have benefitted from a revolution to show easy contempt for those who carried it out in great pathos and at great cost. It is a near industry for the beneficiaries of the modern to decry its scope, purpose, and aims. But still I must say that the crises this revolution fomented for Christology are formidable, all the same.

For Christology the modern has meant a thorough sea change in the relation of deity to humanity in the one Jesus Christ. For most of us living under these conditions of modernity, the story of Jesus Christ is the narrative of a *human life*, somehow and in some mysterious way, at one with God. Again, in Williams's telling phrase, "a human life and will"—Williams is careful, I should note, to not say, "human being"—which "is the performance of the Word of God." Yet to begin with this "human life and will," and to imagine it as an artist searching for a bit of music that will call forth the utmost from her, ennoble her, really, and all us who hear her; to begin here is to make Jesus Christ the event principally and originally of a human being and his destiny. For this reason, I believe, the "historical Jesus"—the search for the reliable deeds and teachings of a first-century Galilean rabbi—has taken such an outsized place in the treatments of most modern Christologies. We look at the Gospels and see a *human life*, and more *a human person*, going about doing good, and we want to know the influences, the thought-world, the likely teachings and controversies of such a Son of Mary. Indeed, we might think of the name used often in more historicizing circles: Jesus of Nazareth. It seems to capture a human being in the days when place names served as surnames: this Jesus, the one from Nazareth. What can the historian know about him, we wonder. Just who was he, we ask; what did he do and why; what can we know and trust of these remnants and sketches of a life we call the Gospels? Certainly such questions are not foreign to a full and fully Chalcedonian Christology. But they represent most decidedly a "Christology from below," starting, that is, from the humanity of Christ and aiming perhaps at a Chalcedonian resolution after all historical work has been fulfilled. In fact, this very phrase, "Christology from below" can be considered an artifact of the dynamics we have explored here in the rupture of the modern. Always there hovers over these treatments of Jesus Christ the aroma of two natures, even two persons, acting on their own, the human being struggling and buckling under the terror of death, the divine at some remove, silent or even absent during those final three hours. Certainly a theologian can solve the problems we have been examining by distinguishing the natures, or more radically, dividing the person! But this cannot serve as a Chalcedonian, a dogmatic solution.

To be sure, we will not make headway in this journey should we abandon attention to the incarnate Christ's life on earth—the "economy of our salvation." But the "economy," as we heard it expounded in Cyril, is quite another domain altogether. His analogy of the divine fire, suffusing and reducing to molten core the iron bar of humanity, is a transformation to another kind, a *metabasis eis allo genos*, as Aristotle would put it. Here the *realization* comes from the fire and *to* the iron bar, even as the eternal Word comes to and creates the humanity that comes to life and is born in Mary. For just this reason is she *Theotokos*, the God-bearer.

The Sacrifice of Jesus Christ

So let me bring this molten coal of fire once again to Gethsemane and to the passion, for this is the destiny and consummation of the incarnate Word of God. I have said several times—a peril, I am sure, of reading much Cyril!— that it is God who acts and who is the foundation, the full personhood of the man Jesus Christ. But I have also stressed the centrality of *sacrifice* as the proper mode and model for the life of the incarnate one. Just how, then, does God die? If anything appears to be a *metabasis eis allo genos*, this is it. The very nature of God is eternal, deathless; for just this reason his Word endures forever. Yet, with Cyril, I want to affirm that this very Son of God groans in prayer in Gethsemane, and he cries out in agony from his deathbed of the cross. As the Cyrillians liked to say: one of the Trinity suffered and died in the flesh. This is critical to Christology, indeed to the Christian faith itself, because God alone saves. A human life, however pure and obedient and sacrificial, cannot save a dying world; only God does that. So it must be that this flesh the Son makes and receives just is *his, God's very own*. In

Cyril's words: "Even though the Word was beyond the power of suffering in his nature as God, he wrapped himself in flesh that was capable of suffering, and revealed it as his very own, so that *even the suffering might be said to be his* because it was his own body which suffered and no one else's."[9] We can see that Cyril struggles in his many formulations of this central point, for he too knows that the divine nature is immutable and human soul and body alone frail, mutable, mortal. Cyril tends to combine bare stipulation—it is so for I said it is so—with ample scriptural citations and with analogies. In the one we have favored: the fire is not damaged by the beating the molten iron receives; yet it remains suffused and underlying the very frailty and creating the vulnerability of the iron to descending blows. Well, this is all very good to say, and helpful as stipulations and analogies are to our all-too-human flesh. But analogies and axioms and likenesses aside, just how can we affirm these central truths of the faith?

You'll notice that I have ruled out from the beginning the notion that God himself suffers. There is *pathos* in God, Karl Barth said, though with guardrails in place, I would say, and Balthasar follows Barth's lead in his remarkable *Mysterium Paschale*. God *suffers*, Jürgen Moltmann said, with the railings stripped away. It is the maxim of many feminist and liberation theologians that the God of freedom is the one who suffers with the oppressed, crucified on the brutal cruelties and indifference of this earth. And we can see what a boon this is to Christology! Of course the Son of God suffers and dies: this is not unthinkable to a God who himself suffers, though in divine fashion. But I am persuaded by Schleiermacher here that a God who suffers becomes conceptually part of the world, an actor within the cosmos, subject to the forces and causalities of the created plane—and that, even if pantheism is expressly denied. So it is not true, I say, that to love is to suffer, or more modestly, that without the possibility of suffering, love cannot be genuine. Rather, in more Thomistic vein, I say that to be perfect love, as is God, is to be immutable, beyond suffering, beyond death and grief and wasting away, the sole, eternal, ever generative Good.

Nor have I imported into this discussion the practice, roundly debated in the Reformation, of the "communication of idioms," in which I attempt to justify or vindicate assigning properties of one nature—the human—to the divine, and in fewer cases, the divine to the human. Of course, this practice is venerable! We see first fruits of it in Cyril or the Cappadocians; it's present in some *quaestiones* of Thomas's *Summa*; and it belongs to many

---

9. Cyril of Alexandria, *On the Unity of Christ* 118; emphasis mine.

of our most ancient hymns, especially those of Ephrem the Syrian. But it becomes a *locus classicus*, an arena of heated debate in the Reformation. There under the guise of eucharistic debates we see the major figures of the new Protestant movement argue about the propriety of assigning human properties to deity, or more controversial still, divine properties to human and created things. But could this simply be a form of verbal gymnastics? Ulrich Zwingli seemed to think so, and held that we predicate some words to Christ's deity—his passion, his frailty, hunger, and thirst—that belong of course to his humanity; but we know that this is simply the "grammar of the faith," a semantic system, not an exchange *realiter*, in substances or natures. Well, that's attractive too! Could we not simply say that the faith statement, "God dies," is a way of speaking about Jesus Christ that acknowledges two natures in him, undivided? It acknowledges the Chalcedonian decree, we might say, and shows us how to speak that language, but it leaves open, undefined and perhaps hesitant, about how all this might work metaphysically. But I am not convinced that "nature" is only a bundle of predicates or properties; it is rather, in Thomas's fine phrase, a mode of substance, that whereby something simply is. Well, you can imagine, this far into this essay, that the proposal of the *communicatio idiomatum*, however rhetorically and grammatically instructive it may be, will not serve the dogmatic, and decidedly metaphysical question I have placed before us.

So we are left where Cyril has placed us: with the eternal Son of God wrapped in his own flesh, such that we know it is his alone, moving in relentless and pitiless determination to a cross outside the city walls. Here all the ambiguities, the ambivalences and conceptual riddles that have accompanied us so far come to their crisis and their fulfillment. Just how can we make the incarnate Word a person and act of sacrifice?

I want to begin my answer to this originary question in an odd place: the medieval notion of Christ's beatific vision. Aloys Grillmeier, in his masterful survey of Christology, *Christ in Christian Tradition*, makes the provocative claim that the *psychology*, the inner life of Christ, is the necessary building block of all true Christologies.[10] It took the early church some little while to see that Jesus Christ must necessarily possess a human mind; the eternal Word could not simply take as his own an inanimate body, as though the Word itself could supply the mind of Christ. No, sometime within the first generation of Nicene theologians, it was clear to all sides in the christological debates that Jesus Christ had to have both rational

10. Aloys Grillmeier, S. J., *Christ in Christian Tradition*, vol 1: *From the Apostolic Ages to Chalcedon (451)*, trans. John Bowden (Atlanta: John Knox, 1975), 361–66.

soul, as the mind was spoken of in those days, and a truly human body. It took somewhat longer to come to the conviction that the human nature of Christ demanded also a human will, and not simply the divine will serving for both natures. But the essential step that Grillmeier discerns in a proper Christology had to wait until the medieval schoolmen, and not surprisingly for a major Catholic thinker, most especially until Thomas Aquinas and his treatise on the person of Christ. In the *Summa* the inner life is finally addressed as a centerpiece of Christology. It is this "rational soul," the mind of Christ that is the meeting point between deity and humanity in the incarnate Son, the place where the eternal sets foot in the temporal. For that reason, Thomas argues, Jesus Christ from the moment of his conception, possessed the beatific vision; that is, he in his human soul saw God face to face, the source of all blessing and beatitude. This entitles Jesus Christ in his earthly life to the rank of "Comprehensor"—one, that is, who does not simply journey toward the vision of God, but rather possesses that vision, now and always.

Now, Thomas knows as do we, that Christ was wearied at midday, as he sat by Jacob's well and thirsted for cool water in the searing heat. Thomas knew that Christ grew in wisdom and stature, his body and his soul maturing in their vocation and obedience. And Thomas knew, and spent many technical paragraphs upon, the truth that Jesus Christ suffered in his police interrogation, his beatings and mockings, and cried out in a loud voice at the very end, in the words of the psalmist, "My God, why hast Thou forsaken me?" In this sense, Christ in his body remained a "wayfarer," a pilgrim as are each of us. Like Cyril, Thomas recognized that Christ suffered a particular horror from Gethsemane forward; yet during that entire last necessary torment for the salvation of the world, Jesus Christ, Thomas says firmly, possessed in the highest region of his mind, his rational soul, the perfect, immediate, and uninterrupted blessing of the vision of God.[11]

Now you might imagine that the modern era has not dealt kindly with this thesis of Thomas Aquinas. It has been widely felt to be "docetic," that is, a denial of the true humanity of Jesus, making him only *appear* to suffer and, in his dying breath, only seem to fear the very state of dereliction. Several learned Thomists, most recently Fr. Thomas Joseph White, have dedicated themselves to defending Thomas from this charge.[12] Given the limitations of

---

11. See Thomas Aquinas, *Summa Theologiae*, ed. English Dominican Province (New York: Benziger Bros., 1947), IIIa, q. 10.

12. Thomas Joseph White, *The Incarnate Lord: A Thomistic Study in Christology* (Washington, DC: Catholic University of America Press, 2015).

this chapter, I don't aim to reproduce those technical and thoroughly scholastic defenses. Rather I would like to propose to you that the underlying *instinct* of this conception of Christ is proper and true, and of critical help in our search for a Christology that is sacrifice for us and for our sake. Christ's inwardness, I propose, is the place where we must begin our answer, and that in a particular version—a nonscholastic version—of the Beatific Vision.

Remember now that the eternal Word is the active agent in the life of Christ. And, that this relation, alone among the divine-creaturely relations in the cosmos, is *competitive*, or better, *consuming*. The very person of Jesus Christ is sacrifice in this strong, unique sense. Now I believe that the Gospels show us a Christ who is ever ready to do his Father's will, to teach, to heal, to exorcise, to obey to the very end, the Father who is explosively alive to this Son of Man. He is God intoxicated, eaten up by zeal for the Father's house. From childhood, Luke the evangelist tells us, Jesus Christ must be in his Father's house or, in another rendering of the Greek, on his Father's business. His food and drink is to do the Father's will. And that meat on which he feeds leads him remorselessly to Jerusalem, to Gethsemane, to Golgotha. During all this earthly sojourn, Jesus Christ in his human inwardness has a direct, uninterrupted vision of this majestic and ruthless face of God. I do not mean here that Jesus Christ was a kind of Franz Kafka *avant la lettre*, that his life was nothing but suffering and despair and torment. No! We see Jesus Christ throughout the Gospels delighting in the company of his friends, especially Mary and Martha and Lazarus, sitting at table with Pharisees and disciples, taking children, those holy gifts of the good God into his arms and blessing them, raising his blessed eyes upon the flowering fields and their glory, and sleeping peacefully in the boat's stern on a night's fishing trip. I do not mean by speaking of Christ's inner life as driven by the God he obeyed in such a way that he could not, nor did not, deeply love and treasure his earthly days in the Galilean hills. I mean rather that the beatific vision for Jesus Christ meant something unique for this Son of Man, something that drove him out into the hills, long nights alone in prayer, something that filled him with the conviction that he must be rejected by his own, betrayed and killed, something that turned his steps always and unmistakably to Jerusalem, the holy city of his holy death. That something in him *terrified* his disciples. The evangelists are quite plain in telling us this, in many ways, small and great. Jesus Christ could be utterly overwhelming to his disciples, majestic in his anger, his stubborn insistence upon suffering, his sublime presence on a windswept sea, his radiance beyond all telling when they ascended with him to the top of Mt. Tabor. Something in him, the evangelists tell us, made his opponents adamantly at war with him; it made his own family consider him out of his mind. He was like all of them; they knew that. Yet he was utterly unlike, a terrifying, majestic, and royal figure, to whom one goes down on one's knees: Go away from me, Lord, for I am a sinner!

That something, I suggest, is the beatific vision of Jesus Christ, his human inwardness beholding his deity, ever with him, wrapping his soul and body around his very transcendent and holy life. But the *visio Dei*, as I understand it, is not the state of the blessed dead who contemplate God in final freedom and delight. Rather, I believe that Jesus Christ, in his own human inwardness, saw the reality of God, its rationality or *Logos*, in its fiery descent into the world, its utterly lowliness. What Jesus saw, or better, what he was, in his own unique person, was the holy fire who is God, cascading down the ladder between heaven and earth, a molten divine Son, who will make his own flesh the sacrifice to be burned to ash on the world's altar. What Jesus Christ in his human soul beheld was not that he, the human life, was to be a sacrifice; that would make Jesus Christ a holy martyr, certainly, but not the Son of God, given for the life of the world. Just this is why we must say that the death of Christ is not abusive, though to be sure it is *terrible*. It is not a human life sacrificed to the gods, not a Dido flung upon the fiery pyre of Carthage. No, it is rather the vision of *God* who empties himself, who tears through the heavens and comes down, the Son whose eternal generation is a *descent*, an outpouring, a self-offering without reserve. Jesus Christ in his humanity looks on *this*, this fiery burning, and he understands that he is to live this terrible descent as his very own life, his very own death. He takes it for his own holy vocation. God the Son will make his way through his own flesh, will rupture and yield it up, and make of his own body and soul, a whole burnt offering, the ash that will redeem a world. Every day, always, Christ sees this, and he knows it is his own deity, his own divine breaking and descent that is the agent, the *dynamis*, the fire that will alight the blaze that is Golgotha. It is God acting, God willing, God lowering and bending down, the eternal generation of the Son, that is seen in all its terrible relentlessness by Christ's inward eye. Just this is what it means for God to save. Just this is what it means for Christ in his person to be sacrifice.

Now I don't pretend that this is an easy or unambivalent vision of Christology. Sacrifice is *terrible*, awe-ful, in the old meaning of the term. I think critics who raise objection to the doctrine of sacrifice as the tradition and as I have laid it out, have put their finger on a deep truth here. There is an element of revulsion—it is that strong, I think—an antipathy, to this act of sacrifice that cannot be pushed aside, however reverently we may hold such a view. It is terrible and shocking enough to watch the tragic Queen of Carthage curse her beloved Aeneas and rip away her own life with her own hands; terrible and shocking to watch the mingled fear and courage of Dr. King as he steps out onto the Edmund Pettus bridge; terrifying to read the stern and fiery sacrifice of Dorothy Day, her rebuke to us and our worldliness; overwhelming to see Archbishop Romero at the altar that day, a martyr to his late-born love of the people; sobering and chilling to hear the Trappist monks in Tibhirine say that the servant is not above the master and await their death and beheading during the Algerian Civil War, some twenty years ago. All these were sacrifices of varied kind; all of them show forth Christ's death until he come. But Christ's death was not like this. He was not a martyr but rather the consummate sacrifice, the divine-given burnt offering for the world's salvation. He saw this; in his person, he was this. He learned obedience through his suffering, Hebrews tell us; and it made him perfect, consummate, the Word's own flesh.

Conclusion

My aim in this chapter has been to reflect upon the *cost* of our redemption. From Torrance to Thomas and Cyril we have tried to take the measure of this cost. The cross is not an easy fact within this world of ours; it does not fit comfortably with the ways we have plowed into this earth. But it is, I believe, the great truth of this cosmos, the divine self-offering for the sake of the world. To say that Christ in his person and in his work just is sacrifice is to place at the heart of Christology the entire sacrificial cultus of Israel, consummated in this one Son, born in heaven and on earth. Perhaps this essay has invited the reader into the vision Torrance proclaims of the "divine omnipotence compassed within our littleness," and that in some small measure, it may have led the reader to a deeper reflection on the mind of Christ, who did not consider equality with God something to be prized, but emptied himself, taking the form of a slave, and found in human form, became obedient unto death, even death upon the cross.

8

Divine Perfection and the Kenosis
of the Son

Thomas Joseph White, OP

Several scriptural passages from the New Testament suggest that Christ, the
Son of God, was subject to self-emptying or kenosis.[1] The most evident of
these is Philippians 2:7, which attributes kenosis to the Son, who though he
was in the form of God, took on the form of a servant and became subject to
suffering under death, so that God has exalted him in the resurrection and
made him recognizable as Lord to all the nations (Phil 2:10–11; Isa 45:22–24).
Whether kenosis in this passage pertains to a preexistent subject who becomes human, and whether it signifies only the taking on of a human form
(i.e., the incarnation) or also designates the obedient suffering-unto-death
are disputed questions. I take it that the preexistence and divinity of the Son
are implicitly denoted by this passage because the Son is said to be in the
form of God prior to incarnation, and that the kenosis in question includes
not only the Son's incarnation, but also his obedience, suffering, and death,
which all follow from his being human. Whether these interpretations are
warranted or not, what is uncontroversial is that these various attributes of
self-emptying, obedience, suffering, and death are attributed to the subject

---

1. The argument of this essay reflects an ecumenical engagement with themes that
Bruce L. McCormack has helped me to consider more closely, and I am grateful to him
for his friendship and contribution to theological conversation, even as he might not
agree with all that I argue below.

of the Son, to his person. Furthermore, they are said to contribute, along with his resurrection and exaltation, to the revelation of his Lordship, to the fact that he has received the name above every other name (Phil 2:9), presumably the divine name, Lord or YHWH, "He who is" (Exod 3:14–15). The kenosis of God is revelatory of his Lordship.[2]

The attribution of divine and human properties to the one person of the Son is historically denoted under the conceptual rubric of the "communication of idioms," or the attribution of names. In its traditional use, as exemplified in figures as diverse as Cyril of Alexandria, Leo the Great, John Damascene, and Thomas Aquinas, I take it that three main regulatory principles emerge for the right use of the communication of idioms. First, there is only one person in Christ (one hypostatic subject), as noted by the Council of Ephesus. Consequently, any property of the divine nature or of the human nature of the Son is attributed personally only to one subject, who is the eternal Son of God.[3] It is the Son and Word of God who created all things, with the Father and with the Spirit. It is the Son and Word who took flesh, suffered, and died. One of the Trinity has been crucified.[4] Historically we can associate this insight with the theology of Cyril.[5]

Second, there are two natures in Christ truly distinct, united not separated, unmixed, unconfused as noted by the Council of Chalcedon.[6] Therefore, the properties of the two natures are not attributed directly to one

---

2. See the exegetical argument of Richard Bauckham, *Jesus and the God of Israel: God Crucified and Other Studies on the New Testament's Christology of Divine Identity* (Grand Rapids: Eerdmans, 2008), 1–59.

3. Consider in this respect the affirmations of the council of Ephesus taken from the Second Letter of Cyril of Alexandria to Nestorius, and the third and fourth anathemas, taken from his Third Letter. Cf. *Compendium of Creeds, Definitions, and Declarations on Matters of Faith and Morals*, 43rd ed., ed. P. Hünermann, ed. for English trans. by R. Fastiggi and A. E. Nash (San Francisco: Ignatius Press, 2012), para. 250–63, including: "we say that the Word, hypostatically uniting to himself the flesh animated by a rational soul, became man in an ineffable and incomprehensible manner" (250).

4. See in this regard the assessment of the Scythian monks' phrase, "one of the Trinity has suffered," made by Pope John II, letter *Olim quidem*, AD 534, *Compendium of Creeds*, 401–2: "God suffered in the flesh."

5. Aquinas associates himself with Cyril's use of the communication of idioms in *Summa Theologiae* IIIa, q. 16, art. 4. References from *Summa Theologiae*, hereafter *ST*, trans. English Dominican Province (New York: Benziger Bros., 1947).

6. See the Letter to Flavian (tome) of Leo the Great, *Compendium of Creeds*, 290–95, and the Council of Chalcedon, *Compendium of Creeds*, 300–303. The latter states, "one and the same Lord Jesus Christ . . . must be acknowledged in two natures, without confusion or change, without division or separation" (302), while the former posits, "The

another. We cannot conclude from the incarnation, for example, that the eternity of God has become temporal, that the divine nature suffers, or that the human nature of God is omnipresent or omnipotent.[7] Thus, we may say that God who is all powerful has taken on human weakness, the eternal one has entered time, and the impassible God has truly suffered. These are not contradictory remarks since the properties attributed to the one person of the Son are ascribed to him in virtue of personal subsistence in distinct natures. Historically we can associate this insight with the theology of Leo.

Third, the two natures of Christ do have distinct operations as noted by the Third Council of Constantinople.[8] Consequently we can ascribe operations of Christ as either God or human to his person, signified by his nature taken not in the abstract but in the concrete.[9] For example, we can call Jesus the person, either "man" or "God," denoting him with these nature terms as a personal subject. In this case it is true to say, for example, that this man created the world, or that God suffers. The latter phrase indicates that one who is God truly experiences human suffering, death, and bodily resurrection. God was born in a cave. God suffered and died on a cross. God was raised from the dead and glorified.

If we approach the mystery of the kenosis of God with this background in mind, it is possible to attribute kenosis to God in three ways: first as to his person, second keeping in mind the distinction of the two natures of the Son, third with respect to his operative actions in the kenosis, as attributed to one who is God and Lord. In the first sense we can say that it was truly the Son of God who emptied himself, and that all that pertains to the kenosis of the Son is attributed rightly to his person. In the second sense we can say that the kenosis pertains to the Son principally in virtue of his human form, and

---

character of each nature, therefore, being preserved and united in one person, humility was assumed by majesty, weakness by strength, mortality by eternity" (293).

7. See the argument by Aquinas, who appeals to previous arguments of Leo the Great and John Damascene, in *ST* IIIa, q. 16, art. 5.

8. See the Third Council of Constantinople, *Compendium of Creeds*, 550–59, which affirmed: "We likewise proclaim in him, according to the teaching of the holy Fathers, two natural volitions or wills and two natural actions, without division, without change, without separation, without confusion" (556).

9. See the argument of Aquinas in *ST* IIIa, q. 16, art. 1 and art. 9. Art. 9: "when we say 'this man,' pointing to Christ, the eternal suppositum is necessarily meant, with whose eternity a beginning in time is incompatible. Hence this is false: 'This man began to be.' Nor does it matter that to begin to be refers to the human nature, which is signified by this word 'man'; because the term placed in the subject is not taken formally so as to signify the nature [in this case], but is taken materially so as to signify the suppositum."

it is carried out through his human life of obedience, suffering, and free acceptance of death.[10] Preceding death he experiences agony, and in death he experiences the separation of body and soul, events that can be considered dimensions of his kenosis. All of this is attributed to the Son in virtue of his human nature, not in virtue of his divine nature. Does it affect or change his divine nature so as to determine anew the identity of God? Does it indicate by analogy what is *already always* (i.e., eternally) the nature of God or does it indicate by analogy the personal properties of the Son that pertain to him eternally? I will return to these questions below and argue that the kenosis of the Son pertains to him personally in virtue of his human nature and that it does not change or alter his divine perfection. It does, however, indicate by created similitude (in his human action of self-offering) something of his personal property as Son, that is, as one who is from the Father, and for the Father, in the spiration of the Holy Spirit as their mutual love. In the third sense of the communication of idioms, we can say that it is truly God who is subject to kenosis, in virtue of his hominization, suffering, and death. Whether this entails an alteration of the divine nature is an open question, as I have indicated. I will argue below that the kenosis of God does not entail any diminishment, alternation, or abandonment of God's perfection, but in fact stems from his inalienable perfection and is an epiphany of the splendor of divine love.

Ontological and Soteriological Principles for Thinking about Divine Kenosis

How might we pursue this line of inquiry, regarding the perfection of the Son who is subject to kenosis? What is this divine perfection, and what

10. See Aquinas, *Commentary on St. Paul's First Letter to the Thessalonians and the Letter to the Philippians*, trans. F. R. Larcher and M. Duffy (Albany, NY: Magi, 1969), on Phil 2:7, 80: "He says, therefore, He *emptied himself.* But since He was filled with the divinity, did He empty Himself of that? No, because He remained what He was; and what He was not, He assumed. But this must be understood in regard to the assumption of what He had not, and not according to the assumption of what He had. For just as He descended from heaven, not that He ceased to exist in heaven, but because He began to exist in a new way on earth, so He also emptied Himself, not by putting off His divine nature, but by assuming a human nature. How beautiful to say that He *emptied himself,* for the empty is opposed to the full! For the divine nature is sufficiently full, because every perfection of goodness is there. But human nature and the soul are not full, but capable of fulness, because it was made as a slate not written upon. Therefore, human nature is empty. Hence he says, He *emptied himself,* because He assumed a human nature."

does it entail? To respond to these questions, it is helpful to recall fundamental points of orientation in Christology, both as regards the ontology of the incarnation and its soteriological consequences, as indeed the topics of who Christ really is and of what he truly accomplishes for human beings are deeply interrelated ones.

Christ Is One with the Father, True and Perfect God

We may begin by noting a classical principle drawn from the Council of Nicaea, based upon the church's common reading of the New Testament, placed in opposition to the famous claim of Arius that the Son of God is a creature. That council stipulated against this idea that Jesus is God, the eternal Son of God become human, God from God, light from light, true God from true God, consubstantial (i.e., *homoousios*: one in being and essence) with the Father.[11] The Nicene principle is obviously important ontologically for it entails the claim that the Son of God, while distinct from the Father personally, is also one with the Father in being and essence, and so too, in light of a Trinitarian reading of the New Testament, is one in being and essence with the Holy Spirit. The kenotic ascriptions we have made in the previous section above presuppose this ontological set of claims, so that we may say that the Son who emptied himself by incarnation, suffering, and death was truly God, one in being with the Father and the Spirit, and also personally distinct from the Father and the Spirit, so that the things we say of him in virtue of the kenosis are truly ascribed to him as a subject, not to the Father or Spirit per se. However, to say just this is also to affirm that the one subject to kenosis, because he is truly God and is one in being and essence with the Father and the Spirit, truly contains in himself as God the plenitude of the divine perfection. It is the ineffable and transcendent *God* who is incarnate, suffers, and is crucified, not a creature or some other subordinate entity. To be God, however, is to possess certain divine and inalienable perfections, which Christ must retain if it is truly God who is with us in the mystery of the incarnation and the crucifixion and not an impostor or a creature upon whom we have projected divinity by error, as upon one whom we merely mistake for God.

Soteriological consequences follow from these ontological considerations. One of them concerns divinization or union with God. Only if Christ

---

11. Cf. the Council of Nicaea, *Compendium of Creeds*, 125–26, and the study by Khaled Anatolios, *Retrieving Nicaea: The Development and Meaning of Trinitarian Doctrine* (Grand Rapids: Baker, 2011).

is truly God has God united himself hypostatically to our human nature. A common patristic argument stipulates that God's incarnation in human nature indicates a soteriological intent on the part of God. He has united himself to our nature so that we may realize that God intends to unite us to his deity, by the adoptive life of grace.[12] As Aquinas restates the argument, if God does something ontologically greater or more magnificent, in becoming human himself, why should we fail to believe that he intends and is capable truly of uniting us to himself in the grace of the beatific vision and the universal resurrection?[13]

A second soteriological consideration concerns solidarity. Only if Christ is truly God can we say that God was crucified and died in solidarity with us in our suffering. Friedrich Nietzsche famously depicts Christianity as the culmination of a tradition of ancient Judaic grievance culture in which the sacerdotal class of an oppressed people created a fictive narrative of a vengeful God who would vindicate the poor and oppressed. This fictive account of divinely approved goods and evils, based on a suppressed will to power (*ressentiment*) on the part of the ancient prophets, functioned culturally to sustain their people by promising eventual triumph, and in doing so also purported to subjugate other cultures to a Judaic standard of measure eschatologically.[14] The narrative of divine pity, centered on the absolute reference of God, was appropriated and intensified by Jesus of Nazareth in his own life of mercy, and after his death that narrative was employed by the paragons of primitive Christianity to subject the noble, beautiful, and stronger cultures of Europe and the Near East to a diseased religious culture of morality by which the weak could emerge as triumphant over the strong. Contemporary narratives of liberation theology often underscore the idea of God's solidarity with us manifest in the mystery of the incarnation of God and the crucifixion of Jesus, and they seek to explore the ethical and political implications of this mystery. However, any such soteriological exploration has a claim to our credence only if God himself has truly become human, so that the liberation or moral exemplarity we appeal to has a basis in reality and is not merely the arbitrary human construction of an aggrieved social class seeking to instrumentalize the lingering cultural influence of the New

12. See Athanasius, *On the Incarnation* 54: "He indeed assumed humanity that we might become God." Translator anonymous (Crestwood, NY: SVS Press, 1944).

13. Aquinas, *Summa Contra Gentiles* IV, trans. C. J. O'Neil (Garden City, NY: Doubleday, 1956), 54.2.

14. See the argument of Friedrich Nietzsche, *On the Genealogy of Morality*, trans. C. Diethe (Cambridge: Cambridge University Press, 2006).

Testament narrative for expedient political purposes, which are ultimately built on untenable philosophical foundations, or the intellectually uncompelling stances of a frustrated morality of resentment.

A third soteriological consideration has to do with the atonement. It matters for the purposes of our redemption whether the man Jesus in his obedience and free acceptance of suffering on behalf of the human race is himself also the Lord and God of Israel. The New Testament suggests that the voluntary suffering of Christ crucified is meritorious of our redemption.[15] The "merit" of Christ as one who is human pertains to the proportionate satisfaction of love and obedience he offers to God in reparation for human disobedience and sin, so as to reconcile us with God justly or in authentic righteousness.[16] However, even if this righteousness of Christ pertains to him formally insofar as he is human, the deity of God present in Christ is also a factor of fundamental importance in the mystery of the atonement. "In Christ, God was reconciling the world to himself" (2 Cor 5:19). Aquinas places emphasis here on the infinite dignity accrued to the humanity of Christ in his passion, in virtue of his deity. The one who obeyed, suffered, was crucified, and died, was truly God, and as a consequence, there is an infinite personal dignity to his human suffering and death, one that makes the holiness of his death unfathomable, and the righteousness of his human self-offering immeasurable.[17] Even if one holds, as Aquinas does, that God did not need to embark on the incarnation and self-offering of the crucifixion to atone for our sins, it is still the case that God's elective decision to atone for human sin in this way is indicative of his wisdom and goodness.[18] This divine wisdom and goodness are manifest in his desire to express his mercy toward the human race precisely by communicating to us a perfect righteousness or justification, built solely on the grace of God, founded in the infinite perfection of Christ, who is God crucified.

---

15. This is the logic of Phil 2:9: Christ's resurrection was merited by his obedience and suffering. See, analogously, Rom 3:25, Rom 5:17; 1 Cor 1:30; and 2 Pet 1:1, all of which intimate a correspondence between the intrinsic excellence of Christ in his human life and the grace of God given to humanity in virtue of Christ's free action.

16. See the argument of Anselm, *Why God Became Man*, in *Anselm of Canterbury: The Major Works*, ed. B. Davies and G. R. Evans (Oxford: Oxford University Press), esp. 2.7, where Anselm notes the relation between Chalcedonian Christology and his understanding of the substitutionary righteousness of the God human.

17. See Aquinas, *ST* IIIa, q. 48, art. 2.

18. See Aquinas, *ST* IIIa, q. 1, art. 2, and q. 46, arts. 1–3, esp. q. 46, art. 2, ad 3.

The Son's Perfection as the Creator

The New Testament not only teaches that the Son is God crucified, but also that the Son is a principle of creation, he through whom God created all things.[19] Within the context of Second Temple Judaism, it is significant that he is depicted as one who is at the origin of creation, the giver of being, and as one to whom worship is rightly directed. These are prerogatives traditionally associated with the God of Israel, which the New Testament newly extends so as to include Christ, as the Alpha and Omega of all things, as he from whom all things come, and as he to whom worship and adoration is owed, now and in the eschaton.[20]

The centrality of this Judaic feature of New Testament Christology is of significance for our reflection on the perfection of the Son. If we read the Old and New Testaments together as a canonical text of inspired origin and thus as a unified source of divine revelation, we should acknowledge that it is God alone who has created all things and who actively sustains all things in being as Creator. In virtue of God's identity as Creator and his ongoing activity of creation, we can and indeed must also logically posit other attributes of God. He is truly the one who communicates being to all things, "He Who Is," the "I AM" who does not exist as we do but who transcends all that we can comprehend of existence. He gives being to things not compulsively or arbitrarily by blind will, but in wisdom, goodness, and freedom. As such he is not ontologically dependent on his creation, such that his identity should be determined and derived from creatures, but rather the contrary is the case: he is the unilateral giver of being to all that is. He alone has the power to create, to author existence into being, and he alone has the power to save, to redeem the world and to raise the dead. As such his eternity as the living God encompasses and fills place and time from within, and his infinite perfection as God is present within the inner depths of creatures, more interior to them than they are to themselves, precisely insofar as he gives all things to be.

If Christ is truly God, then these inalienable features that pertain to God alone as Creator are present in him, even within his filial kenosis of incarnation and obediential suffering unto death. It is truly the Lord God who has suffered, he who is rightly given the name above every other name (Phil 2:9, cf. Isa 45:22–24), he who is rightly worshiped as only the Lord God of Israel can and should be. This reservation of worship to God alone is logically jus-

---

19. See, for example, John 1:1–3; Col 1:16; Heb 1:3.
20. Rev 5:8; 5:13; 7:11; on Christ as the Alpha and Omega, see 1:8; 21:6; 22:13.

tified based on the reality of his infinite perfection, goodness, and creative power, in virtue of which he alone can providently govern all things to their end, effectively. Such worship is also indicative of the church's recognition of God's unique soteriological power, since only one who has the power to create, to sustain in being, and providentially to govern all things truly is one who also has the power to give grace, justify, sanctify, glorify, and save truly. Furthermore, that power to save is manifest in the resurrection and glorification of Christ, not only because God the Creator has raised Jesus from the dead, as a proleptic anticipation of the glorification of all creation, but also because Jesus has in himself the power to raise the dead and to redeem the creation.[21] He is not only the exemplary cause of the new creation as human, but also its efficient cause as God.[22]

It follows from the line of argument offered above that God cannot *not* be the Creator. He alone gives being to the world and cannot transmit this power to another (since it entails an omnipotence or infinite power that only he has as God).[23] He alone sustains in being all things actively and governs them providentially, activities he does not and cannot suspend if he intends to save and redeem the creation in the life of the resurrection. Consequently, God being God, God is always Creator. By that same measure, since the Son is true God, he is always the Creator with the Father, the Word through whom "all things were made" (John 1:3) even when he is the Word "made flesh" (John 1:14). The *Logos ensarkos* is the *Logos* of the Father who was in the beginning, in whom the Father speaks so as to create the heavens and the earth. The God of Israel, then, who is the Creator of all things, who has become genuinely human, has been crucified, suffered and died. "None of the rulers of this age understood this; for if they had, they would not have crucified the Lord of glory" (1 Cor 2:8). We cannot divorce the New Testament Lordship of the Son from the Old Testament Lordship of the God of Israel. Consequently, if we wish to enunciate a doctrine of the kenosis of the Son, we must simultaneously maintain his preexistent Lordship as the Creator of all that is. This entails that he possesses those perfections that are attributable to the Son precisely in virtue of his deity, perfections that are inalienable even in the incarnation and crucifixion. As I have intimated above, these include the perfection of divine wisdom, goodness, love, mercy,

21. John 5:21–22; 10:18; Rev 10:17–18 suggests the divine power of Christ resurrected.
22. Aquinas, *ST* IIIa, q. 56, arts. 1–2.
23. See the arguments of Aquinas, *ST* I, q. 45, arts. 1, 5, and 6, as well as *ST* I, q. 25, arts. 1–3.

justice, holiness, eternity, omnipotence (infinite power) and omnipresence. Truly it is God who has become one of us.

The Son Possesses All That the Father Possesses as God, in a Filial Mode

It follows from the two principles mentioned above (the Son is truly God; God is truly the Creator) that the Son does not become God or develop as God as a consequence of his engagement with creation. That is to say, the incarnation and crucifixion, and indeed the kenosis of the Son in history, is not something that gives being to the Creator. If one were to claim that it did so, this would lead inevitably in some fashion to the denial or obscuring of the scripturally revealed order of derivation: the creative Trinity communicates the plenitude of being to all things in creation out of the plenitude of perfection that the Trinity possesses ontologically prior to creation, and creation does not communicate being or perfection to God. The two are not part of a larger system in which each depends upon the other to contribute to the ongoing processes of the whole, as if God were the living soul of the world. His utterly transcendent freedom to give (that is a dimension of his omnipotence) is a component of his communication of being in and through all time, and in and through all instances, even as he freely begins to sustain creation in being forever in the mystery of the resurrection.

It follows from this idea that the Trinity cannot be perfected essentially, or according to the plenitude of perfection of the divine essence, in virtue of creation, incarnation, kenosis, and resurrection. The mystery of God does not become internally more perfect, infinite, wise, or loving as a result of a developmental or evolutionary process in which God depends upon his relations in creation so as to self-perfect or self-enrich. The giving of God to creation and to human beings that is revealed initially to Israel and brought to fulfillment in Christ is of a wholly other order. God gives to us out of his immeasurable love, and in doing so reveals who he is eternally in Christ. "God is love" (1 John 4:8). He can freely make himself subject to kenosis by becoming human because of the eternal power of his love, and in being truly human, suffering, and dying, he can reveal to us that he is eternally perfect love. He does not undertake kenosis so as to develop as God in a divine life that is to become more loving, more powerful, or more perfectly self-improved. Likewise, the persons of the Trinity do not self-constitute in their eternal relations in virtue of the Son's temporal mission in the economy of taking on a human form. The economy of the Son's descent into our conditions is not constitutive of the relations that constitute the eternal processions of the persons from one another. The Son does not proceed eternally from the Father because of his kenotic incarnation. The Father does not become the Father of the Son in virtue of the temporal kenosis of the Son, and the Spirit does not become the Spirit of the Lord Jesus in virtue of the kenosis of the Son. Rather, the eternal processions of the Son from the Father by way of generation and of the Spirit from the Father and the Son by way of spiration are the transcendent ontological presupposition of the economy, and these processions are made manifest in the temporal missions of the Son and the Spirit.[24] It is because God is eternally triune in an infinite perfection transcendent of his creation that he can freely manifest himself to us and communicate to us a participation in his divine life by grace precisely in the kenosis and exaltation of the Son.

The Fourth Lateran Council drew out an important facet of this teaching in 1215 in response to the Trinitarian theology of Joachim of Fiore, the twelfth-century Cistercian. Joachim held, in opposition to Peter Lombard, that in addition to saying that the Father eternally begets and that the Son is eternally begotten, Christians ought also to say that the divine essence begets and is begotten.[25] As the council noted, this idea leads to the mistaken notion that the divine essence is possessed unequally by the three persons, so that some natural features of the deity are found in one person while other natural features of the deity are found in others.[26] So, for example, one might posit that the Father alone is all-powerful, while the Son is not, or that the Spirit alone is the source of grace, while the Father and the Son are not. Instead, this council underscored the dissimilitude of the three persons when compared with three human persons, who may indeed have distinct natural qualities and who are certainly three distinct individual beings. By contrast, the Holy Trinity is one in being and essence, and each

24. Aquinas, *ST* Ia, q. 43. See the study of this issue by Gilles Emery, "*Theologia* and *Dispensatio*: The Centrality of the Divine Missions in St. Thomas's Trinitarian Theology," *Thomist* 74 (2010): 515–61.

25. See the analysis of Joachim's position in Gilles Emery, *The Trinitarian Theology of St. Thomas Aquinas*, trans. F. Murphy (Oxford: Oxford University Press, 2010), 145–48.

26. See the Fourth Lateran Council in *Compendium of Creeds*, 800–820, esp. 803–8, and particularly these passages: "This reality [the divine essence] is neither generating nor generated nor proceeding, but it is the Father who generates, the Son who is generated, and the Spirit who proceeds" (805); and "One cannot say that he [the Father] gave him [the Son] a part of his substance and retained a part for himself, since the substance of the Father is indivisible, being entirely simple. Nor can one say that in generating, the Father transferred his substance to the Son, as though he gave it to the Son in such a way as not to retain it for himself" (804).

person possesses the plenitude of the divine essence, the deity in all its perfection. Consequently, each person is the one God, and there are not three gods. All that is in one person is in the other two, according to the origin of processional relations. The Father is the fontal origin of Trinitarian life, from whom all comes forth, including the eternal divine life of the Son and the Spirit. The Son is the eternally begotten one, the *Logos* of God who receives all that he has and is as God eternally from the Father, God from God. The Spirit is the eternally spirated love of the Father and the Son, who proceeds from each as from one principle and as the mutual love of each. All that is in the Father that pertains to his deity is communicated to the Son by generation and all that is in the Father and the Son is communicated to the Holy Spirit by way of spiration. Consequently, when each of them acts personally, in any work of creation or sanctification, it is also always all three who act personally, and essentially, as God. The Son in his kenosis as one who is human acts, lives, and dies among us, crucified, but in doing so he also acts as the crucified Lord, one who can communicate grace to the world, even in his death, in virtue of his divine identity. In doing so he acts with the Father, as one who proceeds eternally from the Father, as Lord. He acts also with the Spirit of the Lord, the Holy Spirit who proceeds from him and from the Father, as from one principle, who is sent upon the world from the cross and in the resurrection. Even in the kenotic life of the Son, then, it is all three persons who act to save and redeem. This claim must in fact absolutely be maintained if we wish to affirm that the Trinity is revealed in the cross of God. It is only if and because the three persons act concordantly and in their divine unity as God in the mystery of the self-emptying and crucifixion of the Son that we can in turn say that they are each revealed in the event of the crucifixion, in their real personal distinctness and in their divine unity.

We can conclude this line of argument by noting that just because the Son acts always with the Father (John 5:17), there is a modal distinction of personal action that should be acknowledged when we speak about the life of the Trinity.[27] The Father creates all things as the fontal origin of trinitarian life. However, he also only creates through the Word (John 1:1–3), and in his Spirit of holiness. The relations of origin of the three persons constitute the way in which each of them subsists—that is, as innascible, generated, or

---

27. My argument on this point is influenced by Gilles Emery, "The Personal Mode of Trinitarian Action in Saint Thomas Aquinas," *Thomist* 69 (2005): 31–77.

spirated.[28] As Aquinas notes, the Son is truly God, and he has *in himself* the fullness of the divine power and will, but he does not have this *from himself*, but only ever eternally from the Father.[29] He is also only ever "for" the spiration of their mutual love, just as the Holy Spirit is only ever the mutual gift of the Father and the Son, one who joyfully has all that he is from them and in being so, eternally knows and loves all that is in the Father and the Son. These eternal relations in God are revealed to us by the missions of the Son and the Spirit. While the modal differences of the persons are not constituted or fashioned by the temporal missions of the persons, they are instantiated or rendered concretely present in these missions. The way the Son is God with us in his visible mission of incarnation, then, is distinctively filial in mode or character. All that Jesus of Nazareth does and suffers as a human agent is obliquely indicative of his hidden identity as Son, and so also pertains to his filial way of being. Jesus of Nazareth is one who is always from his Father, and for the Father in all that he does and is, as a person.[30] His life of human lowliness is lived for the Father, and in view of the communication of the Holy Spirit of his Father, to all of humanity. "I came to cast fire on the earth" (cf. Luke 12:49 and Acts 2:3). Likewise, the Spirit who is active in the corporate life of the church is always only the Spirit of the Son and the Father, who alerts us to the reality of the Son present among us in the resurrection, and who in doing so turns us toward the Father of Jesus Christ by way of an adoptive life of grace in the Son.

28. Cf. Aquinas, *ST* Ia, q. 29, art. 4.

29. See the argument to this effect in *SCG* IV, 8.9: "The saying also, then, 'the Son cannot do anything of Himself' [John 5:19] does not point to any weakness of action in the Son. But, because for God to act is not other than to be, and His action is not other than His essence . . . so one says that the Son cannot act from Himself but only from the Father, just as He is not able to be from Himself but only from the Father. For, if He were from Himself, He would no longer be the Son. Therefore, just as the Son cannot not be the Son, so neither can He act of Himself. However, because the Son receives the same nature as the Father and, consequently, the same power, although the Son neither is of Himself nor operates of Himself, He nevertheless is through Himself and operates through Himself, since just as He is through His own nature received from the Father, so He operates through His own nature received from the Father. Hence, after our Lord had said: 'the Son cannot do anything of Himself,' to show that, although the Son does not operate of Himself, He does operate through Himself, He adds: 'Whatever He does'—namely, the Father—'these the Son does likewise'."

30. I have explored this idea in greater depth in Thomas Joseph White, *The Incarnate Lord: A Thomistic Study in Christology* (Washington, DC: Catholic University of America Press, 2016), chap. 5, and in *The Trinity: The Nature and Mystery of the One God* (Washington, DC: Catholic University of America Press, 2022), part 4.

The Kenosis of the Son as a Revelation of the Trinity

In light of these considerations, how might we think about the kenosis of the Son more specifically as a revelation of the Trinity? Some options that have been excluded by the line of argument given above deserve mention in this context.

G. W. F. Hegel developed an original christological ontology in light of his innovative interpretation of the use of the communication of idioms.[31] Prior to Hegel there were significant preexisting strata of debate in the Lutheran tradition regarding the communication of idioms. Luther famously had appealed to the notion of the omnipresence of Christ's humanity in debates regarding the Eucharist, so as to maintain the affirmation of the presence of the risen Christ in the Lord's Supper.[32] His appeal to this idea of a natural omnipresence of the humanity of the Son was disavowed by Calvin, as it was also by influential Catholic theologians.[33] The Lutheran Gießen and Tübingen schools of theology subsequently disputed ways in which natural properties of the deity might be communicated to the humanity of Christ, and either surrendered or concealed for the duration of his visible life in the world as human.[34] Again this debate presupposed that, contrary to the principles we have enunciated above, one might attribute various properties of the divine perfection, such as omnipresence or omnipotence, to the human nature as such. The innovation of Hegel was to invert the perspective so as to ascribe the human attributes to the deity rather than the inverse. In becoming human, God freely adopts finitude, temporality, historical development, experience of evil, death, and nothingness into his own being and nature.[35] On this

31. See, in particular, Hegel, "The Consummate Religion," in *Lectures on the Philosophy of Religion, The Lecture of 1827*, ed. P. C. Hodgson, trans. R. F. Brown, P. C. Hodgson, and J. M. Stewart (Berkeley: University of California Press, 2006), 3:452–69.

32. See Martin Luther, *Confession Concerning Christ's Supper* (1528), trans. R. H. Fisher, in *Luther's Works*, vol. 37, ed. R. H. Fisher and H. T. Lehmann (Philadelphia: Fortress, 1961), 232–33 and 276–81, and *Brief Confession Concerning the Holy Sacrament*, trans. M. E. Lehmann in *Luther's Works*, vol. 38, ed. H. T. and M. E. Lehmann (Philadelphia: Fortress, 1971), 306–7.

33. See, for example, John Calvin, *Institutes of the Christian Religion*, trans. F. L. Battles (Philadelphia: Westminster, 1961), 4.17.16–31, esp. para. 30, where Calvin claims that the attribution of ubiquity to the humanity of Christ violates a right usage of the practice of the communication of idioms.

34. See the analysis in Wolfhart Pannenberg, *Jesus God and Man*, 2nd ed., trans. L. L. Wilkins and D. A. Priebe (Philadelphia: Westminster, 1968), 307–23.

35. See Hegel, "The Consummate Religion," 3:452–69, in which Hegel states: "'God himself is dead,' it says in a Lutheran hymn, expressing an awareness that the human, the

view, the very nature of God is constituted developmentally by God becoming human. Hegel's new metaphysics of divine reason depicts the historical world as an unfolding of the divine life, happening in time and history.[36]

From the point of view of the argument presented above, we may say that Hegel's proposal fails to recognize sufficiently the real distinction of the divine and human natures of Christ, which are truly united in the person of Christ, mysteriously, yet without confusion.[37] As a consequence, Hegel forfeits an adequate theology of God's transcendence and fails to acknowledge sufficiently God in his incomprehensible nature as Creator. Instead of being the one who freely communicates being to all that is, actively present in all things in history as the giver of being, Hegel's God is a process of reason and freedom that develops on the conditional basis of a created history. Likewise, the Trinity is constituted for Hegel by the Son's kenotic human life among us, a view that is inadequate to divine revelation. The history of God as incarnate is not a moment within the development of God's intratrinitarian personhood, such that the processions of the persons would be subject

---

finite, the fragile, the weak, the negative are themselves a moment of the divine, that they are within God himself, that finitude, negativity, otherness are not outside of God and do not, as otherness, hinder unity with God. Otherness, the negative, is known to be a moment of the divine nature itself. This involves the highest idea of spirit. . . . This is the explication of reconciliation: that God is reconciled with the world, that even the human is not something alien to him, but rather that this otherness, this self-distinguishing [of the divine nature through diremption], finitude as it is expressed, is a moment in God himself" (468–69). On historical aspects of the communication of idioms in the Tübingen school, see also Walter Kasper, *The Absolute in History: The Philosophy and Theology of History in Schelling's Late Philosophy* (Mahwah, NJ: Paulist, 2018), 459–65.

36. See Hegel, "The Consummate Religion," 3:417–37, in which Hegel writes: "We consider God in his eternal idea, as he is in and for himself, prior to or apart from the creation of the world, so to speak . . . But God is the creator of the world; it belongs to his being, his essence, to be the creator. . . . His creative role is not an *actus* that 'happened' once; [rather,] what takes place in the idea is an *eternal* moment, an eternal determination of the idea. . . . Specifically, the eternal idea is expressed in terms of the holy *Trinity*: it is God himself, eternally triune. Spirit is this process, movement, life. This life is self-differentiation, self-determination, and the first differentiation of that spirit *is* as this universal idea itself" (417–18). As Karl Barth rightly notes in his critical appraisal, God can only acquire his humanity, for Hegel, by voiding or foregoing divine prerogatives and suspending the activity of his divine attributes, at least in his personal mode of being as the Son of God, *Church Dogmatics* IV/1, ed. G. W. Bromiley and T. F. Torrance, trans. G. W. Bromiley (Edinburgh: T&T Clark, 1956), 179–83.

37. A point helpfully emphasized by Bruce L. McCormack in "Karl Barth's Christology as a Resource for a Reformed Version of Kenoticism," *International Journal of Systematic Theology* 8, no. 3 (2006): 243–52.

to definition or alteration in virtue of the incarnation, passion, death, and resurrection of Christ.[38] Needless to say, we also cannot know of the Trinity by a mere process of philosophical reasoning, something Hegel's philosophy seems to intimate.

Karl Barth perceived a number of the problems with Hegel's proposal, and sought to save his novel proposal regarding the communication of idioms by placing it on different footing.[39] Barth affirms that features of the Son's kenotic life are attributable to his eternal nature as Son, namely his humility, lowliness, obedience, and (arguably also) his suffering, but these features of the Son's natural life as God are not acquired by him in virtue of the kenosis of the incarnation. Rather, they pertain to him in a higher way as God from all eternity, as the precondition for the temporal kenosis. There is a divine self-emptying in God eternally that functions as the transcendent ontological precondition of the temporal kenosis of the Son in time.[40] The obedience and suffering unto death of the Son as human, therefore, can be revelatory of an eternal divine obedience and self-surrender that exists in the deity prior to and independently of the creation.[41]

38. Hegel's metaphysics is one in which the freedom of God is supreme among all divine attributes, such that God can choose to self-identify with his seeming contrary and deploy his nature in a plastic way, to be eternal or temporal, impassible or suffering, omnipotent or powerless, existent or nonexistent, Father or Son. The nature of God is defined then by an all-inclusive process of rational freedom that assimilates and transcends contraries passing through them as historical moments of self-development. This ontology is, however, alien to the biblical notion of God's freedom as something that stems from his nature, and from the Trinitarian mystery of the Father, Son, and Spirit. The divine freedom does not continually re-define God's nature, like a liquid subject submitted to historical process or voluntary whim. Instead the divine freedom is expressive of God's enduring *Logos*, and of his eternal goodness and love, manifest in the work of his Spirit. The Trinity communicates being to and saves the creation, and not the inverse.

39. Barth, *Church Dogmatics* IV/1, 179–210, esp. 182–83.

40. Barth, *Church Dogmatics* IV/1, 209.

41. See Karl Barth, *Church Dogmatics* IV/2, ed. G. W. Bromiley and T. F. Torrance, trans. G. W. Bromiley (Edinburgh: T&T Clark, 1958), 87–89, in which Barth writes: "God is not only love . . . but He loves, and He loves man—so much so that He gives Himself to him. He is not only gracious, but He exercises grace, and He does this by becoming the Son of Man as the Son of God, and therefore in the strictest, total union of His nature with ours. This does not take place at the expense but in the power of His divine nature. It is, however, a determination which He gives it. It [the divine nature] acquires in man its *telos*. Directed and addressed to human nature it acquires a form, *this* form. This is why we cannot possibly maintain that the participation of the two natures in Jesus Christ is only one-sided, that of the human in the divine. In the first instance, indeed, it is that of the divine in the human" (87). See also Barth, *Church Dogmatics* IV/1, 208–10. Barth is

This idea is much closer to classical Trinitarian principles, since it maintains a distinction of natures in Christ, and it does not entail the notions that the life of God is constituted by the historical economy or that the Trinity comes into being or undergoes internal development in virtue of the incarnation. Nevertheless, Barth's position is surprisingly similar to that of Joachim of Fiore, mentioned above, in which it was said that the divine nature generates and is generated. By attributing command and obedience, paternal initiative and filial kenosis to the deity of God itself (the divine nature), Barth posits a real distinction in God of natural attributes and ascribes some attributes of the divine essence to the Son and some to the Father. Various questions arise from this decision. For example, if the Son is truly one in being and essence with the Father, how may the Father have natural capacities the Son does not have, and how may the Son have natural capacities that the Father does not have? If this is the case, each is perfect in various ways that the other is not, so that one may rightly ask whether there is a perfect unity of shared divine life. In fact, the position seems, despite protests to the contrary, to entail that each subject is finite, living within a larger (infinite?) process of becoming, seemingly one realized through the Son's submission to the Father. If this submission takes place at all, it must seemingly do so in the economy, in which case the economy is in fact essential to God's achievement of infinite life. Or likewise: if the Son and Father are constituted by distinct voluntary acts (rather than relations of origin, as is classically affirmed by seemingly all previous influential theological authors before Hegel and Barth), then there are distinct natural characteristics of willing present in the two subjects and even, it seems, distinct wills. If this is the case, can we really speak of a divine unity of will in the Trinity exemplified in acts of creation and redemption, or, as the authors of Lateran IV feared in regard to the thought of Joachim, are we not now dealing with a college of morally autonomous subjects who are not one in essence and will, but who decide to collaborate freely by a perennial repetition of mutually consensual decisions? Or if we say that Barth is merely signaling that the Son receives his eternal willing from the Father and wills what the Father wills, but that the Son is constituted by this obedience to the Father's eternal

---

clearly positing an *analogia relationis* by which God acquires his divine identity in both his nature as God and his personal mode of being as Son through the elective relationship he freely undertakes toward humanity, and the incarnation, but this relationality has its precondition in God's self-determination for Sonship, in virtue of the eternal obedience of the Son toward the Father.

willing, then are we not also committed to saying that the Son is constituted by willing what the Father wills, namely, the missions of the Son and Spirit into the world? In this case, the Son is constituted by willing to incarnate and so the temporal kenosis is in fact determinative of the eternal life of the Trinity and not the inverse.

While these options seem unworkable to me, I do think that they depend upon a resolve to argue that the kenosis of the Son in time is truly expressive of the intratrinitarian life of God. Of course, this must be the case in some way, so one is justified in asking what it would mean to affirm this while upholding the divine perfection of the Son in the way that I have attempted to do in the arguments given above. By way of conclusion, then, I will suggest three ways I think that a theology of divine perfection can maintain and even emphasize rightly that the Holy Trinity is manifest to us in a particularly intensive way in the human kenosis of the Son.

First, on the view I have been exploring in this essay, it should be said that kenosis pertains to the Son alone, not the Father or the Spirit, and that it pertains to him personally in virtue of his human nature, not his divine nature as such. It is only the Son who has become human, been crucified, died, and has risen from the dead in a glorified human nature. We can and must say rightly that God himself underwent kenosis by becoming human, and that God was crucified, and died in agony, but he did so as one who is truly human. The point of kenotic theology is not to submit the deity to becoming but to say that the transcendent God submitted to human becoming. Soteriologically, it matters that God retains his divine perfection, even in his crucifixion. It is the undying and infinite perfection of Trinitarian love that is manifest to us in the death of Christ crucified. The one who suffers in kenosis is the very one who alone can truly save us effectively, in virtue of his hidden eternal power. He who suffered, died, and descended into hell as one of us is the one who can redeem all of us and, indeed, remake creation. Consequently, we must maintain a real distinction of natures in Christ, numinously present, even as we ascribe kenosis to God in virtue of the hominization of the Son.

Second, this kenosis, which stems precisely from God becoming human, is filial in mode. This is the case because Christ is the Son of God, and so all that he does as both God and human is emblematic of his person and is expressed in a filial mode. Following Barth, then, we might think of the gospel's various depictions of the various human loves, desires, intentions, councils, choices, and concrete initiatives of Jesus of Nazareth conducted in obedience to the divine will. Such human actions are not identical to the divine will as such. In his human willing Jesus is submitted to the divine will of the Father, a will that mysteriously abides in him as Lord, and that is fully present also in the Spirit, who acts upon Christ in his human mind and heart, inspiring him from within to conform his life inwardly to this divine will. Thus the human decisions of Jesus transpire in harmony with the divine will and consequently are obliquely revelatory of the Father's designs—designs in which the Lord Jesus Christ and the Spirit share. If all this is true, then the obedience of the Son of Man is indicative of the shared life of Trinitarian communion and inter-personal love. His free acceptance of suffering, his decision to die by crucifixion, and his expiration in love on the cross all indicate and manifest the hidden ground of love, the uncreated mystery of the Father, in whose life he shares fully as his transcendent Word, as the Lord of Israel crucified, spirating the Holy Spirit from the dereliction of the cross, sending that Spirit on mission to all creation as the Spirit of holiness and sanctification.

Third, even as we say rightly that the human self-emptying unto death of Christ can and does truly reveal intratrinitarian personal communion and the uncreated love of God as the fundamental ground of the world, we must preserve the analogical interval between the divine freedom of Christ as God and the freedom of Christ as human, between the uncreated deity in its perfect power to remake all things, and the fragile created nature in which God lives kenotically in solidary with us, in his perfect humanity, subject to suffering and death. Finitude is not a curse that God must reject for himself. It is merely the congenital sign of being a creation with the nobility and limitation that this entails, a finitude that invites us to turn upward in our restless minds and hearts toward a yet higher, infinite source, for which we naturally yearn. The Son does not need to cede his deity of being in the form of God by an impossible alienation of his divine prerogatives in order to take on our finitude and to garner our loyalty. He was not jealous of his divine transcendence. Precisely because of the inalienable perfection of his love and power to redeem, as God, he could become finite and humanly limited without ceasing to be infinitely perfect and divine. Consequently, in imitation of Christ, we should not be jealous of that transcendent perfection he alone has as a man who is God, as if we should require God to evacuate his perfection as Creator as a premise for his rendering himself present to us. Nor, however, should we ignore the distinctive perfection of Christ's humanity. It is a perfection achieved precisely in the lowliness of suffering and death, and in surrender to the divine perfection of the Father, manifest in the obedience of love that characterized his human life. That human perfection was lived out among us in terms that have now become imitable by grace, as Paul tells us

(Phil 2:5). We can therefore set out along the pathway of the Son who took on the form of a servant, and we may do so in the hope of the vision of his glory (1 Cor 13:12), a perfect glory of one who is eternally with and from the Father as Lord (John 17:5), in an eternal communion of life shared with the Holy Spirit. It is to that high place of eternal Trinitarian life that Jesus Christ is now exalted, and it is there that we hope to follow him.

9

Kenosis as Condescension in the Theology of Martin Luther

Matthew J. Aragon Bruce

The Trinitarian and christological dogmas of the Church Catholic were never disputed by the sixteenth-century Protestant Reformers, apart from some initial misgivings concerning nonbiblical terminology. Luther was no exception to this.[1] He unreservedly adopts the dogmas of the early ecumenical councils.[2] While some scholars from previous generations questioned Luther's orthodoxy, largely for polemical purposes,[3] contemporary Luther scholarship

---

1. The following abbreviations for the writings of Martin Luther will be used throughout this chapter: WA: *D. Martin Luthers Werke*, 65 vols. (Weimar: H. Böhlau, 1883–1993); LW: *Luther's Works*, vols. 1–55 (St. Louis: Concordia; Philadelphia: Fortress, 1958–86) and vols. 56–79 (St. Louis: Concordia, 2009–16); AL: *The Annotated Luther*, 6 vols. (Minneapolis: Fortress, 2015–17).

2. See Luther's *On the Councils and the Church*, in WA 50:581–96; LW 41:93–110. Cf. Marc Lienhard, *Luther: Witness to Jesus Christ; Stages and Themes of the Reformer's Christology*, trans. Edwin H. Robertson (Minneapolis: Augsburg, 1982), 232–33; Johannes Zachhuber, *Luther's Christological Legacy: Christocentrism and the Chalcedonian Tradition* (Milwaukee: Marquette University Press, 2017), 76–82.

3. To give but two examples: (1) The Protestant theologian Karl Holl, whose moralizing soteriology did not require a mediator between God and human beings, sought to win Luther to his side and argued that Luther did not subscribe to the traditional dogmas and was both a modalist and subordinationist. See Holl's "Was Verstand Luther unter Religion," in *Luther*, 6th ed., vol. 1 of *Gesammelte Aufsätze zur Kirchengeschichte* (Tübingen: Mohr Siebeck, 1932), 69n4. Marc Lienhard, in what remains the most thor-

demonstrates a remarkable degree of near unanimous consent regarding the following: (1) that Luther adopted the Trinitarian and christological dogmas of the early ecumenical councils in their entirety; (2) that while Luther subscribes to Chalcedon, his Christology has something of an Alexandrian bent (i.e., Luther emphasizes the unity and undividedness of the two natures); (3) that he was resistant to scholastic, metaphysical speculation about the incarnation; and (4) that in some areas he provided "a fresh interpretation" or "further formation" of the precedents set by the Christology of the councils' fathers.[4]

One area in which Luther offers fresh interpretation and further formation is the doctrine of kenosis, the "emptying" that occurs in the incarnation. The idea of kenosis is central to Luther's understanding of the person of Jesus Christ and to his reformational theology as a whole. This is evident from the importance of the great Christ-hymn in Philippians 2 to Luther's work from its earliest stages, not only for his understanding of Christ's person, but also for his understanding of Christ's work, the doctrines of justification and sanctification, his account of the Christian life lived in imitation of Christ, and much more. This can be demonstrated by a glance at two of Luther's more famous

---

ough study of Luther's Christology, has sufficiently debunked Holl on this account; see Lienhard, *Luther*, 110–15, 318. (2) The Catholic theologian Yves Congar accused Luther of what could be described as a monergistic type of monophysitism. According to Congar, the trouble with Luther is not that he understands salvation to be initiated by God alone (something to which Congar was sympathetic), but that the role of the humanity of Christ in the drama of salvation is reduced to such a degree that salvation is due to the divinity of Christ alone. Congar thus summarizes his study: "Luther, in a word, has a Christology of the efficacy of God alone," in "Regards et Réflexions sur la Christologie de Luther," in *Das Konzil von Chalkedon: Geschichte und Gegenwart*, ed. Grillmeier und Bacht (Würzburg: Echter, 1954), 3:486. For responses to Congar's critique, see Vidar L. Haanes, "Christological Themes in Luther's Theology," *Studia Theologica—Nordic Journal of Theology* 61, vol. 1 (2007): 21–46; Zachhuber, *Luther's Christological Legacy*, 62–66; and the magisterial study of Constantio Di Bruno, *Le Rôle Salutaire de L'humanité du Christ à la Lumière des Grands Thèmes de la Christologie de Luther* (Paris: Institut Catholique de Paris, U. E. R. de Théologie et de Sciences Religieuses, 1979).

4. This consent is remarkable given the vast degree of scholarly dispute on other issues. See Bernard Lohse, *Martin Luther's Theology* (Minneapolis: Fortress, 1999), 228–30. In addition to Lohse and the works of Lienhard, Haanes, and Zachhuber cited above, see, for example, Oswald Bayer, *Martin Luther's Theology: A Contemporary Interpretation* (Grand Rapids: Eerdmans, 2008), 232–38; Sammeli Juntunen, "Christ," in *Engaging Luther: A (New) Theological Assessment*, ed. Olli-Pekka Vainio (Eugene, OR: Cascade, 2010), 59–64; Robert Kolb, *Martin Luther: Confessor of Faith* (Oxford: Oxford University Press, 2009), 59–64, 110–17; and Vítor Westhelle, *Transfiguring Luther: The Planetary Promise of Luther's Theology* (Eugene, OR: Cascade, 2016), 95–110, 155–63. These diverse texts are broadly representative of the various schools and factions in Luther research at present.

early writings, the *Sermon on Two Kinds of Righteousness* (1518) and *The Freedom of a Christian* (1520). The former is a sermon that marks one of Luther's first attempts to explain the distinction between alien and proper righteousness, and he does this by means of an extended treatment of Philippians 2:5–11 (supplemented by an appeal to vast number of additional passages from the traditional Pauline epistles). In the latter, we find the famous "two propositions concerning the freedom and slavery of the spirit—*A Christian person is a free lord over all things and subordinate to no one. A Christian person is a subservient slave to all things and subordinate to everyone.*"[5] Luther's distinction in this text between "a spiritual, new, and inner person" and "the corporeal, old, and outer person" is also derived from Paul's distinction between the *forma dei* (form of God) and the *forma servi* (form of a servant) in Philippians 2.[6] For Luther, these distinctions and propositions are not parts of some oppositional dualism; rather they are rooted in the two forms present in the Savior. In the words of the apostle, "though he was in the form of God, he did not regard equality with God as something to be exploited, but emptied himself, taking the form of a servant . . . and . . . humbled himself and became obedient to the point of death" (Phil 2:6–8). Luther sees in these distinctions not merely or even primarily an explanation of the person of Christ, for example, the two natures, but a model for the Christian who is free over all things and subordinate to no one, and who just so—in imitation of Christ—is called not to exploit this freedom but to be a servant to all, God *and* neighbor. In order to understand further Luther's idea of kenosis, we turn first to his exegesis of Philippians 2, followed by attention to his christological reflections in relation to the Lord's Supper and the Christian life.

Luther's Exegesis of Philippians 2

Luther did not write a commentary or lecture on Philippians. Luther's explicit treatment of this passage, apart from a few texts such as *The Freedom of a Christian* mentioned above, is largely contained in his sermons.

It appears that Luther preached five sermons, with a possible sixth, on Philippians 2:5–11.[7] All five sermons were preached on Palm Sunday, the date

---

5. WA 7:21; emphasis original. See LW 31:343–77 for the standard English text, which is actually a translation of the Latin edition; the citation here is from Luther's German version.

6. WA 7:21.

7. These are sermons for which Philippians 2:5–11 is the prescribed text, though Luther reflects on the passage in many other sermons. For example, it would seem the Philip-

this passage was prescribed in the lectionary.[8] The possible sixth sermon is the *Sermon on Three Kinds of Righteousness*, which is closely connected to the already mentioned *Sermon on Two Kinds of Righteousness*; both were written sometime in 1518 or perhaps early 1519.[9] These two sermons are vastly different in form and content, yet they are closely connected, and one seems to be a revision of the other. Just which is which is a matter of some debate, but the more compelling argument is that *Two Kinds* is the later, edited version and Luther's 1518 Palm Sunday sermon.[10] The third is Luther's 1525 Palm Sunday sermon,[11] in which he states in the opening paragraph, "Even though a few years ago a sermon on *Two Kinds of Righteousness* was published in my name, yet the text was not completely explained. For that reason, we will now go through it word by word."[12] Originally preached in 1525, the sermon was included in the Winter Postil published by Luther in 1540. The sermons in the Postil were edited by Luther himself to serve as expositions of Scripture passages in the lectionary. These "sermons" are basically sermon helps on the Gospel and Epistle passages "intended to provide help for preachers with insufficient theological training, and for family reading."[13] The remaining three sermons, Palm Sunday sermons from 1523,[14] 1528,[15] and 1531[16] were not edited for publication by Luther, but were recorded by notetakers. These latter sermons are less reliable because the notetakers often added their own

---

pians passage was on Luther's mind during Lent in 1518, for he preached a sermon on John 9:1–38, about the man born blind, on the Wednesday after Laetare. In this sermon, he undertakes a rather lengthy treatment of the distinction between the form of God and the form of a servant in order to set up his sermon on spiritual blindness; see WA 1:268–69; LW 51:37–38.

8. Philippians 2:5–11 remains a Palm Sunday text today, assigned in the Revised Common Lectionary, Year A.

9. *Three Kinds:* see WA 2:41–47. *Two Kinds:* WA 2:143–52; ET: LW 293–306; AL 2:9–24.

10. There is no small amount of scholarly discussion over which of these two sermons was written first and which is a revision of the other. In addition to the editorial introduction to the Sermon in AL 2:9–12, see Martin Brecht, *Martin Luther: His Road to Reformation 1483–1521* (Philadelphia: Fortress, 1985), 229–31; Robert Kolb, "Luther on the Two Kinds of Righteousness: Reflections on His Two-Dimensional Definition of Humanity at the Heart of His Theology," *Lutheran Quarterly* 13 (1999): 457–58.

11. WA 17/2:237–45; LW 76:415–23.

12. WA 17/2:237; LW 76:415.

13. John W. Doberstein, "Introduction to Volume 51," LW 51:xiv.

14. WA 12:462–71.

15. WA 27:91–95.

16. WA 34/1:181–89.

material and/or edited the sermons, and as such I will not make use of them here.[17] A cursory reading reveals no significant theological departures from the 1525 Postil sermon.

Three Kinds of Righteousness

Three Kinds is rather brief compared to *Two Kinds* (just short of four pages in the WA; further evidence of it being the first edition and *Two Kinds* the revision). Luther says very little about Christ's person in this sermon. What he does is attempt to define what it means to be human "by examining what has gone wrong with humanity" through a series of scholastic-like distinctions between different kinds of sin and corresponding kinds of righteousness.[18]

The sermon begins abruptly: "Threefold is sin, threefold its opposing righteousness." Luther then begins his list of definitions and distinctions, naming and defining each kind of sin and corresponding righteousness. He observes: "First is criminal, i.e., manifest evil which even the secular power punishes such as theft, murder, arson, sacrilege, etc." The contrasting kind of righteousness is righteousness that comes from the law, "civil righteousness," the righteousness in which "a person is good in the presence of people, avoids the punishment of the law, and receives the temporal promises of the law," yet "it does not serve God, but rather itself" and "it makes hypocrites, haughty in the minds of their hearts, bold judges of others." The Christian is "to be dissuaded" from this sort of righteousness and to seek another.[19]

The second kind of sin is the "essential, natal, original, alien" sin that "makes the prior righteousness to be nothing and evil . . . incurable through human powers." In short, this second type is original sin. Its correspondent form of righteousness "is also natal, essential, original, and alien for it is the righteousness of Christ. . . . Whoever is born from God does not sin (i.e. is not able to sin), but the generation from God preserves him." This righteousness is essential and eternal; it is the righteousness of God which Christ gives to the Christian. The Christian receives it from Christ; it is a *passive, saving*

---

17. This is especially the case with the 1531 sermon which exists in two different manuscripts exhibiting many differences. For an overview of the transmission history of Luther sermons, with attention to the various notetakers and their reliability, see the introductions to the new series of LW, vols. 56–58 and 75.

18. Kolb, *Martin Luther*, 66.

19. WA 2:43–44.

righteousness that transforms the Christian from a sinner to a truly righteous person.[20] This second kind of sin and righteousness is "alien" because "just as Adam, through one sin, makes everyone born from him guilty and by that same sin, which is certainly alien to them, gives to them what he has, so Christ, by means of his own righteousness, which is alien to them and unmerited, makes everyone born from him righteous and saved, so just as we are damned by alien sin, we might be liberated by alien righteousness."[21]

The third kind of sin is "actual [*actuale*] . . . the fruit of original." This final type of sin is comprised of the individual sins committed by the fallen, those afflicted by original sin." The correspondent kind of righteousness is termed "active [*actualis*], flowing from faith and essential righteousness." Stating that it is necessary to speak "more extensively" about this third kind of righteousness, Luther begins a detailed description.[22] First, he firmly rejects the meritoriousness of actual acts of righteousness: "Faith is the whole merit, for it is a most empty boast to say that a sudden action might be deserving of eternal life; it is necessary that the person be deserving. Christ has given and merited for us and gives daily." Second, he exhorts the listener or reader not to doubt, but to have faith and act out of faith trusting that so long as they trust that their works are in Christ, these works are pleasing to God, but they are not pleasing on their own: "Whether you sin or do not sin, always rely steadfastly upon Christ and that natural righteousness." Third, the Christian is to engage actively in works that "promote principal righteousness and might minimize original sin . . . from that third righteousness nothing else is sought than that original sin be blotted out and the body of sin destroyed." Fourth, and finally, Christians are called to guard against works that they might choose for themselves, for such works "do not purge sin but rather pollute." Those works that purify are those that God imposes and to which God calls us: these are works of mortification, and Luther observes that "the best are sufferings, sorrows, poverty, ignominy, and death, because here alone God works and the human being suffers, and most perfectly Adam perishes and Christ the vine purifies."[23]

Luther's focus in this sermon is on what it means to be human under the conditions of the fall. Luther states elsewhere that Adam's original righteousness (type 2) was by grace alone even before the fall; Adam did not receive

20. WA 2:44.
21. WA 2:45.
22. WA 2:45.
23. WA 2:46–47.

God's favor by doing good works or keeping God's commands, but he was rather created in a state of righteousness.[24] God gives grace to human beings not because they merit it, but because God loves them. In a Christmas sermon on Titus 3, Luther summarizes his understanding of what it means to be human, properly human, possessed of the righteousness that the loving God gives to his creatures:

> All Christian doctrine, works, and life is briefly, clearly, and completely comprehended in the two terms *faith and love*, through which the human being is placed as a medium between God and his or her neighbor, to receive from above and gift below, becoming as it were a vessel or a channel through which flows the divine goodness unceasingly to other people.... We are children of God through faith, which makes us all heirs of the divine goodness. But we are gods through love, which makes us do good towards our neighbors; for the divine nature is nothing other than pure goodness or as Paul says here [Titus 3:4] friendliness and loving kindness, lavishly pouring out its goodness on all creatures daily.[25]

For Luther, it is the "natal, essential, original, and alien" righteousness—the passive righteousness that God freely and unconditionally gives to human beings out of his grace and love—that is the core of what it means to be human. It is in this passive righteousness, which empowers the Christian to works of active righteousness (obedience to God and love of neighbor), that we come to understand what it means to be human in correspondence with the will of the Creator. After the fall, the source of this passive righteousness is found in the incarnate Christ alone. Righteousness before God "consists of trusting and thus possessing Christ and his righteousness ... won in his death and resurrection, instilled by grace alone as the Father draws us in faith to Christ."[26]

To summarize: Luther's focus in this sermon—which continues to be the primary focus of the subsequent sermons—is on righteousness and not on technical Christology and the divine and human "forms" of the incarnate Son. His primary message is that the active righteousness of the Christian (type 3), which proceeds from the "essential, natal, original, alien" righteousness of Christ (type 2), does not itself merit God's favor and thus salvation. Rather, this righteousness is the response of a loving and thankful child to

24. Cf. WA 42:63–87; LW 1:101–15.
25. WA 10/1:100–101, emphasis original.
26. Kolb, *Martin Luther*, 67.

the loving and merciful Father. It is the passive righteousness of Christ that produces active righteousness in the Christian. God's favor is found in Jesus Christ, his obedience, and his righteousness; and this righteousness is given to the Christian in faith, leading to works of obedience. Luther elsewhere contrasts the "earthly image" of the fallen Adam, "from whom we come," with "the heavenly image" of Christ, who was

> a human being full of love, mercy, and grace, humility, patience, wisdom, light, and everything good. His entire being was so directed that he served everyone and harmed no one. We must also bear this image and be conformed to it. To this image also belongs his death and suffering and everything about him, his resurrection, life, grace, and virtue. Everything is to be likewise directed by those who put on the same.[27]

In subsequent sermons on this theme, as will be seen below, Luther finds that in order to communicate effectively his account of the two kinds of righteousness and of the Christian life lived in conformity with Christ, he has to give a more rigorous account of Christ's person.

Two Kinds of Righteousness

Luther refines his account of righteousness in *Two Kinds*. Notably, he drops the first type of righteousness and now lists only two types, alien or passive righteousness and proper or active righteousness. Moreover, the sermon now treats Philippians 2:5–11 explicitly, with the exhortation "to have the mind of Christ" beginning and structuring the entire sermon. After defining the two types of righteousness, he begins a careful explication of verses 5–8, which includes offering definitions of the "form of God" and the "form of a servant."

Luther first provides definitions of the two forms: "the form of God" cannot mean "the substance of God because Christ never emptied himself of this. Neither can the form of servant be said to mean human substance. . . . the form of God is wisdom, power, righteousness, goodness, and, furthermore, freedom." The form of the servant, on the other hand, refers to the fact that Jesus "subjected himself to all evils and although he was free . . . he made himself to be the servant of all, acting in no other way than as if all our evils were his own." According to Luther, Christ *as a human being* was

---

27. WA 24:50–51.

not naturally subject to the evils, the sins and vices, that plague the rest of humanity. He was free, powerful, and full of wisdom, "preeminent in such attributes that are proper to the form of God." Christ empties himself, not by divesting himself of these attributes, but by choosing not to "use his status against us."[28]

Luther next compares those who do not serve others as practicing a form of "robbery" (*rapina*) in which people fail to give God glory but instead strive to keep such glory for themselves. Luther compares such robbers to the pharisee in the parable of the Pharisee and the Tax Collector (Luke 18:9–14), who was "delighted that others were wretched" and "was unwilling that they should be like him." Such people "are arrogant about themselves—rather they keep and do not give back what clearly is God's (as they should), nor do they serve others with it that they may become like others. People of this kind wish to be like God, sufficient in themselves, pleasing themselves, glorifying in themselves, under obligation to no one, and so on."[29] Luther understands such sin as *concupiscentia*.[30]

For Luther, Christ's emptying himself is not an act whereby he divests himself of some divine attribute, be it power or glory, but rather an act whereby he chooses to serve others by serving them, by seeking their good. He "relinquished that form to God the Father and emptied himself . . . and took the form of a servant." According to Luther, that Christ did not consider himself equal to God "means that he did not want to be equal to God as those who through pride rob it [equality] and (as St. Bernard says) say to God: 'If you will not give me your glory, I shall seize it for myself.'" Aware that he might be understood as subordinating Christ to the Father or even denying the divinity of Christ, Luther qualifies this statement immediately: "The passage, which many have understood affirmatively, is to be understood negatively: he did not think himself equal to God, that is, the fact that he is equal to God, this he did not consider robbery. For this interpretation is not based on a right understanding, since it speaks of Christ the human being."[31]

The remainder of the sermon is focused on how individual Christians should imitate Christ and become servants of one another. Christians are called to empty themselves of anything that might cause them to boast and look down on their neighbor. Luther exhorts those who have health, wealth,

---

28. WA 2:147–48; AL 2:18, translation revised.
29. WA 2:148; AL 2:18.
30. Cf. Lohse, *Martin Luther's Theology*, 55, 71.
31. WA 2:148; AL 2:18–19.

power, honor, and even righteousness to serve their weaker neighbors, forsaking what they have and identifying with the weaker member of the body. Indeed, those who have such gifts given to them by God are to use them to elevate not themselves but their neighbors: "For you are powerful, not that you make the weak weaker by oppression, but that you may make them powerful by raising them up and defending them. . . . You are righteous so that you may vindicate and pardon the unrighteous, not that you may only condemn, disparage, judge, and punish. For this is Christ's example."[32]

Two years later, in *The Freedom of the Christian*, Luther expands the themes of this sermon. Toward the end of this treatise, he writes of "those who have obscured for us the most salutary world of the Apostle having completely misunderstood the apostolic vocabulary ('form of God,' 'form of servant,' 'human form,' 'human likeness') and have applied it to the divine and human natures [of Christ]."[33] For Luther, to apply this passage and the two forms solely to the doctrine of Christ's two natures misses the connection the apostle is making to the life of faith. By contrast, Luther sets out an account of what Paul truly intends:

> Although Christ was filled with the form of God and abounded in all good things—so that he required no work or suffering in order to be righteous or saved (for he had all of this from the beginning), yet he was not puffed up by them nor did he elevate himself above us and assume power over us, although it would have been within his rights to do so. But, he acted contrary to this, living, laboring, suffering, dying just like the rest of humanity, and in human form[34] and action he was nothing other than a human being, as if he lacked all these things and possessed nothing of God forms, yet he did this for our sake, so that he might serve us and so that all the things he accomplished in the form of a servant might become ours.[35]

32. WA 2:150; AL 2:21.

33. WA 7:65; AL 1:522, translation revised.

34. Luther's Latin term here is *habitu*, which is the Vulgate's translation of *schēmati* in Phil 2:7. The NRSV, and most modern Bible translations, translate this as "form." The various English translations of *The Freedom of the Christian* miss this because the translators are trying, understandably because of the importance of the term in Luther's text, to distinguish *habitu* from *forma*, the Vulgate's translation of *morphē*, which the NRSV and most other modern Bible translations also translate as "form." AL goes with "vesture" and LW with "fashion"; both are unsatisfactory because they miss that Luther is simply referencing the biblical text.

35. WA 7:65; AL 1:522, translation revised.

Thus, Paul's purpose is not primarily to provide an understanding of the two natures of the hypostatic union, but rather to exhort Christians to have the same mind as Christ and to live such that everything they do is in service of others.

1525 Postil Palm Sunday Sermon

As noted above, Luther begins this sermon by noting that even though he preached and published *Two Kinds* only a few years before, "the text was not completely explained. For that reason, we will now go through it word by word." This sermon is indeed a verse-by-verse commentary on Philippians 2:5–11. It is doubtful that Luther actually preached this precise sermon. What we have is a version edited to be an expository aid for young and inexperienced Lutheran preachers. Again, while the primary focus is on the Christian imitating Christ and being a servant to all, more is said about the person of Christ, and Luther carefully defines terms such as *forma dei* and *forma servi*.

Luther begins by affirming traditional Christology, stating that Christ is "true God by nature," "infinite good and God himself," who "has lowered himself and become the servant of everyone." But he notes that the term "form of God" is not understood by everyone in the same way. Some understand it as referring to the divine essence or nature in Christ. However, Luther disagrees:

> Although it is true that Christ is true God, yet St. Paul is not speaking here about his divine, secret essence. He uses the word "*morphē*," or "*forma*" later when he says that Christ has taken on the form of a servant. 'The form of a servant' cannot mean the essence of a natural servant who has a servant's nature in himself, because Christ became our servant not by nature but out of his goodwill and grace. For that reason the words "form of God" cannot mean his divine essence.

So for Luther, the terms "form of God" and "form of a servant" do not refer to substances or essences and thus they do not refer to the divine and human natures of Christ. They rather refer to actions, in Luther's words, to "the appearance and manifestation of [an] essence . . . the essence is something, but the appearance does something, or is a deed." To be in the form of God "means that one appears to be God and acts that way, or accepts deity and takes it upon himself." And Christ does act like God in his public ministry as recorded in Scripture, for example, in his miracles, in his forgiving of sins, and so on. But he also acts or appears in the form of a servant, which "means that one appears to be and acts like a servant toward others. *Morphē tou doulou* could be said more plainly as 'servile appearance,' or one who acts like a servant."[36] Christ appeared or acted like a servant during his earthly ministry, above all when he suffered and died for us and for our salvation.

Luther then launches into a discussion of three ways that a form or appearance can occur: (1) an essence can occur without an appearance; (2) an appearance can occur without an essence; (3) an essence can occur together with an appearance. Luther gives examples for each of these three ways with reference to the form of God and the form of a servant.

First, an essence without an appearance: This occurs when God—who is everywhere present—does not reveal himself but withdraws his appearance, perhaps in anger over sin. Luther's further illustrations of this way include a servant who fails to serve but instead lords over others, as well as the devil and the antichrist who presume to take up the form of God.

Second, an appearance without an essence: the form of God cannot so occur. There can be no true appearance of the form of God without the presence of the essence of God—that is, without God himself being present. However, there can be the appearance of the form of a servant without the essence, for example in a king who publicly serves his people. The incarnate Christ is Luther's obvious example.

Third, an essence with an appearance: Luther's examples are God when he shows grace, and a "true Christian" who serves God and neighbor. But his primary example is Christ, who was in the form of God and appeared as God in his earthly ministry.

With these three ways in place, Luther proceeds to explain the passage as follows: "From all this St. Paul's meaning is clear, for he wants to say this: Christ was in the form of God, that is, he had the essence with the appearance. But he did not take up that divine appearance as he took up the form of a servant."[37] In the incarnation, Christ chose not to take up the form of God but instead takes up the form—that is, the appearance—of a servant for the sake of sinners. This is the opposite condition than that in which sinners are themselves, for to be a sinner is to be in a state of wanting to be God and to steal the deity that does not belong to them.[38] Luther makes much of this

---

36. WA 17/2:238–39; LW 76:415–17.
37. WA 17/2:240; LW 76:418, translation revised.
38. See, WA 17/2:240; LW 76:418.

opposition: "Christ empties himself of the form of God in which he was and takes on the form of a servant in which he is not. But we empty ourselves of the form of a servant in which we are and presume to take on the form of God in which we are not."[39]

Luther's position is that Christ is eternally, essentially God. In the incarnation, Christ chooses to appear as a servant rather than to take up the form of God. Christ's deity is thus present but hidden behind the form of a servant. Luther explains the language of "emptying" carefully:

> Christ emptied or got rid of himself; that is, he appeared to be laying aside the deity and would not use it or presume to have it. It was not that he would or could lay aside and put away deity, but that he laid aside the form of the divine majesty and did not act like God. . . . He did not lay aside the form of God in such a way that it could not be sensed or seen, for then no form of God would have remained. Rather, he did not take it or make a show of it against us, but rather served us with it.[40]

Christ's "laying aside" of his form of God was a voluntary choice which was in fact a divine action, an action that flows from the divine wisdom, goodness, and above all love. This love does not seek its own benefit but rather the benefit of the beloved.

At this point, it may seem that Luther has undermined the humanity of Christ. But he takes up the topic of Christ's humanity in the very next section, commenting on the phrases "being born in human likeness" and "being found in human form" separately. Concerning the first phrase, Luther affirms that Christ's being from Mary means that he was "a natural human being." Luther states that this term "human being" must be understood to mean "no more than a human being without anything added. . . . Christ was born like any other human being [with no advantage over others]. . . . Christ came and acted in such a way that no human being is so insignificant that [Christ] was not like him." Concerning the second phrase, Luther affirms that everything Christ did, he did as a human being, "like other people, such as eating, drinking, sleeping," etc., thereby affirming the true and full humanity of Christ. "He could," Luther writes, "have left all of that behind"—that is, all the human actions seemingly unbefitting of deity—"and acted differently as God." But he became fully human and so had all the physical and spiritual

---

39. WA 17/2:241; LW 76:418–19.
40. WA 17/2:243; LW 76:420.

needs of a human being. This includes obedience to God. Luther finishes his exposition of the first half of the hymn by noting that Christ did all that he did, not because we were worthy, but

> because he was obedient to the Father [Phil. 2:8]. Here St. Paul opens up heaven with a word and makes room for us to see the abundance of the divine majesty and to gaze on the inexpressible gracious will and love of the Father's heart toward us, so that we would feel that God from eternity has been pleased with what Christ, the gracious person, would do and now has done for us.[41]

Luther's point is that to have the same mind as Christ means to be at rest in the grace and love of God and just so freed to serve one's neighbor, freed to love others with the same love God demonstrates for us in Jesus Christ.

Luther's Servant Christology in the Lord's Supper and the Christian Life

Luther's understanding of kenosis and of the form of a servant and the form of God in Philippians 2 is basic to that aspect of his Christology perhaps best known by students of the history of theology, that is, his doctrine of ubiquity, the idea that Christ's exalted, post-resurrection human nature is everywhere present, united to the divine nature.[42] This doctrine was the partial cause of the disagreement between the Lutherans and the Reformed at the 1529 Marburg Colloquy and their failure to unify the nascent Protestant movements. In a 1526 sermon—written in response to the Swiss and South German reformers, whom Luther termed "fanatics"—he describes the doctrine thus: "We believe that Christ, according to his human nature, is put over all creatures and fills all things, Paul says in Eph. 4[:10]. *Not only according to his divine nature, but also according to his human nature, is he lord of all things, has all things in his hands, and is present everywhere.* If I am to follow the fanatics who say that this is not fitting, then I must deny Christ."[43] Luther took issue with the early Reformed theologians who denied the ubiquity of Christ's human nature and who asserted that his human nature was like our fallen human nature and thus capable of being present in only one

41. WA 17/2:243–44; LW 76:422.
42. Cf. Lohse, *Martin Luther's Theology*, 230.
43. WA 19:491; LW 36:342, emphasis mine.

spatial location at a given time—even after the resurrection. Luther could not accept this because to him it undermined the real, bodily presence of Christ in the Lord's Supper.

When Luther's Reformed critics appealed for support to the example of Stephen, who looked up to heaven and said, "I see heaven opened and the Son of Man standing at the right hand of the Father" (Acts 7:56), Luther responded:

> How does he see Christ? He need not raise his eyes on high. Christ is around us and in us in all places. These people understand nothing of this. They also say that he sits at the right hand of God, but what it means that Christ ascends into heaven and sits there, they do not know. It is not the same as when you climb a ladder into the house. *It means rather that he is above all creatures and in all and beyond all creatures.* That he was taken up bodily, however, occurred as a sign of this. . . . Although he is present in all creatures, and I might find him in stone, in fire, or even in a rope . . . *he does not wish that I seek him apart from the Word.* He is present everywhere, but he does not wish that you grope for him everywhere. Grope rather where the Word is, and there you will lay hold of him right away. . . . *For this reason he has set down for us a definite way to show us how and where to find him, namely the Word.*[44]

For Luther, God must be sought where he can be found, and God has chosen to be found in his Word, which after the incarnation is in the person of the union and not in the divine Logos or Son alone.

That Luther so understands things is evident from the Marburg debate. At Marburg, Oecolampadius, Zwingli's confrère, denied that Christ was everywhere present in his humanity. Christ is present in the Supper, not bodily, but in the same way that he is present in heaven—namely, in his divine nature, the same way that the Father is present. To this Luther responds: "Indeed, he is [present] in baptism, in the Lord's Supper, in teaching, until the end of the world, until he comes. You may distinguish between humanity and divinity until that time—this is no concern of mine . . . he is present in the sacrament in the same bodily substance as when he was born of the Virgin. I shall not get involved in the matter of his being in heaven and in the bread." Yet Oecolampadius answers, "Don't cling so fast to Christ's humanity and flesh! Raise your thoughts to Christ's divinity!" However, such a notion

---

44. WA 19:491; LW 36:342, emphasis mine.

is utterly contradictory to Luther's understanding, not just of the person of the incarnate Christ, but of how God is known by us, and moreover of how God works for us and for our salvation. Luther thus responds: "I know God only as he became human, so I shall have him in no other way."[45]

Luther continued to develop his doctrine of ubiquity in the continuing disputes with the Zwinglians and others who rejected the real, bodily presence of Christ in the Supper. But his Alexandrian emphasis on the union of the natures and his resistance to any separation of or division between them is an early feature of his thought and is unquestionably derived from Philippians 2. In 1523, Luther wrote *The Adoration of the Sacrament* as part of his dialogue with the Hussites (the conflict with the Swiss Reformed was yet in its infancy), who also argued that Christ was not "present substantially and naturally" in the sacrament.[46] It appears that this treatise is the first text in which Luther gives sustained attention to the words of institution, "This is my body. . . . This is my blood," and articulates his understanding of real presence. In this treatise, Luther defends the practice of the adoration or worship [*anbetten*] of Christ in the sacrament: "He who does not believe that Christ's body and blood are present does well not to worship. . . . But he who does believe . . . can surely not withhold his reverence [*ehrbietung*] of the body and blood without sinning. For I must always confess that Christ is present, if his body and blood are present." There is a distinction, Luther continues, between "Christ sitting up there in heaven, and being in the sacrament and in the hearts of believers." Christ's presence in the sacrament and in the hearts of believers is "not because he wants to be worshipped there, but because residing there he wants to work with us and help us." However, "the reason that he ascended into heaven was certainly because human beings should and must worship him there and confess him to be the Lord, mighty over all things, Phil 2[:10–11]."[47]

The fundamental themes of Luther's Christology can be recognized in these reflections on ubiquity and Christ's presence in the Supper. While adopting the christological dogma of the tradition in its entirety, Luther refuses to think or reflect on the Word of God apart from the person of the union, that is, he rejects any speculation about the being and character of God apart from the incarnation. But he also holds that the work of salvation is not accomplished by the Word of God alone but by the Word hypostati-

45. The dialogue is presented in *Great Debates of the Reformation*, ed. Donald J. Ziegler (New York: Random House, 1969), 94.

46. WA 11:431; LW 37:275.

47. WA 11:447; LW 37:294, translation revised.

cally united to humanity. Luther simply has no interest in any idea or concept of God and God's salvific work independent of the incarnation. Lienhard summarizes Luther's position well: "Luther . . . refused to consider the *logos asarkos*, i.e., the Word, apart from the incarnation. It is in personal union with humanity that the Word saves us. It is this union itself . . . which saves us because this is what accomplishes the work of salvation."[48]

For Luther, there is no place for a theology detached from human sinfulness and the need for salvation.[49] Luther's idea of kenosis is therefore basic to his understanding of both the person and the salvific work of Christ. His Christology is aptly summarized by Dennis Ngien as "God's hiddenness in his opposites."[50] God reveals himself not in power, majesty, and wisdom, but in suffering, weakness, and folly. Luther explains the famous twenty-first thesis of the *Heidelberg Disputation*, "A theologian of glory calls evil good and good evil. A theologian of the cross calls a thing what it actually is," by stating: "He who does not know Christ does not know God hidden in suffering . . . God can be found only in suffering and the cross."[51]

Thus, for Luther, Jesus Christ can save us only if he condescends to our level. Sammeli Juntunen labels this "kenosis as condescendence," arguing that for Luther, not only the incarnation but Christ's entire ministry, death, resurrection, and ascension are an exercise in kenosis.[52] Only the "kenotic Christ"—a Christ who has chosen not to seek his own, rightful, glory and to exercise his natural power, but who has rather given this up and chosen to serve others, loving them such that he is willing to give his own life for them—has the power to save. Christ must humble himself in two ways in order to exercise this power. First, he must become not only a human being, but a human being who does not seek his own glory but serves others in humility and love. Luther explains this in a 1537 *Disputatio*:

> Whoever searches for God in his majesty and divinity may be over-whelmed by God's glory. But after he emptied himself and was made de-lightful and marvelous, a child placed in the lap of the Virgin and in the manger, we can bear him and deal with him. Otherwise, no one will see him and live. But when he is clothed and dressed in human flesh, born

48. Lienhard, *Luther*, 233.

49. Cf. Zachhuber, *Luther's Christological Legacy*, 41.

50. Dennis Ngien, *Fruit for the Soul: Luther on the Lament Psalms* (Minneapolis: Fortress, 2015), 274–75.

51. WA 1:362; LW 31:53.

52. See Juntunen, "Christ," 75–79.

of the Virgin, and incarnate in our flesh, made our brother and our flesh, I cannot dread him.[53]

Second, Christ must condescend to our sinful, contemptible state. In yet another example of "God's hiddenness in his opposites," Luther writes:

> For God became man ... [and] in his last days we discover what we regard as the most terrible evil, [we find him] dying a shameful death. When we consider his entire life, we find that he undertook nothing that the world considered good. ... Now the most precious thing that God has is death and dying, [and] this [Christ] undertook in love and affection, joyfully and voluntarily in obedience to his Father.[54]

Christ must condescend and reveal himself in a lowly state in order to save us from *concupiscentia*, the egotistical, self-determining desire of human beings for what we judge to be good and beautiful. *Concupiscentia* divides things— and more so, people—into the categories of desirable and undesirable, loveable and contemptible. *Concupiscentia* leads us to trust in ourselves and our own goodness rather than in God. It causes us to trust in our own earned merit for our salvation. If Christ had come in his glory and majesty, human beings would consider Christ a reward, something they deserve because of their own goodness. Juntunen summarizes Luther's position: "In order to destroy *concupiscentia* Christ in his *kenosis* became the opposite of all that *concupiscentia* considers good. ... In this way he teaches people to serve others, with a pure divine love, which does not love in order to receive, but in order to give good things to those who lack."[55]

Conclusion

From Luther's treatment of Philippians 2 in his sermons, we see that his Christology turns on the presence of the form of God—a presence hidden but real, not limited or restricted, in the incarnate Jesus. Luther's idea of kenosis is not that the eternal Logos divests himself of his divine attributes or somehow sets them aside in the hypostatic union, nor is it the temporary loss of his eternal divine power and glory in the assumption of human nature. Rather, kenosis means that the form of almighty God is veiled and hidden be-.

---

53. WA 39/1, 484; LW 73:160.
54. WA 1:270; LW 51:40, translation revised.
55. Juntunen, "Christ," 76. Cf. Juntunen, "Christ," 74–76.

hind the form of a humble servant. For Luther—and here he moves beyond the precedent of the tradition—the subject of kenosis is the incarnate Christ, the person of the hypostatic union and not the preexistent *Logos asarkos*.

According to Luther, in the incarnation the form of God is not simply hidden behind humanity as such, but rather is hidden behind the form of a servant (a term that does not simply refer to the humanity of Jesus Christ *per se*). Luther interprets Paul to mean that the incarnate Christ does not use his being in the form of God against us by lording over us, but rather acts for our sake and our salvation. He becomes one with us, subject to the same evils as us: "Although he was free . . . he made himself a servant of all, acting in no other way than as if all evils which are ours were his own."[56]

It is thus easy to see how, so understood, kenosis becomes the basis of a renewed understanding of the Christian life; for Luther, the Christian life is a life of kenosis lived in service of others:

> The Apostle desired that every single Christian, following the example of Christ, should become a servant of others, and if they have wisdom, righteousness, or power that would allow them to excel and glory over others as if in the form of God, they should not keep it, but surrender it to God and become altogether as if they did not have it, and become like one of those who have nothing.[57]

Following Paul in Philippians 2, Luther presents Christ as the model to be imitated by all Christians. Being in the form of God and possessing all divine perfections, Christ empties himself of his privileges and—rather than dominating us like a gentile lord (Matt 20:25), condemning and judging us for our sin—comes to serve and liberate us in love and friendship. In turn, Christians who in faith have Christ's righteousness and are made free, are called to imitate Christ by emptying themselves in service of their neighbors, relating to others as God in Christ relates to them. Faith and works are thus understood as distinct, as distinct as the divine and human natures in the incarnation, but also inseparable, as inseparable as the divine and human natures in the hypostatic union.

56. WA 2:148; AL 2:18.
57. WA 2:148; AL 2:20, translation revised. Cf. Lienhard, *Luther*, 113.

10

The Revisioning of Kenosis after the Critique of Schleiermacher

Paul T. Nimmo

In a brief excursus at the end of the Christology section of his *Christian Faith,* Friedrich Schleiermacher considers the "contrasted *states of humiliation and exaltation*" ascribed to Jesus Christ.[1] He concludes, with characteristic vigor, that this formula

> has its sole basis in one passage of Scripture, whose ascetic and, considered in the wider context, rhetorical character betrays no intention that the expressions occurring within it should be fixed didactically. . . . Thus this formula can rightly with every justification be laid aside in the passing on of doctrine and be committed to history for safe-keeping.[2]

On one reading, this stark judgment might be considered typical of Schleiermacher, the perennial *enfant terrible* of the Reformed tradition who so

---

1. Friedrich Schleiermacher, *Der Christliche Glaube nach den Grundsätzen der Evangelischen Kirche im Zusammenhange Dargestellt: 2. Auflage (1830/31)—Erster und Zweiter Band,* ed. Rolf Schäfer (Berlin: de Gruyter, 2008), §105, Zusatz, 2:161–64. Subsequent references are to GL (*Glaubenslehre*), followed by section number, volume number, and page number. All translations are the author's own.

2. GL §105.Zusatz, 2:164. Schleiermacher identifies the relevant passage in a footnote as Phil 2:6–9 and observes, "All other passages that have been cited on this formula contribute absolutely nothing to the matter" (§105.Zusatz, 2:164n18).

delighted in overturning the carefully laid doctrinal tables in the temples of magisterial and post-Reformation Reformed orthodoxy. It might thus be rejected without much further investigation. And certainly Schleiermacher's radically creative Christology—with its apparent hesitations concerning the preexistence of the Son, its rejection of two-natures doctrine, and its abandonment of penal views of the atonement—offers a surrounding context that would scarcely convince such readers that their rejection was misplaced.

Closer inspection of the arguments that support Schleiermacher's judgment at this point, however, suggests the possibility of a rather different and more generative reading of and response to this material.[3] More detailed analysis demonstrates two noteworthy features of Schleiermacher's rejection of the ideas of kenosis and the two states of Jesus Christ. First, it indicates that at diverse points in his arguments, he echoes and reprises aspects of more traditional Reformed thinking in substantive ways. And second, it evidences that the traditional teaching may indeed have real theological charges to answer in face of Schleiermacher's lines of critique. This in turn leads to the possibility that if kenosis and the two states are to be retained as meaningful tropes of Christology in any way, then creative doctrinal reformulation may be necessary.

It is the purpose of this chapter to outline an argument across these points, in order to take seriously but to move beyond the conclusion of Schleiermacher that the two-states teaching and kenosis should be consigned to doctrinal history. In what follows, the first section explores in greater detail this excursus on the traditional teaching of the two states from Schleiermacher's Christology. The second section brings this position into critical conversation with two treatments of kenosis and the two states downstream of his own work in the second volume of Charles Hodge's *Systematic Theology* and the fourth volume of Karl Barth's *Church Dogmatics*. The conclusion will briefly sketch one possible way forward for considering the kenosis of Jesus Christ.

The Excursus of Schleiermacher on Kenosis

It is important to note at the outset that with regard to this excursus, as often elsewhere, Schleiermacher's investigation of a traditional view proceeds

---

3. For similar ventures in recent literature in respect of other doctrines of Schleiermacher, see among others, Kevin W. Hector, "Actualism and Incarnation: The High Christology of Friedrich Schleiermacher," *IJST* 8, no. 3 (2006): 307–22; Paul T. Nimmo, "Schleiermacher on Scripture and the Work of Jesus Christ," *MT* 31, no. 1 (2015): 60–90; Daniel J. Pedersen, *Schleiermacher's Theology of Sin and Nature: Agency, Value, and Modern Theology* (London: Routledge, 2020).

without reference to his own constructive position.[4] Instead, as will become clear in due course, he seeks principally to question the validity of the doctrine of the two states of Jesus Christ on the basis of a careful critique of its own internal presuppositions.

As a first step in the excursus, Schleiermacher turns to the term humiliation (*Erniedrigung*) and makes the crucial semantic point that "the expression presumes an earlier [existence] that was higher." He acknowledges immediately that "one can certainly call it an exaltation that Christ has become the first-born of the resurrection and sits at the right-hand of God," such that, in comparison, "the earthly state [*Zustand*] can be called a lower one." Given this perception of the relation between earthly and heavenly, one can certainly understand the invocation of the terminology of lower and higher, of mundane and of exalted. However, he continues, "as the person of Christ only began with his incarnation," this first event or state cannot be called "a humiliation." To proceed in this manner, he notes, would be to divide the person of Jesus Christ, considering the "divine in him as a particular being from eternity" and attributing the humiliation to "its descent to earth." The point Schleiermacher is making here is clear: on a traditional two-natures account, the human nature of Jesus Christ, for all that it may be eternally decreed and anticipated, is not actualized until the incarnation; correspondingly, it cannot be the subject of any act of humiliation, for it knows no preceding higher state.[5] Consequently the subject of any humiliation must be the preexistent divine being, in other words, the Logos. However, Schleiermacher notes immediately, "no humiliation can be ascribed to the absolutely highest and eternal—and thus necessarily self-identical—being." Given his resolute defense of an absolutely orthodox doctrine of God, there is no divine mutability in prospect, and to speak of the humiliation of God is simply an impossible exercise in predication.[6]

---

4. The quotations in this section all come from GL §105.Zusatz, 2:161–64. For a historical survey of the doctrine of kenosis, see Rinse Reeling Brouwer, "Kenōsis in Philippians 2:5–11 and in the History of Christian Doctrine," in *Letting Go: Rethinking Kenōsis*, ed. O. Zijlstra (Bern: Peter Lang, 2002), 69–108; David Brown, *Divine Humanity: Kenōsis and the Construction of a Christian Theology* (Waco, TX: Baylor University Press, 2011).

5. As Rowan Williams memorably notes, "the existence of Jesus is not an episode in the biography of the Word"; see *Arius: Heresy and Tradition*, 2nd ed. (London: SCM, 2001), 244.

6. See Daniel J. Pedersen, "Schleiermacher and Reformed Scholastics on the Divine Attributes," *IJST* 17, no. 4 (2015): 413–31. Indeed, Schleiermacher notes, if it were otherwise, one would "all the more" have to speak of "the indwelling of the Holy Spirit in the

Yet what, Schleiermacher considers, if one continues to speak of "humiliation" (*Erniedrigung*)—instead of the more exact (and relative) "state of lowliness" (*Zustand der Niedrigkeit*)—yet does not divide the person of Jesus Christ in this way between divine and human? In this case, he responds, the contrast between the two states would be "mere illusion [*Täuschung*], or at least only an appearance for others, but no truth for Christ himself." Footnoting a slew of references to his favored Gospel of John, Schleiermacher queries how Christ "could have been conscious of a lowliness of his state when he speaks of his relation to God the Father in such a way that even the session at [the Father's] right hand cannot be seen as an exaltation." In other words, he suggests, the perfect God-consciousness of Jesus Christ, abundantly attested in John's Gospel, renders any consciousness of a lowliness of situation unintelligible, even impossible.

At this point, Schleiermacher turns, without explicit signal, to address the specific position of Lutheran Christology—a necessary task given his desire to present a dogmatics for the newly united Prussian church, but one informed in its execution by his avowedly Reformed principles. He thus returns to consider a two-natures Christology, one that includes a "mutual communication of attributes" between the two natures, despite his own typically Reformed rejection of this Lutheran trope. In this conception, he writes, the idea of "humiliation" cannot be ascribed to the union of the natures itself, for the union persists after the human Christ is exalted to the right hand of God. Instead—and given the impossibility of ascribing it to the human nature, as noted above—"humiliation" can be ascribed "only to the divine nature, either in so far as it abstains from the use of its attributes, or in so far as it must embrace the attributes of the human nature."[7] Schleiermacher takes the latter possibility first: this situation is true at every point in the union, including in the state of exaltation; thus it is not possible to ascribe humiliation to the divine nature on this basis. Regarding the former possibility, Schleiermacher is scarcely more sanguine. He notes that this view explicitly presupposes that at some points in the life of Christ in the state of lowliness there were, "by

---

community of believers" and even—given the omnipresence of God—of "creation itself" as a "humiliation." Both are here clearly out of the question.

7. Schleiermacher does not here treat of the possibility—realized in Lutheran doctrine—that kenosis is predicated of the *human nature* in so far as it abstains from or conceals the use of the divine attributes communicated to it in the incarnation. In his own constructive work, Schleiermacher earlier rejects the teaching of the communication of attributes entirely, suggesting in particular that the attribution of the divine attributes in their "infinity" would "destroy" the human nature (GL §97.5, 2:87).

virtue of the free will of Christ, exceptions" to this abstinence.[8] However, Schleiermacher continues, "We cannot at all imagine a more complete use of the same [divine attributes] in the state of exaltation," on the basis that this would render "the human nature in respect of its activity [to be absorbed] by the divine" and "only passive." This would be an impossible outcome, rendering—for example—any conception of the ongoing intercession of the human Christ unthinkable. Thus on neither account can any "humiliation" be ascribed to the divine nature, but only "a less and a more"—language echoing Schleiermacher's earlier reference to "lower and higher."

This leads to the negative conclusion cited above, according to which the formula of the two states, and thus the idea of kenosis, is deemed "completely untenable." The one passage that supports it, according to Schleiermacher, suggests that "the exaltation of Christ is a reward determined for him by God for [his] humiliation" and lacks connection with either the dignity or the work of Christ. At the same time, and more appreciatively, Schleiermacher suggests that "the way in which Paul establishes [*aufstellt*] Christ as a role model agrees very well with the fact that [Paul] started out from only the appearance of lowliness in the life as well as in the death of Christ."

What Schleiermacher advances in this excursus is a series of theological arguments regarding the traditional teaching on the states of humiliation and exaltation of Jesus Christ and the related teaching on kenosis. Nothing that he presents here depends on his own constructive—and controversial—teaching; by contrast, he simply performs an analysis of the ingredient concepts of humiliation and exaltation and adjudicates it impossible to find subjects of whom these epithets could be predicated, *even on the basis of the traditional teaching itself.* It is for this reason alone that Schleiermacher recommends that the doctrine be abandoned and consigned to history; his own constructive doctrine correspondingly moves in a rather different direction.

Such engaged analysis by such a perceptive thinker holds out the possibility that there may be deep-seated problems with the traditional teaching, yet the advice to reject the doctrine was evidently not followed. Indeed, it was in the decades following Schleiermacher that the greatest flowering of

8. In a footnote here, Schleiermacher cites the Solid Declaration from the Lutheran Book of Concord as evidence. He observes that any such abstention must "of course have been voluntary . . . for no compulsion can be done to the divine nature," and further comments that "a coercion to make use of the [divine attributes] against the free will *would* have been a humiliation" (emphasis added).

so-called kenotic theology took place, initially among Lutheran scholars in nineteenth-century Germany, a movement that in turn influenced several theologians in the Anglophone world in important ways. Rather than follow this trajectory, however, two distinctly Reformed responses subsequent to both Schleiermacher and this new development will be considered below.

The Views of Kenosis of Hodge and Barth

The choice to bring Charles Hodge and Karl Barth into conversation with Schleiermacher around these points is purposeful: both scholars were similarly engaged in writing major projects of systematic theology and were similarly located in the Reformed tradition; both figures came later than and interacted with the theology of Schleiermacher, as well—as noted—as with the fresh kenotic trajectory of the nineteenth century; and crucially, both retained the language of the states of humiliation and exaltation. Yet Hodge and Barth are also perceived as representing rather different positions along the spectrum of Reformed theological tradition: Hodge is the more classical traditionalist; Barth is the more constructive innovator. These factors combine to allow them to be brought into conversation with Schleiermacher and his critique of this particular doctrinal teaching in fruitful ways.

Kenosis and the Two States in the Work of Hodge

A significant section within Hodge's Christology in the second volume of his major dogmatic work is given over to a critique of modern forms of the doctrine of the person of Christ, which he accuses of denying "that God and man are essentially different" and of affirming "that God and man are one" to be "the fundamental idea of Christianity."[9] The theologians under suspicion are divided into two groups—the pantheistical, who contend "that man is only the highest existence-form of God," and the theistical, who argue that "the human is capable of receiving the attributes of the divine" (429). Hodge devotes far more attention to the latter group, a broad category that includes not only Schleiermacher (and Dorner), but also Gess and Thomasius, and thus representatives of the new kenotic school of the nineteenth century.[10] Com-

9. Charles Hodge, *Systematic Theology*, vol. 2 (London: Thomas Nelson; New York: Charles Scribner, 1883), 429. Hereafter, page references from this work will be given in parentheses in the text.

10. There would be a raft of questions to be posed to Hodge's sweeping characteriza-

mon to them all, for Hodge, is the affirmation of a "complete identification of the human and divine in the person of Christ," and this takes place either by recurring communications of the Logos to the human soul until the latter becomes "completely divine" or by "a process of self-limitation" in which the Logos "divested Himself of all his divine attributes" (433). Here, in this second mode of identification, is the newly fledged view of kenosis, in which the eternal Logos becomes depotentiated at the point of incarnation.

In a series of objections to these modern forms of the doctrine, Hodge begins by observing bluntly that they simply depart from the faith of the church (437–39). His second criticism is that they do not observe the hermeneutical rule of christological predication, such that anything attributed to the person of Christ "can be predicated either of his human or of his divine nature" (439)—significantly, this was also the working assumption of Schleiermacher's analysis. That Jesus Christ is the object of worship thus "does not prove that Christ's human nature is possessed of divine attributes"; indeed, Hodge laments, "according to the modern doctrine of Kenosis, He has no human nature" (439). On both these points, quite remarkably, Schleiermacher would agree. On the former point, Schleiermacher would affirm resolutely that the humanity of Jesus Christ is certainly neither divinized, nor abolished; on the latter, anti-kenotic point, Schleiermacher anticipates Hodge by recognizing that if the human being is entirely pervaded by the divine nature, the human nature itself is destroyed. Hodge's third objection, moreover, could also have been written by Schleiermacher: regarding "the nature of God," Hodge writes, "He is a Spirit infinite, eternal, and immutable. Any theory . . . which assumes that God lays aside his omnipotence, omniscience, and omnipresence . . . contradicts the first principle of all religion" (439). In a later comment on the satisfaction of the atonement, Hodge correspondingly rejects the Patripassian idea that "the divine nature itself suffered," a view "repudiated alike by the Latin, Lutheran, and Reformed churches"—and, one might add, by Schleiermacher as well (483).

On the one hand, it is hardly a revolutionary understanding of God that Hodge advances at this point; rather, it represents the clear consensus of centuries of prior Christian teaching, to which Schleiermacher subscribes, and rules out *a limine* any ontological kenosis of the divine Logos in the incarnation. On the other hand, it raises again the question posed by Schleiermacher—to be explored further below—of how a kenosis of any sort, or a

---

tion of each of these figures, and perhaps above all of Schleiermacher, for whom the idea that God and human beings are absolutely different is axiomatic *even as* he rejects the doctrine of the two natures of Jesus Christ.

state of humiliation, can legitimately or meaningfully be predicated of the Logos if the Logos retains all its attributes at all points, a question with import not only for Hodge, but also for the broad tradition on which he stands.[11]

In his subsequent treatment of the humiliation of Jesus Christ, Hodge writes that it consists in "his being born . . . in a low condition, made under the law, undergoing the miseries of this life, the wrath of God, and the cursed death of the cross; in being buried, and continuing under the power of death for a time" (610). Yet all these humiliating historical events are predicated explicitly of "the Eternal Son of God," who in the incarnation engaged in "an act of unspeakable condescension" (610, 611). Hodge proceeds to a detailed investigation of each of these material aspects of humiliation, engaging in the process in explicit rejection of the view of traditional Lutherans, who, he esteems, "at the time of the Reformation departed from the faith of the Church on the person of Christ" (621). Thus Hodge disavows the view that the humiliation of Jesus Christ "is limited to the earthly stage of his existence"—if humiliation is true of the earthly stage, it must also be true in relation to the "glorified humanity in heaven," a point again made by Schleiermacher (611). Hodge also explores the Lutheran teaching of the communication of properties between the natures of Jesus Christ, and the resultant debate between the theologians of Tübingen and Gießen as to whether the human nature engaged in a mere *krypsis* (concealing) or an actual *kenōsis* (emptying) of its divine attributes (621–25). The stumbling block with all this for Hodge is that the true subject of kenosis is *not* in fact the human nature of Jesus Christ, but the "eternal Son of whom all that is taught of the humiliation of Christ is to be predicated" (624); thus neither position is acceptable. And at the same time, the modern teaching that the "Eternal Son of God did not assume a human nature . . . but . . . became a man" continues to be utterly repudiated.

Hodge thus rejects—as Schleiermacher does—the attempt to ascribe kenosis either to the human nature of Jesus Christ or to the Logos in the sense of any ontological diminishment. Instead, and with the tradition—and against Schleiermacher—he relates kenosis and the corresponding humiliation of Jesus Christ to the condescension of the Logos in the incarnation and its historical consequences. By virtue of the unity of the natures in Jesus Christ, that which is true of the human nature of Jesus Christ (being of lowly

---

11. Hodge closes his response here by observing that the modern teaching increases rather than removes the difficulties of the doctrine of the incarnation and destroys the humanity of Christ, and he concludes this section with a long critique of Schleiermacher's constructive position: see ST 2:439–40, 440–54.

birth, bound by the law, cursed on the cross, and so on) can be predicated of the person of Jesus Christ, and the hypostasis of this person is the eternal Logos. In the incarnation, then, the Logos assumes a human nature sub-jected to this humiliation.

Precisely here, however, Schleiermacher would object. In so far as the Logos is concerned—according to the traditional teaching and given that for both Schleiermacher and Hodge the new idea of kenosis would be un-acceptable—this undergoes no change at all in the incarnation by virtue of the definition of God as immutable. Therefore it would make no sense to speak here of a humiliation of the Logos or of the divine nature. For this reason, and stretching the bounds of semantic credibility, the traditional solution has been to speak of the kenosis or humiliation of the Logos by way of condescension, as Hodge does, and/or by way of concealment. But it remains difficult, on Schleiermacher's critique, to see either explanation as referring to an actual kenosis or humiliation of the divine Logos at all, and therefore, to see the affirmation of kenosis as anything other than at best metaphorically strained and at worst theologically incoherent. Meanwhile, in so far as the human nature of Jesus Christ is concerned, this has never been anything other than of lowly birth and earthly location under the law. While one might argue that subsequent events in the life of the incarnate Jesus Christ display a continuation or even intensification of such lowliness, on which more below, there is no question here of a dynamic change for the human Jesus *in the incarnation itself*, for there simply was no human nature prior to the annunciation. And thus to speak of a kenosis of humiliation of the human nature in the incarnation makes little sense.

When he turns to treat of the exaltation of Jesus Christ, Hodge identifies four components: the resurrection, the ascension, the sitting at the right hand of God, and the coming again in judgment (626). While the first and fourth movements of exaltation are not specified in terms of predication, the ascension and the session are both ascribed to the whole person of Christ—respectively to "the Theanthropos, the Son of God clothed in our nature" and "the Theanthropos; not the Logos specially or distinctively; not the human nature exclusively; but the theanthropic person" (630).

Yet here again, Schleiermacher would have hesitations. Given that the eternal Son is in essence the absolutely highest, there can be no meaningful way of ascribing exaltation to the Logos. Thus the ascription of exaltation to the person of Jesus Christ must refer to his human nature in particular. Of course, Schleiermacher acknowledges that it might be possible to construe the resurrection and ascension as a move from a lower, earthly state to a higher, heavenly one, and to consider this an "exaltation." Yet even here, he cautions on the aforementioned Johannine grounds, not even Jesus Christ himself considers the session at the right hand of the Father to represent an exaltation.

The result of this exploration of Hodge is twofold. On the one hand, Hodge—a typical representative of a broad tradition of enquiry on kenosis—finds himself in agreement with Schleiermacher at manifold points regarding what it is not possible to say in the doctrine of the two states of Jesus Christ, and particularly so where it comes to dissenting from Lutheran positions. On the other hand, Hodge continues to affirm both doctrines, and therefore he lays himself open to the critiques of Schleiermacher, on which account there can be no ontological kenosis or dichotomous states on the part either of the divine nature or of the human nature. The result of Hodge's account—along with the accounts of much of the tradition—is an affirmation of kenosis or humiliation that is semantically strained, perhaps even to the point of endangering its intelligibility.

Kenosis and the Two States in the Work of Barth

The two states of Jesus Christ serve as one of a number of architectonic principles in the doctrine of reconciliation in the fourth volume of *Church Dogmatics*. In outline, Barth posits that Jesus Christ is "humiliated [*erniedrigt*] as God in order to take our place, [and] also exalted [*erhöht*] as human being in our place."[12] The account of Christology in the first part-volume focuses upon the former, the humiliation of the Son of God; that in the second part-volume upon the latter, the exaltation of the Son of Man.

It is immediately apparent that Barth has set forth a rather innovative approach to this doctrine that contrasts with earlier Lutheran and Reformed positions (IV/1:145 [ET 132–33]). The movements of humiliation and exaltation are not predicated successively of the person of Jesus Christ but simultaneously (IV/1:145–46 [ET 133–34]); and furthermore, each of the two states is ascribed exclusively to just *one* of the two natures—the divine nature is humiliated while the human nature is exalted (IV/1:145 [ET 132]).

---

12. Karl Barth, *Die Kirchliche Dogmatik* (Zurich: EVZ, 1953–1967), IV/1:144. All translations are the author's own, with references provided also for the published English translation (ET), *Church Dogmatics*, ed. G. W. Bromiley and T. F. Torrance, trans. G. W. Bromiley (Edinburgh: T&T Clark, 1956–1969), here at IV/1:131. Hereafter, page references from this work will be given in parentheses in the text.

Barth offers the following explanation for this revision: on the one hand, to say that Jesus Christ as a human being is lowly is simply "a tautology," although it is certainly this lowliness of human being that Jesus Christ comes to address; on the other hand, to say that Jesus Christ as God is in the heights, "free, sovereign, and superior to the whole world," is, again, "a tautology" (IV/1:147 [ET 134–35]). Thus to speak of the humiliation of the Son of Man or the exaltation of the Son of God is simply redundant. Here, the unanimous material agreement of Schleiermacher with Barth on both these points might be noted—albeit on rather different grounds. For Barth, then, it is only God who is "humiliated," in so far as "God became human being while preserving his true deity . . . in highest faithfulness to his divine being," while it is only human being that is "exalted," in the person of one who, "*bound* like all of us and *tempted* like us is free and sinless."[13] Each of these movements will be exposited in greater detail in what follows.

The first point—affirmation of the divine humiliation—represents an immediate and persistent Rubicon between Barth and Schleiermacher, just as it also clearly divided Hodge and Schleiermacher above. With reference to the incarnation, Barth suggests that "God is great, the *true* God proves himself to be such, precisely in that . . . he is able, willing, and ready for this condescension [*Herablassung*]."[14] And more even than this, Jesus Christ as the Son of God "willed to be *obedient* to the Father, and to become the servant of all the world" (IV/1:174 [ET 159]). This view leads to the important premise—which will be revisited below—that "if the human being Jesus is true God, then the true *God* is *obedient*!" (IV/1:179 [ET 165]). And this in turn leads Barth to a first engagement with the kenosis text of Philippians 2 and with several other New Testament passages indicating the lowliness of the human Jesus, "the *suffering* servant," in the flesh (IV/1:180–81 [ET 164–66]). Here, Barth observes, "Jesus would not be Jesus if his way could be different or his work have another character," and suggests that it is right for exegetes "to think through the deity of Jesus Christ precisely on this basis," otherwise there can only result "confusion" (*Verwischung*) (IV/1:181 [ET 166]).

The result of Barth thinking through the deity of Jesus Christ in this way is the view that the Word being "flesh" means existing "with the 'children' of

---

13. IV/1:147–48 (ET 135), reading "*Bewahrung*" for "*Bewährung*" to give "preserving." As will be seen below, the "becoming" here references only a becoming in time of what God already is in eternity.

14. IV/1:173 (ET 159). This marks God out as "different from and superior to" other gods: "God is not arrogant, but humble precisely in his high majesty," 173 (159).

Israel under the wrath and judgment precisely of the electing, loving God" (IV/1:190 [ET 174]). Hence, Barth writes, the history of the Son of God "must be a history of suffering [*Leidensgeschichte*], for God is rightly against him [*hat Recht gegen ihn*]" (IV/1:191 [ET 175]). This history is the way of the Son of God into the far country, the path of divine self-humiliation that leads—not accidentally, but inexorably and purposefully—to the cross. And it is only by looking at this "Christ-event" (*Christusgeschehen*) that one can learn what true deity is, that it includes the self-humiliation of the Son of God grounded in his obedience to the Father (IV/1:193 [ET 177]).

What is crucial for Barth, however, is that this free act in love of self-humiliation does not represent any alteration in God. Barth insists that God is immutable: "God remains God even in his humiliation," on the basis that "The divine being incurs no change, no diminution, no change into something else, no confusion with anything else, let alone any abolition" (IV/1:196 [ET 179]). Here, Barth again returns to the passage in Philippians, indicating its support of his position: "The *kenōsis* consists in his renunciation of an *exclusive* being in the form of God," as "beyond his form in the likeness of God he was able to take the form of a slave," but this "condescension"—this "concealing of his divinity"—does not in any way diminish or change his deity.[15] Barth's wonderful summary description of this account runs simply, "God *can* do this" (IV/1:204 [ET 187]). And this is true not in a bare voluntaristic sense, but in the sense that this act of self-humiliation entirely conforms to who God *is*: "It corresponds to and is completely grounded in his divine nature" (IV/1:204 [ET 187]). The "concealment" and "condescension" of the incarnation are as such "the mirror and the image in which we see [God] as he is" (IV/1:205 [ET 188]). And precisely in this concealment, God is "truly glorious," for "the *freedom* of his *love* that he enacts and reveals in all this is his glory, in distinction from the unfree, loveless glories of all humanly devised gods."[16]

The final step in Barth's argument starts from his observation that the "character of the self-emptying and self-humiliating of Jesus Christ as an act

---

15. IV/1:196–97 (ET 180). Barth here offers a brief sketch of the history of thinking about kenosis, affirming the patristic account and that of Calvin, and rejecting both the "impossible" post-Reformation Lutheran account and the "absurd" nineteenth-century Lutheran kenotic theology, IV/1:196–99 (ET 180–83).

16. IV/1:205 (ET 188). Here Barth returns to Phil 2 to confirm this point, and to draw out—in a way not beyond controverting in light of recent critiques—what he considers to be the secondary, but necessary, consequences for an ethics based on the New Testament, IV/1:205–10 (ET 188–92).

of *obedience* cannot be alien to God" (IV/1:211 [ET 193]). By contrast, this particular exercise of obedience is rooted in a "divine *decree*," indeed, "in the inner necessity of the freedom of God"; and this in turn leads Barth to declare that there is "an obedience that takes place in God" (IV/1:213 [ET 195]). In striking manner, therefore, Barth affirms that "essential to the being of God" there are "an above and a below, a before and an after, superordination and a subordination" (IV/1:219 [ET 200–201]). And the consequence of this construal for the incarnation is that in this self-giving act, God "does not change" but "only acts and reveals himself *externally*, in the world, as well; he is the same in and for *it*, as he is in and for himself . . . in time, what he is in eternity" (IV/1:223 [ET 204]).

Drawing back from this account for a moment, it is clear that Barth wants to affirm in the strongest terms that it is truly God who is at work in Jesus Christ in the lowly situation of the "flesh" in which the divine glory is outwardly concealed. Yet this decreed self-humiliation is revealed to be not at all alien to God: by contrast, "it is just as natural for God to be lowly as to be high, to be near as to be far, to be small as to be great, to be weak as to be strong, to be abroad as to be home" (IV/1:210 [ET 192]). Indeed, more even than this, Barth insists that the glory of the deity in Jesus Christ "consists in its humiliation" (IV/1:142 [ET 130]). There is consequently, Barth avers repeatedly, no change in God in the kenotic act of becoming incarnate; rather, this event corresponds perfectly to the being of God, and it is grounded in the eternal obedience of the Son to the Father.

Yet the question arises for Barth—as it did for Hodge, despite the attendant differences in account—of what purpose the term "kenosis" serves here, given the insistence that there is no change in the divine being. A first answer might lie in the change of context and consequent change of visibility that attend the Son of God becoming flesh, such that—for Barth as for Hodge—the divine glory is now concealed. But if this is true, then again—for Barth as for Hodge—the question arises of whether the language of kenosis is appropriate when it relates to a kenosis that takes place by way of addition (of flesh) and of concealment (of glory) against the explicit backdrop of the divine immutability rather than by way of any genuine emptying. The language of kenosis in this context again risks becoming rather stretched in metaphorical terms.

The hesitation this first answer engenders is further exacerbated in respect of Barth in so far as he himself seems to subvert its plausibility. While Barth does observe that the text of John 17:5 speaks of "a glory that the Son had with his Father before the foundation of the world . . . [and] thus has evidently left behind him," he resolutely affirms that the humiliation of the incarnation is *itself* a glorification, not only of the human being, as will be seen below, but also—and crucially—*of God*. God is glorified precisely in the humiliation of the incarnation, and not to see this is to fall prey to mere human imaginings of what God should be and to ignore the revelation of God in Jesus Christ. Indeed, Barth suggests, "it is from this act of *humiliation*, that all the predicates of his true deity must be filled and interpreted" (IV/1:142 [ET 130]). Along these lines, Barth suggests that to affirm a humiliation of God in the incarnation represents the "contradiction of all human musing about the divine nature," and is helpful on that basis (IV/1:217 [ET 199]). Yet if this logic runs its course, it might be argued that the language of kenosis is only helpful in this broadly didactic vein: in other words, when one starts with the false picture of God, the language of kenosis and humiliation can help one toward a true understanding of God and how God actually works in the world. Beyond such heuristic purpose, however, if it is true that God does not change in the incarnation, that it is as natural for God to be lowly as it is to be high, and that God is glorified in the incarnation, then even the earlier semantic straining seems redundant. Thinking about kenosis and humiliation might then be seen as a didactic ladder by which one ascends to discover Christian truths, but which can be discarded thereafter: such terms are only needed where God is essentially perceived as unfree and loveless.

One further observation might be noted here. It might be suggested, in order to address any lingering concerns about divine mutability, that the terms kenosis and humiliation be deployed to describe not only the incarnate economy of God but also—in some way—the relations within the eternal God. This follows the impulse of Barth, who certainly affirms divine immutability but who also moves to ground the temporal obedience of the Son of God in his eternal subordination to the Father, as was noted above. Such theological manoeuvres to bespeak an "eternal kenosis" are also encountered in the work of other significant thinkers.[17] This move to source the condition of possibility of the incarnation of Jesus Christ in time right in the heart of the divine being is a powerful one, and not one that is here contested. Yet the question arises as to how helpful the language of kenosis or humiliation is in this context of describing an eternal disposition that explicitly does not change. Indeed, it might even be objected—along lines that

---

17. See, for example, Hans Urs von Balthasar, *The Action*, vol. 4 of *Theo-Drama: Theological Dramatic Theory*, trans. Graham Harrison (San Francisco: Ignatius Press, 1994); Bruce McCormack, *The Humility of the Eternal Son: Kenotic Christology in Reformed and Ecumenical Perspective* (Cambridge: Cambridge University Press, 2021).

are implicitly affirmed both in the excursus of Schleiermacher and at points in the positions of Hodge and Barth—that kenotic language, especially given the aorist active form in which it appears in Philippians, is indicative of a temporal and completed act of change that is simply not in view here.

The second point—the exaltation of human being—can be treated more briefly. For Barth, writing of Jesus Christ, "There takes place in and with *his* humiliation (as Son of God) in turn *his* exaltation (as Son of Man)," and this exaltation in turn "exemplarily prefigures and dynamically grounds . . . the exaltation of the human being" (IV/2:19 [ET 19]). There is not only the exaltation of the human Jesus to consider, then, but also the exaltation of all other human beings in him. In other words, as Barth notes later, "In his person, as the *humanitas* of this human being, *humanitas* [in general] is in motion" (IV/2:30 [ET 29]).

Exaltation is thus the history within which there takes place "the movement of the human being "from below *to above*," from the earth as its own sphere, so good as God's creation but so endarkened [*verfinstert*] by humanity, *up to* heaven, the proper sphere of God" (IV/2:30 [ET 29]). This is categorically not a matter of divinization, Barth emphasizes; rather, in this movement, "without ceasing to be human, rather precisely in the creatureliness and corruptness that is assumed and accepted by the Son of God, the human being—this one Son of Man—*returns home*" (IV/2:21 [ET 20]). Hence Barth titles this section "The Homecoming of the Son of Man," which involves a return to true human being, that is, to human being in communion with God, in relation with other human beings, in an ordered existence, and in possession and enjoyment of the appointed salvation (IV/2:21 [ET 20–21]).

This general, and all-too-concise, outline highlights the key contours of Barth's account of the exaltation of the human nature of and the human being in Jesus Christ. It might be noted at a general level that both Schleiermacher (in his excursus) and Hodge (in his exposition) in their own ways affirm Barth's instincts regarding the plausibility of the term exaltation to describe a movement in Jesus Christ from below to above, from earth to heaven. Moreover, all three figures would be adamant that the movement of exaltation in no way compromises his humanity. Yet there are manifest differences.

The most obvious difference for the present purpose is that, in his excursus, Schleiermacher writes of the movement of exaltation relating to the resurrection and the ascension, a position explicitly affirmed by Hodge. For Barth, in contrast, the exaltation of the human being takes place across the whole incarnate history of Jesus Christ, including his life, passion, and crucifixion as well as his resurrection and ascension. Ironically, Schleiermacher's own constructive account might sit closer to this affirmation of dynamic movement here, given his own insistence upon the development of the human life of Jesus progressively revealing the perfection of humanity that is contained within Jesus from his birth.[18] Despite such difference, however, it remains the case that the issue of exaltation is rather less controverted or complex than that of humiliation. There does seem to be a broad and semantically unstrained affirmation that the incarnation of Jesus Christ leads both to his own elevation in some way and to an opening up of new and higher possibilities for the sinful human being, in this world and/or in the next. Even the critical excursus of Schleiermacher thus has very limited traction at this point.

Conclusion

In the foregoing analysis, a remarkable degree of consonance has been uncovered between the critical excursus of Schleiermacher on kenosis and the positive expositions of Hodge and Barth in respect of a number of issues: on the affirmation of divine immutability, on the impossibility of divine exaltation, on the affirmation of the lowliness of the human Jesus, on the exaltation of the human Jesus, and on the rejection of any exaltation by way of divinization. At the same time, there remains one area of substantive difference—regarding the humiliation or kenosis of the Son of God in the incarnation. Schleiermacher is dismissive of this language and its use in the tradition, but both Hodge and Barth seek to retain its ascription to the Son of God by way of positing a kenosis of addition (of human nature) leading to concealment (of divine glory). The questions were posed above, however, as to whether such an affirmation of these terms is not rather strained semantically, in so far as adding and concealing is scarcely the same as emptying, and as to whether the terms were not ultimately subverted by Barth himself in his positive construction. If these questions are answered positively, then it might even be conceded that Schleiermacher had a point after all, and that the terms could safely be laid aside and committed to history.

Yet the scriptural witness of Philippians 2 will not be laid aside quite so easily by many, and the question arises as to whether an alternative ascription of kenosis and humiliation to the person Jesus Christ might both be theologically possible and avoid the critical conclusions of Schleiermacher. The starting point of one such reading might be to affirm, with all three of the figures considered above, the principle of divine immutability and—consequently—to deny the possibility of an ontological kenosis of the divine nature. Such a read-

18. GL §93.3-5, 2:45-52.

ing might also reject the position of Hodge and Barth in so far as they predicate kenosis of the divine nature regardless, by way of concealment and/or addition, on the basis that the language of emptying in such cases is strained.

This leaves open the possibility, however, of offering an alternative, theologically provocative reading of this passage that affirms a kenosis of the *human nature* of Jesus Christ. Such an affirmation is never seriously pursued by Hodge or Barth, and indeed is rejected by Barth and Schleiermacher. With Schleiermacher, such a reading might recognize that the intrinsic lowliness ascribed to the incarnate state of Jesus Christ arises synchronically with the incarnation and thus cannot usefully be described by the term kenosis or humiliation. Yet there is another possibility that lies to hand.

One way forward would be to suggest that the definitive movement of kenosis and humiliation in the life of the human Jesus takes place not at his birth, but at another point in his life at which there takes place a significant emptying. The obvious candidate is the unfolding crisis that encounters Jesus in the passion narrative, and specifically the growing human experience of God-forsakenness in the course of the passion that reaches its nadir on the cross (Matt 27:46; Mark 15:34), itself the direct consequence of the obedience of Jesus to the will of the Father (Luke 22:42). This prospect of affirming an experiential emptying of the hitherto uninterrupted relationship of God to the human Jesus, at the point where Jesus Christ voluntarily and obediently takes on the full ambit of human sin and careens toward the ultimate humiliation of death upon the cross, is at least an intriguing prospect. Certainly, there is no ontological kenosis in view here: it might be argued with Barth that this event is divinely and eternally elected, thus there is no divine mutability; meanwhile the human Jesus remains absolutely the fully human Jesus, living in the lowly context of human corruption. But what changes is that this human Jesus now, for the first time, experiences the complete abandonment of the Father and embraces the full assumption of human sin. It is this event that might be termed the kenosis of the human Jesus—not the incarnation as a whole, but this unique and far-from-glorious exchange: from the experience of the fullness of life with the Father to the humiliation of bearing the sin of the world.[19]

It might be objected, however, that such an emptying is not ontological but only experiential. This is certainly true, and it may be that on this account

---

19. The experience of God-abandonment may not be unique to the human Jesus, although one might argue that in respect of its intensity Jesus yet stands alone; however, in so far as the concomitant bearing of the sin of the world is concerned, it might certainly be claimed that Jesus stands alone.

it escapes Schleiermacher's critical conclusions. At the same time, it also sets forth a kenosis in time that may nonetheless prove to be a critical constituent in the effecting of human salvation. Here, after all, is the final step on the path of the suffering servant, as Jesus obediently agrees to enter the experience of God-abandonment and to take on the burden of sin—a final and absolute humiliation, a definitive emptying of that fullness and security that had prevailed before. Ascribed to the human nature alone, this leads to the deepest moment of kenosis and humiliation, as the Son becomes "obedient to the point of death—even death on the cross" (Phil 2:8). Unlike Hodge and Barth, whose versions of kenosis seek to combine an affirmation of divine immutability with a meaningful kenosis of the Son of God, this account argues instead that at the heart of reconciliation is the event in which the human Jesus is rendered bereft of all assurance and consolation at the climax of his passion. In this way, it identifies an event of kenosis in the history of Jesus that does justice to its simple meaning of emptying.

It should be acknowledged in closing that, even if such a constructive proposal were to avoid the fire of Schleiermacher's excursus on kenosis, it would fall entirely foul of his desire to affirm the uninterrupted God-consciousness of Jesus Christ.[20] But the tentative exploration of such a reading of kenosis and humiliation may yet inform a viable pathway, if not to resolving the conundrums posed by Scripture, nevertheless to investigating them with new vigor and insight. And on the merits of that outcome, it might be noted, Schleiermacher, Hodge, and Barth would wholeheartedly agree.

---

20. See GL §§101.2, 101.4, 2:113–15, 117–20, in the last of which Schleiermacher writes: "But here again it is a magical caricature of this when an idea locates the reconciling power of his suffering precisely in the fact that he voluntarily gave up his blessedness and became truly unblessed, even if only for moments, misconceiving completely the necessity of an unshakeable blessedness in Christ" (2:118).

11

Kenosis and the Humility of God

David Fergusson

The flourishing of kenotic Christology provides a curious episode in the history of doctrine. Having emerged in its modern form in mid-nineteenth-century Germany, it later took hold among English and Scottish theologians. It is not too much of an exaggeration to describe it as a default setting, at least in British Christology in the late Victorian and Edwardian periods. Surprisingly, however, kenoticism quickly fell out of fashion, being subjected to a range of objections that were widely regarded as decisive.[1] Donald Baillie's seminal *God Was in Christ* is a useful barometer in this respect. Published in 1946, Baillie's text registers three criticisms of kenotic Christology that he presents as the settled opinion of the time.[2]

First, what was the Word of God doing in the cosmos during Christ's earthly life? The inconvenient implication of a temporary setting aside or muting of the Word of God's incommunicable attributes during the years of Christ's earth life led to inevitable speculations about an administrative reorganization within the life of the Trinity. The result was that the effort to

1. For valuable surveys of the field see David Brown, *Divine Humanity: Kenosis Explored and Defended* (London: SCM, 2011), and David R. Law, "Kenotic Christology," in *Blackwell Companion to Nineteenth Century Theology*, ed. David Fergusson (Oxford: Wiley-Blackwell, 2010), 251–79.
2. Donald M. Baillie, *God Was in Christ* (London: Faber, 1948), 94–98.

circumvent the metaphysical difficulties surrounding the Chalcedonian formula led to some egregious conceptual entanglements. Such division, when introduced into the life of the Godhead, was disruptive of the classical ideas of divine simplicity and oneness. As William Temple had earlier insisted, this question admits of no answer.[3]

Second, does kenosis simply give us a temporary divine theophany in which God appears in human disguise—a metamorphosis rather than a true union? This negative feature of the kenotic tradition seemed to point to its religious inadequacy rather than its conceptual incoherence. If some essential elements of divinity need to be concealed or relinquished as a condition of the possibility of the incarnation, then does the assumption of flesh actually *reveal* as opposed to hide God? A distinction between the moral and metaphysical attributes might alleviate this problem, but again this generates difficulties around divine simplicity. The attributes do not belong to God contingently or as real distinctions within the divine being. In any case, can divine love be stripped of divine power without weakening its capacity? Paul's insight is that divine power is manifested in the foolishness of the cross, not that it is abandoned or lost in this event. If the fullness of God is here to be revealed, then kenosis, whatever else it is, cannot be construed as a divestment of divine identity in the incarnation. If Christ reigns from the tree, then he reigns.

Baillie's third complaint follows from this second. The eternal humanity of Christ, a feature of the classical doctrine of the ascension, appears impossible to maintain within a kenotic Christology. If we are to identify the Son of God with Jesus, not only then but now, then the kenotic arrangement should be permanent. Yet the intention of the theory was to view the self-adjustment within the life of God as requisite only for the duration of Christ's earthly life, on the apparent assumption that at the end of this life the Son of God could resume a full divine status. With its presupposition that full divinity and humanity cannot be simultaneously conjoined, kenotic Christology must view these as successive states. The exalted Christ must therefore have ceased to be human or else be disjoined from the Word of God. Admittedly, we enter upon quite speculative territory here in postulating an eternal humanity of Christ. Yet the language of resurrection and exaltation which suffuses the New Testament writings points us in just this direction. A kenotic theory that seeks to explain a historical incarnation seems to generate even more problems than it solves.

3. See William Temple, *Christus Veritas* (London: Macmillan, 1924), 142–43.

As Bruce McCormack has pointed out, one of the ironies of kenotic Christology is that while these criticisms were being forcefully articulated in Germany, the movement began to flourish elsewhere, particularly in the United Kingdom.[4] Though sympathizing with its motivation, Isaak Dorner had already raised some acute difficulties, noting several problems created by kenotic theories. Not only were they conceptually obscure, under critical inspection they also generated new complications that resembled those of the older christological heresies.[5]

Partly under the influence of Ritschl and his school, Christology in Germany became more preoccupied with historical issues and less inclined to metaphysical abstraction. Yet in Scotland and England, kenoticism prospered through the late nineteenth century and into the twentieth century. In what follows, I shall argue that, in the case of Anglican theology at least, the movement was animated by more than a concern to formulate a conception of the divinity and humanity of Christ adequate to the historical conditions of his earthly life. In ascribing an act of kenosis to God, this theology sought to characterize the divine being as itself possessing an essential kenotic aspect. Marked by its indebtedness, even if only indirectly, to Hegelian idealism, this resonated with a wider account of the God-world relationship in both nature and history.[6] As a result, kenosis came to be viewed more as a characteristic of God than as an instrumental mechanism for the incarnation of the second person of the Trinity. In what follows, I shall explore this distinction between an "instrumentalist" and an "ontological" kenoticism, noting that the latter, now more favorably viewed, is already latent in the former. I shall also argue that kenoticism as an ontological claim can be viewed as recovering elements of a spiritual theology that lie deep within the traditions and practices of the church. How the self-abasement of God can also be understood as an expression of divine power will be the theme of some concluding reflections.

---

4. Bruce L. McCormack, "Scottish Kenotic Theology," in *History of Scottish Theology*, ed. David Fergusson and Mark W. Elliott (Oxford: Oxford University Press, 2019), 3:28.

5. Isaak Dorner, *History of the Development of the Doctrine of the Person of Jesus Christ*, trans. William Lindsay Alexander and D. W. Simon (Edinburgh: T&T Clark, 1892), 3:249–56. This volume was first published in German in 1845.

6. David Brown highlights the influence of idealist philosophy on Anglican kenoticism. See *Divine Humanity*, 128–33.

Kenotic Christology in Anglican Thought

The hinterland of much late-nineteenth-century theology in England was shaped by idealist philosophy, particularly in Oxford, where J. R. Illingworth, Charles Gore, and Henry Scott Holland were influenced by T. H. Green at Balliol College.[7] (William Temple would similarly be influenced by Green's pupil, Edward Caird.) Idealism allied to political radicalism provided the appropriate religious response to skepticism and materialism. God, as the eternal consciousness, is manifested through human consciousness and moral agency. Green's account of the self-expression of God in the world of nature and history may not have accorded with orthodox dogma, but it offered a religious vision that could combat more reductionist trends in philosophy. The world of nature and history could be viewed as a manifestation of the divine, particularly in the evolution of human consciousness. Within this religious worldview, the incarnation emerged as the epitome of the relationship between God and the world; it was emblematic of a universal truth. In this late-nineteenth-century setting, idealist philosophy could provide an interpretation of Darwinian evolution that was patient of theistic concerns while also underpinning the political vision of an organic society in which corporate relations were arranged for the benefit of each and every individual. The attractions of idealism to budding theologians, seeking to combat materialism and to engage in social reform, were thus considerable.[8]

Those theologians influenced by idealist philosophy did not by any means subscribe to all its tenets. Although a theist, Green was distant from the claims of Christian orthodoxy. Yet, as one writer quipped, "The philosopher's honey was carried off to the Tractarian hive."[9] This is especially evident in approaches to the incarnation. Within the general ethos of idealist thought, the concept of a divine kenosis could be less narrowly confined to a mechanism enabling the incarnation of the Son of God under the limitations of historical existence. Its wider location belonged to the God-world relationship in which the divine is poured out, expressed, and comes to itself through nature and history. The work in which God relates to the world

7. See *T. H. Green: Ethics, Metaphysics and Political Philosophy*, ed. Maria Dimova-Cookson and William J. Mander (Oxford: Oxford University Press, 2006).

8. For a recent study of this movement see William J. Mander, *British Idealism: A History* (Oxford: Oxford University Press, 2011).

9. Quoted by J. K. Mozley, *Some Tendencies in British Theology: From the Publication of* Lux Mundi *to the Present Day* (London: SPCK, 1951), 18.

is kenotic by virtue of an unchanging divine essence. This view already emerges in the essays of *Lux Mundi* (1889), though it becomes clearer with the subsequent publications of Charles Gore and others. In his contribution on Christology, J. R. Illingworth is driven more by philosophical concerns to establish a view of the incarnation that avoids the errors of pantheism and deism. The former blurs the distinction between God and world whereas the latter accentuates it to the extent of concealing their relationship. According to Illingworth, patristic theology regards the incarnation as "the climax and keystone of the whole visible creation."[10] In this respect, the incarnation is the highest and most fitting expression of the way in which God relates to the world. The special revelation in Christ is continuous with, yet surpassing, God's general revelation across space and time.

In this intellectual setting, the person and work of Christ were articulated in evolutionary terms. Both Illingworth and Aubrey Moore welcomed these as an advance upon earlier conceptual schemes that tended to represent divine action as sporadic rather than constant and continuous. Moore's oft-quoted remark illustrates this succinctly; Darwinism, though appearing in the disguise of a foe, did the work of a friend.[11] He goes on to comment: "It seems as if in the providence of God, the mission of modern science was to bring home to our unmetaphysical ways of thinking the great truth of the Divine immanence in creation, which is not less essential to the Christian idea of God than to a philosophical view of nature."[12] For Moore, however, this is not a novum but a return to the classical teaching of Irenaeus, Athanasius, and Augustine. The mechanistic theology represented by Paley departed from this sense of divine immanence in creation. But now, through the prevalence of evolutionary patterns of thought, a retrieval of a more thoroughly incarnational approach becomes possible.

The only explicit reference to kenosis in *Lux Mundi* appears in Gore's discussion of the inspiration of Scripture. Noting that Jesus employs assumptions that were standard in the Judaism of his day—e.g., the literal truth of certain events recorded or the Davidic authorship of the Psalms—Gore then asks whether this forecloses various critical questions. In resisting this inference, he argues that the kenosis of the Son of God in the incarnation involves

10. J. R. Illingworth, "The Incarnation in Relation to Development," in *Lux Mundi: A Series of Studies in the Religion of the Incarnation*, ed. Charles Gore, 2nd ed. (London: John Murray, 1890), 185.

11. Aubrey Moore, "The Christian Doctrine of God," in *Lux Mundi*, 99.

12. Moore, "The Christian Doctrine of God," 100.

his entering fully into the circumstances of human existence in the time and place in which he lived. He writes that "the Incarnation was a self-emptying of the Son of God to reveal himself under conditions of human nature and from the human point of view. We are able to draw a distinction between what He revealed and what He used."[13] Gore is in no doubt that Christ is the fullest revelation of God, yet this revelation is mediated through the words and thought forms of the people among whom he lived. Self-emptying here might be thought of in terms of God's accommodation in Christ to our creaturely estate. But it plays only a minor role in Gore's essay and seems far removed from its more systematic elaboration in the German kenoticists.

In his subsequent writings, Gore addresses the history of kenotic Christology while appearing dissatisfied with most of its formulations.[14] We find him repeating some of the criticisms already leveled by Dorner. In Christ, God is revealed, not concealed. At no point do the cosmic Christologies of Paul and John suggest that there was an interruption in the sustaining of the world by the Son of God. On the contrary, their use of these cosmic references is intended to identify the eternal Word or Son with the human Jesus. The crucified, risen, and exalted Jesus is none other than the eternal Word or Son. This is not to deny that in the life of Jesus there is a self-restraint by which the Son of God adapts himself to the circumstances of a truly human existence—Gore's allegiance to anything resembling a kenotic Christology does not really proceed beyond this single claim. By virtue of its affirmation, his Christology seeks a path between the traditional but ahistorical position that Jesus enjoyed the full beatific vision from the time of his conception, and the opposite claim that his divine identity was so discarded that he ceased to be conscious of his divine Sonship in leading a fallible and peccable life. Yet Gore's limited employment of the concept of kenosis is clearly distinguished from prevailing views in Germany and England. Indeed, his own position is one that is perceived to be compatible with a strong affirmation of two-natures Christology—it is never presented as an alternative to a more Chalcedonian approach.

My purpose here is not to explore the coherence and adequacy of Gore's Christology. Instead, I merely want to indicate that the commitment to kenotic forms of expression in *Lux Mundi* and elsewhere reflects a rather different philosophical and theological orientation from the one that shaped

13. Charles Gore, "The Holy Spirit and Inspiration," in *Lux Mundi*, 359.

14. See Charles Gore, "The Consciousness of Our Lord in His Mortal Life," *Dissertations* (London: John Murray, 1895), 71–97, 183–95.

much kenotic Christology in Germany. The idealist hinterland enabled its exponents to see kenosis as an element of all God's dealings with the world.[15] In this kenotic movement there is an impartation of the divine to the creaturely realm, an expression of God's eternal being everywhere in the world but most intensely in the incarnation. In moving in this direction, Gore and others appealed both to the traditions of patristic theology and to what they regarded as the proper meaning of the Christ-hymn in Philippians 2:5–11 with its reference to the self-abasement of the divine Son in the life of Christ. Interestingly, Baillie himself, in the aforementioned critique, has a footnote in which he acknowledges the possibility of an alternative approach to kenosis. Drawing upon the modern Orthodox tradition, he quotes Sergius Bulgakov: "It is essential to realise that, contrary to the various kenotic theories of Protestantism, our Lord in His abasement never ceased to be God, the second person of the Holy Trinity."[16] This remark suggests a rooting of kenosis in the life of God itself, so that the incarnation becomes its fullest historical expression. Instead of an instrumental act in which the divine is converted into a state appropriate to the conditions of human life, the kenosis of the Word of God in Christ corresponds to a love that characterizes the very being of God; this is radiated outward in the economy of creation and redemption. In this way, kenosis becomes the "natural" rather than the "unnatural" expression of the divine life; it has an eternal, rather than an episodic character. For Bulgakov, the kenosis of the divine in the human nature of Jesus is possible because of a created human openness to receive divinity. Already analogously related, the divine and the human are united in ways that are natural for both. In the unique receptivity of Jesus, this human capacity finds its natural fulfilment.[17]

After the demise, if not the disappearance entirely, of the older kenotic theories, this theme became more prominent in a succession of thinkers in the twentieth century. In his doctrine of God, Karl Barth insists upon self-abasement as a revelation rather than a concealment or temporary suspension of essential divine attributes. With his resolute determination to avoid

15. In Scotland, one of the few theologians to dissent from the prevailing kenotic trend was the idealist John Caird. See his work *The Fundamental Ideas of Christianity* (Glasgow: Maclehose, 1899), 2:127–34.

16. Sergius Bulgakov, *Sophia: The Wisdom of God, An Outline of Sophiology*, rev. ed., trans. Xenia Braikevitic, O. Fielding Clarke, and Patrick Thompson (Hudson, NY: Lindisfarne, 1993), 89.

17. In employing curiously similar expressions, Baillie triggered a charge of adoptionism among some of his critics.

a "God behind the God of Jesus," he insists that the incarnation is grounded in the essence of God and not merely in the form in which the Son of God appeared. Hence kenosis cannot be construed as either a hiding or an adjusting of deity in order to make the incarnation possible. Its possibility is grounded in the actuality of the Word become flesh: "This self-emptying and self-humbling has nothing to do with a surrender or loss of his deity."[18] The lordship of Christ displays his free self-offering; at least for faith, it is not disguised.

William Temple had already adopted a similar approach in the aforementioned *Christus Veritas*, first published in 1924. After criticizing the kenotic formula of Mackintosh, he offers his own account: "The Incarnation is an episode in the Life or Being of God the Son; but it is not a mere episode, it is a revealing episode. There we see what He who is God's wisdom always is, even more completely than any Kenotic theory allows."[19] Insofar as it goes, this seems right as a corrective to the speculations and entanglements of earlier kenotic theories. Nevertheless, it is worth pausing to note how closely Temple aligns himself with the concerns of these approaches. He speaks about attributes or functions incompatible with humanity not being exercised by the Eternal Son.[20] And, in doing so, he affirms unequivocally that Christ was a person of his own time and place. He lacked knowledge of modern science, grew in experience and wisdom, experienced temptation, faced the vicissitudes of contingency, and with us became a fellow learner. In affirming these human characteristics, Temple sides with the kenoticists in denying omniscience and omnipotence to the incarnate Word. He seems to agree that this would make the incarnation a charade, while rendering impossible a contextual-historical reading of the Gospels. For Temple's critics, this raised the question of whether his earlier dismissal of kenoticism in Mackintosh et al. was too swift.[21]

At the very least, Temple here faces a formidable problem. If traditional approaches to two-natures Christology cannot be followed all the way, for example in ascribing the beatific vision to Jesus from the moment of his conception, and kenoticism as a theory is a dead end, then how is the incarna-

18. Karl Barth, *Church Dogmatics* II/1, ed. G. W. Bromiley and T. F. Torrance, trans. T. H. L. Parker et al. (Edinburgh: T&T Clark, 1957), 516.

19. William Temple, *Christus Veritas* (London: Macmillan, 1924), 144.

20. Temple, *Christus Veritas*, 144.

21. For example, J. M. Creed, "Recent Tendencies in English Christology," in *Mysterium Christi*, ed. G. K. A. Bell and D. Adolf Deissmann (London: Longmans, Green, 1930), 136.

tion to be described? Even in the absence of full explanation, some coherent suggestions are needed. Although increasingly elusive at this point, Temple offers two proposals that sit somewhat uneasily together. The first is to insist upon the two wills of Christ. As human, Christ has a will that is subject to the ordinary processes of temptation, nescience, and moral progress. But, in describing the Son of God, we cannot attribute such terms of him: "We cannot predicate moral progress of God the Son; we must predicate such progress . . . of Jesus Christ."[22] Here Temple leans in a Nestorian direction with his affirmation of a complete union of purpose and action between Jesus and the divine Word. Yet he avoids the dualist tendency inherent in such formulae by speaking of a single personality that emerges from this union. This enables him to describe this human life as the very life of God. He elaborates this claim through introducing a notion of corporate personality by which Jesus and the Son of God become united as a "concrete universal" or "Second Adam." This new identity is forged in the incarnation and leads to the further notion of the body of which Christ is Head. As its members, we can find our true human identity in this wider corporate whole.

Whether these proposals survive close scrutiny is uncertain.[23] We might wish to speak of Jesus as being uniquely absorbed into the life of God as a prototype or harbinger of a new humanity; yet this generates some difficulties for both Christology and ecclesiology. According to New Testament accounts, the risen Jesus remains a discrete human person after his resurrection, honored as the Son of God. But it seems a stretch to characterize him as a "concrete universal" despite whatever else is said of his enduring significance. Similarly, although Christians belong to the body of Christ, they do not lose their personal identities by becoming its members. Indeed, the Pauline insistence upon discrete members and functions suggests a clear individuation of multiple persons in the community of faith. Temple's christological formulae oscillate uneasily between Antiochene and Alexandrian tendencies, though he is hardly alone here. Donald Baillie's use of the paradox of grace to describe the constitution of the incarnate person may be more consistent, yet his approach also has attracted the criticism of Nestorianism or an incipient adoptionism.

It seems that much modern Christology is here impaled upon the horns of a dilemma. The elucidation of the full humanity of Christ that is now a

22. Temple, *Christus Veritas*, 150.
23. Creed argues that in the end Temple was forced into retaining elements of the kenotic Christology that he regards as discredited ("Recent Tendencies," 136).

condition of biblical criticism requires some departure from a tradition that assumed that Jesus had full exercise of divine powers from the outset of his life. And the kenotic formula that was intended to circumvent this problem while maintaining a strong affirmation of divine identity has been found seriously deficient. It is hard to see where this goes, except through a juxtaposition of different christological models that will soon require appeal to paradox and mystery. Kenotic Christology is an attempt to understand how two (a divine nature and a human nature) could have a single instantiation. But, according to its critics, its outcomes are an attenuation of the person of Christ that undermines what it seeks to articulate—namely, the disclosure of his divinity—and a sundering of the Trinitarian persons with tritheistic consequences.

My intention in this essay, however, is not to pursue these difficult christological questions but instead to underscore the real gains that are made by emphasizing kenosis in terms of divine humility.[24] In fairness to the earlier exponents of kenotic Christology, we should recognize that this was always part of their intention. Kenosis was never reduced entirely to a mere strategy or mechanism by which the divine Son could live a brief earthly life. The act of kenosis was intended as a reflection and impartation of the moral properties of God, particularly in later exponents such as Forsyth and Mackintosh who sought to avoid earlier difficulties. Thus, in homiletic mode, Mackintosh writes: "So dear were human souls to God that He travelled far and stooped low that He might thus touch and raise the needy. Now this is an unheard-of truth, casting an amazing light on God, and revolutionizing the world's faint notions of what it means for Him to be Father."[25] Among its best exponents, the kenotic theory, for all its deficiencies, sought to accentuate divine lowliness as essential to a christologically-shaped doctrine of God. This was revelation not concealment. And part of its rationale was that this disclosure was too often shrouded in more Chalcedonian approaches and their popular

24. It should also be acknowledged that kenotic Christology continues to have some distinguished exponents in the contemporary field. See, for example, several of the essays in *Exploring Kenotic Christology: The Self-Emptying of God*, ed. C. Stephen Evans (Oxford: Oxford University Press, 2006).

25. H. R. Mackintosh, *The Doctrine of the Person of Jesus Christ*, 2nd ed. (Edinburgh: T&T Clark, 1913), 467. See also P. T. Forsyth, who remarked, "The Godhead that freely made man was never so free as in becoming man. His self-limitation was so far from impairing his being that it became the mightiest act of it that we know. It was not limitation so much as concentration." *The Person and Place of Jesus Christ* (London: Independent Press, 1909), 315–16.

reception. This sense of kenosis as a useful theological *concept* rather than a christological *theory* has retained its prominence in the field; it deserves further appreciation both as a form of retrieval and as a corrective strategy.

The Homeliness and Courtesy of God

> Not in that poor lowly stable
> With the oxen standing by,
> We shall see him but in heaven
> Set at God's right hand on high.[26]

Much Christian devotion has suffered from thinking of God and Christ preeminently in terms of their heavenly glory. Within this paradigm, the thirty-three years of Christ's life and passion have been viewed as a *katabasis* that performs a divinely initiated rescue mission on a fallen world. Christ's true home is above not below; his appearance among us is brief but decisive. In returning to God, he resumes his natural place of exaltation. To fulfill a necessary work of atonement, the Son of God must come down from glory, but only for a season. His work accomplished, he can resume his heavenly status.

> Ride on! ride on in majesty!
> Thy last and fiercest strife is nigh;
> The Father on his sapphire throne
> Awaits his own anointed Son.[27]

Notwithstanding elements of caricature in my description, there lurks in the Christian mindset an aversion to any sense of divine humility as the expression of an essential attribute rather than an expedient measure. The Anselmian model of the atonement can sometimes reinforce this train of thought with its pivotal notion of a satisfaction that requires the death of one who is both divine and human. The necessity of an infinite offering can only be met by the divine person undergoing a life of perfect obedience and then submitting his death to satisfy the honor of God. While this theory can be inflected in more constructive ways, its tendency is to view the incarnation

26. From the closing verse of Frances Alexander's carol, "Once in Royal David's City."
27. From the third verse of Henry Hart Milman's Palm Sunday hymn, "Ride On! Ride On in Majesty!"

instrumentally with its orientation toward the death of Christ as a convenient necessity, rather than as the expression of the eternal being of God.

Yet, as noted above, an approach that integrates incarnation and atonement more thoroughly is better equipped to view the former as the manifestation of self-giving love. The lowliness of God in identifying with the crucified figure is a revelation, not a concealment. God is humble, not as a means to an end, but as the God who is for us and with us. The incarnation reveals a love that indwells the creation and works in all things for good.

This emphasis upon incarnation is characteristic of those theologies that continued to deploy kenotic concepts not instrumentally but ontologically. Several emphases are typically evident in such strategies—the identification of God with the material world, divine passibility, the involvement of the church in the wider sociopolitical realm, a reconfiguring of the relationship between the church and the kingdom, and the stress on a constant divine indwelling more consonant with evolutionary patterns of thought than earlier Paleyan notions of occasional intervention. Much liturgical revision and hymn-writing have reflected this shift, though these trends were already evident in theological work undertaken in *Lux Mundi* and elsewhere during the previous century.[28]

"God with us" is a familiar claim that characterizes much Christian preaching and pastoral counsel today. Although its roots are deeply scriptural, it requires some further exposition in this context. A standard criticism of the essays in *Lux Mundi* was that they were preoccupied with the "religion of the incarnation" rather than the incarnation itself. The concept tended to function as a general principle rather than as the description of a particular event, even though these were generally assumed to be mutually supportive. This raises the question of whether the incarnation of Christ was merely an instance of a general principle, a signifier for what was generally true of the created order, that is, that it was indwelt by God. And, if so, then what was the significance of both the event and the general principle?[29]

28. This is discussed at greater length by Rowan Williams, *On Christian Theology* (Oxford: Blackwell, 2000), 225–38. The liturgical outputs of the Iona Community in Scotland also reveal an emphasis upon incarnation and divine indwelling; by contrast, more traditional accounts of the atonement are muted.

29. This criticism of *Lux Mundi* was made in a footnote by A. M. Fairbairn, *The Place of Christ in Modern Theology* (London: Hodder and Stoughton, 1893), 451. He also observes that "From the Lutherans the notion [of the incarnation] has filtered through various channels into the modern Anglican consciousness, which loves to describe Christianity as 'the religion of the Incarnation,' the church as naturally of a piece with it, and continuing

Running parallel with these lines of inquiry is a pastoral issue. If God is with us, what difference does that make? If God accompanies us in our joys and sorrows, of what benefit is that to us? And how does the suffering of Christ shape a response to these questions? While such queries might harbor impious sentiments, they cannot be avoided. Two possible answers need to be viewed with varying degrees of skepticism.

The first is that by virtue of the event of the incarnation, God understands what it is like to be human, to suffer, and to face death. This response fails on at least two grounds. The circumstances of Christ's life do not encompass the full gamut of human experience—for example, he was a man not a woman, a child but not a parent, and he did not live to enjoy or suffer old age. But, more importantly, God does not have to become incarnate to have maximal knowledge of human experience. Divine discernment needs no bodily or sensory mediation to comprehend the life of creatures. The empathetic powers of God are not dependent upon a hypostatic union for their realization. If they were, some very radical revision of the doctrine of God would be required.

A second type of response is more promising. We might view the incarnation as a striking revelation of what occurs across all space and time, namely, that God knows, accompanies, and loves each creature. The realization of this good news delivers us from unnecessary fear and anxiety about the intentions or character of God. There are some real gains here in dispelling misconceptions that can arise from earlier formulations or a deeply ingrained, even pathological, sense of guilt and unworthiness. But is this sufficient? Consider the following proposition: "God understands and is with you in your suffering." There may be some comfort to draw from this knowledge of divine accompaniment. After all, a friend who has experienced something of the same sickness, distress or calamity that has befallen us can be a valuable source of consolation and counsel, probably more so than one not similarly afflicted. Yet we need to ask if what is disclosed in the incarnation is exhausted by claims about divine accompaniment, presence, and indwelling.

If incarnation is not merely a general rule or historical type, then the revelation of the universal will be more dependent on the particular than is here stated. The gospel story has a specificity that is not readily reduced to an

its work." The critique is further developed by Alasdair Heron in "The Person of Christ," in *Keeping the Faith: Essays to Mark the Centenary of Lux Mundi*, ed. Geoffrey Wainwright (Philadelphia: Fortress, 1988), 99–123. (This volume was later dubbed *Lux Tuesday*.)

illustrative example of a general principle. Attention to the particular must make a difference to our understanding of the mode of God's presence, so that it remains a constant point of return. Here some insights can be gleaned from the practice of prayer and spiritual devotion.

Significantly perhaps, it is among writers who have approached the subject of kenosis from this angle that most light has been shed. In his *Mysterium Paschale*, Balthasar explores ways in which ancient patristic insights can be developed in an ontological approach to the subject. He notes the strenuous efforts of Origen, Chrysostom, Cyril, and Hilary to describe how God's omnipotence is revealed in the humility of the cross: "In the incarnation the triune God has not simply helped the world, but has disclosed himself in what is most deeply his own. . . . It is in this perspective that many of the assertions of the Father become fully luminous for the first time."[30] Balthasar's appeal to the theologians of the early church is an instructive example of how their doctrine of God had to be fashioned by the passion of Christ. Instead of simply adopting Hellenist themes and yoking these to creedal tenets, former assumptions had to be fundamentally reshaped in accordance with scriptural interpretation, devotional practice, and Christian ethical teaching. For Balthasar, kenosis can even be traced upstream to the life of the Trinity with its eternal processions.[31]

In extending this kenotic insight to the theology of creation, W. H. Vanstone, another Anglican writer, argues against accounts of the God-world relationship that are dominated by notions of sheer power. In the making of the world, there is a divine expense that he describes as "precarious" in the form that God's rule takes. Although this is a general assertion, it proceeds from a theology of the cross. Vanstone's claim is that the entire creation must be viewed as the domain of God's kenosis, not through an act of abandonment but in a redeeming process that takes place from within and awaits the response of creation to the display of that love. At times, his language suggests problematically that God's sovereignty has been irretrievably compromised, especially in hinting that final outcomes may be tragic. But the salient point

30. Hans Urs von Balthasar, *Mysterium Paschale* (Edinburgh: T&T Clark, 1990), 29. See also Donald M. MacKinnon, *Themes in Theology: The Threefold Cord* (Edinburgh: T&T Clark, 1987), 143: "Christ's self-submission to these conditions is to be seen not as an abdication of divine omnipotence but rather as its only authentic human manifestation."

31. The spiritual theology of Augustine also provides a rich resource for reflection upon divine humility together with its affective and active consequences for the Christian life. See, for example, Stephen Pardue, "Kenosis and Its Discontents: An Augustinian Account of Divine Humility," *Scottish Journal of Theology* 65, no. 3 (2012): 271–88.

in this context is that if the kenosis of God in redemption is a disclosure of who God really is, then we must commit to the view that the same kenotic love sustains the entire creation. Vanstone writes: "Christianity should have no hesitation in attributing to God that authenticity of love which it recognises in His Christ—in attributing to the Creator that authenticity of love which it recognises in the Redeemer."[32]

Two related problems have emerged in discussions around this recent reappropriation of kenotic insights. The first is the charge, strikingly rehearsed in some feminist criticism, that an excessive stress on kenosis will encourage a culture of suffering in silence, victimhood, and acquiescence in abusive practices.[33] Notwithstanding its appeal to Christ's example, advocacy of a kenotic acceptance of suffering may simply reinforce oppression, especially when delivered by a masculine clergy. There is a real risk here that is worryingly supported by some historical and contemporary examples, not least in the strategies that have been employed to protect the reputation of the church in the face of public scandal.[34] Unless kenotic practice can be viewed as a form of empowerment, then it will be unable to withstand the force of such criticism. A theology of cross and resurrection together is required here for the sake of underscoring the transformed agency that characterizes the Christian life. Excessive emphasis upon passivity will miss the point that the weakness of Christ in his suffering enables a new form of activity in the world. Without a properly accentuated account of Christian agency, this criticism will stand.[35]

A related difficulty surrounds the perceived implication that a practice of kenosis must involve the renunciation of all forms of power, as if this were at odds with an ethic of love. This becomes a particularly acute difficulty in the

32. W. H. Vanstone, *Love's Endeavour, Love's Expense: The Response of Being to the Love of God* (London: Darton, Longman & Todd, 1977), 59.

33. See, for example, Daphne Hampson, *Theology and Feminism* (Oxford: Blackwell, 1990), 155.

34. An excess of loyalty to an institution or profession can too easily result in strategies that compel obedience and demand silence of victims and office bearers. See, for example, Marie Keenan, *Child Sexual Abuse and the Catholic Church: Gender, Power, and Organizational Culture* (Oxford: Oxford University Press, 2012), 223–24.

35. I take this to be one of the central points argued by Sarah Coakley in her nuanced defense of kenosis. See "*Kenōsis* and Subversion: On the Repression of 'Vulnerability' in Christian Feminist Writing," in *Powers and Submissions: Spirituality, Philosophy and Gender* (Oxford: Blackwell, 2002), 3–68. Linn Tonstad raises further questions about a possible conflation of vulnerability and dependence in *God and Difference: The Trinity, Sexuality, and the Transformation of Finitude* (London: Routledge, 2016), 108–10.

realm of public theology if a disjunction is formed between a kenotic *imitatio Christi* and political activity. The risk of course is that the latter ceases to be informed by any distinctively Christian account of agency, as in some constructions of the two-kingdoms doctrine.[36] A legitimate response will again seek to inflect rather than eschew all possibilities of a genuinely Christian exercise of institutional authority. Constraints are necessary, for example, by appropriate checks and balances, the holding of office on a temporary basis on trust rather than right, the combining of justice with mercy, and practices of amnesty.[37] A kenotically grounded ethic of service should be seen as demanding a chastened account of political or other institutional forms of agency, not as negating their very possibility or so relentlessly exercising a hermeneutics of suspicion that the field is effectively conceded to other forces. The articulation of a public theology in this register will also counter the aforementioned charge of so overstating vulnerability as to welcome all its manifestations.[38]

As is now well known, Julian of Norwich survived a life-threatening disease as a young woman.[39] Her visions of the crucified Christ subsequently shaped her devotional life, her writing, and her public witness in Norwich. In describing her deepened relationship with God after this time of intense suffering, she refers to her discovery of the "homeliness" and "courtesy" of God. These terms come from different medieval social contexts. "Courtesy," a chivalrous notion, denotes a proper respect and self-bearing, whereas "homeliness" describes a familiarity and intimacy, a willingness to make one's permanent dwelling in a place where one's weaknesses and idiosyncrasies are most exposed. Julian does not hesitate to describe this presence of Christ in motherly terms. Gentle but persistent, it transforms her life yet without overwhelming her identity or sense of self: "Our courteous Lord

36. "The danger of the metaphor of kenosis is . . . that it should be thought that the new higher life of loving and humble service has no point of contact with the necessarily structured life of ordinary society or that involvement in society can be conducted on higher principles." Stephen Sykes, "The Strange Persistence of Kenotic Christology," in *Being and Truth: Essays in Honour of John Macquarrie*, ed. Alistair Kee and Eugene T. Long (London: SCM, 1986), 371.

37. See Oliver O'Donovan, *The Ways of Judgment* (Grand Rapids: Eerdmans, 2005), esp. 84–100.

38. Karen Kilby addresses this danger of esteeming vulnerability in "The Seductions of Kenosis" in *Suffering and the Christian Life*, ed. Rachel Davies and Karen Kilby (London: T&T Clark, 2020), 163–74.

39. The relevance of Julian's theology in this context is suggested by Jane Williams, *The Merciful Humility of God* (London: Bloomsbury, 2018), 49–57.

willeth that we should be as homely with him as heart may think or soul may desire. But beware that we take not so recklessly this homeliness that we leave courtesy. For our Lord himself is sovereign homeliness, and as homely as he is, so courteous he is: for he is very courteous."[40]

This homely presence is not merely passive and consoling for Julian. Its energizing qualities enable her to undertake new forms of service and witness. She reflects upon and writes up her experiences. Centuries later, the manuscript is uncovered and circulated to a wider audience. And, during her remaining years despite a reclusive location, she is available to others. Worshippers and pilgrims come to her window to receive counsel and spiritual direction for their own lives.

The presence of God is here characterized in terms that require a christological specificity. Without attention to the figure of the crucified Jesus, these revelations would have little meaning. Yet their significance is universal—all manner of things shall be made well. The reach of the unbounded love of God is not limited to the faithful nor even to the human creature: "All thing that he hath—For well I wot that heaven and earth and all that is made is great and large, fair and good; but the cause why it shewed so little to my sighth was for that I saw it in the presence of him that is the Maker of all things."[41] This recognition of the universal homeliness and courtesy of God is not merely passive; these have an active quality that redirects her life, bestowing a new meaning and purpose upon it.

Here we can discern something about the power of God in the foolishness of the cross, together with the reasons why Jesus pronounced the blessedness of the poor, the meek, the bereaved, and those who hunger for justice. The energizing force of this faith permeates the New Testament, standing as a permanent challenge to a wearied church that regards its best days as past. The presence of God when determined by the particularity of the life and work of Christ becomes a power manifested in weakness. Any account that we offer of an incarnation or indwelling of God in the created order takes its bearings from this unsubstitutable narrative of the gospel story.

The kenosis of God is the outpouring of a divine love, yet in this entering into weakness it manifests a strange new power. The dispossessed are forgiven and restored. The church gathers those who were of little worldly repute and transforms them as witnesses of God. The seeming insignificance

---

40. Julian of Norwich, *Revelations of Divine Love*, ed. Dom Roger Hudleston, 2nd ed. (London: Burns Oates, 1952), long text, chap. 77, 157.

41. Julian of Norwich, *Revelations of Divine Love*, chap. 8, 15–16.

of Christ's early followers is countered by their long-term impact upon societies that once dismissed them. The struggles of the oppressed can display an indomitable spirit and mercy that expose the shallowness of so much else. And the arc of history, though long and often confusing, bends slowly toward God's justice. The task of a spiritual theology of kenosis is to make some conceptual sense of this power that is displayed in weakness, of the victories that can be won from the underside by God's grace.

I have sought to argue that, as a theological theme rather than a christological theory, kenosis should be regarded as an enduring expression rather than a concealment of divine love. This notion, however, requires careful handling—whether theologically, liturgically, or pastorally—if it is to prove a constructive element in Christian confession. But in articulating a fundamental element of faith at its Christ-focused center, it becomes a powerful theme that disturbs assumptions about divine power and our ways of living.

12

Is There a Kenotic Ethics in the Work of Karl Barth?

Georg Pfleiderer

In contrast to their predecessors in the sixteenth, seventeenth, and nine-teenth centuries, present debates on kenoticism as discussed mostly among Anglophone Protestant theologians are—in my judgment—driven not so much by specific problems of Christology but by fundamental questions of the doctrine of God as to whether God really became human in Christ and whether God can suffer. Even if such questions were already at stake in the former versions of the debate, the character of these questions has changed. The new quest for God's true humanity is no longer driven by largely specu-lative interests in establishing God's real presence in the Eucharist by means of metaphysical concepts but rather by more practical ones. We are now interested in the humanity of God in the sense of God's emotional participa-tion and compassion, in this humanity as an interhuman capacity.[1] From this perspective, the present debate on kenoticism could be understood (at least with regard to some of its participants) as a dogmatic version of the many attempts to modernize the Christian image of God from an authoritarian icon of repressive religious pedagogy to a God fitting our modern under-standing of God as a social, compassionate personality. Such tendencies are even noticeable among evangelicals.

1. See, for example, the "Big Five-Model" or "OCEAN-Model" used frequently in per-sonality psychology.

Such an interpretation of the debate should not be understood as a critical denunciation. Our common modern ideal of God as a compassionate personality can be used to uncover aspects of the biblical God and traditional dogmatics that were entombed under the rubble of repressive interpretations of Christian dogmatics and ethics. The dogmatic dressing of this debate should also not be understood as camouflage. It may rather function as a bulwark against problematic "liberal" attempts to adapt, in a merely external manner, essential contents of Christian morality and ethics to the spirit of the age.

If this explication of present debates on kenoticism is true, then it might also illuminate the fact that a particular theological work is often used as a touchstone in this debate, a work whose author denied being a kenoticist even though he presented a theology that actually fits such interests very well: Karl Barth.[2] There are, as Bruce McCormack has pointed out,[3] good reasons to call Barth—so to speak (echoing a famous dictum of Schleiermacher)—a kenoticist "of a higher order." According to Barth, God's atonement with humanity in Jesus Christ is based in God's interior essence, which therefore must be conceived as a "being in becoming,"[4] as a "being in action."[5] And this character of God's essence is described as "the way of the son of God into the far country."[6] Barth illuminated the principal meaning of this narrative metaphor in a famous interpretation of his own theology in a 1956 lecture where he coined the popular phrase "the humanity of God."[7] This expression should be understood not only in the sense of (refurbished) traditional dogmatics (namely, as referring to the doctrine of God's two natures), but also in the sense of a contemporary modern conception of God as a compassionate (human) personality. Barth is not only a kenoticist but also a liberal "of a higher order."[8] His dogmatic theology has an explicitly ethical point, which is the theological foundation of an understanding of

2. See Karl Barth, *Church Dogmatics* IV/1, ed. G. W. Bromiley and T. F. Torrance, trans. G. W. Bromiley (Edinburgh: T&T Clark, 1956), 180–83; Karl Barth, *The Epistle to the Philippians*, trans. James Leitch (London: SCM, 1962), 60–64.

3. Bruce L. McCormack, "Karl Barth's Christology as a Resource for a Reformed Version of Kenoticism," *International Journal of Systematic Theology* 8, no. 3 (2006): 248–51.

4. Eberhard Jüngel, *God's Being Is in Becoming*, trans. John Webster (London: T&T Clark, 2014).

5. Paul T. Nimmo, *Being in Action: The Theological Shape of Barth's Ethical Vision* (London: T&T Clark, 2007).

6. Karl Barth, *Church Dogmatics* IV/1:157.

7. Karl Barth, "The Humanity of God," *CrossCurrents* 10, no. 1 (1960): 70–79.

8. See Karl Barth, "Liberale Theologie (Ein Interview)," in *Letzte Zeugnisse* (Zurich: EVZ, 1969), 33–48.

human freedom and self-determination as empathic responsibility for others. If Barth's christological theology is, as McCormack has shown, kenotic (and I agree with him), then Barth's ethics is, too. For it is Barth's intention to unfold ethics as an integral part of his dogmatics according to his basic understanding of God's self-revelation in Jesus Christ.

Ethics as Kenotic Dialectics

In this chapter, I want to examine the precise structure of the kenotic shape of Barth's ethics.[9] This is a specific version of investigating the epistemological structure of Barth's theology and of his ethics in particular. Like many other scholars, I believe that Barth's intellectual roots in Marburg neo-Kantianism contributed strikingly to his theological method.[10] However, I have a specific understanding of Barth's transformation of this intellectual heritage. I am convinced that Barth uses a specific method of *theological argumentation*. It is the particular aim of this argumentation to make clear, by means of its manner of progression, that readers should conceive of themselves (and their existential self-understanding) as involved in the unfolding of this argumentation. Like a sermon (and taken from this literary genre), Barth's theology is a theology essentially addressed to someone; it reflects the steps of a theological self-explication of faith understood as a fundamental process of interpreting the self, life, and the world in light of God's self-revelation in Jesus Christ. Barth could thus also be called a Schleiermacherian "of a higher order." His method of argumentation possesses, however, more similarities with the method of Schleiermacher's famous philosophical opponent in Berlin: the dialectics of Georg Wilhelm Friedrich Hegel. So, and this is my last variation of the phrase, Barth could also be called a Hegelian "of a higher order."[11]

In his commentary on the Epistle to the Romans and also in his *Church Dogmatics*, Barth's theological method is a specific method of dialectical ar-

---

9. I use the term "kenotic" in the following to denote Barth's understanding and unfolding of his central christological idea of God's self-alteration in Jesus Christ—that God *"emptied himself* (of that [divine] form) *and took on the form of a servant, became like men"* (Karl Barth, *Epistle to the Philippians*, 63)—and the consequences of this idea for his ethics.

10. See Georg Pfleiderer, *Karl Barths praktische Theologie: Zu Genese und Kontext eines paradigmatischen Entwurfs systematischer Theologie im 20. Jahrhundert* (Tübingen: Mohr Siebeck, 2000), 158–63, 190–205, 233–39, 268–70, 317.

11. See, e.g., Michael Welker, "Barth und Hegel: Zur Erkenntnis eines methodischen Verfahrens bei Barth," *Evangelische Theologie* 43 (1983): 307–28.

gumentation.[12] It is dialectical, first, in the sense that it logically unfolds an argument, going from position to counterposition to their mediation, or (with Hegel) from the universal to the particular to the singular, or (with Barth himself) from the position of God, the Father, to that of God, the Son, to that of God, the Holy Spirit, or (also with Barth and his understanding of the Anselmian ontological argument) from the divine idea to its realization (in Jesus Christ) to its pronunciation to us and the world. As such, Barth's dialectics should also, second, be understood as a practical, rhetorical dialectics, which means that it describes a divine speech-act—"the Word of God"—by performing it and its structure with human words. It therefore has the double character of both theological reflection and practical sermon. It is, in other words, a dialogue with the (intended) reader (as opponent and potential follower), a performed discourse. In this mode, it is a sermon for professional religious intellectuals, for pastors. In a Schleiermacherian idiom, it performs theology as a function of the task of leading the church. It has, at once, the structure of both metapractical, theoretical reflection *and* practical action. Its intention is that it be used as a pattern of practical annunciation guided and structured by the theoretical reflection presented in Barth's *Church Dogmatics*.

Due to its character as a (meta)practical speech-act, Barth's dialectics should be understood, third, as an ethical dialectics, as a dialectical unfolding of ethical action and reflection, precisely, of ethical judgment. Particularly this ethical dimension of Barth's dialectics makes strong universal truth claims. It is not a theology merely for a particular religious people (for Protestant Christian pastors, although it remains primarily directed to them); it intends rather to be taken as theological reflection for all human beings. As such a practice of theory, it is the (intended) realization of the categorical imperative: the truly good human action is the proclamation of the Word of God, an action that is reflected on and performed in Barth's *Church Dogmatics*.

In the following, I will try to evidence and unfold this interpretation through analysis of a specific section of Barth's ethics: some paragraphs on the foundation of his general ethics in *Church Dogmatics* II/2. It will turn out that in these paragraphs Barth unfolds the general intention of his theology and ethics: to overcome (in a Hegelian sense of the word) Immanuel Kant's concept of practical reason.[13] The kenoticism of Barth's ethics will prove to entail the key argument of this theological and philosophical intention.

12. Karl Barth, *The Epistle to the Romans*, trans. Edwyn C. Hoskyns (Oxford: Oxford University Press, 1968), and Barth, *Church Dogmatics*.

13. In doing so, Barth follows in the footsteps of his liberal predecessors, Albrecht Ritschl and Wilhelm Herrmann.

It is a disadvantage of my way of interpreting Barth that it demands a very close, if not microscopic, reading of his texts. Yet this way is particularly necessary to trace how Barth reduplicates his technique of argumentation within itself, such that it not only determines the sequence of parts and paragraphs in *Church Dogmatics* but also the argumentation in every paragraph. In many cases, this technique is even reduplicated within chapters, sections of chapters, and sentences.

This highly artificial technique is, on the one hand, easy to detect since just a glance at the table of contents enables one to notice it. On the other hand, Barth's descriptive attitude, lengthy narrative, and metaphorical style often veil the precise systematic progression of the argumentation.[14] There is no discrete methodological discourse in *Church Dogmatics*; there is only its practice. "Spectators" (653, 656, 767, etc.)[15] are not allowed in this theology; they are abolished.[16] Nevertheless, in order to understand the true intellectual and religious depth of this theology, we cannot avoid behaving as its spectators, or better, as its observers. In order to "follow the acting of *God* attentively,"[17] we have to observe Barth's way of argumentation attentively and therefore also critically.[18] The interpretation cannot avoid the semblance of committing a theological sin; it is dependent upon divine—and human—pardon.

The Kenotic Structure of the Foundation of Barth's Ethics (CD II/2)

The particular points that we the readers should understand in §§36–39 of *Church Dogmatics* are (1) that we (our entire existence, which is our entire acting) are involved in the acting of God in Jesus Christ, (2) why we are involved in it, and (3) for what purpose we are involved in it. The divine speech-act reconstructed and presented here is a speech-act that aims to be reduplicated by our own acting and thereby to be proclaimed to all human-

14. With regard to this methodological or stylistic aspect as well, Barth's theology may be called "kenotic."

15. Here and in the following, the page numbers inline refer to Barth, *Church Dogmatics* II/2.

16. See Pfleiderer, *Karl Barths praktische Theologie*, 29–138.

17. See the last sentence of Karl Barth, "Der Christ in der Gesellschaft (1919)," in *Vorträge und kleinere Arbeiten 1914–1921*, ed. Hans-Anton Drewes (Zurich: Theologischer Verlag, 2012), 598.

18. This uncomfortable situation may itself be called a "kenotic" problem of Barth interpretation: the dialectics of veiling and unveiling of God in his revelation has an analogy in the (same characteristics of the) transparency of Barth's theological method.

ity. Barth thus intends to unfold the humanity of God in a conceptional way as a liberating command for all human beings. His basic claim is that the "idea of responsibility, rightly understood, is known only to Christian ethics. This alone teaches a true and proper confrontation of man" (642). This is a theological statement that as such contains a strong philosophical claim.

It is easier to gain a comprehensive view of Barth's method of dialectical argumentation if we present the headings of the four paragraphs (actually: one plus three) and their (in each case threefold) subdivision in a table with some interpretive remarks:

	§36 Ethics as a Task of the Doctrine of God		
	(ontological)	1. The Command of God and the Ethical Problem	
	(epistemological)	2. The Way of Theological Ethics	
(position [vertical and horizontal])	(Father: general claim [personal imperative])	(Son: particular realization of the claim [in general])	(Holy Ghost: mediation of claim and decision)
	§37 The Command as the Claim of God (God is the source/subject and object of human responsibility)	**§38 The Command as the Decision of God** (God makes himself responsible for us—we must make ourselves responsible for others)	**§39 The Command as the Judgment of God** (God judges us by judging the conformity of our judgments to his gracefully being responsible for us)
(Father: basis, presupposition)	1. The Basis of the Divine Claim	1. The Sovereignty of the Divine Decision	1. The Presupposition of the Divine Judgment
(Son: content, concrete realization)	2. The Content of the Divine Claim	2. The Definiteness of the Divine Decision	2. The Execution of the Divine Judgment
(Holy Ghost: teleological aspect: form, quality, purpose)	3. The Form of the Divine Claim	3. The Goodness of the Divine Decision	3. The Purpose of the Divine Judgment

I will show that the kenoticism of Barth's ethics can be found generally in the progressive, dialectical character of the argumentation. In this framework, it is hidden in the second, christological element of the threefold structure: in the "definiteness," namely, in the exclusive and also inclusive (!) concreteness of God's command. This (claim of) concreteness will turn out to be the core of Barth's anti- (or meta-)Kantian approach.

Ethics as a Task of the Doctrine of God—CD II/2, §36

Barth outlines the fundamental ideas of his ethics in §36. Ethics is part of the doctrine of God since the being of God must be understood as acting. Ethics is thus "the theory of this divine praxis" (531). Analogically to the being of God, the personal existence of human beings must be conceived as acting too.[19] As such, personal human existence is characterized by "self-determination" (510–11) by means of a particular form of reflection: "responsibility."[20] Barth's ethics is an ethics of responsibility, and it unfolds as a reflection that is characteristic of such responsibility. Fundamental to this kind (and process) of reflection is the insight that it is based on God's acting. Concretely, it is based on the covenant character of God's self-alteration in Jesus Christ; covenant is interpreted here as making "Himself responsible for man" (511). The noetic character of human responsibility (as practical reflection) is thus ontologically grounded in God's acting. As such, this reflection has a certain structure: the structure of taking responsibility for somebody else. Ethical reflection is itself an ethical act; it is the reflective aspect of acting.

Ethical reflection reflects the acting of God in Jesus Christ and as Jesus Christ.[21] This divine acting must be interpreted as the divine practice in which man is "made responsible" by God in Jesus Christ.[22] In this initial

19. Barth writes, "For it is as he acts that man exists as a person" (516), and again, "To exist as a man means to act" (535). This definition is essential for Barth's anthropology; it follows directly from his fundamental epistemological presuppositions. I abstain here from discussing the plausibility of this definition of human being, even though such a discussion is in fact necessary and controversial!

20. For Barth, "It is in and with man's determination by God as this takes place in predestination that the question arises of man's self-determination, his responsibility and decision, his obedience and action" (511).

21. Barth states: "He exists because Jesus Christ exists. He exists as a predicate of this Subject, i.e., that which has been decided and is real for man in this Subject is true for him. Therefore the divine command as it is directed to him, as it applies to him, consists in his relationship to this Subject. Therefore the action of this Subject for him is the right action or conduct which we have to investigate" (539–40).

22. For Barth, "What 'there is' is not as such the command of God. But the core of the matter is that God gives His command, that He gives Himself to be our Commander.

chapter, Barth defines acting itself as "choosing" and "deciding" (535). In §38, he refers to the second aspect ("deciding"). The "choosing" aspect seems to be the subject of the first paragraph (§37). The subject of §39 is "judgment." Judgment seems to be practical, performed reflection as an act (or the moment of an act) in which the elements of choice and decision become practically reflected, which means they become expressed (orally performed and made valid).

The Command as the Claim of God—CD II/2, §37

The following paragraph, §37, does not speak of choice but of claim. *Claim* refers, however, to the aspect of an act of choosing that binds a chosen subject (as object) legally or morally. This is exactly what is meant here, since in the narrow sense the choosing (more precisely, electing) aspect of God's acting was already reflected in the doctrine of election. For this reason, *claim* refers to the choice involved in the demanding or binding dimension of God's acting, and it is this dimension of God's acting which is the subject of ethics. In this context, it should be noted that the English word *claim* does not exactly reproduce the semantic notion of the German word *Anspruch*. *Anspruch* belongs to the semantic field of *sprechen* ("to speak," "to talk to somebody"). It means "to address someone" (orally) in the sense of addressing him or her as the object of a claim. *Anspruch* is the moral and legal version of *Ansprache* ("speech"; actually: "speaking to somebody or an audience"). Thus, as a claim on and to somebody, *Anspruch* itself denotes a speech-act. In the context of a text that is meant as the theory of a practice (see 548) and at the same moment as the practice of this theory, this text also performs this claim on human beings (to be precise, it entails the claim to perform this claim).[23]

As depicted in the diagram above, Barth's unfolding of the first aspect of God's command as the "claim of God" is threefold. It distinguishes between

---

God's command, God Himself, gives Himself to be known. And as He does so, He is heard. Man is made responsible" (548).

23. In this context, it should be recalled that the term *Verantwortung* (as well as its English translation "responsibility") is also a rhetorical notion. It is an intense form of giving an answer to somebody (the prefix *Ver-* intensifies the relational dimension). Both terms originally refer to the situation of a defendant in court. Even though the term *Verantwortung* generally became a key concept in the humanities and theology in the German-speaking world in the twentieth century, it has a specific character in Barth's performative, rhetoric theology of the Word of God.

(1) the "basis," (2) the "content," and (3) the "form." This terminology is often used by Barth to denote the three aspects of his dialectical method.

The Basis of the Divine Claim

The English translation of *Grund* as "basis" does not quite reflect the connotations of the German term. "Der Grund des göttlichen Anspruchs" denotes a legal foundation that is in this case based on an absolute authority who is the source of all justice. These associations are indicated in the introduction, according to which the "present enquiry concerns the basis and justice of this claim, the majesty with which the command of God is proclaimed and heard in this circle" (556). It is obviously the logical or argumentative position of God the Father that is indicated here. The argument is: human responsibility in a strict and universal sense can only be maintained if it can refer to the absolute source of all moral and legal bindings, which we call God, specifically "the majesty of His will" (560). The philosophical claim implied in this theological argument is that a categorical imperative must be founded on the absolute authority of an absolute will. Finite human reason cannot serve as such a basis because it does not have the power of an absolute will.

An absolute will must have the power of absolute self-determination. Where can such self-determination be found? It can be found (only) in an actual fact that reveals itself as such a fact: in God's presence in the life and fate of Jesus Christ in the form of his free obedience. Hence, Barth writes, "In this event [*Geschehen*] God uttered His command" (560). Slightly different from the English *event*, the German term *Geschehen* denotes a temporally limited proceeding in time. The whole biography of Jesus of Nazareth, "what happened in Bethelehem, at Capernaum and Tiberias, in Gethsemane and on Golgotha, and in the garden of Joseph of Arimathea" (559), is viewed here as a realization of "the obedience of the free man to the free God" (561). As such, it has the character of a "valid model for the general relationship of man to the will of God" (562). Again, the German *exemplarisch* is stronger than the provided translation "valid model"; it refers to the idealistic concept of *Allgemeinheit* (universality). In the life of Jesus Christ, understood as a permanently realized obedience to God, the paradigmatic realization of humanity is present. Since this perfectly realized obedience is transparent to the grace of God, it can be said that "When grace is actualized and revealed, it always means that the Law is established" (562). It is established in this "*Geschehen*" as an absolute authority, as a strictly binding command, as a categorical imperative.

The Content of the Divine Claim

When—that is, under which conditions—is a command strictly binding? It is only binding in this sense if it can be shown not only that it is based on an abstract absolute authority but also that it is concrete in every particular moment of life. If the command is just a general categorical imperative, the moral agent is in the position of a subject who reflects on the derivation of a situational, hypothetical imperative. In the moment of such reflection, the categorical imperative is actually modified into a hypothetical imperative. It must, therefore, be shown that the divine command has "teleologic power" (566).[24] "There is no divine claim in itself (literally and stressed: "*as such*," which means "in general"). There are only concrete divine claims. For it is the grace of God which expresses *itself* [emphasis mine] in these claims" (566). To understand the biography of Jesus Christ as the outcome of perfect human obedience and thus as divine self-expression implies to "become obedient to Jesus" (568), and this implies "actually to become obedient to God, not a conceived and imaginary God, but to God as He is in His inmost essence" (568–69). The distinctiveness that is recognized in God's command if we look at Jesus's life is the aspect that makes his demand and the categorical imperative concrete and therefore really demanding: "Jesus Himself is the divine demand which confronts us as a genuinely compelling demand and which is also rigorous in the sense that it can be fulfilled only willingly or not at all" (569). Thus, the life of Jesus answers the question of the content of the divine demand: "What are we to do? We are to do what corresponds to this grace" (576). What does this mean? Barth explains, "What God wants of us and all men is that we should believe in Jesus Christ" (583). Belief in Jesus Christ is the concrete, kenotic form—that is, the content—of fulfilling God's demand, the categorical imperative.

The Form of the Divine Claim

The divine claim is only fully understood in its progressive structure if we understand that it has not only a majestic basis and concrete content but also a concrete addressee who must fulfill the demand to believe in Jesus Christ

---

24. This transition to the next subchapter is striking. It demonstrates how essential the dialectical progression is for Barth's argumentation. Position (a) (the absolute basis) would actually be denied if the argumentation did not go on to the second moment, the moment of content.

personally and concretely. Barth writes, "Our present question is how man—corresponding to the basis and content of the command of God—becomes its addressee and recipient" (583). How does this happen? It happens if and when we understand that it is concretely we who have to identify with these addresses, that we are meant, that "I [!] belong to Jesus" (610). As long as I (each reader: you!) do not actually perform this act, everything said beforehand "would be a construction that does not reach our actual life, and is of no use to it" (606). How and when does the command of God reach our actual life? It does so when we realize that it has a specific "form," namely, "the special form which is its secret even in the *guise* of another command, . . . the fact that it is permission—the granting of a very definite freedom" (585; emphasis mine). It does so in the person of Jesus Christ: "It is in this person and only in Him that the identity of authority and freedom is accomplished" (606), and this accomplishment is the ground of our freedom. Thus, the fundamental claim of Kant's theory of practical reason, the realization of individual autonomy by its orientation to the absolute demand of the categorical imperative, is here (according to the intention of the author) theologically reproduced and criticized.

Nevertheless, it is the implication and condition of this theological overcoming to understand that the command of God "demands everything, the totality of my life" (610). As an act of total self-determination, it "demands a genuine decision" (609) that "can and must be continually repeated and confirmed" (612). In the following, it will be necessary to analyze in which way this moment of a (permanently repeated) human decision is based on the respective property of the divine command itself. This is explained in §38.

The Command as the Decision of God—CD II/2, §38

This paragraph, §38, is crucial to the foundation of Barth's ethics and to the interpretation presented here. It unfolds the christological (God as Son) aspect of the whole argumentation. Its interpretation should therefore give the most specific answer to the question of the sense in which we can speak of a kenotic structure in Barth's ethics. It is in this paragraph that the central argument supporting his fundamental claim to overcome a philosophical (namely, Kant's) theory of human ethics is presented. This overcoming is realized in the form of a theological reconstruction of the concept of "responsibility." Barth tries to demonstrate here that God's command must be understood as the founding structure (actually, the founding process) of the realization of human responsibility, which must itself be understood as the embodiment of free human personal existence.[25] It is exactly this identification of the divine command as the basis of autonomous human life that we can rightly call the kenotic structure of Barth's ethics. We could also call it Barth's theological version of a transcendental theory of human acting, a theory whose purpose is to overcome Kant. Its key operative idea is an analysis of the meaning of *decision*. The argumentation proceeds as follows:

The Sovereignty of the Divine Decision

God's command is not only "a claim [*Anspruch*] on men, the divine command is a statement [*Ausspruch*] about him" (631). The German term *Ausspruch* means "statement" in the sense of "explication," which makes the reference to the "content" (632) (of the divine command) clearer. However, as a divine explication, it is not only a passive or theoretical description, "it [rather] moves and changes, marks and qualifies him" (631–62) actively. In contrast to all other (relative) claims, the divine command moves and changes "man in his innermost self" (631). It would not be divine (absolute) if it were not to do so; it leaves no room for an arbitrary freedom of obeying or not obeying. "In virtue of its distinctive [*einzigartig*; better: "unique"] validity it so concerns man that by this claim he in some way becomes a different man from what he would be without it" (631). Barth refers to this transforming (performative) aspect of the divine description of the human being as "God's decision concerning us" (633). It is the decision of God's self-revelation in Jesus Christ in favor of us, the decision of grace.

Thus, in Barth's use of the term, a decision is not simply the definite result of consideration but also its actual execution as "willing and acting" (632). In other words, a decision includes the execution of the act itself. Given its characteristics as a "claim" and its "content" (proposition), this act is a speech-act. It has the twofold structure of acting and interpreting itself. As such it is acting (and speaking) addressed to someone; it is "God's decision concerning us" (633).

It is essential to Barth's argumentation that it states the analogical structure existing between the decisions for God's acting and those for human acting, for this structure grounds the human conduct of life in general. Barth writes, "'We' are the men who stand before God as creatures, who for their part exist in willing and acting, in the venture of a series of decisions which is as long or

---

25. It is here, in the first chapter of §38, where Barth's central proposition is presented: "The idea of responsibility, rightly understood, is known only to Christian ethics" (642).

short as our temporal life" (632). Thus, he continues, "The claim of the divine command is concerned with these decisions both as a whole and in detail. It is in these decisions that we give our witness to the fact that we belong to God" (632). Our human decisions (as the speech-acts core to our human acts) contain an explicit or implicit reference to the (speech-)acts of God concerning us: "Whatever may be our attitude to Him, because it is our attitude to Him, it always includes in itself a definite attitude on the part of God to us" (633).

This—in fact very remarkable—assertation of an inclusion of God's decision in ours is the essential point in Barth's entire argumentation. It states that, despite our knowledge or our ignorance, personal human acting always includes (presupposes and demands) God's gracious decision upon us. In this respect, Barth can even say: "In some sense it is itself the realization of this divine attitude. In our attitude and conduct we emerge always as those who are known by God as He gives us His command" (633). It is this structure of implicit (or explicit) reference to the divine decision that pertains to all human acts or decisions that can be called their responsive (sub)structure, the structure of responsibility.[26] Our decisions are good and free insofar they reflect (the knowledge of) their dependence upon the divine decision concerning us (which is God's graceful acting upon us).[27]

To put it philosophically, human decisions (and acts) are good insofar as they reflect the knowledge that the absolute (of practical reason) is not merely a human idea, construction, or demand (the categorical imperative) but a (divine) reality (and its graceful acting upon us), which we (must and do) always presuppose while acting autonomously and responsibly (which are the same). Barth notes, "The obligation revealed and grounded in the person and work and lordship of Jesus Christ fulfils the idea in all its strictness. It is a categorical imperative, not merely in name, but in fact. And as such—unlike the Kantian imperative—it reveals the fact that to obey it is not merely the highest duty but also the highest good" (652). In other

---

26. Barth writes: "It is the idea of responsibility which gives us the most exact definition of the human situation in face of the absolute transcendence of the divine judgment. We live in responsibility, which means that our being and willing, what we do and what we do not do, is a continuous answer to the Word of God spoken to us as a command. It takes place always in a relationship to the norm which confronts and transcends us in the divine command" (641).

27. For Barth, "It does not really affect the freedom of our own decisions. It is our own free decisions whose character God decides even as we ourselves make them. It is they which are claimed and measured by His command. It is the use of our freedom which is subjected to the prior divine decision" (633–34).

words, there is no free, autonomous responsible acting without trust in the accommodating grace of forgiveness. Therefore, Barth observes: "The idea of responsibility, rightly understood, is known only to Christian ethics. This alone teaches a true and proper confrontation of man" (642).

The true reason for this far-reaching philosophical claim is nothing other than the kenotic structure of Barth's ethics. To put it theologically, it is the precise content of God's decision to divest himself in the decisions of human beings. "The Christ . . . being in the form of God did not regard equality with God as spoil,"[28] but delivered himself to the predators. This exactly is "the sovereignty of the divine decision." According to Barth, it and it alone is able to explicate the binding character of ethics: "Every non-Christian view of human life, i.e., every view which does not have a christological basis, will betray itself as such by the fact that while it may perhaps arrive at the idea of a certain claim upon man—although without making clear how or why it is binding—it will not attain to the idea of true and proper responsibility and therefore the conception of the uninterrupted responsibility in which we stand" (642). For this reason—the implicit philosophical character of his theological argument—Barth can postulate that "Christian ethics itself cannot limit its validity to Christians only, i.e., to those who are aware that their life is essentially and objectively a life in responsibility" (643).

To summarize, it is specifically the "definiteness of the divine decision" (661) that actually bears the claim of outperforming the abstract character of a categorical imperative in Kant's sense.

The Definiteness of the Divine Decision

In order to expose the distinctness and objectivity of God's command as a divine decision and the respective effects on the structure of human responsibility,[29] Barth refers to a specific implication of the sovereignty of God's decision: its total inclusion of all acts of human life—in Kantian or Hegelian wording, its generality.[30] This generality can be understood as the power

28. Karl Barth, *The Epistle to the Philippians*, 60.

29. Barth posits that "The conception of the divine decision, and the corresponding conception of human responsibility to it, must now be particularly considered from the standpoint that the divine Word is given to us, and that it is concretely filled out, that it is given with a definite and specific content" (661).

30. For Barth, "That God is gracious to us in Jesus Christ means a total divine claim to our obedience and a total decision concerning good and evil in the choice of our decisions" (662).

to determine every single act in human life. God's command is "*mandatum concretum* or rather *concretissimum*" (662).

Again this is meant as a criticism of Kant and his categorical imperative. Barth argues: "The categorical imperative as such will never be a command. It can become this only when we receive, not this formula, but a real imperative—distinguished by the fact that it corresponds to the formula—and we bow or do not bow before this real imperative—but not the formula" (666–67). It should be noted that Barth argues here (in a quite long section [666–68]) as a philosopher! His philosophical argument is that as a general rule of judging, the categorical imperative does not present an intrinsic aspect of acting or deciding but an instrument of evaluating future or past acts: "it is not yet a command, but at best only a perspicuous discussion and description of the command" (667). In its generality, Barth argues, the categorical imperative leaves space for interpretation. Capturing this space, the interpreter acts (in Barth's eyes) as an observer evaluating his own past or future (realized or potential) acts. In such moments, he does not act as an agent but as a spectator (of himself). To abolish any evaluative distance from the inner circle of ethical obligation and moral acting, Barth declares: "It [the divine command as the only real, true command] does not need any interpretation, for even to the smallest details it is self-interpreting" (665).

What Barth is arguing for is a theological version of what we nowadays would call moral realism, but in its most specific and most situational version. For Barth this absolute ethical concretism is necessary to expose God's demand as a demand in the logical, intrinsic sense of the word: "An 'I' which is distinct from and confronts my own I is quite indispensable to the concept of the command" (667). It is noteworthy that Barth argues here with the intrinsic semantic logic of the concept of command—in general![31] His idea is that a command (in general) is only a command that is definitely binding if the one who utters it is, first, another person that, second, possesses an authority of binding force. The embodiment of such a person—that is, the embodiment of such a command in its genuine sense—can only be God as absolute otherness, absolute subjectivity.

The problem with this theological argument based on the logic of semantics is twofold. First, the reference to God as absolute otherness or

---

31. The English translation "concept of the command" is a literal reproduction of the German "Begriff des Gebotes"—see Karl Barth, *Kirchliche Dogmatik* II/2 (Zurich: Theologischer Verlag, 1980), 744. Nevertheless, it is misleading: "*Begriff des Gebotes*" means "concept of command," and the definite article *the* does not refer—as the context shows—to the specific command of God. If it did, the argument would be lost.

an absolute authority does not reflect the christological—or precisely, the kenotic—structure of divine otherness; second, the argument pushes Barth into declaring an ethical concretism and absolutism, which, taken literally, should have quite odd consequences: either a rough biblicism or a theopneumatic decisionism in material ethics, which would potentially block all the criteriological effects of the foundations of material ethics. In fact, in respect of the latter, Barth's general actualistic, ontological reservation of God's free acting beyond all human ethical and theological conceptions of it does indeed leave space for precisely such consequences. Nevertheless, a close reading of Barth's material ethics in the context of the doctrine of creation in volume III/4 of *Church Dogmatics* or in the context of the partial ethics of reconciliation in volume IV/4 would show that Barth's procedure there is analogous to what is practiced in volume II/2: Barth's material ethics can thus be understood as a reflected theory of theological judgment along the lines of the foundations laid out in his general ethics.

Similar observations can be made regarding the former, the supposed biblicism. Barth states "two facts: (1) that the divine law in the Bible is always a concrete command; and (2) that this concrete commanding to be found in the Bible must be understood as a divine command relevant to ourselves who are not directly addressed by it" (672). Nevertheless, the seemingly postulated concretism of ethics is rather to be understood as a theological postulate that does not in fact legitimate a rough biblicism or a rough spiritualism of ethics. Barth writes: "This Lord in the fulfilment of His work is Himself the divine command. And by the very fact that He is the divine command, the latter is concrete and specific and relevant to every moment and action of every human life. Therefore the Bible is the source and norm and judge of all ethical disciplines, not as a pack of cards, not as it is divided and dissolved into a multiplicity of timeless revelations of the divine will unrelated to history, but in the historical unity of its content" (705).

In this paragraph, however, which contains the acme of the methodological kenoticism of Barth's ethics, a systematic problem actually emerges. There is, ultimately, at least an imbalance between the postulated intrinsic objectivity of biblical commands, the postulated relevance of these commands for each individual today, and the unavoidable individual interpretations—in their diversity and disharmony—of divine commands mediated by the Bible. This would indicate a deficiency of Barth's claim to base the process of responsible individual moral judgments on theological grounds. In other words, one might ask: what is the value of God's self-delivery in human flesh if this self-delivery remains separate from the sphere of fallible attempts at ethical decision making? These questions should be addressed in the chapter in which the pneumatological aspect of divine decision is reflected. This is the subject of the last section.

The Goodness of the Divine Decision

To present the pneumatological dimension of divine decisions, Barth uses the concept of goodness. Allow me to interpret Barth's basic formulation with interjected commentaries:

> The goodness [quality or effect on us] of the divine command is some-
> thing universal [the aspect of the Father]; the universal truth and validity
> of God in this specific relationship [the aspect of the Son]. That God is
> kind in His commanding and forbidding is always and everywhere im-
> portant for every man in every situation [the aspect of the Holy Ghost]
> because in this truth [epistemological dimension] consists the inalien-
> able and unchangeable substance of all His commanding and forbidding,
> because His goodness is His very essence [divinity of the Holy Spirit!].
> Because God is rich in His goodness [interior trinitarian mediation], His
> commanding and forbidding are not uniform [the aspect of the Father in
> a negative connotation], but particular [the aspect of the Son!; remem-
> ber: decision is itself the Christological aspect of divine command], and
> therefore [!] so manifold [pneumatological aspect]. (710)

On this basis, we can expect that Barth will prove the proposition that the goodness of the divine command consists in its inherent ability to ground and illuminate any individual ethical truth seeking and therefore also prove the essential plurality of such attempts. Does he actually do this? Partially! Actually, the main priorities set here are slightly different and stand in fact in a certain tension to the quoted proposition. The chapter has a transparent threefold structure.

First, the universal (Father) aspect (of this pneumatological dimension of divine decision) runs like this: "Because God and His command are good in this full sense of the term, the divine will may not be atomised, as though in the last resort it consisted in, or could be resolved into, the fact that different men in their different times and situations received specific divine intimations; as though it could be related closely, and even identified with the needs and urges and instincts of the individual life" (711–12). "Atomizing" had been a key, widespread antiliberal term in conservative social philosophy since at least the 1920s. Barth used it in his commentary on Romans;[32] in 1942 it is still present.

Second, Barth writes: "Because the command of God is good, this means that, in spite of all the diversity of its claims on men it unites them. . . . Moral fellowship can and will arise where people see and know that they are in the same situation and in the same ground to the extent that they recognize themselves to be placed under the sovereign and definite decision of God" (716). The Son aspect also stresses the unifying, anti-individualistic aspect of morality resulting from the divine command. The English "moral fellowship" leaves even more space for internal diversity than the German "*sittliche Gemeinschaft*." What about the moment of particularity (of difference, of alteration, of criticism, etc.), which could be expected here? Why does Barth not at least emphasize that an attribute and criterion of the legitimacy of the Christian community is its potential to integrate—and thereby affirm—individual differences? Without referring to this, how can Barth state that the "Christian fellowship is the essence of all fellowship" (724)?

Third, Barth states: "Finally, because the command of God is good, it unifies each individual man in himself. At this point too—and supremely—there is the threat of contradiction, conflict and chaos. It is because man is not at one in himself that we are not at one with each other. It is because inner consistency and continuity are lacking in the life of the individual that there is no fellowship among men" (726–27). "Well roared, lion!" we might say. The intrinsic unification of each individual may rightly be understood as a result of the healing quality of God's command. However, again the emphasizing of "inner consistency and continuity . . . in the life of the individual" sounds one-sided and lacking in complexity. What about the right to become a different person (Dorothee Soelle)? What about Bonhoeffer's sensitivity for the brokenness and fragility of modern biographies? Would such sensitivity not fit better in a kenotic interpretation of the divine command than the proclamation of an unbroken continuity of the kind that Bonhoeffer connected to the experience of the generations of the nineteenth-century bourgeoisie?[33]

An Outlook

For reasons of limited space, we have to stop our close reading of Barth's kenotic ethics at this point. We have to abstain from an analogue interpre-

---

32. See Barth, *Epistle to the Romans*, 53.
33. See Dietrich Bonhoeffer, *Widerstand und Ergebung: Briefe und Aufzeichnungen aus der Haft*, ed. Eberhard Bethge, 11th ed. (Munich: Chr. Kaiser, 1980), 149.

tation of the third, pneumatological aspect of divine command, to which Barth refers by the concept of the "judgment of God" (§39, 733). To abstain from this interpretation is a pity in so far as this paragraph would show how Barth uses this aspect—as is often the case in pneumatological sections of *Church Dogmatics*—for a critical self-relativization of the discourse presented before. The judgment of God is also a judgment about theological discourse itself! For example, Barth writes there: "In place of every weak theory of our relationship to God and to His command there comes the powerful theory of this practice—the theory of our actual relationship to God. And in place of the weak self-judgment in which we cause ourselves to be exculpated there comes the powerful self-judgment in which we must and will declare that we are guilty, because we ourselves, as the sinners we are, can only repeat the divine sentence, adding to it not at all either for good or evil" (750). A close reading of this paragraph would actually show how Barth overturns (in the Hegelian sense of suspending [*aufheben*]) the theoretical theological discourse into a religious (my word, of course) speech-act. For good reasons, the last words of the pneumatological chapter of this pneumatological paragraph in Barth's foundational theory of ethics are the exclamation: "Veni Creator Spiritus!" (781). The knowledge that we cannot even utter this cry without the help of this "Creator Spiritus" is the theological signature of our kenotic existence.

13

Kenosis and the Mutuality of God

Cambria Kaltwasser

Virtually whenever the doctrine of kenosis is invoked today by pastors, Christian educators, or theologians, it is used to answer the conundrum of how an almighty and omniscient God can become the subject of a finite human life without overwhelming and either partially or fully annihilating it.[1] Indeed, this is why I mention kenosis exactly once per semester to my undergraduate students, whose assumptions about Jesus are still basically docetic. Some account of God's self-emptying seems necessary for them to begin to grapple with all that is entailed in the affirmation that Jesus grew "in wisdom and in years, and in divine and human favor."[2] Kenosis offers an enticing, if all-too-easy, safeguard for the integrity of Jesus's full humanity.

Detractors of this theological framework have pointed out the myriad inconsistencies involved in thinking of God as "giving up" divine attributes,

---

1. Sometimes the term kenosis is applied more generally, to speak of the many ways in which God adopts limitations in order to work within God's finite creation. In these instances, the problem of the integrity of the created order is seen as parallel to the christological conundrum named above. See *The Work of Love: Creation as Kenōsis*, ed. John Polkinghorne (Grand Rapids: Eerdmans, 2001). Within this volume, Sarah Coakley's comments on these "generalized approaches" are particularly insightful. See Coakley, "Kenosis: Theological Meanings and Gender Connotations," in *The Work of Love*, 192–210, 200–203.

2. Luke 2:52 (NRSV).

whether they be "essential" or "nonessential."[3] This concept seems to imply a transformation in God that compromises divine integrity, or, worse, challenges the gospel affirmation that in Jesus Christ we have to do with the very fullness of God.

A second strand of criticism has arisen among feminist theologians in recent decades. They worry that God's supposed self-emptying is a destructive model for the Christian life, in so far as it encourages women to sacrifice themselves on the altar of service to others.[4] While kenosis may be a fitting model for men, it is a damaging exemplar for those already lacking in power and privilege.

Notice that these perspectives merge over their respect for the integrity of a moral agent, whether it be Jesus, God, or humanity at large. Critics of modern kenoticism ask how a Christ emptied of divine prerogatives can be the self-same God whom Christians worship as Creator and Lord. Feminists ask, in parallel, how Christians can obey Paul's exhortation to "let the same mind be in you"[5] without losing themselves in the process. Meanwhile, the very aim of the modern conception of kenosis has been to safeguard the human agency of Jesus from domination by the divine personality. Is the man Jesus no more than an object commandeered by God? Finally, these concerns are not unrelated, I suggest, to worries regarding the status of the human covenant partner in relation to God. Can the Christian life itself be perceived as a form of domination of the individual by God?

How can we understand both God's self-humiliation in Jesus Christ and God's ongoing relation with us as empowering rather than overpowering or manipulative? In examining these perennial christological conundrums with the themes of agency and domination in mind, it becomes clear that the concept of kenosis is by no means immune from danger. The correction must consist, not only in tracing kenosis back to the inner being of God and to something essential to the human person as such, but also in redescribing kenosis less violently.

---

3. Bruce McCormack offers a succinct summary of this debate in "Kenoticism in Modern Christology," in *The Oxford Handbook of Christology*, ed. Francesca Murphy (Oxford: Oxford University Press, 2018), 444–58, especially 451–54.

4. This worry is traced and addressed by Sarah Coakley in "'*Kenōsis* and Subversion': On the Repression of 'Vulnerability' in Christian Feminist Writing," in *Powers and Submissions: Spirituality, Philosophy, and Gender* (Oxford: Blackwell, 2002), 3–39. For a constructive proposal addressing these concerns, see Aristotle Papanikolaou, "Person, Kenōsis and Abuse: Hans Urs Von Balthasar and Feminist Theologies in Conversation," *Modern Theology* 19, no. 1 (2003): 41–65.

5. Phil 2:5 (NRSV).

In what follows, I begin by turning to Sarah Coakley for help in bringing to light the ways that agential integrity and power dynamics show up in the history of kenotic theology. Latching onto the insight of Bruce McCormack that the Son's kenosis ought to be conceived of as a receptivity toward the life of the man Jesus, I suggest a model of kenosis as reciprocity or shared life, a model whose implications move beyond Christology into our shared life with God in Christ. In the process, I seek to answer the following questions: What portrait of Jesus's life results from this understanding of Christology, one in which Christ comes not to dominate but to share in our life? What portrait of God results from this Christology and the interdependence of Jesus and his fellows that is part and parcel with it? Finally, are there any ongoing consequences for the God who wills to share our life in this way? Drawing from Karl Barth, I highlight two different "kenotic" moments that are intrinsic to this new understanding: Jesus's reciprocity with his fellows and God's reciprocity with us as we pray.

Sarah Coakley on Kenosis, Power, and Vulnerability

The theological debate over kenosis presents us with real questions about how God can share life with us while safeguarding the integrity of both divine and human agents. By tracing the ways that this worry over intelligible agency arises such that kenosis has been named both an antidote and a culprit, we can clarify one of the central stakes of a debate that bears upon our doctrines of God, Christ, and humanity.

Coakley frames her historical investigation of the doctrine of kenosis as an intervention in the discordant usage of the term by modern feminists.[6] At issue is whether the act of self-emptying should be lauded as an appropriate check on masculinist power or disdained as a form of masculine compensation inappropriate for women. Coakley shows that criticisms such as the latter do not latch on to every version of kenosis. In her exacting analysis of the history of the doctrine, she presents evidence that kenosis has never meant just one thing, and that its various associations are at times completely at odds.[7] Yet Coakley's deeper motivation is to recover a useful model of power-in-vulnerability that she believes lies at the heart of Christology: "Here, if anywhere, Christian feminism has something corrective to offer

---

6. Coakley, "'*Kenōsis* and Subversion,'" 4.

7. Coakley identifies no fewer than six different versions of kenosis in the history of biblical and theological reflection. Coakley, "'*Kenōsis* and Subversion,'" see especially 11, 14, 19.

secular feminism."[8] Her feminist analysis of different versions of kenosis illumines the various power deformations at work. Of these, I highlight only two: the overt compensatory guilt of modern kenoticism and the docetic tendency of Alexandrian Christology.

The feminist worry about inappropriate models of self-abnegation finds its target in the modern version of the doctrine first put forth by late-nineteenth-century Lutheran theologian Gottfried Thomasius. This is the first version of kenosis to posit that in the incarnation God the eternal Son temporarily sets aside certain divine attributes.[9] Aside from the logical difficulties this theory raises (Is there such a thing as a nonessential attribute of God? Divested of certain traits, does God remain fully God?), the idea of self-limitation rightly raises worries that the Christian life directs us toward self-neglect or abnegation. Perhaps this model is appropriate only for men, who can "afford to seek some compensatory 'loss.'"[10] The latter objection gains even more credibility when Coakley examines the metaphors employed by subsequent British kenoticists, replete with sexist and classist assumptions.[11] For Coakley, whether or not these metaphors render the Son's kenosis logically coherent is not the only matter of importance. At issue is how the power dynamics implicit in these metaphors lay bare our assumptions about God's manner of relating to us, in this case, doing little to assuage our worry that divine condescension is really a covert exercise of privilege, rather than its relinquishment.

The kenosis of Alexandrian Christology, while immune from the charge of glorifying self-abnegation, is no better than modern iterations from a feminist outlook. For, whereas the Alexandrian account never contemplated a divestment of power on the part of God, it tended to make an object of Jesus's human nature.[12] For Cyril, kenosis entails God's self-subjection to

8. Coakley, "'*Kenōsis* and Subversion,'" 4.
9. Coakley, "'*Kenōsis* and Subversion,'" 19.
10. Coakley, "'*Kenōsis* and Subversion,'" 20.
11. It is a parade of classist, largely Eurocentric tropes that include "an African king," the son of a commanding officer (see F. Weston, *The One Christ* [London: Longmans Green, 1914], 166–87); a sultan, a concert violinist, and a "promising philosophy student" (see P. T. Forsyth, *The Person and Place of Jesus Christ* [London: Hodder & Stoughton, 1909], 296–300). Coakley, "'*Kenōsis* and Subversion,'" 20–22.
12. McCormack registers a similar worry when speaking of the "instrumentalization" of Jesus's humanity by the Logos. See McCormack, "Karl Barth's Christology as a Resource for a Reformed Version of Kenoticism," *International Journal of Systematic Theology* 8, no. 3 (2006): 250. McCormack points out that the dilemma stems from the patristic commitment to divine impassibility, a topic about which Coakley remains curiously silent (248n4).

the conditions of humanity, while in no way impairing anything proper to God. Suffering is experienced by the Son of God only indirectly, according to his human nature,[13] and only in a highly controlled manner. Coakley draws attention to the highly managed nature of Christ's human affections in Cyril's account. According to Cyril, at "times" Christ "*permitted* his own flesh to experience its proper affections [and] *permitted* [his human] soul to experience its proper affections."[14] Coakley interprets this handling of Jesus's human nature by the Logos in the language of domination:

> The spectre raised here of a divine force that takes on humanity by controlling and partly obliterating it (all, seductively, in the name of *kenōsis*) is thus the issue that should properly concern us where the further outworkings of the "Alexandrian" tradition are concerned: it is a matter of how divine "power" is construed in relation to the human, and how this could insidiously fuel masculinist purposes, masculinist visions of the subduing of the weaker by the stronger.[15]

The question of whether or in what sense it is fitting for God to "use" Jesus's humanity opens up a number of complex theological questions. For our purposes it is enough to recognize that there is something unseemly about God commandeering Jesus's humanity, allowing it to exercise its ordinary functions only at "times," while remaining sealed off from it. For Coakley, these descriptions "hover . . . uncomfortably close" to docetism, a suspicion that only deepens with the addition of John of Damascus's eighth-century stipulation that the communication of attributes flows in only one direction (from Christ's divine to his human nature).

As Coakley's analysis has helped to clarify, in each of the versions of kenoticism examined above, problems of coherency lie close at hand. Moreover, while the problems are unique to each specific version of keno-

13. Cyril compared the relationship between the Logos and his human nature to the relationship between a human soul and body. He suggests that just as the soul can be said to suffer what the body suffers, so can the Logos be said to suffer what the man Jesus suffers. This metaphor made sense of Cyril's more paradoxical statements about Christ's suffering, since, according to Frances Young, at the time the soul was thought to be impassible. Frances M. Young and Paul Parvis, *From Nicaea to Chalcedon: A Guide to the Literature and Its Background* (London: Hymns Ancient & Modern, 2009), 318. If the soul's impassibility is called into question, however, as was inevitable in the modern period, this metaphor no longer serves to immunize the Logos against the sufferings of Christ.

14. Cyril, *De recta fide ad Augustus* 2.55, quoted in Coakley, "'*Kenōsis* and Subversion,'" 15, Coakley's emphasis.

15. Coakley, "'*Kenōsis* and Subversion,'" 15–16.

sis, in both cases, the threat of domination menaces. With regard to modern kenoticism, the threat is two-sided. On the one hand, as Coakley has shown, the concept of divine divestment has spurred a number of more or less thinly veiled sexist and classist tropes wherein "kenosis" serves more to mask privilege than to bestow it. On the other hand, to the extent that God surrenders God's identity in the incarnation, not only is such self-emptying of questionable worth to the human partner, it also presents an unhealthy model of self-abnegation that makes an easy tool for the domination of the weak at the hands of the powerful. With regard to Alexandrian Christology, although we cannot speak of two "subjects" of the incarnation, it nonetheless seems appropriate to describe the instrumentalization of Jesus's human nature by the Logos as a kind of domination, or, at least, as an objectification that smacks of the manipulation of other human subjects. Here it is questionable whether Jesus's humanity makes a contribution to the atonement, or whether it is something like a prop serving as a kind of object lesson by God the Son. The question arises here: In what sense does God become the subject of a truly human life?

For her own part, Coakley is less optimistic about the prospect of ascribing a form of kenosis to the divine Logos and more interested in ascribing it to the human Christ, where it can achieve greater resonance for feminist ethics today, offering "a vision of christological *kenōsis* uniting human 'vulnerability' with authentic divine power (as opposed to worldly or 'patriarchal' visions of power) and uniting them such that the human was wholly translucent to the divine."[16] This form of human surrender ought not to be seen as exemplary only for men. Coakley suggests that the way to theological tropes that are wide enough to include the flourishing of women (and not only women, but persons of color, the poor, and anyone on the losing side of power) is not to reverse the current by giving women a license to acquire (masculinist) power and men an obligation to relinquish it, but rather "via a reformulation of the

---

16. Coakley appeals to the New Testament literature that sees any suggestion of divine self-divestment as anachronistically applied to Philippians 2. More importantly, she is wary of the logical inconsistencies that arise from speculation about the Son's self-emptying, and moreover worried about the possible losses incurred for the classical doctrine of God. She suggests that the conundrums surrounding the *communicatio idiomata* can best be avoided by doubling back to the Antiochene Christology wherein the person of the union is confected from both human and divine natures, and not to be identified with the Logos simpliciter. Coakley, "'*Kenōsis* and Subversion,'" 18. Coakley credits the Giessen Lutheran school of the seventeenth century with this proposal.

very notion of divine 'power' and its relation to the human."[17] Whereas Coakley addresses this power dynamic from the human side only, in what follows, I take up the task with regard to God's exercise of power.

Bruce McCormack on the Receptivity of God the Son

Coakley's interest in the dynamics of divine and human power in the incarnation may initially seem a uniquely feminist concern. On closer examination, however, her analysis highlights tensions long present in the debate over the meaning of kenosis. This becomes all the clearer when we shift our attention to the systematic register. The resonance between Coakley's worry and that of Bruce McCormack, although his is more dogmatic than ethical, reveals once more the interrelation between Christology and ethics.

McCormack is concerned with the intelligibility of the incarnation and of our affirmation that God in Christ shared our suffering. He chronicles the history of kenosis from its interpretation by the church fathers up through its modern reformulations, highlighting how the tradition has been hamstrung by its unwillingness to ascribe suffering to God.[18] McCormack argues that, under the pressure of the doctrine of divine impassibility, orthodox Christology tended to treat the human nature of Jesus as an instrument of the Logos, a subject in its own right that could be made a buffer between God the Son and Jesus's human passions.[19] This claim parallels Coakley's ascription of a quasi-docetism to Alexandrian Christology. Their concerns, while ostensibly different—McCormack is concerned with the intelligibility of the incarnation and Coakley with the proper disposition of human creatures vis-à-vis God and one another—are united by an underlying concern for the integrity of the human person. Both wish to rule out the possibility that at decisive moments Jesus's humanity is merely an instrument or object of God's.

McCormack's aim is to articulate a version of divine kenoticism that avoids the problematic suggestions of divine divestment but still speaks to the suffering of God. He follows the tradition in saying that this must be a kenosis by addition, but he declines from sealing off the being of God from the experience of Jesus's human weakness, suffering, and death. McCormack proposes instead a kenosis of "complete and total receptivity toward

17. Coakley, "'*Kenōsis* and Subversion,'" 22.
18. McCormack, "Karl Barth's Christology as a Resource," and "Kenoticism in Modern Christology."
19. McCormack, "Karl Barth's Christology as a Resource," 248n4.

everything that comes to [the Logos] through his human nature."[20] Mc-Cormack's proposal addresses Coakley's concern that God not parody the human covenant partner by taking up a human nature only to control and partly obliterate it from the position of security. Just where Coakley shifts her attention to our "receptivity" to the divine life, McCormack speaks of God the Son's "receptivity" to the human Jesus.

What does this receptivity in God imply about the necessary reformulation of divine power to which Coakley alluded? How can it escape the vicious pendulum swing of masculinist power passing over to compensatory guilt and loss? McCormack is clear, with Barth, that kenosis represents no self-abnegation on the part of God. In order to suffice as an account of divine power that makes space for human agency, however, there must also be a correlative activation of the human partner. How might we think of God's self-emptying not as disempowerment but as empowerment of God's human covenant partners? I suggest that to such "receptivity" there be added an account of the ongoing *reciprocity* between God and God's human covenant partners. Indeed, Barth gives us the beginnings of just such a picture.

Karl Barth on Jesus's Reciprocity with His Fellows

For a portrait of the incarnation that assumes a form neither of patriarchal domination nor of compensatory self-abnegation, I turn to Barth's portrait of Jesus's humanity, embedded within his doctrine of creation. In taking up this question, I necessarily take for granted moves that Barth makes elsewhere regarding Jesus as the self-revelation of God. In his doctrine of reconciliation, Barth's basic move is to insist that God does not abandon Godself in the act of becoming humble: Instead, "the *kenōsis* consists in a renunciation of His being in the form of God alone."[21] God can be God in both glory and humility precisely because humility is already an attribute of the triune God in the eternal obedience of the Son. Barth's doctrine of humanity, with Jesus as the prototype for humanity, is not the place to find Barth's technical solution to the problem of how God can take on a finite human life without compromising Godself. Here, we see rather Barth's understanding of the *consequences* of that decision—for Jesus, in particular, but also for the triune God. Specifically, it gives us the beginnings of a description of the shared agency in which

20. McCormack, "Karl Barth's Christology as a Resource," 249.

21. Karl Barth, *Church Dogmatics*, IV/1, ed. G. W. Bromiley and T. F. Torrance, trans. G. W. Bromiley (Edinburgh: T&T Clark, 1956), 180.

God wills humanity to participate. In *Church Dogmatics* III/2 Barth offers an account of Jesus's mutuality with other human beings that is highly suggestive for rethinking God's exercise of power in the act of incarnation.[22]

Here, Barth presents Jesus's humanity both as the "concrete correlative" of his divine mission and as the fullness of what God intended humanity to be.[23] In paragraph 45.1, Barth's concern is to show that Jesus's humanity (and therefore ours) is a fellow-humanity (*Mitmenschlichkeit*)—that, in fact, it is Jesus's relationships with others that make his humanity what it is. Here we get a portrait of what power in responsibility—what reciprocity—looks like. Barth speaks of the man Jesus as not only determinative of the existence of all others, but also, in some profound sense, *determined by* them.

The radicality of Barth's description of Jesus's dependency was not lost on the students in my undergraduate theology course. In a recent discussion of this section, the designated discussion leader paused over the statement that Jesus "is pleased to be called by [his neighbors] to His own life, to be given the meaning of His life by them."[24] Had not Barth taken his description of Christ's solidarity with us a step too far, he wondered. Should it have been enough to say that Jesus's *love* for his fellow human beings made his life what it was? Instead, Barth seemed to place Jesus's identity in the hands of others. In what sense is Jesus "determined by" or "given the meaning of his life by" his fellows?[25] Is Jesus's identity tenuously tethered to human agents such that his mission hangs, willy-nilly, at their whim? Has Jesus, in fact, given himself away? Or, alternatively, are these phrases merely another way of describing Jesus's unilateral saving action on our behalf, action taken without us and for us? In what sense is the man Jesus really determined by his fellows?

---

22. Karl Barth, *Church Dogmatics* III/2, ed. G. W. Bromiley and T. F. Torrance, trans. Harold Knight et al. (Edinburgh: T&T Clark, 1960), §45, "Jesus: Human Being for Other Human Beings" (translation revised). I could well have turned to *Church Dogmatics* IV for a more conceptual treatment of the Son's relationship to Jesus's humanity. I did not do so for a couple of reasons, the first being that Bruce McCormack has taken up this material to that end in much more depth and rigor than I could possibly do here. See McCormack, *The Humility of the Eternal Son: Reformed Kenoticism and the Repair of Chalcedon* (Cambridge: Cambridge University Press, 2021). The second reason is my conviction that a certain clarity is achieved regarding these conceptual relationships by turning to descriptions of the concrete enactment of Jesus's humanity. Ultimately, this move reflects my conviction that God's tangible manner of relating to us in Jesus Christ (and in the ordinary activities of the Christian life) is the litmus test for these conceptual relationships.

23. Barth, *Church Dogmatics* III/2:210.

24. Barth, *Church Dogmatics* III/2:215.

25. Barth, *Church Dogmatics* III/2:216.

Barth suggests that in order to be able to make our cause his own, Jesus had to be like us in respect of our reliance on each other. Because Jesus's life is *pro nobis* from beginning to end, this mutuality was the case at every moment of his life, and not only when he deemed to take it up: "He is originally and properly the Word of God to men, and therefore His orientation to others and *reciprocal relationship* with them are not accidental, external or subsequent, but primary, internal and necessary."[26] From the beginning, then, the Son's solidarity with us entails entering into reciprocity with us. Whatever else this means, it cannot be that Jesus engaged us only unilaterally, acting upon our humanity while himself remaining untouched by it. What sort of reciprocity, then, does Barth see at work in the life of God incarnate that might reframe our whole understanding of divine power?

To begin with, Barth draws upon the many instances in Scripture where Jesus is described as *affected* by his fellow human beings. Barth names the many times in the Gospels when Jesus reacts with emotion to the plight of his fellows. Jesus is frequently said to have "had pity," wherein "the suffering and sin and abandonment and peril of these men not merely went to the heart of Jesus but right into His heart, into Himself, so that their whole plight was now His own, and as such He saw and suffered it far more keenly than they did."[27] In illuminating contrast to Cyril's sense that Christ gave permission in time to the spiritual and bodily affections of his human nature, Barth explicitly states that Christ's affections are aroused by his fellows without any anticipation on his part:

> There is not in Him a kind of deep, inner, secret recess in which He is alone in Himself or with God, existing in stoical calm or mystic rapture apart from His fellows, untouched by their state or fate. He has no such place of rest. He is immediately and directly affected by the existence of His fellows. His relationship to His neighbours and sympathy with them are original and proper to Him and therefore belong to His innermost being. They are not a new duty and virtue which can begin and end, but He Himself is human, and it is for this reason that He acts as He does.[28]

Barth would likely agree with Cyril when it comes to the integrity of the Son's original choice to humble himself. Barth insists that Jesus's humilia-

26. Barth, *Church Dogmatics* III/2:210, emphasis added.
27. Barth, *Church Dogmatics* III/2:211.
28. Barth, *Church Dogmatics* III/2:211.

tion is an offering and not a fate suffered.[29] The question here, however, is about the existence of a divine consciousness hovering over the earthly life of Jesus, giving or withholding its assent to human emotions and physical reactions as they arise. When it comes to Jesus's sympathy toward us, Barth is explicit that the Son's original choice to unite with our flesh means that he participates in all of our human experiences. He stands at no remove from these experiences. In fact, they are a constitutive part of his mission.

In Barth's terms, the way in which Jesus's fellows affected him was not just in the sense of emotional or physical reactions that arise unbidden. According to Barth, Jesus was also subject to the claims of those around him, particularly as these claims invoked his saving mission. Barth insists, in fact, that Jesus's glory consists in none other than his being "fully claimed and clamped by His fellows."[30]

Barth's description of Jesus's disposition toward his neighbors implies two levels of agency. On the one hand, Jesus is always already *for us*, because as the Son of God he is determined for just this saving mission.[31] On the other hand, as human, he is "immediately and directly affected" by his fellows in time. It is his shared experiences with others that call him again and again to his Father's mission. We see this play out, for instance, when his mother insists he provide wine for wedding guests, when the Canaanite woman requests healing for her daughter, and when the hemorrhaging woman grabs his attention through a tug on his garment.[32] The vast majority of Jesus's healing ministry, in fact, is a matter of his *responding* to the needs and claims of others that confront him unbidden. The fact that in each of these instances it is women in particular—those on the underside of cultural power—who call Jesus to his mission underscores God's willed mutuality with us. God in Christ dignifies human beings by treating them not merely as recipients of grace, but as partners.

The sense in which Jesus Christ is "for us" is not *merely* that he imposed his will to save us, that he accomplished something on our behalf whether we liked it or not. No doubt, God the Son *did* impose his will to save; his mission never hung in the balance. However, he did so in such a way as to

29. Barth, *Church Dogmatics* III/2:214.

30. Barth, *Church Dogmatics* III/2:215.

31. Barth writes: "He is originally and properly the Word of God to men, and therefore His orientation to others and *reciprocal relationship* with them are not accidental, external or subsequent, but primary, internal and necessary," *Church Dogmatics* III/2:210, emphasis added.

32. Matt 15:22–28; John 2:1–11; Mark 5:25–34.

take responsibility for us in our real plight, to be *responsive* to our plight, and so to draw men and women into participation in God's mission. In this concrete, moment-by-moment sense, then, Jesus "is pleased to be called by them to His own life, to be given the meaning of His life by them."[33] In Jesus Christ, God the Son became interdependent on us, not in the sense that he gave himself away, but in the sense that he allowed his earthly life to be co-determined by us and allowed himself to become subject to the claims of his fellows that, in big and little ways, made his mission what it was.

Without this reciprocity, this give and take, the incarnation becomes a form of playacting, with Jesus's humanity a kind of object lesson that is merely performed and does not really engage us. Coakley's designation of "docetism" for this transactional vision of the incarnation is apt. Moreover, if God were to treat Jesus's humanity *only* as an object, then we might have reason to fear that God has similar designs for the Christian life. We might be justified in suspecting that, since it takes place over our heads, salvation barely concerns us. It is the *reciprocity* of the Son of God with us that suggests a more adequate concept of divine power than Coakley found in Alexandrian Christology, because it paves the way forward for a picture of our covenant partnership with God in Christ.

Prayer and the Reciprocity of God

Although Barth does not give us a fully fleshed answer to the question of how the Son's kenosis might reformulate our concept of divine power, his account of Christ's "reciprocity" with us, involving Jesus being "affected," "determined," and "claimed" by us, is highly suggestive for an account of divine power-in-responsibility. Ultimately, the question to be answered is whether there are any ongoing effects of the incarnation, not only on humanity's side, but on God's. Is the history of Jesus Christ a transaction, accomplished and then set aside? If so, this history would lend itself, if not to Coakley's worry about divine domination, then at least to an unwelcome kind of paternalism. The alternative to this transactional version of Christ's work is an account of God's ongoing responsiveness to us.

I argue that Barth gives us the beginnings of an account of divine reciprocity, but that it is not found in the place one might think. It is not found in his doctrine of sanctification or his treatment of Christian love. It is found rather in his doctrine of prayer, pieced out over the *Church Dogmatics* in his

33. Barth, *Church Dogmatics* III/2:215.

doctrines of creation and reconciliation. In this doctrine, Barth gives a fuller and richer account of the mutuality of God's life with us.[34] Jesus's mutuality with us discloses a God who invites our participation in Christ's kingly office. In his doctrine of prayer in *Church Dogmatics* III/3, Barth describes our share in Christ's governance, and in the posthumously published fragment *The Christian Life*, he makes that shared governance a matter of God's allowing and enabling us to co-determine God's actions. God's reciprocity with us poses no threat to God's sovereignty, since God both empowers our prayers and transforms them for the purposes of God's kingdom.

Perhaps the most characteristic feature of Barth's doctrine of prayer is the objective significance Barth attributes to our prayers. Barth refuses to treat prayer as though it were exhausted on the side of human subjectivity. He reserves his strongest criticism for theologies that

> can speak only poetically and not properly of an invocation of God by man, and . . . cannot speak at all of a corresponding hearing on God's side, for this kind of *reciprocity* between God and man, this kind of codetermination of a divine action by a human action . . . is thought to be totally out of keeping with the sovereign nature of God and the absolute dependence upon him of all the reality that is distinct from him.[35]

Barth insists that our prayers have an objective consequence on God's side. Only such an understanding preserves the central fact of prayer as a two-way dialogue between God and God's covenant partners. Because of this realism, Barth's account of prayer holds great significance for our understanding of God's ongoing mutual relationship with us in Jesus Christ. Prayer envisions an irreducible reciprocity between God and God's human partner by grace. As such, it calls into question any picture of divine sovereignty as domination or coercion.

34. I am not intimating that God's sovereignty is in any way limited by what God chooses to share with us. I take it for given that, for Barth, our salvation is accomplished entirely from God's side, that our participation itself is brought about from beginning to end by the work of the Holy Spirit. This is possible because I believe that Barth possesses a noncompetitive understanding of divine and human agency, wherein full human participation poses no challenge to divine sovereignty. What is at issue here is not a curtailment of divine power, but rather a divine inclusion of human action within the exercise of that power.

35. Barth, *The Christian Life* (London: Bloomsbury T&T Clark, 2017), 154–55, emphasis added. In the passage under consideration, Barth has Schleiermacher in mind.

Barth's first foray into the doctrine of prayer is embedded in his doctrine of providence, where he spells out the details of divine *concursus*—God's working in and through human actions. Human action is treated under the headings of faith, obedience and petitionary prayer, but it is only the latter which, according to Barth, gives us a full account of human "co-operation in the doing of the will of God."[36] In other words, here, in the doctrine of prayer, we see the fullest picture of the relationship between divine and human agency. Barth's daring claim in this section is that in prayer, the Christian acquires "a genuine and actual share in the universal lordship of God."[37]

Of course, God works in and through all world events, and, in that general sense, in and through all creatures, to achieve God's purposes. What is unique about the Christian's participation in God's governance, as it is exemplified in prayer, is that she participates in God's rule not just "from without" but "from within, as a creature which not only experiences this rule in practice but perceives and acknowledges and affirms and approves it, which is in fact thankful for it and wills to cleave and conform to it."[38] In other words, the Christian is the one who is gifted with the knowledge of God's will for the created order, and who is freed to endorse God's will and to make God's will her own.

The concept of co-operation is illumined by Barth's wedding of prayer to friendship with God, a theme he reiterates throughout his doctrine of providence: "In obedience the Christian is the servant, in faith he is the child, but in prayer, as the servant and the child, he is the friend of God, called to the side of God and at the side of God, living and ruling and reigning with Him."[39] In what sense is participation in God's rule by prayer a kind of friendship with God? The implication of this section is that friendship entails partnership toward a common end. Barth's view bears a resemblance to Aquinas's understanding of friendship as mutual well-wishing that involves concord between wills.[40] As Jesus says in John 15:15, "I do not call you servants any longer, because the servant does not know what the master is doing; but I have called you friends, because I have made known to you everything that I have heard from my Father." The intimacy of Christians with God is such that they are, however imperfectly, privy to God's will in a way that the rest

---

36. Barth, *Church Dogmatics* III/3, ed. G. W. Bromiley and T. F. Torrance, trans. G. W. Bromiley and R. J. Ehrlich (Edinburgh: T&T Clark, 1960), 286.

37. Barth, *Church Dogmatics* III/3:285.

38. Barth, *Church Dogmatics* III/3:239.

39. Barth, *Church Dogmatics* III/3:286.

40. See Daniel Schwartz, *Aquinas on Friendship* (Oxford: Clarendon Press, 2017).

of creation is not. Moreover, Christians are those empowered to participate in the fulfillment of that will, through prayer and prayerful action.

Barth's description of God's responsiveness to our prayers emphasizes God's prior determination to be affected by our prayers in a way that mirrors his statements of Jesus's responsiveness to his fellows:

> The will of God is not to preserve and accompany and rule the world and the course of the world as world-occurrence in such a way that He is not affected and moved by it, that He does not allow Himself to converse with it, that He does not listen to what it says, that as He conditions all things He does not allow Himself to be determined by them.[41]

Like the incarnate Christ, God does not hold himself aloof and apart from God's human covenant partners. Like Jesus by his fellows, God is "affected" and "determined" by those who pray to God in faith. At least in consequence of the incarnation, God's sovereignty cannot be conceived as *autarchy*, a steamrolling of the wills of those affected by it or a proceeding with no interest in their wants or desires.

This kenotic movement entails no relinquishment of power on the part of God. God does not hand over the reins to humans nor toss the ball into our court. Barth makes clear in this section that divine and human agency are not competitive: "There is no creaturely freedom which can limit or compete with the sole sovereignty and efficacy of God. But permitted by God, and indeed willed and created by Him, there is the freedom of the *friends of God* concerning whom He has determined that without abandoning the helm for one moment He will still allow Himself to be determined by them."[42] Therefore, the account of divine reciprocity that I am drawing from Barth has little in common with open theism, which suggests that human choices can be real only if utterly independent from outside influences. In fact, this kind of absolute self-sufficiency is precisely the kind of autarchic agency that I am ruling out, on both God's side and on ours.[43]

Many of the conclusions of Barth's doctrine of *concursus dei* are reiterated and given fresh emphasis in *The Christian Life*. Barth confirms that the goal

41. Barth, *Church Dogmatics* III/3:285.
42. Barth, *Church Dogmatics* III/3:285.
43. As Coakley emphasizes, the idea that we must have an "incompatibilist freedom . . . the type supposedly free from conditioning control by another" is "a false form of hubristic human power." Sarah Coakley, "Kenōsis: Theological Meanings and Gender Connotations," in *The Work of Love*, 205–6.

of the covenant of Jesus Christ is the establishment of covenant partnership whereby God invites participation in God's work and rule. Barth rejects a view of God as working unilaterally:

> He does not just speak to them. He wills that he also be spoken to, that they also speak to him. He does not just work on and for them. As the Founder and the perfect Lord of this concursus . . . he wills their work as well. He for his part will not work without them. He will work only in connection with their work.[44]

If there was a danger or a potential danger identified by Coakley in Cyril's account of the incarnation, it was the unilateral nature of the union, such that the Logos acted upon the man Jesus but was not in turn affected by him. The question would then arise whether God is similarly only capable of such unilateral relating when it comes to relationship with us. Here, Barth answers that question directly: "God does not just speak," but is "*spoken to.*" God "does not just work *on and for*" us, effectively over our heads. God also works in our work. Finally, God

> is not so omnipotent or, rather, so impotent, that as they call upon him, liberated and commanded to do so by him, he will not and cannot hear them, letting a new action be occasioned by them, causing his own work and rule and control to correspond to their invocation.[45]

Even of our shortsighted, imperfect, and quite often misguided petition, Barth avers, God "does not despise it in this inadequacy. He lets himself be touched and moved by it."[46]

Conclusion

The purpose of this essay has not been to propose a new solution to a perennial christological debate, but rather to trace one of the implications of the debate itself to a different theological locus, namely, the Christian life. One of the suggestions of this study is that how we think about the relationship of God the Son to our humanity bears upon the range of ways we can imagine God relating to us in our ordinary efforts at responding to the gospel.

44. Barth, *The Christian Life*, 155.
45. Barth, *The Christian Life*, 155.
46. Barth, *The Christian Life*, 158.

Coakley has illuminated the ways in which kenosis—whether as a christo-logical doctrine or as an ethical ideal—comes prepackaged with assumptions about divine and human power that may serve to underwrite dominating relationships within and without the church. Avoiding the detrimental effects of these assumptions entails revising our understanding of divine power. One way of understanding the momentous contribution of Barth's theology is to see it as just such a revision, as offering a different account of divine power wherein God reveals God's majesty in humility. In his portrait of Jesus's humanity, that majesty-in-humility is fleshed out in Christ's reciprocity with his fellows.

The test of this revised conception of power, however, is whether there are any ongoing consequences of the incarnation for God's relating to us. In his doctrine of prayer Barth gives us just such consequences. Barth characterizes petitionary prayer as an acquired right whereby, "without abandoning the helm," God makes the goal of God's saving work a shared partnership with us:

> In the human world as in all other spheres of His creation He could in His omnipotence direct everything according to His will for the best, perhaps for man too, but over his head and without consulting him. He could simply be a Questioner waiting for man's answer, a Commander looking for his obedience. And it might be asked whether it would not be better for all concerned if God were to act in this manner. In fact, however, He does not do so. He considers man worthy that He should confront him as his Commander and stand on his level as Partner with partner.[47]

This theology of covenant partnership implies a kind of reciprocity about which Barth is rarely explicit, but which comes to its most concrete expression in his doctrine of prayer.

The consequences of this move are far-reaching. Not only does an account of divine reciprocity provide a portrait of the Christian life that goes beyond divine paternalism, suggesting a richer account of Christian formation and growth. It also serves as a model for humility and mutuality among Christians and between Christians and non-Christians that is in keeping with Paul's exhortation to "let the same mind be in you that was in Christ Jesus."[48]

---

47. Barth, *Church Dogmatics* III/4:649. Barth writes: "God as the Lord of this history not only wants man to be the object of His action and the recipient of His blessings, but also to have him as a responsible partner" (*Church Dogmatics* III/4:75).

48. Phil 2:5 (NRSV).

In an illuminating essay on Barth's theme of covenant partnership, Wolf Krötke implies that God's elevation of the Christian to the role of partner ought to cause us to treat others with greater dignity as we invite them to the gospel.[49] A witness shaped by Barth's conviction that the basic anthropological category is that of *covenant partner* cannot proceed by tactics of control or manipulation but only by way of "signs of invitation."[50] Such a theology is contradicted by "relationships of domination in the church, which *per se* deny the fact that every human being is called to be a partner of God and may 'come to life again' as a human being in the community."[51] Here is an account of divine humility that rules out equally an instrumentalization of others and an annihilation of self, and so answers the feminist complaint about false as well as destructive displays of self-abnegation. Where God is understood not merely to act *upon us without us,* but to act *with us,* both empowering our actions and responding to them, there is a powerful incentive to recognize the agency of even the most vulnerable others and to make space for them as agents capable of and responsible for discerning and pursuing God's will in the life of the community.

49. Wolf Krötke, "Gott und Mensch als 'Partner': Zur Bedeutung einer Zentralen Kategorie in Karl Barths Kirchlicher Dogmatik," in "Zur Theologie Karl Barths: Beiträge aus Anlaß seines 100. Geburtstags," supplement 6, *Zeitschrift für Theologie und Kirche* (1986): 171.

50. This phrase, *"Einladende Signale,"* is from Krötke, "Gott und Mensch als 'Partner,'" 171.

51. Krötke, "Gott und Mensch als 'Partner,'" 171, citing Barth, *Church Dogmatics* IV/3.2, ed. G. W. Bromiley and T. F. Torrance, trans. G. W. Bromiley, 529, translation revised.

14

Kenosis and Divine Continuity

Keith L. Johnson

The doctrine of kenosis considers both the claim that Jesus Christ "emptied himself" (Phil 2:7) and the acts of humility, obedience, and suffering that result from this emptying. Debates about Christ's kenosis often focus on the question of how these specific acts relate to Christ's divine being. Are these actions *revelatory* of Christ's divinity, such that they should be considered a true and faithful expression of his divine nature? If so, then how do these actions relate to traditional affirmations about divine immutability, impassibility, and simplicity? Do these actions *contradict* Christ's divinity, such that they should be considered strictly human actions that are inconsistent with the qualities essential to Christ's divine nature? If so, then by what criteria does one discern which qualities of Christ's human life are, and are not, revelatory of God? And what would it mean to say that the crucified Christ is "the power of God and the wisdom of God" (1 Cor 1:23–24)? Or are these actions *neutral* in the sense that they neither reveal nor contradict Christ's divinity but instead simply reflect Christ's true humanity? Should these actions thus be placed in the same category as Christ's acts of eating and sleeping, which are not typically seen as revealing or contradicting his divine nature?

This chapter seeks to illuminate how these questions have shaped the Christian tradition by tracing one line of this discussion through key figures in both the fourth and twentieth centuries. The story begins with the debates that led to the Council of Nicaea. The conflict between Arius and Alexander turned upon their divergent accounts of the continuity between Christ's kenosis and his being. Arius argued that this continuity indicates that Christ was a creature; Alexander rejected this conclusion, but he struggled to offer his own coherent account of this continuity. Athanasius later took up this challenge, and his arguments about Christ's kenosis set the trajectory for the Nicene tradition. Some matters remained unresolved, however, and an undercurrent of ambiguity ran through the tradition that led to ongoing tensions. Sensitive to these tensions, Karl Barth sought to address them by extending the claims of Nicaea beyond the Nicene tradition itself, leading him to a unique and controversial approach to the continuity between kenosis and divinity. Then, by standing both with and against Athanasius and Barth, James Cone turned the question of continuity on its head and set a new agenda for discussing the relationship between kenosis and divinity.

Arius and the Pro Nobis

Arius's conflict with Alexander was animated by ambiguities that Arius perceived in the church's talk about two key claims: (1) the ontological distinction between God and creation and (2) Jesus Christ's central role in salvation. For Arius, the question concerned the relationship between these two claims. How does Christ reconcile humans to God without undermining the distinction between divine and created being? Arius's arguments about Christ and salvation mark his attempt to answer this question in line with his reading of Scripture.

It was his particular way of reading Scripture that led to the confrontation. One of the striking aspects of the conflict is that Arius and Alexander agreed about nearly all of the underlying dogmatic issues. They both presuppose that, as Creator, God is self-sufficient and absolute, and thus distinct in essence from everything created. "Our faith from our ancestors," Arius writes to Alexander, "which we learned also from you, is this: we know one God—alone unbegotten, alone everlasting, alone without beginning . . . immutable and unchangeable."[1] They also both describe salvation in line with the biblical narrative about Christ's suffering. This suffering is linked to Christ's kenosis, his self-emptying to take on human flesh, embrace pov-

---

1. Arius, "Letter to Alexander of Alexandria," 2. Citations are drawn from the translation in *The Trinitarian Controversy*, Sources of Early Christian Thought, trans. William G. Rusch (Philadelphia: Fortress, 1980), 31–32.

erty, and submit to death in obedience to the will of the Father (Phil 2:6–9; 2 Cor 8:9). Their disagreement concerned the relation between Christ's kenosis and the divine being. The nature of this relation had vexed theologians for two centuries, and by the early fourth century, two trajectories of thought had emerged stemming from two distinct modes of biblical exegesis. Arius represented the tradition of what John Behr calls "univocal" exegesis, an approach that applies Scripture's claims about Christ "in a unitary fashion to one subject, who thus turns out to be a demi-god, neither fully divine nor fully human—created but not as one of the creatures."[2] Alexander stood in the tradition of "partitive" exegesis which interprets Scripture's claims about Christ in a twofold manner, with some claims held to refer to Christ's divinity and others to his humanity.

The uneasy tension between the two traditions broke when Alexander, in an attempt to solidify his authority as bishop of Alexandria, confronted the popular presbyter Arius about his teaching. When pressured to renounce his views, Arius refused and insisted that his teaching corresponded to the fathers, Scripture, and Alexander's own preaching.[3] In his letter responding to the charges, Arius focuses his defense on the uniqueness of the divine being, the biblical language of the Son's begetting, and the implications of Christ's kenosis. "God, being the cause of all, is without beginning, most alone," he writes, "but the Son, begotten by the Father, created and founded before the ages, was not before he was begotten."[4] If the Son were equal to the Father, he argues, then there would be "two unbegotten causes" and God would be "compounded, divided, mutable, and a body." Worse still, if the Son were divine—and if he also suffered and died—then the "incorporeal God suffers things suitable to the body."[5]

Alexander responded by focusing on the unchanging relationship between the Father and Son: "The Father is always the Father. But he is the Father of the always present Son, on account of whom he is called Father."[6] The eternal nature of this relationship means that the distinction between "unbegotten" and "begotten" is not identical to the distinction between Creator and creature. Rather, God's singular and immutable divine being

2. John Behr, *The Formation of Christian Theology*, vol. 2, *The Nicene Faith*, part 1, *True God of True God* (Crestwood, NY: St. Vladimir's Seminary Press, 2004), 14.
3. Arius, "Letter to Alexander of Alexandria," 4.
4. Arius, "Letter to Alexander of Alexandria," 4.
5. Arius, "Letter to Alexander of Alexandria," 4, 5.
6. Alexander, "Letter to Alexander of Thessalonica," 26. Citations are drawn from the translation in Rusch, *Trinitarian Controversy*, 33–44.

includes within itself the relation between the Father and the Son, leaving the relation shrouded in mystery for the human knower. The Son, according to Alexander, is begotten

> inexplicably and indescribably . . . since his *hypostasis* happens to be be-yond investigation of every originated nature, just as the Father himself is beyond investigation because the nature of rational ones does not allow the knowledge of the divine generation by the Father. Those moved by the Spirit need not learn these things from me, since the voice of Christ echoes in us and anticipates us, teaching, "No one knows who the Father is except the Son, and no one knows who the Son is except the Father" (Matt 11:27).[7]

The effect of this argument is to locate knowledge of God in the affirmation of the deity of the Son, because if knowledge of God is first a matter of the eternal relation between the Father and Son, then access to God requires confessing the existence of this relation.[8]

When Arius refused to make this confession, Alexander expelled him from the church. Arius responded by holding public meetings and gather-ing support from other local presbyters and laity. According to Alexander, Christ's kenosis played a key part in Arius's arguments during this period: "They keep in their memory statements about the Savior's sufferings, hum-blings, emptying, and so-called poverty, which by addition the Savior ac-cepted on our account. They quote these as evidence for impugning his highest and essential divinity."[9] Eventually these meetings caused enough of a stir that Alexander forced Arius and his supporters out of the city. Arius settled in Palestine, declaring that he had been "unjustly persecuted" and writing to bishops around the empire for support.[10]

These letters stoked the controversy, and the fact that they found a re-ceptive audience is informative. As a presbyter, Arius possessed little eccle-siastical authority, and his writings do not seem to have been particularly influential on later thinkers.[11] He seems less to have created a theological

---

7. Alexander, "Letter to Alexander of Thessalonica," 46.

8. Khaled Anatolios, *Retrieving Nicaea: The Development and Meaning of the Trinitar-ian Doctrine* (Grand Rapids: Baker Academic, 2011), 83.

9. Alexander, "Letter to Alexander of Thessalonica," 37.

10. Arius, "Letter to Eusebius of Nicomedia," 1. Citations are drawn from the transla-tion in Rusch, *Trinitarian Controversy*, 29–30.

11. Behr, *The Nicene Faith*, part 1, 26.

movement than to have revealed it. As supporters rallied to his side—and as the conflict with Alexander eventually led to a council chaired by Constantine—Arius became the visible symbol of a theology that had operated within the church for decades.[12] This theology had adherents because it provided a way to address tensions in the church's account of Christ and salvation that theologians like Alexander failed to address.

Arius rightly discerned that a coherent account of Christ's saving work should correspond to Christ's being, such that *what Christ does* reflects *who Christ is*. He also rightly interpreted Scripture to say that Christ's saving work takes place *pro nobis*, for us. He then concluded that Christ's work *pro nobis* must have its origins in Christ's being. The problem is that Alexander could not draw the same conclusion without resorting to ambiguity. Since Christ's saving work takes place through Christ's suffering and death, Alexander located the origin of this work strictly in the economy, at the point when Christ takes on human flesh as an "addition" to his divine nature.[13] This left a gap between who Christ is in his eternal relation to the Father and what Christ does *pro nobis* in his human flesh. In the midst of this gap is Christ's kenosis, and Alexander wraps this event in the ineffable mystery of the divine. But where Alexander saw mystery, Arius saw only the gap. From his vantage point, Alexander's description of Christ's saving work stands in discontinuity with Christ's being because the actions central to that work do not correspond to the nature of divinity.

Arius's theology resonated because it explained the continuity of Christ's being and work without an appeal to mystery. His logic is intuitive, in part because he begins with the actual object of the Christian confession: the man Jesus Christ, the human *creature*, who suffered, died, was buried, and raised from the dead.[14] His argument is simply that these creaturely actions correspond to Christ's being. Christ's kenosis is not a mystery but a disclosure, because his lowliness and suffering show that Christ is a creature. Christ is an utterly unique creature, however, because he was created by the Father before all time to serve as the mediator between the Father and the rest of creation. This mediation begins as Christ ushers the rest of creation into existence, and the same work of mediation takes visible form when he takes on human flesh in order to save human beings. Arius describes the nature of this mediation in his *Thalia*:

---

12. Rowan Williams, *Arius: History and Tradition*, 2nd ed. (London: SCM, 2001), 166.
13. Anatolios, *Retrieving Nicaea*, 93.
14. Anatolios, *Retrieving Nicaea*, 45.

God himself then, as he is, is inexpressible to all.
He alone has none equal or like himself, none one-in-glory.
We call him unbegotten, because of him who is begotten by
    nature.
We praise him as without beginning because of him who has a
    beginning;
    and adore him as everlasting, because of him who in time has
      come to be.
The one without beginning established the Son as a beginning
    of things created,
    and having engineered him bore him as his own son.
He has nothing proper to God, as a real property.
For he is not equal to, nor yet one-in-essence with him . . .
For God is inexpressible to the Son, for [God] is what is to [in/
    for] himself,
    that is, unspeakable.
So that no words expressing comprehension does the Son know
    to speak,
    for it is impossible for him to search out the Father, who exists
      in himself.[15]

As Arius depicts it, human knowledge of God takes place through the mediation of the Son because, apart from the Son, humans could not know God *even as the unknown*. But this is the precise knowledge that the Son is able to provide. Even though the Son does not have direct knowledge of God because the Son too is a creature, as the first and greatest creature he possesses unique and unsurpassed access to the divine being. In this sense, precisely through his creatureliness, the Son directs humans to the ineffable mystery of God and enables them to join him in adoring it. His entire existence, both before and during his human life, is *pro nobis*.

From the perspective of Arius and his supporters, this account of salvation has the benefit of consistently maintaining the ontological distinction between God and creation, affirming that Christ's saving work *pro nobis* corresponds to his being, and maintaining a straightforward reading of the biblical description of Christ—none of which, in their view, Alexander's account does.

---

15. Arius, *Thalia*, in Behr, *Nicene Faith*, part 1, 140–41.

Athanasius and Divine Character

The ambiguities within Alexander's theology help explain why the tentative consensus that emerged from the Council of Nicaea dissolved within a decade. In the conflict-riddled years that followed, Athanasius took up Alexander's arguments in order to address the tensions Arius had exploited. His goal, particularly in his early writings, is to prove that Christ's saving work corresponds to his deity by demonstrating that the Son's kenosis *reveals* rather than contradicts his divine nature.

This argument is the thesis of *On the Incarnation*.[16] Athanasius frames the book as a defense of the fittingness of the incarnation, one that shows how Christ's "apparent degradation . . . provides a greater witness of his divinity."[17] The key to this argument's refinement of Alexander's theology is to pay attention to how Athanasius reconfigures the *pro nobis*. He agrees with Alexander, in contrast to the Arian position, that the Son is not essentially *pro nobis*, because he thinks this would mean that the Son exists "to be an instrument of our need."[18] Yet he also recognizes that, if he follows Alexander by locating the *pro nobis* strictly in the economy without connecting it directly to the divine being, then the gap between God and salvation that Arius filled with a creaturely Son would remain open. To close this gap, Athanasius needs to explain how Christ's kenosis is grounded in his eternal divine nature. He accomplishes this by turning to God's character: "by the love for humankind and the goodness of his own Father he appeared to us in a human body for our salvation" (1). The Son emptied himself, not because the Son is essentially *pro nobis*, but because this particular action accords with God's love and goodness.

Athanasius develops this claim by clarifying the nature of the relationships between God and creation, the Father and the Son, and the Son and

---

16. Khaled Anatolios observes that, while Athanasius does not mention Arius by name in *On the Incarnation*, both the date of its composition and its arguments indicate that it is a "veiled attack on Arius and his supporters." This is particularly true of the second half of the treatise, which focuses on refutations of arguments by the "Jews" and "Greeks" that parallel Arian claims. See *Retrieving Nicaea*, 101–2.

17. Athanasius, *On the Incarnation*, 1. All citations refer to the paragraph numbers of the text and are drawn from St. Athanasius the Great of Alexandria, *On the Incarnation*, trans. John Behr (New York: St. Vladimir's Seminary Press, 2011). Hereafter, references from this work will be given in parentheses in the text.

18. Athanasius, *Against the Arians* 2.30. Citation drawn from the translation in Khaled Anatolios, *Athanasius* (New York: Routledge, 2004), 124.

human beings. Arius had posited that Christ was created by the Father to serve as the mediator between the Father and the rest of creation, such that the Son is the direct cause of creation. Athanasius rejects this gap between the Father and creation: "How then do they introduce a creation alien to the Father? For if, according to John, encompassing all things in saying, 'all things were made by him and without him nothing was made' (Jn 1:3), how could there be another creator besides the Father of Christ?" (2). Here God's act of creation is linked to both Father and Son in a manner that reflects their eternal relationship: there are not two creators but one, and the act of creation comes *from* the Father *through* the Son.

Why did God create? Athanasius locates the answer in God's goodness: "For God is good, or rather the source of all goodness, and one who is good grudges nothing, so that grudging nothing its existence, he made all things through his own Word, our Lord Jesus Christ" (3).[19] So creation is not necessary to God, as if God's relation to creation implies some sort of divine dependency upon it. Rather, God acts freely for the sake of creation by granting it existence. This act of grace happens through the Son, but—in distinction from Arius—this act is grounded in *God's* being rather than strictly in the being of the Son. Since this act proceeds from the Father through the Son, it reflects their divine relationship—and thus the Son's deity. And because the act of creation occurs by grace rather than necessity, it reflects the divine goodness. Note how these moves shift the terms of the discussion. By framing God's relationship to creation in light of the communicable attribute of God's goodness instead of the qualities that make God distinct from creation—such as God's immutability and impassibility—Athanasius is able to connect God's acts in creation to God's eternal being, including the eternal relationship between the Father and Son, without undermining the distinction.

This connection frames Athanasius's discussion of Christ's relationship to humanity. He argues that, since God wanted humans to exist eternally, "[God] granted them a further gift . . . making them according to his own image, giving them a share of the power of his own Word, so that having as it were shadows of the Word and being made rational, they might be able to abide in blessedness" (3). So like the rest of creation, humans are created out of nothing by a free divine act that proceeds from the Father through the Son. Humans are distinct from other creatures, however, because they

---

19. He later writes: "having a nature that did not once exist, they were called into existence by the Word's advent and love for human beings" (4).

are granted a unique relationship to God through the Word, who provides humans the ontological stability they lack by giving them a participation in the divine life. This means that the Son's unique role as mediator is not a sign of the Son's creatureliness—as Arius argued—but the Son's *divinity*, since the Son's relation to humanity is determined precisely by his ontological distinction from creation.[20]

This is the ground from which Athanasius argues that the Son's kenosis corresponds to his divine being. He explains that, when humans sinned against God, their participation in the Word was broken and they began to experience corruption and death. This result raised questions about God's consistency with respect to creation. Since the creation of humanity was an act of God's goodness, permitting humans to fall into nonbeing would be "improper to and unworthy of the goodness of God" (6). At the same time, if God permitted sinful humans to live despite their disobedience, then God "should appear a liar for our profit and preservation" (7). What, then, should God do in order to remain consistent with his divine character? For Athanasius, the answer is the incarnation. The Word of God took on human flesh and bore the consequence of human sin in his death so that, through his resurrection, God could re-create what he had created while remaining consistent in both word and deed. Athanasius writes: "For him it was once more both to bring the corruptible to incorruptibility and to save the superlative consistency of the Father. Being the Word of the Father and above all, he alone consequently was both able to re-create the universe and was worthy to suffer on behalf of all and to intercede for all before the Father" (7). Here we see Athanasius's refutation of Arius's central argument: Christ's saving work stands in continuity with Christ's divine being because his kenosis does not contradict but reveals the immutability of God's character. "And thus," he writes, "taking from ours that which is like, since all were liable to the corruption of death, delivering it over to death on behalf of all, he offered it to the Father, doing this in his love for human beings, so that . . . he might turn them again to incorruptibility and give them life from death" (8). Christ's saving work *pro nobis* stands in continuity with his nature because this work "supremely befitted the goodness of God" and reflects God's love (9).

Athanasius then extends his argument to challenge Arius's theology further. Not only does the Son's kenosis correspond to his divine being and bring salvation to humanity, but it also gives humans knowledge of the Father that Arius believes impossible. When God created human beings, the

---

20. Anatolios, *Retrieving Nicaea*, 105.

difference between God and creation meant that human nature "was neither sufficient of itself to know the Creator nor to receive any knowledge of God." However, by their participation in the Word who is the image of the Father, humans were by grace "able to receive through him a notion of the Father" (11). After the fall, the grace was lost, and instead of setting their minds on things above, humans looked down to created things and crafted idols out of them. And so, out of his own divine goodness and love, the Son takes on human flesh for their sake.

> No longer were human eyes held upward but downward. So, rightly wishing to help human beings, he sojourned as a human being, taking to himself a body like theirs and from below—I mean through the works of the body—that those not wishing to know him from his providence and governance of the universe, from the works done through the body might know the Word of God in the body, and through him the Father. (14)

In Arius's theology, Christ exists between God and humanity as a semidivine figure, and from this position he provides a negative knowledge of God that enables humans to stand alongside him in adoration of the unknowable Father. For Athanasius, in contrast, the divine Son stoops down from above to unite his divine being to human flesh so that humans can be lifted up with him and participate in his own knowledge of the Father. This act displays God's consistency because it is a reiteration of God's original intent. Just as God created humans to know God through their participation in the Word of God, he re-creates humans so that they can know God through this same Word. And since this knowledge comes as a gift from God's goodness and love, the divine act by which it occurs corresponds to God's being.

Barth and Differentiated Unity

Athanasius's arguments about the continuity between Christ's kenosis and the divine being provide the theological framework within which the Nicene tradition's claims about Christ's deity and his saving work operate. Centuries later, as he considers this tradition in light of the church's history, Karl Barth agrees with these claims but insists they are "not enough."[21]

21. Karl Barth, *Church Dogmatics* IV/1, ed. G. W. Bromiley and T. F. Torrance, trans. Geoffrey W. Bromiley (Edinburgh: T&T Clark, 1956), 183. Barth argues that the church will maintain the Nicene tradition, not by slavishly repeating its claims, but by seeking to

> In calling this man [Jesus of Nazareth] the Son or the eternal Word of God, in ascribing to this man in his unity with God a divine being and nature, it is not speaking only or even primarily of him, but of God. It tells us that God for his part is God in his unity with this creature, this man, in his human and creaturely nature—and this without ceasing to be God, without any alteration or diminution of his divine nature. But this statement concerning God is so bold that we dare not make it unless we consider seriously in what sense we can do so. . . . And at this point the traditional theology of the Church gives rise to an ambiguity. . . . The ambiguity is one which needs to be removed.[22]

Barth thinks this ambiguity stems from an unexamined presupposition behind the tradition's claim that Christ's kenosis corresponds to his deity. To identify it, Barth says the church must look behind the question "Why did God become human?" and address the one that undergirds it: "How did God became human?"[23] Or, put differently: before the church can explain *why* God became incarnate in Christ, it must explain *how* God can become incarnate in the particular way that Christ does—in the humility and obedience that led to his death on the cross—without contradicting his divine nature.

Barth believes the tradition's silence with respect to the *how* of the incarnation undermines its answer to the *why*. The problem is that, in connecting Christ's kenosis *pro nobis* to the divine being by means of God's goodness and love—qualities that the Father, Son, and Spirit equally possess—no explanation is given about how Christ's acts of humility and obedience correspond to his divine nature. An act of humility assumes the existence of one who is above and one who is below; an act of obedience presupposes that there is one who acts before and one who acts after. Since the Nicene tradition had no place for such distinctions in its account of the divine being, theologians tended to view Christ's acts of humility and obedience strictly in relation to his human nature and not as revelatory of his divinity. As a result, much of the tradition viewed the very qualities Christ displayed on his way to the cross as inconsistent with God's nature, as if God was acting "in discontinuity

---

draw the same conclusion anew in the present. While the Nicene Creed shows the church "the direction we have to look," we have to "go further in this direction, not losing contact with the dogma but again following our own path" (200).

22. Barth, *Church Dogmatics* IV/1:183–84.
23. Barth, *Church Dogmatics* IV/1:184.

with himself" in this event. "In himself," Barth says of the tradition, "[God] was still the omnipresent, almighty, enteral, and glorious one, the all-holy and all-righteous who could not be tempted. But at the same time, among us and for us he was quite different."[24] This discontinuity between Christ's saving work *pro nobis* and his divine being meant that, even as it recited the claims of Nicaea, the church risked returning to the ambiguities that prompted the council.

To correct this problem and actually achieve the aims of Nicaea, Barth argues that the church must focus again on the concrete particularities of Christ's human life, starting with the fact that Christ became incarnate *as a Jew*. "The Word did not simply become any 'flesh,' any man humbled and suffering," Barth writes: "[The Word] becomes Jewish flesh. The church's whole doctrine of the incarnation and the atonement becomes abstract and valueless and meaningless to the extent that this comes to be regarded as something accidental and incidental."[25] He explains that God's covenant with the people of Israel—a people who once were slaves—revealed that God is not too high to identify with the lowly: "He is the same high God who in his supreme humility elected himself as the God of this one small people."[26] And God's faithfulness to this covenant despite Israel's disobedience shows that, when God takes on human flesh to serve as David's royal heir, God is willing to bear the consequences of Israel's sin for their sake: "He accepts personal responsibility for all the unfaithfulness, the deceit, the rebellion of this people and its priests and kings."[27]

The royal humility and faithfulness of God in relation to Israel is the context within which the continuity of Christ's kenosis with the divine being can and must be understood.[28] Barth argues that Christ's kenosis

corresponds to and is grounded in his divine nature that in free grace [God] should be faithful to the unfaithful creature who has not deserved it and who would inevitably perish without it, that in relation to [his crea-

24. Barth, *Church Dogmatics* IV/1:184.

25. Barth, *Church Dogmatics* IV/1:166.

26. Barth, *Church Dogmatics* IV/1:169.

27. Barth, *Church Dogmatics* IV/1:72. He continues: "for in this one Israelite Jesus it was God himself who as the Son of the Father made himself the object of this accusation and willed to confess himself a sinner, and to be regarded and dealt with as such."

28. As Barth puts it: "For a knowledge of this continuity of the being and activity of God, of his condescension, the Old Testament is indispensable as the presupposition of the New" (*Church Dogmatics* IV/1:173).

ture] he should establish that communion between his own form and cause and that of the creature, that he should make his own its being in contradiction and under the consequences of that contradiction, that he should maintain his covenant in relation to sinful [humanity]—not surrendering his deity, for how could that help? but giving up and sacrificing himself—and in that way supremely asserting himself and his deity.[29]

So when the Son empties himself to take on Jewish flesh, adopts the form of a humble slave, and remains obedient even to the point of his death, these actions correspond to how God always has related to his people Israel within their covenant relationship. Even more so, they display God's faithfulness to himself, his immutability in contrast to the nature of ever-changing and wavering creatures.

Barth believes this background puts the church in position to address the question of *how* God can become incarnate in Christ without contradicting his divine nature. He begins by laying out his central presupposition: "Let us grant . . . that what the New Testament says about the obedience of Christ on his way of suffering has its basis . . . in his divine nature and therefore in God himself."[30] He acknowledges that this presupposition raises the specter of Arius, since the notion of "obedience" would seem to imply the existence of two distinct beings, with one superior to the other. But such a path is forbidden if it is in fact true that "God was in Christ reconciling the world to himself" (2 Cor 5:19). "No," Barth writes, "not in unequal but equal, not in divided but in the one deity, God is both One and also Another, his own counterpart, co-existent with himself."[31] The notion that God exists as his own "counterpart" makes sense if God's oneness includes within itself the differentiation of the Father, Son, and Spirit. Barth explains that, in the triune life, the Father and Son exist in an ordered relationship marked by the Son's obedience to the Father; yet this obedience does not compromise the Son's perfect equality with the Father because the Spirit exists in both Father and Son precisely in their unity with one another. The being of the one triune God thus exists "in the totality, the connection, the interplay, the history of these relationships" that include the Father's command and

---

29. Barth, *Church Dogmatics* IV/1:187, translation slightly altered. He continues: "If God is in Christ, then this aspect of the self-emptying and self-humbling of Jesus Christ as an act of obedience cannot be alien to God" (193).

30. Barth, *Church Dogmatics* IV/1:195.

31. Barth, *Church Dogmatics* IV/1:201.

the Son's obedience.[32] This is the precise point where the church can draw a connection between the concrete qualities associated with Christ's kenosis and the divine being. The humility and obedience that the Son displays during the incarnation do not mark a change in the Son's divinity, nor are they merely human traits. Rather, Christ's acts of humility and obedience are a revelation of his divinity, and thus an unveiling of the history of the triune life. Barth concludes: "He is as man—as the man who is obedient in humility, Jesus of Nazareth—what he is as God. . . . That is the true deity of Jesus Christ, obedient in humility, in its unity and equality, its *homoousia*, with the deity of the one who sent him and to whom he is obedient."[33]

Cone and Liberative Kenosis

As James Cone considers the arguments of Athanasius and Barth, he argues that their accounts of Jesus Christ's divinity are irrelevant to the experience of the Black church.[34] He explains that Black Christians "do not ask whether Jesus is one with the Father or divine and human, though the orthodox formulations are implied in their language. They ask whether Jesus is walking with them . . . whether he was really present at the slave's cabin, whether slaves could expect Jesus to be with them as they tried to survive the cotton field, the whip, and the pistol" (13). To address these questions, Cone insists that theologians must show how Christ relates to their actual, lived experience of oppression. Athanasius offers little help, because he begins with an abstract account of Christ's divinity and then uses it to understand Christ's humanity. As a result, the concrete deeds of Christ's historical life— such as his ministry to the poor, his proclamation of freedom to captives, and his identification with the restorative promises of Israel's prophets— make no difference for Athanasius's description of Christ's person and work (106).[35] For Cone, Barth never fully overcame—not even in his final work

---

32. Barth, *Church Dogmatics* IV/1, 203.

33. Barth, *Church Dogmatics* IV/1, 204, translation revised.

34. The arguments presented here represent the early stage of Cone's theological development, which includes his dissertation "The Doctrine of Man in the Theology of Karl Barth" (1965), *Black Theology and Black Power* (1969), *A Black Theology of Liberation* (1970), and *God of the Oppressed* (1975). Cone later noted that his theology shifted in the years after 1975. See James Cone, *God of the Oppressed*, rev. ed. (Maryknoll, NY: Orbis Books, 1997), xvi. Hereafter, page references from this work will be given in parentheses in the text.

35. Cone explains: "I respect what happened at Nicaea and Chalcedon and the theo-

outlined above—the problems of his earlier dialectical theology. Specifically, in Cone's estimation, Barth's emphasis on God's absolute distinction from creation never allowed him fully to take into account the history of Christ's human life in his doctrine of God (107).

To fix these problems, Cone argues that the theology of Athanasius and Barth needs to be turned "right-side-up."[36] This process begins with paying attention to the voices of the lowly and humiliated. Black Christians start with the stories of Christ's humanity—particularly his suffering and death—as interpreted in light of their experience of oppression (109–10). Their theology develops as they move dialectically between this experience and Scripture.[37] When the biblical stories are heard within the context of oppression, Cone says, these stories have the "power to point to the One whom the people have met in the historical struggle for freedom" (101). Black Christians recognize that this previously unknown "other" is the risen Jesus Christ:

> Through the reading of Scripture, the people hear other stories about Jesus that enable them to move beyond the privateness of their own story; through faith because of divine grace, they are taken from the present to the past and then thrust back into their contemporary history with divine power to transform the sociopolitical context. This event of transcendence enables the people to break the barriers of time and space as they walk and talk with Jesus in Palestine along with Peter, James, and John. They can hear his cry of pain and experience the suffering as he is nailed on the cross and pierced in the side. (101)

Here Cone depicts human experience as the starting point but Scripture as the norm. The Bible functions as a mirror in which the oppressed see, not merely a reflection of themselves, but the image of the risen Christ who is with and for them in the midst of their suffering. Christ's identification with them in their suffering reconfigures their relationship to time, space, and place by connecting their present lives to Christ's life.

---

logical input of the Church Fathers on Christology, but that source alone is inadequate for finding out the meaning of black folks' Jesus" (13).

36. See James Cone, *My Soul Looks Back* (Nashville: Abingdon, 1982), 45: "As Barth had turned liberal theology up-side-down, I wanted to turn him right-side-up with a focus on the black struggle in particular and oppressed people generally."

37. Cone notes that this occurs either from one's personal experience of oppression or one's solidarity with those who are oppressed, although this second mode occurs only rarely. See *God of the Oppressed*, 221–22.

Jesus's Jewish identity plays a decisive role in this approach because it locates Christ's human life within the context of the exodus and thus connects it to God's liberation of the enslaved Israelites out of Egypt (124). Cone explains: "Israel's election cannot be separated from its servitude and liberation. Here God is disclosed as the God of history whose will is identical with the liberation of the oppressed from social and political bondage" (60). In Israel's Scriptures, God confirms his identification with the oppressed by sustaining them through the wilderness and dwelling with them in their land. As God defends Israel from powerful enemies, they are called to obey his commands, which include caring for the poor and weak in their midst. When Israel fails to do so, God's prophets condemn them for idolatry as well as injustice, because their acts of oppression reveal that they no longer know God rightly (61–66). Through these same prophets, God promises that he will restore Israel by liberating the oppressed, caring for the poor, and establishing a kingdom marked by justice.

When Jesus arrives on the scene, he identifies his ministry as the fulfillment of these royal, divine promises. "This is what the incarnation means," Cone writes: "God in Christ comes to the weak and helpless, and becomes one with them, taking their condition of oppression as his own and transforming their slave existence into a liberated existence" (71). The cross shows the extent of God's solidarity with the oppressed, because in this event Christ submits to the power of death so that he can free his people from its reign. This liberation takes place in and through his resurrection. "When God raised Jesus from the dead, God affirmed that Jesus's historical identity with the freedom of the poor was in fact divinity taking on humanity for the purpose of liberating human beings from sin and death" (115). Christ's resurrection means that he can transcend the limits of history and be present with the poor and oppressed in the contemporary moment. In this sense, Cone says, "the Risen Lord's identification with the suffering poor today is just as real as was his presence with the outcasts in first-century Palestine" (124). And as Jesus declared in Nazareth, he has come to bring good news to the poor and freedom for the captives. Black Christians interpret these promises to mean that, in the midst of their dehumanization, Christ affirms their dignity. He identifies with them in their suffering, and his promises provide hope beyond their earthly life. He shows them that their poverty is temporary rather than permanent; that their resistance against their oppressors reflects rather than contradicts God's order for creation; and that their often-hindered pursuit of justice eventually will be fulfilled by the just judgment of Jesus.

This account of Christ's presence puts us in position to see the implications of Cone's account for the debates about the relationship between kenosis and divinity. Like Athanasius and Barth, Cone believes that *what Christ does* must stand in continuity with *who Christ is*, such that Christ's saving work *pro nobis* corresponds to his divine being. But the way he affirms this continuity is quite different. Athanasius had located the *pro nobis* strictly in the economy, because it allowed him to connect Christ's kenosis to God's character without undermining God's distinction from creation. Barth pressed beyond this argument by grounding the concrete qualities associated with Christ's kenosis—humility and obedience—in the triune being, so that he could affirm that Christ's act *pro nobis* at the cross reveals rather than contradicts his divine nature. For both Athanasius and Barth, then, the continuity between kenosis and divinity is established by starting with the incarnation and then looking *backward* to God's eternal life in distinction from creation. Because Athanasius locates the consistency between kenosis and divinity in God's character rather than God's being, Christ's humble and obedient embrace of death at the cross stands in an ambiguous relationship with the qualities of the divine nature. By connecting kenosis to the eternal relationship between the Father and Son, Barth is able to relieve this ambiguity, and he ends up with an account of God that makes submission and obedience essential to the divine life.

Cone reconfigures these distinctions in light of the tradition of the Black church. As he depicts it, Black Christians do not confess that Christ is divine on the basis of the tradition's philosophical and theological arguments, nor does their confession depend upon their ability to draw a connection between Christ's human life and his divine being prior to the incarnation. While these matters are important, they are not decisive. Rather, Black Christians confess Christ's divinity because of the correspondence they discern between the Bible's account of the human life of Jesus and their own present experience of God's power in their struggle for liberation. So, in distinction from Athanasius and Barth, Cone establishes the continuity between Christ's kenosis and divinity by looking *forward* from Christ's incarnation to the risen Christ's present life as Christ continues to work toward the future God has promised.

Cone's central concern is discerning how Christ's present actions stand in continuity with Christ's past actions and with what God will do in the future. This leaves him largely uninterested in the ambiguities that drove the debates surrounding Nicaea, and it also leaves him uninclined to follow Barth's deductions about the inner life of the Trinity. Instead, Cone's focus is on God's faithfulness amid human suffering. In this light, Christ's kenosis testifies to God's consistency. When Christ "emptied himself" to take the form of a slave, he revealed that God not only hears the cries of the lowly, but he also fully identifies with them. When Christ "humbled himself and became obedient to the point of death," he showed that God would go to any depth to liberate his people from the forces that hold them in captivity. And the fact that God exalted this same Christ to the highest throne serves as the ground for the hope of the oppressed: if the lowly Christ has been lifted up, then the God who raised Christ will be faithful to raise them as well.

15

The Generosity of the Triune God and the Humility of the Son

Christoph Schwöbel

When one surveys the last decades of christological discussion, one is struck by the changes in the themes, methods, and modalities of christological conversations. While the debate around *The Myth of God Incarnate* (1977) seriously considered the possibility of interpreting the language of the incarnation as a mythological expression of belief in Jesus Christ, which deemed following the path of the formulation of christological dogma to be decidedly unpromising, recent contributions to Christology have taken up the task of defending the Christology of the ecumenical councils, offering a retrieval of classical Christology. While the technicalities of the christological debate in patristic, scholastic, and Reformation theology were in the closing decades of the twentieth century regarded as offering no way forward in Christology, recent debates have centered on the conceptual issues raised by the Chalcedonian Definition (451) as the midpoint between the Councils of Nicaea, Constantinople, and Ephesus and their continuation in the second and third Councils of Constantinople and the Second Council of Nicaea. The question of how the Chalcedonian formulae were interpreted, in modification and amplification, in scholastic and Reformation theology, including the era of seventeenth-century scholasticism, be it Roman Catholic, Lutheran or Calvinist, forms a major focus of christological debates.

This shift in the modalities of the discussion reflects a significant change in the ways of doing theology. While the debates around *The Myth of God*

Incarnate can be seen as the apex of theological efforts to engage with the challenges of modernity, the more recent conversations seem to be fueled by the feeling that postmodernity, for all its ambiguities, has opened possibilities for reengaging with classical debates without the restrictions that the modern development of historical investigation and philosophy had imposed on Christology. Appeals to whatever is regarded as "classical," such as "classical theism," have become common parlance. While this promises a real theological liberation, especially for christological thought, it also seems to lead to a relative neglect of those theological strands of twentieth-century theology for which critical engagement with modernity shaped every aspect of the theological enterprise. The theological achievements of Karl Barth, Rudolf Bultmann, Paul Tillich, Karl Rahner, and Hans Urs von Balthasar and the constructive way in which their theological concerns were creatively continued and transformed by theologians such as Jürgen Moltmann, Wolfhart Pannenberg, Robert Jenson, and Eberhard Jüngel are, so it seems, sometimes disregarded at our peril.

One may wonder whether the recent shift in focus and style of christological thinking has already contributed much to overcoming the fundamental crisis of Christology since the Enlightenment.[1] At the risk of oversimplification, one can characterize this fundamental crisis as the fragmentation of Jesus Christ, the subject matter of Christology, be it in worship, personal faith or theological reflection, into the three distinct entities of the Jesus of history, the Christ of faith, and the Son of God of Trinitarian and christological dogma. The severing of the links between history, saving faith, and dogmatic affirmation seems still the major challenge that confronts Christology today. We cannot ignore this challenge, because the very character of Christian faith demands that we connect history, faith, and dogma. Can contemporary christological reflection contribute to the healing of the fractures that modern thought in its various guises has inflicted upon Christology?

In Christology, one reason for "the strange persistence of Kenoticism"[2] is that it appears to offer the promise of such healing, of providing a way in which the requirements of a historical picture of Jesus as the Christ, the confession of faith in Jesus the Lord and Savior, and the dogmatic assertions

---

1. Cf. for this analysis Christoph Schwöbel, "Christology and Trinitarian Thought," in *Trinitarian Theology Today*, ed. Christoph Schwöbel (Edinburgh: T&T Clark, 1995), 113–46.

2. Cf. Christoph Schwöbel, "'Taking the Form of a Servant': Kenosis and Divine Self-Giving in Thomas Aquinas and Martin Luther," *Angelicum* 98, no. 1 (2021): 43–66.

about the being of the Son of God can be held together. The term kenosis is taken from the so-called Christ hymn in Philippians 2:6–11, which states about Christ Jesus: "who, though he was in the form of God, did not regard equality with God as something to be exploited, but emptied himself [*heauton ekenosen*], taking the form of a slave" (Phil 2:6–7a). Whereas in patristic and scholastic debates this text was mainly referenced to support the ethical demand for Christians to adopt the attitude of Christ—"Let the same mind be in you that was in Christ Jesus" (Phil 2:5)—it was first applied to the being of Christ and the divine attributes he shared with God the Father in post-Reformation christological discussions. The famous debate between the Lutheran theologians of Gießen and Tübingen, often quoted but rarely studied, was focused on the question whether Christ willingly suspended the exercise of his divine attributes during the incarnation (kenosis).[3] The Gießen position, mostly discussed with regard to Christ's possession of omnipresence, assumed that during the incarnation Christ could adapt to different modes of presence by his will. The Tübingen position insisted that there was no suspension of the exercise of the divine prerogatives, but that they were hidden (*krypsis*) during the incarnation. The background of both positions was the Lutheran conviction that because of the personal union of divine and human natures in Christ, Christ's humanity participated after the ascension in being everywhere ("ubiquity"), so that wherever the Lord's Supper was celebrated Christ could be really present in, with, and under the elements of bread and wine.

When the keyword kenosis was again taken up by Lutheran theologians in the nineteenth century, it was as a response to the challenges of the early "life of Jesus" research, presented in its most critical form by David Friedrich Strauß, which maintained that the historical picture of Jesus could not substantiate the metaphysical claims made by christological dogma.[4] Now kenosis was taken to refer to the suspension or the surrender of divine attributes or, at least, the exercise of the divine attributes during the incarnation. The subject of this act of self-emptying was no longer "Christ Jesus," the incarnate Lord, but the eternal Logos who surrendered what made him equal to God the Father before the incarnation. If this move was successful,

---

3. Cf. Jörg Baur, *Luther und Seine Klassischen Erben: Theologische Aufsätze und Forschungen* (Tübingen: Mohr Siebeck, 1993), and Ulrich Wiedenroth, *Krypsis und Kenosis: Studien zu Thema und Genese der Tübinger Christologie im 17. Jahrhundert* (Tübingen: Mohr Siebeck, 2011).

4. Cf. Martin Breidert, *Die Kenotische Christologie des 19. Jahrhunderts* (Gütersloh: Gütersloher Verlagshaus Gerd Mohn, 1977).

it was hoped, one could both hold fast to christological dogma and adapt
to the findings of historical Jesus research. This attempt at maintaining allegiance to the dogmatic tradition, the Christ of faith, while at the same time
doing justice to what the historical investigation offered as a picture of the
historical Jesus, quickly spread from its birthplace in the Lutheran theology
at Erlangen to Denmark, Scotland, and England. However, already in the
early stages of the debate in the nineteenth century, it became clear that this
version of kenosis involved crucial questions concerning the doctrine of
God. Does the act of self-emptying on the part of the Logos extend only to
God's "relative" attributes, the attributes God has in relation to the created
world (like omnipotence, omnipresence, and omniscience), or to all divine
attributes, including the attributes that God has "absolutely," apart from
God's relation to the world (like God's love and goodness)?

It is this relationship between Christology and a Trinitarian doctrine of
God that forms the focus of the most recent debates in the twentieth century
and at the beginning of the twenty-first century. Karl Barth had offered a
decisive stimulus by insisting that the conventional conjunction between the
divine nature and the human nature and the states of exaltation and humility
might be misconceived in most traditional Christologies. Is it not the core
of God's self-revelation in Christ that the Lord takes the form of a servant,
traveling the way into the far country, and so lifts humanity to the exalted
state of "royal humanity"? While Barth did not develop this into a kenotic
Christology, others were inspired to inquire into the conditions of possibility
of a kenotic incarnation in the being of God. Is it necessary to assume a primordial kenosis, an *Ur*-kenosis, in the relation between the Father and the
eternal Son in order to make the incarnation as kenosis real?[5] Does the fact
that Christ "became obedient to the point of death—even death on a cross"
(Phil 2:8) demand surrendering the dogmatic assumption of impassibility in
God? And does this not—almost automatically—necessitate giving up the affirmation of divine immutability? If one considers the popularity of Dietrich
Bonhoeffer's phrase that God suffers with us, one is tempted to speak of a
new dogma of divine passibility in the twentieth century. Can this move heal
the fragmentation of Jesus Christ and, with the unity of Jesus Christ regained
by suspending the affirmation of divine impassibility and immutability, also
offer the image of a compassionate God?

5. A concise overview of the debate and thoughtful suggestions toward its resolution
are offered by John Betz, "The Humility of God: On a Disputed Question in Trinitarian
Theology," *Nova et Vetera* 17 (2019): 769–810.

In his magisterial study *The Humility of the Eternal Son*,[6] Bruce McCormack, who has already provided perceptive accounts of the history of kenoticism,[7] has offered a programmatic proposal for reformed kenoticism and the repair of Chalcedon. His proposal is Reformed in that it takes up the Reformed emphasis on the integrity of the divine and human in Christ during the incarnation, although he offers a strong account of the incarnate Son as the one subject in the incarnation, mirroring the Cyrilline emphasis on the integration of the divine and human in Christ. McCormack's conception is placed under the heading of kenoticism, although he insists that it has only the name in common with the kenoticisms of self-surrender of the nineteenth century. It is, however, kenotic in that he assumes an essential humility in the relation of the eternal Son to the Father as the condition of possibility of a kenotic incarnation. McCormack's main interest, however, is the repair of Chalcedon, since the Definition, he asserts, falls short of solving the problems of pro-Nicene Christology by allowing only an active relationship of the eternal Son to Jesus, because the parties at Chalcedon all remained bound to the presuppositions of divine simplicity and impassibility.

If It Ain't Broke . . . ?

What is it about the Chalcedonian Definition that requires repair? The notion of repairing suggests that, on the one hand, there is really something about the Definition that requires fixing, because otherwise it will not work, but, also, on the other hand, that there is enough that is worth retaining in it such that one can repair it and does not need to replace it. There are two "pressures" at work in formulating the Definition, McCormack contends. One is to insist on a "unified subject" so that the Nestorian challenge could be warded off by bishops who in their majority followed the Cyrilline position of developing a Christology of integration, stressing the necessity of having one person as the subject of the whole of Christ. Following this trajectory, the unified subject must be "the preexistent Logos *as such*—a subject who

---

6. Bruce L. McCormack, *The Humility of the Eternal Son: Reformed Kenoticism and the Repair of Chalcedon* (Cambridge: Cambridge University Press, 2021), 29. (Further references to this book are in parentheses inline.)

7. See Bruce McCormack, "Kenoticism in Modern Christology," in *The Oxford Handbook of Christology*, ed. Francesca Aran Murphy and Troy A. Stefano (Oxford: Oxford University Press, 2015), 444–57. See also Bruce McCormack, "Scottish Kenotic Theology," in *The Long Twentieth Century*, vol. 3 of *The History of Scottish Theology*, ed. David Fergusson and Mark W. Elliott (Oxford: Oxford University Press, 2019), 19–34.

acts through and even upon (in the resurrection and exaltation) His human 'nature'" (29). The second pressure, though equally anti-Nestorian, pushes in the opposite direction. Taking up Gregory of Nazianzus's axiom that "the unassumed is the unhealed," McCormack posits that "no account of human nature that failed to give due attention to intellect, memory, and agency could be fully adequate" (29–30). Trying to accommodate both pressures, there appear on McCormack's account two possibilities. One could assume that the Logos suspended his self-activating activity through and upon Jesus when fundamentally human passions and actions are ascribed to Jesus, raising immediately the possibility that during these moments there are two subjects. If one tries to counter this, one can only maintain that the Logos acted upon Jesus in an uninterrupted fashion, but that, of course, makes the Jesus of the Gospels with his true humanity disappear, because that could never be compatible with assuming that the person of the union is the preexistent Logos who is simple and impassible. And here is, in McCormack's analysis, the core of the problem: "The aporia is this: Jesus of Nazareth contributes nothing to the composition of the 'person' in which two natures are said to 'subsist'. . . . Jesus has no constitutive relation to the Logos" (31).

The chief motivation for McCormack's attempt at repairing Chalcedon is to develop a Christology and, indeed, a Christian theology, for which Jesus matters—matters in the deepest sense that the identity of the Logos cannot be determined ontologically without a constitutive reference to Jesus. The danger of a purely formal adherence to Chalcedon is, indeed, that one maintains all the concepts it offers without excluding those interpretations that would have the effect of either denying implicitly the significance of Jesus for Christology or of fragmenting the unified subject of the clauses of the Definition. To achieve this via a doctrine of the *anhypostasia* of the humanity of Jesus Christ or to see it, following Leontius of Byzantium, as being enhypostatized in the Logos only duplicates the effect of seeing the preexistent Logos from the start as the unified subject of all of the christological assertions in the Definition and either takes away something that is crucial for understanding the humanity of Jesus or turns it into something that has only a figurative significance, but does not form part of what needs to be said ontologically of Jesus Christ.

The attempt at repairing that McCormack undertakes consists in showing that reference to Jesus is constitutive for the meaning of the "one and the same" who is the grammatical and logical subject of the determinative phrases of the Definition. For this, he contends, this term must be interpreted in such a way that it allows theological space for Gregory Nazianzen's "the unassumed is the unhealed," not only in an abstract sense, but as expressing the concrete humanity of Jesus in his relation to God the Father. What one could perhaps call the "implicit dyotheletism" of the Definition is for McCormack "a most sound instinct" (254). Likewise, McCormack is—rightly—keen to retain the language of the terms "hypostasis" and the "hypostatic union" given its ability to accommodate "the suggestion that the Son has an eternal relation to Jesus that has now been actualized (rendered concretely real) through uniting in time" (255). Similarly, the concept of the Son's being "consubstantial with the Father as regards his divinity, and the same consubstantial with us as regards his humanity" is for McCormack to be retained as an expression of the *homoousios* of the Nicene Creed in the sense that "Christ is 'one' with the Father and 'one' with us," although this will have to be expressed "without resorting to the concepts of divine and human substance" (256). All these elements must be retained to provide the basis for a repair.

What, then, needs to be replaced or, at least, interpreted in a way different from those ways of understanding the Definition that make reference to Jesus seem redundant? McCormack is clear that the idea of "an *independent* Logos *asarkos* . . . without a determination for incarnation" is something about which the Bible knows nothing. He writes: "Let us not mince words: the preexistent Logos *as such* is a pure postulate, a human invention, alleged to be complete without regard for its activity *ad extra*. It is an 'idol' by any other name" (253). One should not overlook the qualifiers. It is the idea of an "*independent* Logos *as such*" that is being criticized here. This is surely right, because in the scriptural witness it is the Logos who is by no means independent, but in the beginning "was with God, and the Word was with God" (John 1:1), and it is this Word who "became flesh and lived among us, and we have seen his glory, the glory of a father's only son, full of grace and truth" (John 1:14). These scriptural phrases exclude both the idea of an independent Logos and, even more so, the idea of a Logos "as such." Similarly, McCormack objects to the concept of two "natures," not only for Schleiermacher's reason that the divine and the human cannot be comprehended under one concept,[8] or for Alvin Plantinga's reason that a being that does not belong to any genus cannot rightly be said to have a nature.[9] The real

---

8. Cf. Friedrich D. E. Schleiermacher, *The Christian Faith*, ed. H. R. Mackintosh and J. S. Stewart, trans. Terrence Tice, Catherine L. Kelsey, and Edwina Lawler (London: Bloomsbury T&T Clark, 2016), §96.1, 392.

9. See Alvin Plantinga, *Does God Have a Nature?* (Milwaukee, WI: Marquette University Press, 1980).

difficulty, for McCormack, lies in the unspecified language of a "human nature," and he expresses his sympathy for Karl Barth's move "in historicizing
the 'natures'—rendering them in terms of a single, shared history" (255).

It is worth noting that such an assessment of what needs to be retained in
order to repair always involves both historical and systematic criteria with
regard to the development of the doctrinal debates to which Chalcedon responded and with regard to the doctrinal development that responded to the
Chalcedonian Definition. Bruce McCormack's work is an outstanding and
challenging example of how the systematic questions open up the historical
debates in a way that focuses on the inner logic of the theological arguments,
entangled in complex debates, and so provides an essential context for the
contingent historical encounters.

"Ontological Receptivity"—A Repair Manual

The point where Chalcedon needs repairing, for McCormack, is simply
this: the Chalcedonian emphasis on the one christological subject must be
retained while at the same time the gospel story of Jesus must be given constitutive significance for the definition of the identity of the Logos. This is
achieved by making "Jesus in the power of the Holy Spirit to be the performative agent of all that is done by the God-human" (257–58). It is this move
that necessitates that "the Logos . . . be understood as relating to the human
Jesus *receptively*," receiving all that Jesus did and suffered into the eternal life
of the Logos. This could only be coherent if this "ontological receptivity" is
"itself an active relation," fulfilling what is the *telos* of the being of the Logos
in the Trinity from the beginning (258). This sense includes the idea that the
Logos is from eternity *incarnandus* and becomes *incarnatus* in time as the
actualization of this eternal determination. This does not imply a violation
of divine immutability, although it deviates from some conventional understandings of the impassibility of the divine essence by rendering "the being
of God affective" (258). McCormack's proposal for repairing Chalcedon is
extremely parsimonious. His repair manual consists of but one page, but it
has a considerable appendix of implications and consequences.

The implications of introducing ontological receptivity are far-reaching,
for Christology as well as for the doctrine of God. For Christology, the mode
in which the Logos actively receives the experiences of Jesus must be specified with regard to the character of the experience even in its utmost abyss,
the experience of dying the death of a human life. For this experience of Jesus
to be an event in the divine life of the Logos, one must say that this human

experience is taken up into the "unquenchable, inexhaustible" eternal life, an event that McCormack describes as "absorption" (259). This already implies that the life of God stands beyond the alternative of life or death that characterizes all created life, so that the overcoming of death in the cross of Christ can only be understood as the death of death as ultimate separation from God as the source of life, and so a participation in the eternal life of God, as this finite one. Similarly, McCormack explains that the human experiencing of Jesus in its discursive character is received in the knowledge of the Logos as a mode of "'illuminating' (intensifying) the knowledge that is his as divine" (260). Analogically, the struggle of Jesus in the Garden of Gethsemane to accept the Father's will in his active obedience must be understood to be received by the Logos in the sense that "divine acts of willing have been 'illuminated' through the experiences of having been 'completed' in a human act of willing that is deliberative and conditioned by internal and external factors" (260). One can already see that the ontological receptivity that is elaborated christologically sets the agenda for a discussion of the divine perfections that does not define human and divine attributes as logical complements, as if one must be seen as the negation of the other.

The introduction of ontological receptivity in the relationship between Jesus and the eternal solves, McCormack claims, a whole series of problems. Once this composite subject of the gospel story is introduced, one can retain the dyothelite insistence on two wills but insist on only one operation. Once a "composite subject" is established, the necessity of developing a doctrine both of the *communicatio operationum* and of the *communio idiomatum* is no longer given: "this entire discussion (including its later Lutheran and Reformed versions needs, in my judgment, to be consigned to the dustbin of history" (263). Positively, this means that the properties of the human Jesus belong to the personal properties of the Logos. They are not something that needs to be added. One can, however, wonder whether these earlier debates do not have a crucial function in the development of this doctrine of the divine perfections that takes the ontological receptivity of the eternal Son into account and so allows the Jesus of the Gospels to make a difference to the way the divine attributes are conceived. McCormack illustrates this point with regard to divine omnipotence, which in his account leads to reflections on the use of power in weakness and not on the nonuse of power (267).

The most surprising effect, however, is that the introduction of ontological receptivity redefines how the divine kenosis of Philippians 2:6–8 is to be understood: "The *divine kenosis* borne witness to in Phil 2:6–8 is ontological receptivity" (263). There is, therefore, no need to entertain the notion of a divestment of power or a surrender of divine attributes. McCormack's recommendation for repairing Chalcedon thus renders the discussions of the nineteenth-century kenoticists redundant, because what they tried to achieve, reconciling classical patristic Christology with the new pictures of Jesus in history, can be more easily achieved through the introduction of ontological receptivity. If ever there was an application of Ockham's razor in the history of christological thought, this must be seen as an exemplary case.

There is one implication that still needs to be mentioned. If one affirms the ontological receptivity to Jesus of the eternal Son, this results in a different view of the hiddenness of God in God's self-revelation. In the self-revelation of the eternal Son in Jesus the hiddenness of God is no longer to be placed beyond the boundaries of the humanly knowable, nor in a "mystery" that transcends what is humanly knowable and sayable—the classic case of "tight-corner apophaticism." The hiddenness is rather the mode of divine self-revelation, which as concealment discloses something essential about the being of God the Son: the humility of the eternal Son in his self-revelation (272–73).

There is, of course, much more to be said with regard to Bruce McCormack's proposal for repairing Chalcedon. It is, in a way, a minimalist proposal with maximal effects. It allows us to retain the whole of the Chalcedonian Definition (with the possible exception of the language of natures that is, at least, in need of reinterpretation) by suggesting that we take as the subject of the Definition the one divine-human subject that is constituted through the ontological receptivity of the Son to Jesus and to see this receptivity as grounded "from the beginning" in the humility of the eternal Son. As such, McCormack's proposal goes a long way in healing the fragmentation of Jesus Christ into the disjointed parts of the Son of God of christological dogma, the Christ of saving faith, and the Jesus of history. It might, however, be helpful for a conversation with McCormack to try to place his proposal within a wider framework of questions on the interplay between Christology and the doctrine of God.

The Starting Point of Christology

There has been a long discussion in modern Christology on the appropriate starting point for Christology. Should it start "from above," from the Second Person of the Trinity, and then follow the way of the Son to the incarnation in Jesus, through his life, death, and resurrection to the ascension? Or should it start from "below," from the Jesus of history, and then proceed through the way in which the resurrection enabled believers to see in Jesus the Christ of faith and the eternal Son incarnate? McCormack has described the structure of his planned series of three volumes, starting with Christology and then moving to the doctrine of God in order to develop the doctrine of the atonement in the third part, as "a dialectical movement in thought 'from below to above' and only then and on that basis, 'from above to below'" (2).

It seems to me that the proper starting point of Christology, and perhaps of the whole of Christian dogmatics,[10] is Christian worship today, which, just like the witnesses of the New Testament, is characterized by trust that believers today live in an enduring communion of life with their crucified risen Lord, a communion that is celebrated in the Eucharist and the proclamation of the gospel, and that believers participate in the Spirit in Christ's filial relationship to God the Father. One of the reasons why this starting point for Christology seems most appropriate is that it tries to start with what in the celebration of worship is joined together, and not with one of the parts that have been put asunder by the criticism of the Enlightenment. In worship, reference to Jesus is constitutive for the celebration of the Eucharist and the proclamation of the gospel, which places the celebrating, listening, witnessing, and praying community in the context of the whole narrative of God's ways with God's creation, from Alpha to Omega, from creation to the eschatological consummation. The Christ of faith is the one with whom communion is kept through trust in the promise of the gospel and the celebration of the Eucharist. We can only hope that this opens the way to our eternal salvation, if we trust that Jesus Christ is indeed the Son of God of Christology who "for us human beings and our salvation came down from heaven, was incarnate of the Holy Spirit and the virgin Mary and became a human being," as the Nicene Creed professes. The biblical testimonies are in this way taken up in the use of the Bible as Scripture, which leads to the adoption of scriptural ways of speaking of God in Christ through the Spirit; this in turn enables contemporary speaking to God through Christ and in the Spirit. The dogmatic tradition is taken up in the profession of the Creed and, hopefully, in the exposition of Christian teaching as part of the

---

10. In modern theology this view was first programmatically developed by Geoffrey Wainwright, *Doxology: The Praise of God in Worship, Doctrine and Life; A Systematic Theology* (London: Epworth, 1980). I have sketched the implications of such an approach for Christology in "Wer sagt den Ihr, dass ich sei? (Mt 16,15). Eine systematisch-theologische Skizze zur Lehre von der Person Christi," in *Christologie*, ed. Elisabeth Gräb-Schmidt and Reiner Preul, Marburger Jahrbuch Theologie 23 (Leipzig: Evangelische Verlagsanstalt, 2011), 41–58.

proclamation of the gospel. Reference to the Jesus of history, to the Christ of faith, and to the Son of God of the creeds is in this way embedded in the practice of worship, which presupposes the situation of the co-presence of the assembled congregation with the triune God.

This focus on worship as the context and starting point of Christology and, indeed, of all theology, should not be understood as a reduction of theology to liturgy. Rather, it views Christian worship as the point of integration of the different dimensions of Christian faith. Christian theology as faith thinking is crucially concerned with developing a view of reality that is grounded in the self-communication of the triune God who alone is to be worshipped. Most of the classics of Christian theology are rooted in Christian worship and are concerned with developing criteria, something like liturgical rubrics, for worship that is appropriate to the self-communication of God. Christian ethics as faith acting relies centrally on the formation of Christian persons in community, not least in a worshipping community, as the foundation for an ethics of goods, virtues, and obligations. Therefore, theology is not so much concerned with spelling out the *implications* of liturgical actions in Christian beliefs, with regard to our understanding of God, our view of what it means to be human, and our interpretation of the world, as with elucidating how these beliefs are *enacted* in the liturgy, involving the whole embodied personal being of the worshipers.

If, however, the emphasis is in this way on the enactment of beliefs in the speech acts and life acts of worship, then the content of such beliefs cannot be abstracted from the form of their communicative enactment. The being of the God who is worshiped cannot be separated from the forms of divine self-communication that form the foundation of worship. The being of God's human creatures, created in the image of God, cannot be properly determined without attention to the ways in which they respond to being addressed by God. Worship presupposes God as a self-communicating being and shapes the response to such self-communication in forms of human communication. These forms of communication—one can paradigmatically point to prayer as praise, thanksgiving, petition, and lament—have an ontological import that shapes the forms of communication and finds expression in the community's understanding of God, humanity, and the world.

Christian worship in all its forms understands itself as responsive action in answer to God's address in word, act, and being. This pattern of address and response is understood as rooted in God's being itself, if God's being is the being of the Father, the Logos/Son, and the Spirit, and it makes creatures in every dimension of their being communicative creatures, addressed and challenged to respond in every dimension of their life. Christian worship conducted "in the name of the Father, the Son and the Spirit" understands itself as going along the way in which God extends God's communication to us—from the Father, through the Son, in the Spirit—returning in the Spirit, through the Son and to the Father. In its most radical sense, worship is not just a celebration of a "word event," but a celebration of who we, the worshipers, are in relation to who God is for us and in Godself.

The point of this lengthy (but still far too sketchy) contextualization of the starting point of Christology is simply this. If we place Christology in the context of worship, in the communicative relations that constitute Christian worship, "ontological receptivity" is a central category. It applies to all that we receive from God and is at the center of many liturgical actions. We are who we are as creatures, as fallen creatures, reconciled with God in Christ, and destined for sanctification through the Holy Spirit in communion with the triune God, because of ontological receptivity. Being a creature is defined by ontological receptivity. That constitutes the fundamental asymmetry in the reciprocal relationship with God. On the other hand, the practice of worship also presupposes that God is receptive to humans relating to God in worship. Otherwise directing our prayers of praise, thanksgiving, lament, and petition to God would not make sense. But we do so in a specific sense that involves the triune God, by offering our prayers in the Spirit and through the Son, appealing to Christ as our intercessor before God the Father. How does the specific ontological receptivity of the eternal Son to Jesus, which McCormack gives the central place in his Reformed kenoticism, relate to the radical receptivity in which we stand in relation to God?

Threefold Divine Self-Giving and the Kenosis of the Son

Martin Luther famously summarized the Creed in the Large Catechism in a formula describing God's Trinitarian self-giving. While the Ten Commandments "teach us what we ought to do, the Creed tells us what God does for us and gives for us."[11] While the Ten Commandments make clear that we cannot fulfil what the law demands, the Creed, writes Luther, "brings pure grace and makes us righteous and acceptable to God." The knowledge of God's grace is the restitution of the human capacity that enables us to do what the commandments command. The "pure grace" that the Creed offers is then

---

11. *The Book of Concord: The Confessions of the Evangelical Lutheran Church*, ed. Robert Kolb and Timothy J. Wengert (Minneapolis: Fortress, 2000), 440.

summarized in the formula of God's threefold self-giving, "because we see here in the Creed how God gives himself completely to us, with all his gifts and power, to help us keep the Ten Commandments: the Father gives us all creation, Christ all his works, the Holy Spirit all his gifts."[12]

Luther's adaptation of the Augustinian language of the gift presents divine giving in terms of both Trinitarian self-donation and Trinitarian self-disclosure. He writes, "God himself has revealed and opened to us the most profound depths of his fatherly heart and his pure, unutterable love." This conjunction between God's self-donation and self-disclosure not only makes us gifted creatures, but also discloses our *telos* as it is defined in the depth of God's heart as love, revealing the purpose of the creation of human creatures: "For this very purpose he created us, so that he might redeem us and make us holy, and, moreover, having granted and bestowed upon us everything in heaven and on earth, he has also given us his Son and His Holy Spirit, through whom he brings us to himself."[13] God's threefold self-giving is aimed at our sanctification in being brought into communion with the triune God. This, however, does not involve us unawares as the objects of divine action, but involves us in such a way that we can recognize the trinitarian giver in God's self-giving and so trust in God ultimately. Luther writes: "we could never come to recognize the Father's favor and grace were it not for the Lord Christ, who is mirror of the Father's heart. Apart from him we see nothing but an angry and terrible judge. But neither could we know anything of Christ, had it not been revealed by the Holy Spirit."[14]

It is to be noted that this description of the generosity of the triune God in God's threefold divine self-giving combines an ontological dimension, expressing the relation of God's self-giving being to our created being, with an epistemic dimension, according to which God reveals God's being so that we know and recognize and are in this way brought to God the Father. This calls, as the appropriate form of reflection, for an ontology of communicative relations that is at the heart of the Christian understanding of God, humanity, and the world. This view is firmly rooted in the biblical traditions, and it has been rooted in the traditional language of the Son (as Logos) and the Spirit from the very beginning of Christian theologizing. One may wonder whether it has been possible to retain this interlacing of ontology and epistemology

12. *Book of Concord*, 440.
13. *Book of Concord*, 439.
14. *Book of Concord*, 440.

consistently throughout the history of Christian thought. The protracted discussion of the *communicatio idiomatum* may be a case in point.

We can see "Barth's 'rule'," as McCormack calls it (2), as an apt expression of this interlacing: "statements about the divine modes of being antecedently in themselves cannot be different in content from those that are to be made about their reality in revelation."[15] If we follow that rule, we will always have to start from the Spirit in Christian theology, from the place where God's revelation in Jesus Christ has come to its point in creating faith in us, so that we can recognize Jesus as the Christ and see him as the "mirror of the Father's heart." Luther was surely right in insisting that we could not know anything about Christ, "had it not been revealed by the Holy Spirit," for the Spirit reveals the Gospel of Christ through the word of Scripture, authenticated for us by the internal testimony of the Spirit to us as the truth of God's relationship to the world. What the Spirit gives us to know, is, however, precisely the Gospel of Christ, especially if we start from the Spirit in the structured interweaving of perspectives "from below" and "from above," which is at the heart of Christian worship.

Summarized in its most elementary form, what is communicated to us in the promise of the gospel and the celebration of the sacraments is the story of one personal subject, Jesus of Nazareth, who is confessed as the Christ, the Son of the living God. A reading of the gospel or a celebration of the sacraments that attributes certain aspects to the divine nature and others to the human nature necessarily destroys the narrative unity of the subject of the gospel. However, the story of this one person, Jesus of Nazareth, is narrated in such a way that everything he does is done in the authority of the God he calls Father and for those who without God are lost in God-forsakenness. There are thus two relationships that constitute the unity of the person of Jesus of Nazareth: the relationship to God, which is grounded in the relationship of God the Father to Jesus through the Spirit, and Jesus's relationship to the addressees of his life's witness to the coming of the king-dom of God. Everything that is told in the story of this one person—his life and his death, his deeds and his suffering, his message and his communica-tive acts—is an enactment of his relationship to God through the Spirit in his relationship with other human persons in the context of their cultural and natural settings in order to establish anew their relationship in the Spirit to God the Father. The relationship to God the Father in the Spirit "frames" the

15. Karl Barth, *Church Dogmatics* I/1, 2nd ed., ed. G. W. Bromiley and T. F. Torrance, trans. G. W. Bromiley (Edinburgh: T&T Clark, 1975), 479.

personal relationships in which Jesus as the one person of the gospel lives to other persons. Conceived by the Holy Spirit, born of Mary, called to his ministry by the Father in the Spirit, he lives his life as the "mirror of the Father's heart" and dies in active obedience to God the Father. Luther's image of the mirror is an apt expression for the fact that we see the relationship of God the Father in the Spirit to us through the way in which Jesus relates in the Spirit to God the Father. The resurrection of Jesus from the dead and his ascension to eternal life with God vindicate his message of the coming of the kingdom of God as the actualization of God's relationship to God's creation and disclose the unbroken relationship of God to Jesus, even in Jesus's death. The narrative unity of the story is maintained in that Jesus's relationship to God the Father in the Spirit is the way in which God the Father's relationship to Jesus and through Jesus to the whole of creation is disclosed.

This ultra-brief sketch serves to make one point with regard to what Christians mean when they talk about Jesus being truly God and truly human. On the basis of the gospel story we must claim that the divinity of Jesus is his relationship to God the Father in the Spirit as the eternal Son. The identity of Jesus as the Son is a strictly relational identity, comprising the elements of distinction in his pointing to God the Father as the ground and source of his being as the Son and his communion with the Father in the Spirit. The *locus* of the divinity of Jesus is his identity as the Son, which is enacted in his relationship to the Father in the Spirit, which, in turn, discloses the relationship of the Father to him. Only in this way, through the personal relationship between Jesus and the Father can one talk about his exemplifying the divine "nature," a concept that is, indeed, in need of heavy qualification if it is to be applied to God. Furthermore, Jesus's divinity as his divine sonship is oriented toward communicating this filial relationship to God the Father in the Spirit to others, who through him and in the Spirit participate in this filial relationship as God's children (cf. Rom 8:15–17).

Similarly, Jesus's humanity is not simply his possession of a "human nature," used as a concept of classification for whatever it means to be human. Rather, it is the actualization of true humanity in this particular Jew of the first century. The way in which Jesus practiced his humanity in relation to others makes clear that humanity is only ever actualized as a particular personal human identity, in which the personal particularity of human life as it is grounded in God becomes the matrix of speaking about the human, always concretely and always particularly. What is striking about the Gospel story is that Jesus's humanity is portrayed not so much as exemplifying an individual archetype of what it means to be human in abstraction from all the relationships in which Jesus lives. Rather, Jesus's true humanity is relational in the sense that, in encountering Jesus, the true humanity of others is restored, reinstated, and recognized as the inalienable dignity conferred to every human being in that their personal identity is rooted in the triune God. Jesus's humanity is underdetermined when it is just interpreted as factual humanity or as individual archetypal humanity. Dietrich Bonhoeffer's view of the pro-existence of Jesus, which he summarized in the formula "being there for others" (*Dasein für andere*),[16] seems to point in the right direction when it sees the humanity of Jesus as the way in which true humanity is communicated to those who encounter him.

The point of this brief exploration is to indicate a way in which the divinity and humanity of Jesus can be expressed in a "noncompetitive" relationship precisely by conceptually redefining Jesus's divinity as his Sonship in relation to God the Father in the Spirit and his humanity as the actualization of what humans are meant to be in relation to others as their identity is grounded in the relationship of the triune God to them. The divinity and the humanity of Jesus are both enacted in one personal life in which Jesus's divinity, his relationship to God the Father in the Spirit, is disclosed precisely in this human life in the relationship he has to others.

How should one approach the question of kenosis in this framework? Can the exhortation to be of the mind of Christ (Phil 2:1–5) which Paul supports with the hymn to Christ Jesus, contrasting Christ Jesus's self-emptying (Phil 2:7) with God's exaltation of Christ (Phil 2:9), find a place in the christological sketch that we have introduced all too briefly? We can take our direction again from Martin Luther. In his exposition of the Christ hymn in Philippians 2, he interprets the "taking the form of servant" by interpreting it as acting in the "gesture" of a servant. Luther uses the German word *Gebärde*, which is the communicative enactment of a content through all available semiotic means without words. Luther discusses the various ways in which the essence of a being comes to expression in the gesture of its life, in its self-manifestation. While Christ was in the form of God in which his form of existence corresponded to his being, he chose a form of existence that did *not* correspond to his being, but underlined the character of his being.[17] Luther contrasts the self-emptying of Christ in order to become obedient unto death (Phil 2:8) with the self-exaltation of the first humans in Genesis 3.

16. See Dietrich Bonhoeffer, "Outline for a Book," in *The Bonhoeffer Reader*, ed. Clifford J. Green and Michael P. DeJonge (Minneapolis: Fortress, 2013), 813.
17. See in more detail Schwöbel, "Form of a Servant," 61–64.

Whereas Eve, in her desire to be like God and following the promise of the serpent by doubting God's word, is attracted to the fruit because it seems good and beautiful and promises true knowledge (the three transcendentals being apprehended apart from their ground in God), Christ Jesus regards to be equal with God not as something to be usurped, and empties himself in order to take the form, the appearance of a servant. This self-emptying is only possible because he has received equality with God, but he chooses this form of self-manifestation, the Son's self-giving in his obedience unto death, to manifest the Father's love as self-giving love. Both stories end in enlightenment: Adam and Eve recognize that they are naked; Christ Jesus is acclaimed by all as the Lord, to the glory of God the Father (Phil 2:11). For Luther, the contrast exists between the desire for self-elevation of the first humans and the self-humbling of Christ Jesus, who in this way, as a servant, obedient unto death, is elevated by God. The self-disclosure of God under the opposite is for Luther a central aspect of divine self-giving.[18] It is a way of disclosing the being of God in the form of a servant that reveals God's true glory as the glory of the one who stoops down to raise the poor from the dust and seats them with princes (Ps 113:6). In the Christ hymn of Philippians, a summary of Jesus's story in worship, Christ Jesus manifests in this way God's relationship to his creation that he calls into being from nothing, justifies the sinner through God's own creative justice, and perfects those who cannot perfect themselves by perfecting them in communion with God's glorious being. Christ Jesus's self-emptying is the self-disclosure appropriate to the self-giving of the triune God. The kenosis is an expression of the *plērōsis*, the abundance of God's trinitarian generosity.

If we follow Barth's rule that "statements about the divine modes of being antecedently in themselves cannot be different in content from those that are to be made about their reality in revelation," where does that leave us with regard to the eternal Trinity? It seems that the biblical witness challenges us to locate ontological receptivity in the very heart of the being of the triune God. When the unbegotten Father "begets" the Son, the Father communicates the fullness of the divine essence to the Son, thereby freely positing the other as distinct from the Father's being, yet of one essence with the Father. Actively begetting on the part of the Father implies passively being begotten for the Son. Similarly, the procession of the Spirit from the Father makes the Spirit the one who passively proceeds, but who does not initiate

---

18. See Steven D. Paulson, "Luther on the Hidden God," *Word & World* 19, no. 4 (1999): 362–71.

an active procession.[19] With regard to the relations of origin, there is a place for ontological passivity in the Trinity. However, these relations do not yet establish ontological receptivity, for this requires the active recognition of the begottenness of the Son across all the active relations of the Son to the Father, exemplified in the Son's active obedience. Moreover, the biblical witness seems to require that we see the trinitarian relations just in this sense as asymmetrical, but also as reciprocal, which would also demand ontological receptivity in the Father. Exactly this seems to be required if we understand the triune God as the living God, a community of mutual love. If we want to maintain that God is love, ontological receptivity must be seen as inscribed in the eternal communicative being of the Trinity. If we follow this route of thought, we would not have to postulate with Hans Urs von Balthasar an *Ur*-kenosis in the eternal trinitarian life of love. The acknowledgment of the generation from the Father in the Son does not involve any emptying, any self-abnegation or any self-divestment at all. It is simply the recognition of a freely given hypostatic identity in essential communion with the Father. It is the actuality of divine self-giving and receiving that constitutes the life of the triune God of love, the primordial generosity anchored in the very being of the triune God. It is this which opens up the possibility of interpreting the kenosis of the Son as the actualization of divine *plērōsis* in the divine economy in a form appropriate to fallen creatures who have fallen as they attempt to elevate themselves apart from God.

It seems that with this systematic move we have followed Bruce McCormack's suggestion to recast the question of kenosis *as ontological receptivity* far too well by locating ontological receptivity in the life of the whole triune God, Father, Son, and Holy Spirit, and not only with regard to the ontological receptivity of the eternal Son to Jesus. How can we account for the specific point of concern of McCormack within the wider scheme we have suggested? This brings us back to McCormack's original question of how Jesus, the Jesus of the Gospels, can matter for Christology and for our understanding of the triune God, conceived along the lines of repairing the Chalcedonian Definition without collapsing the divine processions, which constitute God's eternal being, into the trinitarian missions in relation to creation in time and space. There are two implications of the way in which we have reflected on McCormack's proposal that seem to be relevant here. If ontological receptivity is eternally constitutive of the being of the trinitarian life of God and so also of the eternal Son, the ontological receptivity of the

19. For a paradigmatic account see Thomas Aquinas, *Summa Theologiae*, trans. English Dominican Province (New York: Benziger Bros., 1947), Ia, q. 28, ad. 4.

eternal Son is what essentially characterizes the Trinity as a communion of love in the personal property of the Son. The ontological receptivity of the eternal Son is thus one exemplification of what constitutes the life of the Trinity as a whole. Furthermore, if we understand God's being from all eternity as being constituted in the communication of the divine essence in the "begetting" of the Son and the "proceeding" of the Spirit, God's being is not only "being in communion," but also "being in communication." If the incarnation is the free self-communication of the triune God to creation, it must also be that the economic self-communication of God in the asymmetrical ontological reciprocity we have sketched above is included in the immanent self-communication of God's own being. The relationship of Jesus to God the Father in the Spirit is the self-manifestation of the relationship of the eternal Son to the Father in the Spirit and as such cannot be excluded from the reciprocal communication which constitutes the life of the eternal Trinity.

There is, however, a problem here. In the picture we have developed, it is not the ontological receptivity of the eternal Son, but the asymmetrical reciprocal relationship of Jesus and the Father in the Spirit that constitutes the self-manifestation of the eternal Trinity in the economic Trinity. Just as the Gospel tells us, Jesus relates to the Father in the Spirit and not to the *Logos asarkos*. Bruce McCormack has reminded us that Scripture tells us nothing about the *Logos asarkos*. It is a human construct to clarify the relationship between Jesus and the God he addresses as Father. It is not a separate entity such that the Son existed during the incarnation as a double identity of a *Logos asarkos* and a *Logos ensarkos*, the Jesus of the Gospels. McCormack has already indicated that the Logos must be understood from eternity as the Logos *incarnandus* whose being is actualized in time as the Logos *incarnatus*.[20] We have no other way for the identification of the Logos than the Gospel story of Jesus. However, this temporal story, located at a particular location in space and time, is determinative of the identity of the Son. Talking about the Logos *asarkos* is a particular and often misunderstood *mode* of speaking about the Logos *ensarkos* which has the point of underscoring that what needs to said about the relationship of Jesus to God the Father in the Spirit is true of the relationship of the eternal Son to God the Father in the Spirit. To make this point is the goal of McCormack's suggestion for the repair of Chalcedon. Chalcedon leads to all the difficulties that were the subject of the post-Chalcedonian debates if the subject of the Definition, the "one and

---

20. Bruce McCormack is not alone in this; see Wilfried Härle, *Outline of Christian Dogmatics: An Evangelical Dogmatics* (Grand Rapids: Eerdmans, 2015), 337–38.

the same Son," is identified with the Logos *asarkos* and not with Jesus as the person of the union. It seems to me that the problematical consequences of speaking of the Logos *asarkos* in abstraction from the Gospel story can only be avoided if one interprets Chalcedon, as the Definition itself insists, strictly within the framework of the Nicene-Constantinopolitan Creed, which makes the relationship to God the Father the defining relationship of the "one Lord, Jesus Christ." Could it be that the later controversies concerning the *extra Calvinisticum* belong, well, perhaps not in the "dustbin of history," as Mc-Cormack has suggested with regard to the *communicatio idiomatum* (263), but on the laboratory table of theological analysis—to see whether perhaps in speaking of the *Logos asarkos* one *mode* of *speaking* of the "one Lord, Jesus Christ" has been turned into a separate mode of *being*.

This last remark already indicates that McCormack's work has made a distinctive and immensely valuable proposal for the solution of the problems that have exercised christological discussion for centuries. One of his suggestions, to distinguish clearly between divine impassibility and divine immutability, must be embraced wholeheartedly. Divine passibility in the sense of divine ontological receptivity in the immanent and the ontological Trinity and in their relationship must be clearly asserted. The biblical witness makes this task imperative. This does not, however, apply to divine immutability, which is equally as well supported in Scripture as divine passibility. Could it be that divine immutability is not just a moral attribute, identical with God's faithfulness, but rather the eternal persistence of the mutual, reciprocal (therefore including passibility), but also *asymmetrical* relationships in the divine life that constitute both the persons of the Trinity and their communion in the one essence?

An Afterthought

In working through the questions that Bruce McCormack has presented in such magisterial fashion and in reflecting on his answers, the question occurred to me more than once whether the traditional terminology especially of the doctrine of the Trinity, but also of "classic" Christology must be reconsidered. Wolfhart Pannenberg already pointed out that the language of "begetting" and "proceeding," "breathing," and "sending and gift" can hardly claim scriptural support in the way they are presented in the classical expositions of doctrine.[21] In recent years, I have been more and more per-

---

21. See Wolfhart Pannenberg, *Systematic Theology*, trans. Geoffrey W. Bromiley (Edinburgh: T&T Clark, 1988), 1:304-8.

suaded by Martin Luther's way of recasting traditional trinitarian language in terms of a conversation in which the Father is from eternity the Speaker, the Son the Word that the Father speaks, and the Holy Spirit the Listener—in McCormack's terms the eternal *exemplar* of ontological receptivity.[22] I wonder whether such a view of the immanent Trinity could not more easily be employed for what needs to be said on the basis of the scriptural witness to a creation that is spoken into being such that whatever is, is part of God's vocabulary,[23] of the Word that becomes human, of the word of the cross that promises our salvation, which we would then, with Luther, have to imagine as God's speaking to us eternally. Would such a conceptuality, firmly binding being and meaning together in an ontology of communicative relations, help to solve some of the problems with which we have been struggling?

These are just notes for a conversation with Bruce McCormack. I am sure that I will have much to learn in such conversation. And perhaps, if Luther is right and God is conversation, we may hope that our theological conversations resonate with echoes of the object of such conversations.

22. See Christoph Schwöbel, "Martin Luther and the Trinity," in *Oxford Research Encyclopedia of Religion* (Oxford: Oxford University Press, 2017), http://religion.oxfordre.com, accessed July 1, 2021, and for the systematic implications, Christoph Schwöbel, "God as Conversation: Reflections on a Theological Ontology of Communicative Relations," in *Theology of Conversation: Towards a Relational Theology*, ed. Jacques Haers, Bibliotheca Ephemeridum Theologicarum Lovaniensium 172 (Leuven: Peeters, 2003), 43–67. See also Christoph Schwöbel, "Einfach Gott. Trinitätstheologie am Anfang des 21. Jahrhunderts," *Neue Zeitschrift für Systematische Theologie* 62, no. 4 (2020): 519–41.

23. See Christoph Schwöbel, "We Are All God's Vocabulary: The Idea of Creation as a Speech-Act of the Trinitarian God and Its Significance for the Dialogue between Theology and Sciences," in *Knowing Creation: Perspectives from Theology, Philosophy, and Science*, ed. Andrew B. Torrance and Thomas H. McCall (Grand Rapids: Zondervan, 2018), 47–68.

16

The End of Humanity
and the Beginning of Kenosis

Hanna Reichel

"That's one small step for a man, one giant leap for mankind," Neil Armstrong famously declared as he landed on the moon. But how do we know according to which scale we should measure this event, and which horizon best describes its significance? Which particularities do we pick out in characterizing an event? If we describe Armstrong's leap with regard to physical distance crossed, the objectively true measurement will only miss what makes the step remarkable. Contextualizing it as "stepping out of a spacecraft unto solid ground" would at least clarify that comparing it with jumps of Olympic athletes is beside the point. Only calibrating the scale of measurement to the hitherto uncrossed boundary between "earth" and "moon" allows us to understand what set this leap apart.

However, once we discern this salient boundary, we might wonder whether "mankind" really picks out the subject well, or whether Armstrong might more precisely be described as an "earthling" stepping onto the moon. Then again, in the fierce international competition that characterized the "race to the moon," a Russian observer might register the incident as "an American" having set foot on the moon. Does the narrower national lens obscure the historic achievement? Or is the generalization more misleading, since it insinuates a united effort that did not historically exist? Conceptual calibration matters, not only in terms of accuracy, but also in terms of the ramifications it brings into view or forecloses.

290 / *Hanna Reichel*

(Cur) Deus Homo, *or How to Measure a Leap?*

How to measure a leap? How to understand a crossing? Different descriptions are not only a matter of scale; they also open up meanings pertaining to different reference systems. Consider the claim, "Esmeralda swam across a river before giving birth to a baby girl." From this characterization, we might infer that an existential, life-changing event took place. Recalibrating the statement to "a Mexican woman crossed the Rio Grande before giving birth to a baby girl" clarifies that the crossing was not merely a strenuous exercise, but the overcoming of a national boundary with legal consequences. Both descriptions are correct, and both might indeed be adequate in different contexts. The former might be more relevant in a medical assessment of Esmeralda's physical condition. But the latter will be more helpful in ascertaining the citizenship of the newborn baby. Conceptual calibration thus prefigures what meanings we may discern in an event.

The incarnation marks a very particular crossing. The measure of this "leap" defines the Christian understanding of God and constitutes Christian hope for redemption, salvation, and the promise of communion between creator and creature. *Which* categories ought to bear theological weight in its description, and *what* comes into view by drawing them out? In reference to widespread assumptions about God—what God *ought* to be like in order to be God—three "scandals of particularity" come into view: the incarnation's historical singularity, its indelible materiality, and its irreducible suffering.[1] From Chalcedon's focus on "human nature" through Anselm's *Cur Deus Homo?* to contemporary theologies of God becoming human,[2] we are so used to describing all three scandals of this crossing in terms of the "humanity of God" that it almost seems ridiculous to ask whether this is, in fact, the most precise and useful theological calibration of the incarnation. Nevertheless, I ask: Can we be sure humanity is indeed its most salient horizon? What alternative calibrations are possible, and what overlooked theological ramifications would they bring to the fore?

Let me state from the outset: I am not saying that God did not become human. I am not saying that Jesus was not human. I am not saying that the incarnation does not have ultimate significance for humanity. My caution is twofold: (1) identifying the incarnation with "becoming human" has led

1. Cf. Niels Henrik Gregersen, introduction to *Incarnation: On the Scope and Depth of Christology*, ed. Niels Henrik Gregersen (Minneapolis: Fortress, 2015), 4.
2. Reinhard Feldmeier and Hermann Spieckermann, *God Becoming Human: Incarnation in the Christian Bible*, trans. Brian McNeil (Waco, TX: Baylor University Press, 2021).

to the (potentially misplaced) reification of the category of humanity as a theological universal, even as a soteriological category in itself; and (2) permitting ourselves to recalibrate the same event with reference to other categories might afford valuable theological insights. I draw out these concerns in two rounds. Building on Rosemary Radford Ruether, I ask whether foregrounding the "humanity" of Christ might miscalibrate the particularity of the incarnation in a similar manner as stressing his "maleness" would. With Gregory Nazianzen's soteriological axiom, I then inquire whether spelling out the comprehensive significance of the incarnation in aspects pertaining to "human nature" might miscalibrate the universality of the incarnation.

The rest of this chapter is a thought experiment. Revisiting the biblical testimony without the habitual predetermination to interpret it along the lines of "humanity," it is surprising how little salience the category has in the testimony of the New Testament. (Due to the limited scope of this chapter, I focus primarily on Paul and John.) The New Testament foregrounds three concentric horizons with regard to which the relevance of the one incarnational "leap" is typically expressed: there is an almost indexical insistence on the redemptive movement of God in the *singular* person of Jesus Christ (the scandal of singularity); then, his relevance for the cosmic, *universal* horizon of "the world," "the *kosmos*," "all flesh" is clearly proclaimed (the scandal of materiality); and finally, the incarnation obviously has immediate relevance in the adoption of those who "belong to Christ" into the *particular* horizon of God's history with God's people, where God's redemptive presence is already historically effective. Even as all three of these horizons can obviously be described with reference to humanity, it is clear that none of them precisely maps onto the boundaries of humanity. But even so, the third, intermediary category is surprisingly challenging to pin down. I ultimately find its horizon not to be constituted by a creaturely particularity at all, but by the particularity of God: behind the scandal of suffering lies the scandal of God's essential kenosis.

Can a Male Savior Save Women? Miscalibrating Particularity

Many foundational documents in Western history talk about "man" as an anthropological universal: "We hold these truths to be self-evident, that all men are created equal."[3] More contemporary declarations have typically corrected masculine equivocations of humanity to read, "All human beings are born free and equal in dignity and rights."[4]

---

3. US Declaration of Independence 1776, Preamble.
4. UN Declaration of Human Rights 1948, art. 1.

Rosemary Radford Ruether's provocative question, "Can a male savior save women?," is an excellent example of questioning such a miscalibration in theology. Ruether points out how an anthropological ontology according to which "only the male represents the fullness of human potential" justified itself by reasoning: in Christ, God assumed male flesh, therefore only male flesh could adequately represent the divine.[5] With reference to the particularity of incarnation, it thus foreclosed the admission of non-males to church offices.

Ruether's question was obviously rhetorical. Soteriologically, the tradition she critiqued clearly held that Christ's soteriological significance was universal. Her question thus exposed that interpreting Christ narrowly through the particularity of his (historically presumably accurate) masculinity was as ridiculous as suggesting that he was only the savior of human males. Ruether questioned whether the anthropological, ecclesiological, and ethical conclusions drawn actually attached relevance to the right category of his earthly existence. She insisted that the incarnation needed to be recalibrated to be about God's humanity, not about God's masculinity, and thus she stripped the sexism rampant in much of the tradition of any theological warrant.

Ruether's intervention thoughtfully exposed what we may call a fallacy of misplaced concreteness. The Whiteheadian term describes the equivocation of an (otherwise helpful, even necessary) abstraction with the object it was supposed to represent.[6] This diagnosis of unhelpful reification also allows us to inquire: Which particularity should qualify for abstraction in any given process of conceptual modeling, including theological reflection? Regarding salvation in Christ, it may seem rather obvious that masculinity is a misplaced concreteness. While there is little reason to doubt that the historical Jesus was male, it also seems clear that isolating and reflecting on his maleness will not provide an adequate account of the incarnation. Similarly, we may ask, are we sure that we are not committing a similar miscalibration when picking out the salient particularity as "God becoming *human*" in Christ?

Quod non assumptum, non sanatum? Miscalibrating Universality

Which particularities "matter" in the event, how, and to whom? That the incarnation "matters" (pun intended), and matters tremendously, is what

---

5. Rosemary Radford Ruether, "Christology and Feminism: Can a Male Saviour Save Women?," in *To Change the World: Christology and Cultural Criticism* (New York: Cross-road, 1981), 45.

6. Alfred N. Whitehead, *Science and the Modern World* (New York: Macmillan, 1925), 74.

Christian faith has always assumed, and nothing less than the non-docetic efficaciousness and comprehensive scope of salvation is at stake: "God [sent the Son into the world] in order that the world might be saved through him" (John 3:17). Gregory Nazianzus famously claimed, "The unassumed is the unhealed, but what is united with God is also being saved."[7] Presupposing *that* the incarnation had comprehensive significance, Gregory thus historically maintained against Apollinaris of Laodicea that Christ needed to be "fully" human, i.e., endowed with all human faculties and capacities in order that all of these might be reconciled in the incarnation.

Gregory's dictum is often called "the soteriological axiom," and it has become a widely invoked theological touchstone for calibrating the incarnation. On closer examination, there seem to be several separate theological assumptions wrapped up in it. In order to warrant the conclusion that Christ must have been "fully human," Gregory implicitly stipulates: (1) only God can save; (2) God saves through uniting what is to be saved to Godself in Christ ("assuming"); (3) uniting one specimen to Christ redeems its "nature," i.e., the redemptive effect extends to all members of its class; (4) the whole human being is in need of salvation; (5) all that is necessary for salvation has been accomplished in Christ. Leaving aside other questions that could be raised about these assumptions, I want to point out that as Gregory meant to safeguard effective, comprehensive salvation (5), he did so in terms of the particularly *human* condition (4). While none of the consequences drawn may be incorrect, the calibration to humanity leads to an implicit identification of "the whole human being" and "all that is necessary for salvation." Ever since the early christological controversies, the full humanity that is assumed by Christ has thus been reified as the scope of salvation. Other calibrations have dropped out of view.

If "full humanity" was used in the ancient church and beyond as signaling the comprehensive significance of the incarnation, we might question whether it casts the horizon of its significance wide enough. Narrowing our reflection to the incarnation's significance engenders an anthropocentrism that at least excludes the nonhuman creation from view, but can also inform its treatment as other, subordinate, and fit for exploitation. Just as Ruether questioned whether the logos exclusively assumes *male* flesh, we may thus

---

7. Gregory of Nazianzus, *On God and Christ: The Five Theological Orations and Two Letters to Cledonius*, trans. Frederick Williams and Lionel Wickham (Crestwood, NY: St. Vladimir's Seminary Press, 2002), 158.

ask whether Christ's flesh is exclusively *human*, or rather, more generally creaturely—with potential ramifications for all creatures?[8]

Furthermore, identifying the scope of salvation with the scope of the human being inadvertently leads to the reification of humanity as in and of itself a soteriological category. "He was made human so that he might make us gods,"[9] as Athanasius described the soteriological goal of the incarnation. Contemporary theologies prefer to speak of "the God who became human—and our becoming human."[10] Somewhere in the history of interpretation the conviction that "only God can save" has become congruous with "(true) humanity" as redemptive. Slippage between taxonomic (humanity as species) and moral meanings (humanity as virtue) testifies to this shift.

We may be careful to define true humanity christologically as, for example, Karl Barth has famously done, and subsequently emphatically endorse universal human rights on theological grounds.[11] Even so, we are still reifying the category and imbuing it with soteriological significance, engendering the need to negotiate what (and, more importantly, who) *counts* as human. History teaches us that postulated humanity does little to make those lives we habitually disregard grievable or recognizable as human. Postulated humanity creates economies of salvation according to who is able to "achieve" common humanity, e.g., along lines of racialization or ability. Is "humanity" really the best heuristic to calibrate redeemed being? What is won—and what (and who) slips from sight—by using "humanity" as the primary category to calibrate redeemed being?

Which Particularity? Whose Universality? And What Salvation?

Hermann Cremer helpfully reminds us, "All errors committed in the discussion of . . . God have to do with the fact that one does not begin with its actuality as it can be perceived and experienced in the self-affirmation of God in his revelation, but seeks to gain knowledge of it a priori."[12] His

---

8. David Clough, *On Animals: Systematic Theology* (London: T&T Clark, 2012), insightfully elucidates the arbitrariness of traditional anthropocentric readings with regard to the incarnation, and across doctrinal loci, offering the first full-fledged systematic theology that reflectively takes into account the nonhuman creation.

9. Athanasius, *On the Incarnation*, translation anonymous (Crestwood, NY: St. Vladimir's Seminary Press, 2011), 54.3.

10. Feldmeier and Spieckermann, *God Becoming Human*, 367.

11. Cf. Karl Barth, *The Humanity of God*, trans. Thomas Weiser and John Newton Thomas (Louisville: Westminster John Knox, 1999).

12. Hermann Cremer, *Die Christliche Lehre von den Eigenschaften Gottes* (Giessen:

caution applies to any theological axiom, including soteriological ones. In our search for an adequate understanding of particularity and universality for describing the incarnation, we thus turn to its singularity: Jesus Christ, as attested by the Scriptures.

The Incarnation's Anti-Particular Singularity: "Christ Jesus"

First and foremost, the New Testament testimonies gesture toward a scandalous singularity: that God incarnates into an—otherwise not very remarkable—individual creature and insists that something happened *here* that does not equally happen anywhere else. God's willingness for relationship with God's creation as well as God's boundary-crossing humility and love—which is well-attested throughout God's history with God's people—incarnationally intensifies, culminates, and becomes definitive of who God is in a singular, unprecedented, and inimitable manner: in the person of Christ Jesus. Gregersen calls this the "strict sense view" of incarnation, reserved to Jesus alone.[13]

For Paul, Christ demonstrates that God is "God for us" (Rom 8:31), "that is to say, as the one who addresses this world to save it."[14] While Paul never directly attributes divinity to Christ, he acclaims him as *Kyrios Jesus Christos* and integrates him into a christologically reformulated *Shema Yisrael* (Phil 2; 1 Cor 8:6).[15] He thus indicates that this individual is irreducible to the understanding of who God is and how God is at work in the world. This significance extends beyond those who believe in him to the whole of creation (cf. 1 Cor 8:6; 2 Cor 5:17; Gal 6:15). For Paul, the point of the Christ-event is soteriological, and its particular quality becomes apparent in the word of the cross (1 Cor 1:18–2:16) and the Philippians hymn (Phil 2:6–11): God's love scandalously upends the hierarchies of the world. Through the eternal Son, God adopts believers as children of God so that they become new creatures, a vanguard of the newness of all creation. God's transvaluative election of that which is weak, foolish, and poor in the eyes of the world is transformative for, and communicatively effective beyond, the elect.

John goes even further than Paul in describing the singularity of Christ. From the prologue to the witness of Thomas, he refers to Christ in terms

---

Brunnen, 2005), 83, famously adopted by Karl Barth as his own "rule" in *Church Dogmatics* I/1, 2nd ed., ed. G. W. Bromiley and T. F. Torrance, trans. G. W. Bromiley (Edinburgh: T&T Clark, 1975), 479.

13. Gregersen, "The Extended Body of Christ: Three Dimensions of Deep Incarnation," in *Incarnation*, 238.

14. Feldmeier and Spieckermann, *God Becoming Human*, 250.

15. Feldmeier and Spieckermann, *God Becoming Human*, 247.

that are usually exclusively reserved for the one God of Israel. Even more, he ascribes to him eternal preexistence, co-creatorship, and equal originality with the Father. John affirms, as Feldmann and Spieckermann note, "that one cannot speak appropriately about God if one prescinds from his relation to the Logos and hence to Jesus Christ."[16] For John, in fact, there are three distinct realities: God, the coeternal Logos predestined to become human, and the whole of the cosmos, "a reality that will likewise be a central element of the Gospel from now on: 'everything' as all things without distinction."[17] That "God is love" manifests itself in God's passion for the world and in Christ's passion at the cross. This love, however, is also communicative of the reciprocal immanence between the Father and the Logos to the believers. John describes the Logos both as origin and as goal of creation. He is, Feldmann and Spieckermann observe, the "path towards a new closeness on the part of God," first "to make creatures into children of God" and eventually "overcoming of the separation between the creator and the creature."[18]

One might be tempted to parse out Christ's singular significance in the particularities of this creature's existence. If *this* person reveals who God is and what God is like, then what about Jesus is theologically significant? As even our initial, theologically more inconspicuous examples of Neil Armstrong or Esmeralda demonstrate, some particulars of Jesus Christ will obviously seem more salient than others. His shoe size? Obviously not. His gender? Probably not. His Jewishness, however, well . . . !

While modern quests for the historical Jesus in particular have been interested in demonstrating his extraordinary qualities (if in different registers—as prophet, teacher, moral example, healer, revolutionary, and so on), the first New Testament testimonies are notoriously indifferent to the particulars of Jesus's earthly existence, and the ancient church maintained that parsing out Jesus's creaturely particularities does not lead to theological insight. While it thus generally resisted spelling the incarnation out in terms of particulars of whatever kind, the church did pick out Christ's humanity as the only particularity that "counts" in the incarnation. Thus, the "crossing" effected by the incarnation was described as the one between God and humanity. But can we be so sure that the church understood Christ's humanity as a *particularity*, even? They seem to have used it as the most generic category available: Humanity was rather de-particularized into representing the universal horizon of the incarnation.

---

16. Feldmeier and Spieckermann, *God Becoming Human*, 314.
17. Feldmeier and Spieckermann, *God Becoming Human*, 315–16.
18. Feldmeier and Spieckermann, *God Becoming Human*, 320, 322.

The tradition thus pointed indexically to this person as the site of the incarnation and maintained that "Jesus Christ" is untranslatable into categories of whatever kind, whether pertaining to characteristics of the historical Jesus of Nazareth or to conceptual abstractions. Any theology that calls itself Christian can only legitimate itself by pointing to Christ and by anchoring its interpretations in his singularity. It is the gesture that insists that it is here that God is to be found, "in, with, and under" Jesus's flesh, "unconfused, undivided, unchanged, unseparated," rather than attempting a translation into a specific *what*ness. And we have seen that once we reread Jesus's humanity as a particularity, it might quite quickly belong in the same category as his masculinity: a historical fact, undeniably, but in and of itself not more revelatory of the divine than other personal particulars. The singularity of Christ in that sense indeed entails an almost kenotic renunciation of any particularity that would make Jesus seem significant in and of himself or comparable to other historic figures.

The Incarnation's Anti-Particular Universality: "All Flesh"

Eponymous for the theological notion of "incarnation" is, of course, John's "the Word became flesh" (1:14). Interestingly, this pivotal text does not invoke humanity. Why then is the humanity of Christ the category that has traditionally been foregrounded in establishing the event's significance?

The Greek *sarx* and the Hebrew *basar* have both a wider and more specific meaning than "human." Neither reducible to a merely physical, material aspect of life, nor necessarily carrying a negative connotation (cf. Ezek 11:19; 36:26), *basar* typically refers to the psychosomatic unity of the creature in its finitude and transience.[19] This quality might be felt especially acutely by human beings, but it is not unique to humanity. While *basar* can metonymously stand for the human being, its use for nonhuman animals and even the totality of living creatures is well-documented (Gen 6:12, 13, 17; 7:21; 9:11–17; Num 18:15; Ps 136:25; Dan 4:9; Job 34:15). Similarly, *sarx* clearly ranges across the diversity of creaturely life (1 Cor 15:39–40). While it can be deployed in opposition to *pneuma*, it cannot be reduced to mere matter. Rather, it stands for existence within a "worldly" horizon, as marked by interdependence, vulnerability, and transience (1 Cor 7:28; 2 Cor 4:11; 7:5). While not in and of

19. Thorsten Klein, "Fleisch (NT)," in *WiBiLex: Das Wissenschaftliche Bibellexikon im Internet* (May 2017), https://www.bibelwissenschaft.de/stichwort/48865/, accessed July 1, 2021.

itself negative, *sarx* is thus also the aspect in which the creature is "chronically endangered" and "self-endangering" concern for self-preservation makes creatures notoriously vulnerable to hubris, self-dependence, and sin.[20]

Incarnation literally signifies the scandalous fact that the Logos enters this world of flesh. In the singular, concrete body of Jesus of Nazareth, it embraces the materiality, sociality, vulnerability, transience, and death that mark fleshly existence at large.[21] The incarnation's materiality has always been scandalous because it posits the revelation of God in that which is, according to received wisdom, most remote from being divine. It finds the transcendent in immanence, the eternal in a temporal existence, the infinite in very finite conditions, the omnipotent in vulnerability. What is scandalous is that God does not insist on "God-likeness" in counter-distinction and even opposition to God's creation. Who God really is thus reveals itself, kenotically, in the apparently "ungodlike" temporal, material, creaturely existence that the preexistent, transcendent, divine Logos makes its own.

This kenotic enfleshment has breathtaking implications. The creator overcomes the all-defining boundary and even the split between creator and creation as such, to become truly present in, with, and for the created world. Henceforth, nothing "will be able to separate us from the love of God" (Rom 8:38–39). Incarnation in the flesh signals redemption of all flesh. John can almost interchangeably speak of the Son coming into the "the world," indicating the realm of creation as a whole rather than a specific emphasis on humanity as such (cf. 3:16), and attest Christ's soteriological authority "over all flesh" (1:3; 17:2). Paul describes the whole creation as waiting for redemption in Christ (Rom 8:19–23) and envisions the *anakephalaiōsis* as "gather[ing] up all things in him, things in heaven and things on earth" (Eph 1:10). Christ promises new life to those who already belong to him, and eventually the whole "kingdom" and "all things," everything that would have been subject to death. Colossians paints Christ as "the firstborn of all creation . . . in whom all things hold together" and in whom God reconciled "all things, whether on earth or in heaven" (Col 1:15, 17, 20). Recognizing this cosmic horizon, Johnson thus discerns a promise of "deep resurrection" that extends to "every creature that passes through death."[22]

---

20. Cf. Michael Welker, "Was kann theologische Rede von Inkarnation und Auferstehung zur Anthropologie beitragen?," in *Verkoerperung als Paradigma theologischer Anthropologie*, ed. Gregor Etzelmüller and Annette Weissenrieder (Berlin: de Gruyter, 2016), 316–25.

21. Gregersen, "Extended Body," 225, 232.

22. Elizabeth Johnson, *Ask the Beasts: Darwin and the God of Love* (London: Bloomsbury, 2014), 209.

In Gregory Nazianzen's term, the Scriptures seem to imply all along that "creatureliness" rather than "humanity" has been assumed in Christ as they sketch "creation" rather than "the whole human being" as the scope of God's healing action. Might reading the incarnation as "God becoming human" instead of "God becoming flesh" be a similar miscalibration as earlier generations' talk about "men" instead of "humanity"? Pondering Neil Armstrong's leap, we earlier considered replacing "man" with "earthling" for added precision. If the Logos's "becoming flesh" is not *merely* about "humanity," then conceptually recalibrating the incarnation "as God stepping over the boundary between creator and creation and taking on creatureliness" would more adequately capture the extension and significance of the incarnational leap.[23] Pushing Ruether's provocative question further, we thus ask critically: *Can a human savior save the nonhuman creation?* Focusing narrowly on Jesus's humanity only obfuscates the scope, boundary, and relevance of the incarnation.

Against possible suspicions that "deep incarnation" leads to panentheism,[24] I want to state very clearly that recalibrating the incarnation this way is not necessarily any more panentheistic than the Chalcedonian formula has been all along. It continues to describe the same, singular act of the second person of the Trinity making the full creaturely existence of Jesus of Nazareth its own. The recalibration simply picks out "flesh" instead of "humanity" as the scale according to which one and the same "leap" is best measured.

The recalibration is also ethically significant. Instead of turning "true humanity" into a soteriological category and from there into a norm of right relationship, we might reflect on what embracing "true creatureliness" would look like. Many of the commitments traditionally treated under "true humanity" would retain their place—the relationship as a creature with one's creator, the embrace of one's own finitude, interdependence, and particularity as a creature—but we would additionally be challenged to envision relations of co-creatureliness with the beyond-human creation of which humans are part and parcel, rather than extend habitual anthropological supremacy.

While I am convinced that such a recalibration has important theological and ethical potential, we should also be cautious that, in exchanging one perceived universality for another, we are not just falling into a different

---

23. Clough, *Animals*, 103. A similar move is proposed by contemporary advocates of "deep incarnation."

24. This suspicion was confronted head-on by the main proponents of deep incarnation in the 2011 symposium "Is God Incarnate in All There Is?," whose proceedings were published as Gregersen, *Incarnation*.

misplaced concreteness. Any particular calibration is always in danger of reifying—and deifying—the respective particularity theologically, resulting in "a strangely blinkered underestimate of the scope and grandeur of God's creative and redemptive purposes" as well as problematic ethical consequences.[25] The cosmic horizon of the incarnation calls into question any proprietary claim under the name of human (or other) particulars. However, we also need to be cautious against reifying the "soteriological axiom" instead of the incarnation it was meant to interpret: starting from an *a priori* assumption that "all" *must* be saved, merely to discern the most comprehensive category imaginable to fulfill this definition. In other words, while we have shed light on the incarnation's scandalous singularity and materiality, we still need to gain more clarity about the incarnation's particularity.

The Particularity That Was Singular: "Imago Dei"?

Is there not, after all, a *particular* creature of *particular* interest to the creator? Is the incarnation not aimed at humanity in a special (if not altogether exclusive) way, as healing that *particular* split between God and that creature created in the image of God who wanted to be *more* and therefore became *less* than God's image? Such is obviously the most widespread account of the incarnation.

Indeed, the New Testament emphasizes that the incarnation overcomes the rift worked by sin, which finds its most intensive and extensive expression in the actions and attitudes of human beings, even as all of creation is seen as suffering under it.[26] And indeed, the Hebrew Bible speaks of the human being as created specifically and uniquely "in the image of God" (Gen 1:27). In an essential or relational interpretation of this *imago*, the tradition has typically insisted that the human being retained it after the fall, and that God becoming human in Christ redemptively opened the way for us to become true images of God once more.

25. Clough, *Animals*, 103.

26. For the "groaning of creation" for redemption, cf., e.g., Christopher Southgate, *The Groaning of Creation: God, Evolution, and the Problem of Evil* (Louisville: Westminster John Knox, 2008); Johnson, *Ask the Beasts*. For interdisciplinary research that challenges the assumption that sin is an exclusively human affair, cf. Clough, *Animals*, 105–30; Gregor Etzelmüller, "The Evolution of Sin," *Religion & Theology* 21 (2014): 107–24; Joshua M. Moritz, "Animal Suffering, Animal Sin, Theistic Evolution, and the Problem of Evil," in *Anticipating God's New Creation: Essays in Honor of Ted Peters*, ed. Carol Jacobson and Adam Pryor (Minneapolis: Lutheran University Press, 2015), 280–93.

But what if the *imago dei* was instead *the only thing* that was lost in the fall? If, as current exegetical scholarship widely agrees,[27] the image is not an essential quality of the human being, but rather a function, a role, a commission—of the vicarious presence in God's place on earth, attending to and preserving the goodness of God's creation—then the actuality of this presence and the capacity to fulfill that role were indeed impaired by sin. And what makes us so sure that the incarnation aims at *restoring that function*, which was never quite as central in biblical anthropology in any case? In the whole canon, only Genesis 1:26–27 and 9:6 refer to the human being as image of God, and the New Testament reserves that title for Christ (most prominently, 2 Cor 4:4; Col 1:15).

Reconsidering the scale of calibration allows us to consider that the incarnation might, in fact, signal God's gracious *taking away* humanity's responsibility for creation from humanity at large, and conferring it directly and exclusively upon Christ. Christ manifests God's presence on earth and preserves (even restores) the goodness of creation. Christ thus conclusively fulfills that function. Humanity is neither a condition nor the ontological realization of the *imago dei*, neither its boundary nor as such even its site. The *imago dei* then pertains to the incarnation's singularity rather than identifying its particular scope with humanity.

Indeed, a "most beloved creature,"[28] a distinct and distinguished addressee within creation, God's elect exists, and it is the *singular* person of Jesus Christ. Yes, Christ opens the door for Christ's creaturely siblings to become children of God in and through Christ. Other creatures may thus be enabled for participation in Christ as Christ's extended body—but the *imago dei* is mediated exclusively christologically, not anthropologically. It does not afford a theologically distinguished position of humanity *qua humanity*.

We remain convinced that the need for redemption is intensified among (yet surely not restricted to) *homo sapiens*. It also stands to reason that human writers would describe the significance of Jesus Christ in human terms. But is it conceivable that acclamations of Christ as "the light of all people" (John 1:4) or "mediator between God and humankind, Christ Jesus,

---

27. Feldmeier and Spieckermann, *God Becoming Human*, 12. Centuries of scholarship have been unable to find an essential quality that would clearly set the human being apart from the rest of creation (a delightful survey of candidates can be found in Clough, *Animals*, 63–65). Wentzel van Huyssteen thus ascertains a growing consensus on functional or relational interpretations; cf. *Alone in the World: Human Uniqueness in Science and Theology* (Göttingen: Vandenhoeck & Ruprecht, 2006), 128–32.

28. Feldmeier and Spieckermann, *God Becoming Human*, 367.

himself human" (1 Tim 2:5) would retain their meaning if we took them to be speaking about the recognition of the creator by the creature and the mediation of the divide between creator and creature? Even in talk about Christ as the "second Adam" (1 Cor 15; Rom 5:12–21), we might recognize that Adam is the proverbial, literal, and exemplary "earthling." Would our recalibration allow us to appreciate most biblical references to humanity as synecdoches for the incarnation's singular and universal significance, rather than its particular extension?

This Particularity That Is Not One—The Scandal of Particularity

Still, there is a particular horizon to which the incarnation "matters," a realm where it becomes *actually* effective historically. However, it is not humanity at large.

The Unparticular Particularity of "the People of God"

The category of "the people of God" that comes into view here is an important site of theological negotiation in the New Testament. Kinship metaphors serve to inscribe Jesus into a particular history of a particular people, and at the same time to mark transgressions of categorical boundaries rather than their reification. In short, they speak of election more than of anthropology.

The New Testament describes Jesus's particularity in terms that firmly locate him in the story of God with God's people, e.g., as son of David (Rom 1:3), descendant of Abraham (Heb 2:14–17), or descendant of Israel (Rom 9:5). The image of Sonship in particular links Jesus equally firmly to the Father *and* to the created order—often in one and the same breath—to mark a communicative effect. Paul talks about God sending "his Son, born of woman, born under the law, in order to redeem those who were under the law, so that we might receive adoption as children" (Gal 4:4–5). The point of the divine Son becoming "son of woman" is that it allows others to become his siblings, and thus, by extension, children of God (cf. Gal 3:26; 2 Cor 6:18; Rom 8:14). John similarly uses kinship language to carve out an extension of the incarnation into a community: "to all who received [Christ], who believed in his name, he gave power to become children of God" (John 1:12; cf. 1 John 3). The nearness of God in Christ is communicative. The singular radiates out and establishes a particular horizon of the incarnation, integrating those who belong to Christ into the history of God with God's people. It thus marks a reality that is presently distinct—particular—and yet gestures toward the eschatological, universal horizon where, ultimately, "all things" belong to Christ (John 17:2) and "what happens to the children of God now becomes, for the waiting creation, the ground of its own hope for redemption."[29]

Paul adopts the ancient image of the social body and transforms it christologically, signaling that, in a certain sense, "the incarnation of God in Christ continues in the community of those who believe in Christ."[30] God's singular incarnation in Christ that promises a universal reconciliation of "all things" already transformatively expands the body of Christ to the participation of other creatures. This body of Christ is obviously rather *more particular* than "humanity" at large: God's election, into which those who believe in Christ are adopted, is the realm in which God's closeness becomes communicatively and transformatively effective and efficient in history.

This body also has notoriously, scandalously indeterminate boundaries. The emergent community is not simply the universal horizon of the incarnation's reach, nor is it based on the particularities of Jesus's earthly existence. It is not constituted by a shared characteristic with him (whether calibrated in terms of shoe size, profession, gender, religion, species). If we look for fixed categories that define the horizon of particularity that engenders "the church" or "the people of God," we will be sorely disappointed. This horizon of particularity is surprisingly *un-particular*. In Galatians 3:26–29, Paul even emphatically declares the non-salience of any particulars as qualifiers of belonging or standing: "There is no longer Jew or Greek, there is no longer slave or free, there is no longer male and female; for all of you are one in Christ Jesus." In fact, negotiating the counter-intuitive de-particularization of this emergent community and the relativization of any boundary markers centrally characterizes Paul's work in his letters and the development of the early church according to Acts.

This intermediary horizon does not indulge those who are looking for a particularity in the sense of a particular property that could be turned into a possession. Those who inscribe themselves into this history orient themselves between two fixtures—the cosmic horizon of creation and the singularity of Christ—and negotiate their own strangely de-particularizing existence in between. Sharing in the "promise" for all flesh, and taking on the name of "Christ-ians" strips all their particulars of relevance or turns their meaning into its opposite (1 Cor 1:18–25), just as God's election has

29. Feldmeier and Spieckermann, *God Becoming Human*, 259.
30. Feldmeier and Spieckermann, *God Becoming Human*, 265.

tended to do throughout the story of Israel. This unparticular tendency of God is neither an erasure of difference nor necessarily an inversion of all hierarchies. Instead, it is the non-insistence on sameness as a condition of redemptive unity.

The Particularity of God: Essential Kenosis

Have we thus abolished all particularity in the incarnation? By no means! What we have called into question is the assumption that the particularity of the incarnation is definitively expressed in the "humanity" of Christ. Human beings and communities share in the promise of the children of God, and they share the creaturely transience and interdependence of "all flesh" with the rest of the nonhuman creation. But humanity defines neither the incarnation's *universal* horizon nor the *particular* extension of this story. As a category of reference, it says either too much or too little.

The particular horizon we *have* identified as engendered by the incarnation—the engendering of a "people" who participate in that union—is remarkably undistinguished by particularity, and even actively departicularizing. The incarnation's particularity does not come into play as a specific property of the flesh of Christ or of those who belong to him. Instead, it is signaled by the irreducible elements of the story of God's faithfulness to God's election, into which Jesus in his life, suffering, and resurrection is inscribed as God's servant, God's messiah, God's wisdom, God's word, and God's elect. If anything, then, one could describe this particularity as that of Jesus's *Jewish* flesh, and this is indeed the only particular "property" of Jesus that is of theological significance. Even so, this scandal of particularity is not primarily one of *Jesus's* fleshly particularity but one of *God's* particular character. It thus even exceeds the "Jewish flesh" (while never being separable from it)—and throws the story wide open for those who "belong to Christ"—that is, ultimately, "all things"—to participate in it.

The name of this particularity, which is the particularity of God's own being, is kenosis. We have already found its traces in the singularity and the universality of the incarnation. Now it is time to spell it out as the true scandal of particularity at work in the incarnation.

The Philippians hymn (Phil 2:6–11), most likely the earliest concise Christology,[31] describes a particular double movement: of self-emptying and

---

31. Cf. *Where Christology Began: Essays on Philippians 2*, ed. Ralph Martin (Louisville: Westminster John Knox, 1998).

humiliation from godlikeness to death on a cross, and of subsequent exaltation in cosmic authority under divine name. The poles of the movement are marked by the antithesis of "the form of God" and "the form of a slave." Even as the passage highlights Christ's humanity explicitly, it is clear that the point is not the particularity of the species, but the humility manifested in the incarnation: references to his human "likeness" (*homoiōma*) and "form" (*schēma*) are but the "factual side" of the "form of a slave" that reflects the "'quality' of his incarnation."[32] Indeed, Paul can equally use metaphors of impoverishment to describe the same movement: "though he was rich, yet for your sakes he became poor, so that by his poverty you might become rich" (2 Cor 8:9).

Put differently, the point the hymn is making is not about humanization but kenosis. The references to poverty, servanthood, death, and the cross mark something particular, but not the particularity of Jesus's humanity in and of itself. Rather, they mark the particularity of God—the particularity of God's self-giving love, manifested in the incarnation. Indeed, biblical scholars have stressed that the humility indicated in the hymn is *not* the renunciation of the Son's divinity, but its expression: "For in 'pouring himself out' and 'humbling himself to death on the cross,' Christ Jesus has revealed the character of God himself. Here is the epitome of God-likeness: the preexistent Christ was not a 'grasping, selfish' being, but one whose love for others found its consummate expression in 'pouring himself out.'"[33] Kenosis is precisely how Christ enacts his being "equal with God."

Kenosis, then, is not about "divestiture of something (whether divinity itself or some divine attributes)" nor about "self-limitation regarding the use of divine attributes."[34] Neither is it about the exchange of properties between different "natures." Kenosis is not even primarily about "humility" or "downward mobility"—although both will be its typical and recurrent expressions. Before it is any and all of these things, kenosis is about the "not regard[ing] equality with God as something to be exploited" (Phil 2:6b). This "mindset"—this quite particular "way of thinking, acting, and feeling"[35]—is what allows Christ to humble himself. Christ's insistence on the non-salience of sameness, and thus the non-

---

32. Gordon Fee, *Paul's Letter to the Philippians* (Grand Rapids: Eerdmans, 1995), 213.

33. Fee, *Philippians*, 197.

34. Michael Gorman, *Inhabiting the Cruciform God: Kenosis, Justification, and Theosis in Paul's Narrative Soteriology* (Grand Rapids: Eerdmans, 2009), 21.

35. Michael Gorman, *Becoming the Gospel: Paul, Participation, and Mission* (Grand Rapids: Eerdmans, 2015), 118.

limitation by particulars, allows for crossing over into, and uniting with his own being, that which is "different." This particularity is what makes incarnation into that which is not-God possible, and even essential to who God is: essential non-insistence on sameness, turned into active insistence on the non-salience of sameness, reconciles the irreconcilable. Kenosis is both the condition of possibility of unity across difference, and the resulting shape of the union described in incarnation, redemption, and communion.

This understanding of kenosis as primarily the insistence on the non-salience of sameness also clarifies why the second part of the hymn does not constitute a reversal but an extension of the same movement.[36] It does not describe Jesus's promotion to divine status, but "indicates that God has publicly vindicated and recognized Jesus's self-emptying and self-humbling as the display of true divinity that he already had."[37] Bruce McCormack has insightfully pointed out that, in giving God's name to the Son and withholding nothing in terms of power and authority, the hymn even reports "a kenosis of the Father."[38] Kenosis, then, is not a particular property of the Son alone; kenosis is the particularity of God: "God . . . is essentially kenotic."[39]

This realization exposes the mistake in looking for a particularity on the side of the incarnated flesh to explain or define the incarnation. Such a search rests on the assumption that the horizon of the incarnation needs a particularity to define its perimeter. But kenosis does not require a fixing of its horizon to become effective. Similarity or affinity on the side of the creature, shared experience and shared identity do not constitute its condition. Rather, God's kenotic disregard of God's own sameness creates the conditions of solidarity, creates the conditions of shared experience. Shared particularity and even shared identity are the effect of kenotic solidarity, not its presupposition.

The particularity of God in Christ *becomes* the particularity of those who are communities "in Christ." Kenosis communicates the particularity *that it is* to those it draws into its movement. Constituting solidarity by conviviality, it permits shared experience, which eventually even turns into shared identity "in Christ." The paraenetic context cannot be divorced from the hymn:

36. Gorman, *Inhabiting*, 32.
37. Gorman, *Inhabiting*, 28; cf. Fee, *Paul's Letter*, 196.
38. Bruce L. McCormack, *The Humility of the Eternal Son: Reformed Kenoticism and the Repair of Chalcedon* (Cambridge: Cambridge University Press, 2021), 207.
39. Gorman, *Inhabiting*, 28.

it is engendered by the kenotic movement that prompts kenotic concretions. A curious double exhortation can thus be discerned in the introductory verse 2:5: a direct prompt to take Christ's mind as one's own example, and an indirect one in which they build networks of examples for each other with each other.[40] This is a participation in the kenotic movement more than a particular *imitatio Christi*: it is the enactment of the very particularity by which one finds oneself constituted, not an ethical demand.[41] Indeed, focus on imitation might put undue focus on the particularities of Jesus's life—but what the Philippians (and we with them) are called to imitate is not the life of Jesus, but the "mindset" of Christ—essential kenosis. The result will be lived in a plurality and diversity of concretions in a proliferating network of lived examples of kenotic existence.[42]

We can thus now also make sense of the curious non-particularity of the communities that come into view as the particular horizon of the incarnation. Its de-particularizing effect forbids the reification of particularities into soteriological categories. In Christ, they are constituted by and participate in kenotic non-insistence on sameness that does not reify the boundaries of the community but acts to form shared experience. This non-particularity is an expression of their own particularity, as the particularity of the one to whom they belong. For those who become communities "in Christ," kenotic solidarity is not a denial of oneself and one's identity, but its exercise: their "becoming the gospel" as the social body of Christ.[43]

Kenosis as an Alternative to Becoming Human

The incarnation is not about humanity. It is not about becoming truly human. It is not even about true creatureliness. The incarnation is first and foremost an expression of who God is. God's essentially kenotic character does not insist on sameness. Instead, it insists on the non-salience of sameness—even that of divinity. This kenotic insistence of God is what becomes salvific, since it is what creates communion regardless of difference. The primary, most salient, and universally relevant unity achieved kenotically

---

40. Peter Wick, "'Ahmt Jesus Christus mit mir zusammen nach!' Imitatio Pauli und Imitatio Christi im Philipperbrief," in *Der Philipperbrief des Paulus in der Hellenistisch-Römischen Welt*, ed. Jörg Frey, Benjamin Schliesser, and Veronika Niederhofer (Tübingen: Mohr Siebeck, 2015), 313–14.

41. Wick, "'Ahmt Jesus Christus . . . nach!,'" 319.

42. Wick, "'Ahmt Jesus Christus . . . nach!,'" 316.

43. Cf. Gorman, *Inhabiting*, 23.

is the reconciliation of creator and creature in the person of Jesus Christ. All other differences are encompassed in this singularity, and they can be spelled out along the universal horizon of "all flesh." In the meantime, the category of the human can be safely relegated to a low-threshold biosocial status, because it bears little theological or moral weight.

The incarnation has a particular horizon, too, but it is not established by a particularity of the flesh of Jesus or of those who belong to him. The particularity of the incarnation is the kenotic *particularity of God* as manifest in Christ Jesus. Kenosis is essentially communicative, writing itself into and drawing out the history of God with God's people. It thus engenders communal realities that are presently distinct—particular—while being drawn into the same kenotic movement. Their notoriously, scandalously open boundaries do not point to a lack of particularity; rather, they express their particular, their essentially kenotic, character.

The particularity that is kenosis renders our search for the "right" calibration of the incarnation moot. The question is neither whether a male savior can save women nor whether a human savior can save the nonhuman (or *even* the human) creature. Of course, interpretive calibrations will always be necessary. They will have to be negotiated contextually between the singular and the cosmic horizon of the incarnation as kenotic concretions themselves. In all this, the insistence on the non-salience of sameness opens the way for communion that does not ask creatures for their passport. Belonging to Christ, Christ's kenotic particularity becomes our own. We too, then, do not have to compete for "true humanity." We, too, may then participate in the extension of intermediary horizons—networking solidarity with other creatures, human or otherwise. We, too, will not regard sameness as something to be grasped and exploited, and insist instead on its non-salience— until "all things" may be restored.

Epilogue

Kenosis as a Spiritual Practice

Kevin W. Hector

Bruce McCormack has recently argued that doctrines of kenosis tend to fall into two camps: *ontological* doctrines that aim to explain how the historical Jesus could be divine yet apparently lack certain divine attributes, and *ethical* doctrines that see kenosis as a description (and recommendation) of Jesus's way of life. The problem with these approaches, on McCormack's telling, is that both leave intact an understanding of divine nature that is incompatible with the lowliness involved in Jesus's human, all-too-human life: the onto-logical approach responds to this incompatibility by suggesting that the eter-nal Son temporarily emptied himself of certain divine attributes, whereas the ethical approach responds not by addressing these incompatibilities, but simply by shifting our focus to the exemplarity of Jesus's life. Over against these approaches, McCormack contends that an adequate doctrine of keno-sis must begin by rethinking these taken-for-granted understandings of the divine nature, for it is only in light of such rethinking that we can do justice to the fact that God remains immutable even in the act of self-emptying and, so, to the fact that God becomes incarnate precisely in the lowly, humble, all-too-human life of Jesus.

McCormack's own work on kenosis thus aims to rethink the theological ontology that has been taken for granted in most approaches to this doctrine. Interestingly, though, his work also opens up the possibility of rethinking the ethical approach to kenosis, for once we have revised our theological ontology, we can return to the latter sort of approach, not as a way of sidestepping ontology, but precisely as a way of working through its consequences. This paper sketches one such outworking, by considering what it might mean to treat kenosis as a spiritual practice—a practice, in other words, that is designed to transform our way of seeing and being in the world.

***

Before explaining what such a practice might look like, we first need to say a few words about "kenosis." As is well known, in the most basic sense kenosis means "emptying," though in the context of Philippians 2, such emptying is further characterized as a not-grasping or a letting-go. Importantly, this passage also emplots kenosis in a dramatic arc, in which a downward movement of emptying, not-grasping, and humbling is followed by an upward movement of being exalted—and thus filled—by God.[1] Even more importantly, Philippians 2:9 uses the word "therefore" (*dio*) to join these two movements, which suggests that the upward movement is a *consequence* of the downward—that is, that Jesus is exalted and filled by God *because* he emptied himself, humbled himself, and did not grasp for such exaltation. The implication, then, is that kenosis is a matter not just of emptying oneself, but of emptying oneself so that one can be filled by God. This is apparently the lesson that Paul means for the Philippians to draw, namely, that instead of trying to exalt themselves, they should let go of their attempts at self-exaltation in order to let themselves be exalted by God.

There is much more to be said about kenosis itself, of course, but let us suppose that it involves a sort of self-emptying for the sake of being filled, and, in particular, for the sake of being filled by God. If so, how might one put such kenosis into practice? Paul provides us with one crucial answer, namely, that we set aside our competitive, self-seeking desires vis-à-vis others. In this paper, however, I want to consider another answer, the inspiration for which comes from Simone Weil's notion of "attention." Weil characterizes attention in the following terms:

> Attention consists of suspending our thought, leaving it detached, empty, and ready to be penetrated by the object; it means holding in our minds, within reach of this thought, but on a lower level and in contact with it,

---

1. As is well known, this is an example of *katabasis* and *anabasis*; on this, see John Reumann, *Philippians: A New Translation with Introduction and Commentary*, Anchor Bible 33B (New Haven: Yale University Press, 2009), 334–35.

the diverse knowledge we have acquired which we are forced to make use of. Our thought should be in relation to all particular and already formulated thoughts, as a man on a mountain who, as he looks forward, sees also below him, without actually looking at them, a great many forests and plains. Above all, our thought should be empty, waiting, not seeking anything, but ready to receive in its naked truth the object that is to penetrate it.[2]

On Weil's account, then, one practices attention by letting go of one's preconceptions in order to let oneself be filled with the singular reality of a particular object. As Weil is quick to clarify, however, the letting-go in question is not a matter of emptying one's mind of all its concepts, but of holding one's concepts loosely, so to speak, by letting them be shaped and even selected by whatever it is to which one is attending. (Though Weil does not mention it, this procedure is relevantly similar to Friedrich Schleiermacher's "hermeneutical circle": in order to make sense of a text's parts, one must have some idea of the whole to which they contribute, but one must continually revise the latter in light of the former.)[3] At the most basic level, accordingly, to practice attention is to loosen the grip of one's preconceptions in order to see a particular object in all its particularity and, so, to let one's mind be filled with that object's peculiar reality.

To get a better sense of what Weil has in mind here, it might be helpful to consider the example of a poet like Marianne Moore.[4] Moore is justly famous for treating every creature as an entire world, filled with wonders; William Carlos Williams thus aptly remarked that, when reading her poems, "in looking at some apparently small object, one feels the swirl of great events."[5] We see a nice example of this in Moore's poem "The Jelly-Fish":

2. Simone Weil, "Reflection on the Right Use of School Studies with a View to the Love of God," in *Waiting for God*, trans. Emma Craufurd (New York: Putnam's Sons, 1951, 2009), 62.

3. For this, see Friedrich Schleiermacher, *Hermeneutics and Criticism and Other Writings*, ed. and trans. Andrew Bowie, Cambridge Texts in the History of Philosophy (Cambridge: Cambridge University Press, 1998), §20.1, 24.

4. Weil had no familiarity with Moore, as far as I know, but she does see poetry as exemplifying the sort of attention she has in mind; she thus claims, for instance, that "the poet produces the beautiful by fixing his attention on something real" (*Gravity and Grace*, trans. Emma Crawford and Mario von der Ruhr [London: Routledge, 1999], 119). Moore's poetry neatly instantiates exactly this sort of attention.

5. William Carlos Williams, "Marianne Moore," in *Selected Essays* (New York: Random House, 1954), 294.

Visible, invisible
A fluctuating charm,
An amber-colored amethyst
Inhabits it; your arm
Approaches, and
It opens and
It closes;
You have meant
To catch it,
And it shrivels;
You abandon
Your intent—
It opens, and it
Closes and you
Reach for it—
The blue
Surrounding it
Grows cloudy, and
It floats away
From you.[6]

Moore is here making use of ordinary concepts, but she does so in such a way that these concepts are selected and bent and refashioned for the sake of illuminating the singular reality of a singular encounter with a jellyfish. The poem is thus an act of attending to—and drawing our attention to—the latter's particular reality. The poem also intimates the elusiveness of this reality: as the reader reaches out to grasp the jellyfish, it pulls away; then, just when one has given up on catching it, the jellyfish gives another tantalizing glimpse of its splendor, thereby enticing one to reach for it again before it ... floats away. Here as elsewhere, then, Moore's poetry attends to particular creatures *as* the particular creatures they are, and in so doing evinces a sort of wonder at them. It is as if each poem says, *I caught a glimpse of this creature, and it is a marvel—this very creature, in all its ordinariness, is so extraordinary that it stretches my descriptive capacities to their breaking point.*

Poets are not the only ones who practice attention, of course; among many others, we see something similar in photographers, who train themselves to

6. Marianne Moore, "A Jelly-Fish," *The Lantern* 17 (Spring 1909): 110. Note that this is the longer version of Moore's poem; a shorter version was published as "A Jellyfish" in *O to Be a Dragon* (New York: Viking, 1959).

pay exacting attention to light and color and every intricacy of detail within a visual field. In so doing, many also train themselves to perceive that which is extraordinary in ordinary, everyday life. To take just one example, this is exactly what Yasumi Toyoda's "Super Ordinary" project aims to do, namely, to "notice more," as she likes to put it. One of the chief reasons that we do not notice more, of course, is that we have simply become used to seeing (and, so, not seeing) the things around us, which is why Toyoda's photography draws its material from the most anesthetizing, routinized aspect of her existence: the daily commute. Many of her photographs themselves are striking, but the most important feature of her work, for our purposes, is her practice of giving herself little projects, instructing herself to be on the lookout for certain phenomena within her surroundings. She thus sets out, for instance, to photograph (and so notice!) instances of a particular color such as yellow or mint green, or of seams and joints, or corners, or corrugation, or even peculiar objects like hoses or handpumps. By giving herself these assignments, she primes herself to notice these features within her surroundings; as a result, features that she would otherwise have hurried past are lit up with salience. She thus ends up noticing more and more of the things worth noticing in her daily life, which means, in turn, that she notices more and more of the richness and texture of her surroundings. (Think of what happens when she encounters a corner where yellow corrugated metal is joined to a flat, mint-green wall.) What is more, once one begins to give oneself assignments like this, it quickly becomes evident that there is no end, in principle, to the assignments one *could* give oneself; one could thus be on the lookout for droplets or spidery cracks or circles or sun-faded colors or literally any number of other things, each of which would equally merit one's notice. By giving oneself the task of noticing certain phenomena, then, one trains oneself to notice how many phenomena are worth noticing, which is to say that noticing can beget noticing. Hence, whereas poetry can teach us to let our concepts be bent and chosen by particular objects, a photographic project like Yasumi Toyoda's can loosen the grip of routine and, with it, our routinized *not*-noticing of the world around us. And in helping us see more of the richness of that world, photography can thereby enable us to see more of its wonders; in this connection, Toyoda is fond of quoting the Hungarian photographer, Brassaï: "If reality fails to fill us with wonder, it is because we have fallen into the habit of seeing it as ordinary."[7]

Examples aside, the point is that attention requires us to let go of the concepts and frameworks through which we ordinarily filter our surroundings,

---

7. Toyoda quotes this passage on her website, *Super Ordinary Life*, at superordinarylife.com/blog-1, accessed June 24, 2021.

so that we can open ourselves to the richness and peculiarity of the world around us. In attending to an object, in other words, one tries to empty oneself of one's preconceptions and predeterminations and then to let oneself be filled by the reality of the object itself. The echoes of kenosis here should already be apparent, though I will make the connection more explicit in due course.

* * *

With that, we can now consider a few ways in which such attention might count as a *spiritual* practice. First, as we have already seen, attention can open us up to wonder at our surroundings and, just so, train us not to take the world as a given but to experience more and more of it as creation. In our everyday lives, this is not how we experience our surroundings; we tend to experience the things around us either as part of our routine or as at our disposal, and thus end up taking them for granted and reducing them to what they are *for me*.[8] We thereby fail to appreciate the richness and goodness of the world around us, just as we fail to wonder at the fact of its existence.[9] As Augustine insists, we should constantly be amazed at God's creative work, yet "his miracles, by which he governs the whole world and administers all creation, have lost their impressiveness by constant repetition, so that almost no one deigns to notice the wondrous and stupendous works of God in any grain of seed."[10] The fact that a grain of seed grows into a tree or flower or blade of grass is astonishing, as is the growth of each leaf and each branch on the tree. Yet we are so used to seeing trees and flowers and grass and clouds and water and countless other wonders that we seldom even notice them, much less stand in awe of the one who created them. Attention can be a spiritual practice, then, insofar as it trains us to notice more of the world around us and, so, to appreciate more of its richness and wonder, for this is

8. So Rudolf Bultmann: "In my everyday work, in the use of my time, etc., I regard the world as at my own disposal. The world and my action in it are godless throughout. . . . But the concept of wonder radically negates the character of the world as the manageable world of everyday work" ("The Question of Wonder," in *Faith and Understanding* [New York: Harper & Row, 1969], 251, 255).

9. Karl Barth thus claims that "wonder occurs when someone encounters a spiritual or natural phenomenon that he has never met before. It is for the moment something uncommon, strange, and novel to him. He cannot even provisionally assign it a place in the previous circle of his ideas about the possible" (*Evangelical Theology* [Grand Rapids: Eerdmans, 1963, 1979], 64).

10. Augustine, Tractate 24 (on John 6:1–14), *Tractates on the Gospel of John, 11–27*, trans. John Rettig (Washington, DC: Catholic University of America Press, 1988), 1.1, 231.

part of what it would mean to treat the world as created. Insofar as attention trains us to experience the world in these ways, accordingly, it is part of what I have termed a *practical* doctrine of creation: a doctrine of creation, that is, that focuses on the dispositions that one would have to cultivate in order to respond to the world as the creation of a loving God. After all, if one believes, with the angels in Isaiah 6:3, that the whole earth is filled with God's glory, then one must not only assent to the truth of that belief, but actually *see* the world as so filled. The practice of attention can help us do just that.

To be sure, the mere fact that one attends carefully to something does not mean that one will wonder at it; after all, sometimes the act of photographing something is an attempt to domesticate it—we thus speak, tellingly, of using a camera to "capture" an image or a moment. What must be added to mere attention, then, so that it will cultivate in us a sense of wonder and appreciation? Sometimes, nothing: we are simply stopped in our tracks by some phenomenon, taken by surprise, arrested by it. (I cannot help but react this way upon seeing a deer, for instance, no matter how many times they cross my path.) In such cases, we cannot help but wonder; then our job is simply to linger in that wonder, to let it sink in, and, just so, to do justice to whatever wondrous thing we have beheld. In most cases, however, we will spot that which is wondrous about the world around us only if we have put ourselves on the lookout for it. To see how this works, consider an instance where someone calls my attention to something by saying, "Oh, wow, look what's behind you." In that case, when I turn to look behind me, I will be primed to see something *as* wow-worthy. To be sure, I may zero in on something other than what which my interlocutor was calling to my attention: they may have been reacting in wonder to a brilliantly colored goldfinch, for instance, whereas I may so react to the shagbark hickory on which it is perched. The point is that if I am primed to perceive something wondrous—to perceive something *as* wondrous—then I will be much more likely to do so. The key to perceiving the world around us with a sense of wonder, then, is to prime ourselves to do so, which is to say that we will be much more likely to experience wonder if we are expecting to. This means, in turn, that wonder tends to beget wonder, for the more we are on the lookout for things that are wondrous, the more we will not only perceive things as wondrous, but the more disposed we will become to perceive them as such and, so, to treat the world not as given but as creation.[11] By training us to

11. John Calvin puts this nicely: "There is no doubt," he insists, "that the Lord would have us uninterruptedly occupied in this holy meditation; that, while we contemplate in

notice more of the wonders around us, accordingly, attention can function as a spiritual practice.

That brings us to a second respect in which attention is a spiritual practice: the better we get at attending in this way to the world around us, the better we will get at contemplating God, both because we are better at contemplating per se, and because we are seeing more and more of God's glory. Weil makes the former point explicit in her theology of education: "The key to a Christian conception of studies is the realization that prayer consists of attention. It is the orientation of all the attention of which the soul is capable toward God. . . . Of course school exercises only develop a lower kind of attention. Nevertheless, they are extremely effective in increasing the power of attention that will be available at the time of prayer."[12] By disciplining one's powers of attention, one becomes capable of attending more fully to objects, which means, in turn, that one becomes capable of attending more fully to God. As Sarah Coakley has pointed out, contemplative prayer requires considerable discipline, not least because we are so easily distracted.[13] Coakley's own approach to distraction focuses on the practice of contemplative prayer itself, but it stands to reason that if we practice attention in our everyday lives, we will better be able to pay attention when we turn to God. After all, once we have learned to attend well to one thing, we have a better idea of what it looks like to do so and how to go about doing it, not to mention an improved capacity for focusing our sustained attention on something. By getting better at attending to the world around us, accordingly, we can develop some skills and dispositions that will help us attend better to God.

In attending to the world around us, we can also expect to see more and more of its beauty and, in turn, more and more of *God's* beauty. The logic here goes something like this: (a) the world around us is filled with beauty;

---

all creatures, as in mirrors, those immense riches of his wisdom, justice, goodness, and power, we should not merely run over them cursorily, so to speak, with a fleeting glance; but we should ponder them at length, turn them over in our minds seriously and faithfully, and recollect them repeatedly. . . . Therefore, to be brief, let all readers know that they have with true faith apprehended what it is for God to be Creator of heaven and earth, if they first of all follow the universal rule, not to pass over in ungrateful thoughtlessness or forgetfulness those conspicuous powers which God shows forth in his creatures, and then learn so to apply it to themselves that their very hearts are touched," in *Institutes of the Christian Religion*, ed. John T. McNeill, trans. Ford Lewis Battles, Library of Christian Classics (Philadelphia: Westminster, 1960), 1.14.21.

12. Weil, "Right Use," 57.

13. On this point, see Rupert Shortt's interview with Sarah Coakley in *God's Advocates: Christian Thinkers in Conversation* (Grand Rapids: Eerdmans, 2005), 67–85.

(b) if God is infinitely beautiful, then the world's beauty must be included in and an expression of God's own beauty, rather than outside that beauty;[14] (c) beauty is such that, as soon as we notice it, we want to linger on it and contemplate it; (d) as we contemplate the beauty of the world around us, we are simultaneously contemplating God's beauty, whether we realize it or not. When I behold the sun setting over the ocean, lighting up the sky with bands of pink and purple, I cannot help but watch; I am transfixed; I want to take in as much of that moment as I can. The argument here is not simply that we should be similarly transfixed by the splendor of God, though that is surely true. Rather, the argument is that God's splendor is infinite and, so, that all creaturely beauty is a reflection of God's own beauty. In beholding the former, accordingly, our sense of the latter should be stretched and en-riched. If so, then attention turns out to be a kenotic practice in two further respects. On the one hand, if attention is a way of emptying ourselves in order to be filled with more and more of God's beauty, and if God's beauty is an aspect of (or maybe even equivalent with) God's glory, then it follows that the practice of attention follows precisely the logic of Philippians 2: we empty ourselves in this way in order to be filled by God. On the other hand, to be so filled is already to be exalted by God, for the more we take in of God's glory, the more we emulate and are conformed to the Son of God who eternally beholds and delights in the glory of God the Father—we are thereby lifted up, in other words, to receive a share in the self-knowledge and self-delight that characterize the very triune life of God, which is to say, again, that we are thereby exalted.[15] Attention thus turns out to be a practice of kenosis in a material, and not only a formal, sense.

***

Before proceeding, I need to address a question that may occur to some readers: Does this account entail that poets and photographers and scientists and countless others are practicing kenosis? And that they are being filled with God's glory? To address this question, we need to emphasize a crucial

14. The logic here echoes that of Spinoza (*Ethics*, part 1, especially def. 6 and prop. 16) as reworked by Schleiermacher (especially in his second *Speech*). I elaborate this logic a bit further below, as well as in chapter 3 of *Theological Project of Modernism: Faith and the Conditions of Mineness*, Oxford Studies in Analytic Theology (Oxford: Oxford University Press, 2015), 75–125.

15. Here I am intentionally echoing Karl Barth, especially *Church Dogmatics* II/1, ed. G. W. Bromiley and T. F. Torrance, trans. T. H. L. Parker et al. (Edinburgh: T&T Clark, 1957), 67–75.

point: in order to contribute to a practical doctrine of creation, what matters is not simply that one engages in practices of attention, but that these practices cultivate (and are expressions of) particular *dispositions*, especially the disposition to *appreciate* or *wonder at* the world. There is a vital difference, after all, between a person who observes an ant colony simply in order to chart its various branches, circumstance-responsive changes, etc., and someone who does these things with a sense of how interesting or impressive or mind-boggling or well-designed or beautiful it is. Insofar as practices of attention cultivate and are expressions of the latter sensibilities, then they, too, dispose one to treat the world as God's creation, and just so contribute to what I am calling a practical doctrine of creation.

And while I cannot do justice to the point here, I would argue that they can so contribute even if the person practicing them does not realize that they are doing so. We could defend the point by appealing to an externalist account of reference, but for now I will simply offer an analogy. Suppose a picture that my daughter has painted, or a robot she has built, is on display somewhere, and that the people looking at it are admiring its use of light, marveling at its design, or whatever. Even if they mistakenly think the painting and robot were created by one of her teachers—or if they have no thought whatsoever about who created them—they are still appreciating and wondering at her creations, and their doing so redounds to her praise even if they themselves are not in position to realize it. And while it would surely be better if they knew who the creator was and so rightly directed their admiration to her, it does not change the fact that they are admiring *her creation* all the same. I would say the same of practices of attention: so long as they cultivate and are expressions of a sense of appreciation for and wonder at the world, they train one to treat the world as God's creation. Better still, of course, if their practitioners could not only treat but also recognize it as such; yet these practices can contribute to a practical doctrine of creation even absent such recognition.

***

That brings us to one further, and altogether vital, respect in which attention can be a spiritual practice: it trains us not only to see the world around us differently, but to see other people differently, too. Here especially, we can do so only if we hold our preconceptions loosely, for unless we do so, we are liable to see a distorted picture of another's reality. As Kierkegaard puts it, "When it is a duty in loving to love the people we see, *then in loving the actual individual person it is important that one does not substitute an imaginary idea of how we think or could wish that this person should be.* The person who does this does not love the person he sees but again something unseen, his own idea or something similar."[16] Hence, if we see someone in light of concepts we associate with certain groups, for instance, and if these concepts are either distorting or unresponsive to that person's particularity, then we will have a hard time (at best) getting to know them as they are and, so, loving them in their own right. (To wit: I see someone wearing fancy clothes and so assume that they are a rich person, and I associate "rich person" with snobbiness, insensitivity to the plight of others, being entitled, etc. If the latter associations make it harder for me to see the ways this person does not fit with my concept of them, then my concept gets in the way of seeing them for who they are.)

So how do we see others in their particular reality? If, following the theological tradition, we identify their fundamental reality as the image of God, then it is by looking for that image that we open ourselves to their reality. To be sure, there is more than one way of thinking about how humanity bears God's image. Some theologians have claimed that we reflect God's image insofar as we are rational; others, insofar as we are inherently relational; still others insofar as we exercise dominion over the world. The mere fact that a person is rational, relational, or in charge does not mean that they bear much resemblance to God, however; after all, a CEO who exploits their employees in order to maximize profits exhibits all three traits but does not thereby resemble God. What is missing from these accounts, arguably, is God's *character*: to bear God's image is not simply to reflect certain formal traits such as rationality, relationality, or dominion, but material traits such as wisdom, justice, love, mercy, creativity, and the like. There is a reason why traditional accounts have focused on formal rather than material traits, of course, namely, the fact that we are sinful and so, apparently, have defaced our material likeness to God; in Athanasius's famous analogy, humanity is thus like a painted portrait that has become covered with stains and, in consequence, no longer bears a clear likeness to the portrait's original subject.[17] This does not mean, however, that we no longer bear *any* likeness to God's character; it means, rather, that the image of God is, properly speaking, an eschatological notion: only in the consummation of all things, and as a

16. Søren Kierkegaard, *Works of Love*, ed. and trans. Howard V. Hong and Edna H. Hong (Princeton: Princeton University Press, 1995), 9.156, 164.

17. Athanasius, *On the Incarnation of the Word*, §14.1.

crucial aspect of that consummation, will we truly bear God's likeness.[18] This means, on the one hand, that no matter how bad or ungodly a person presently is, this badness cannot be thought to define them, for the simple reason that there always remains an eschatological hope that they will be restored to God's likeness. On the other hand, because eschatological fulfillment stands in continuity as well as discontinuity with the present—as I argue elsewhere[19]—then it stands to reason that we can already be on the lookout for foretastes of this fulfillment. Such "being on the lookout" is what attention looks like when it comes to other persons.

Here is one way of thinking about what such attention might look like. If God's character is infinitely good, then there are infinite ways that it *can* be reflected—and since it is infinitely good, there are infinite ways that it *should* be reflected, since that is what it would mean for all creation to be filled with God's glory. If so, then it stands to reason that each human being is meant to reflect God's goodness in their own, unique way—not only because they are meant to reflect this goodness in response to unique circumstances, but because they are to do so in a way that bears the stamp of their individuality. Simply stated, then, to look for the image of God in others would be to look for glimpses of the way they are meant to reflect God's goodness. We see a helpful analogue of this in the way good parents and teachers often interact with children: they are actively on the lookout for signs of goodness and promise in kids—signs of talent and good character, as well as signs of their values, interests, peculiarities, and even the "projects" that might have their name written on them—and may then encourage children to see these things in themselves and, indeed, to grow into them. Parents and teachers thus see children with a sort of proleptic, prophetic vision. To look for the image of God in others is to do much the same thing.

To look for the image of God in others thus means that we should assume that each person is meant to embody that image and, so, to be on the lookout

---

18. This seems to be what Calvin has in mind, for instance, in the following passage: "even though we grant," he writes, "that God's image was not totally annihilated and destroyed in him [i.e., Adam], yet it was so corrupted that whatever remains is frightful deformity. Consequently, the beginning of our recovery of salvation is in that restoration which we obtain through Christ, who also is called the Second Adam for the reason that he restores us to true and complete integrity. . . . The end of regeneration," accordingly, "is that Christ should reform us to God's image" (*Institutes* 1.15.4).

19. I argue this in "Eternal Fulfillment: Some Thoughts on the Afterlife," *Journal of Religion* 101, no. 1 (2021): 8–26; and in chapter 7 of *Christianity as a Way of Life: A Systematic Theology* (New Haven: Yale University Press, forthcoming).

for the way that they do so.[20] To cite just one precedent, we hear something along these lines in Friedrich Schleiermacher's influential "phenomenology of the Infinite."[21] Schleiermacher there argues that we first apprehend the Infinite—which was his then-preferred name for God—by coming to see other persons as unique and irreplaceable expressions of Humanity; we recognize, that is, that each person contributes something particular to the full expression of Humanity and, so, that Humanity would be lacking something without that expression. Schleiermacher likewise claims that the particular expression of each contributes to the Humanity that can be taken up and expressed by others, from which it follows that every such expression is a microcosm of Humanity and that the Humanity of each is constantly enriching the Humanity of all (and vice versa). Humanity itself is thus a microcosm of the Infinite, as is each individual human, though Schleiermacher hastens to point out that Humanity is not *the* Infinite. For our purposes, the key point here is that one should always be on the lookout for the ways that the Infinite is expressed in others and, if possible, one should contribute something to that expression. Insofar as one does so, one will be more open to the way someone bears the image of God and, so, to their fundamental reality (assuming, with the tradition, that these coincide).

The more we see the image of God in others, moreover, the more disposed we will be to look for it and the better we will be at spotting it; just as an experienced birdwatcher will notice more and more birds in their surroundings, and more and more varieties among these birds, so a person who looks for the image of God in others will come to see it in more and more of the people around them and, in turn, see more and more of the richness and endless variation with which this image can be expressed. One who

20. It also means that we can never simply identify someone with whatever is worst about them, much less that we would be on the lookout for that which is worst about them, for no matter how bad they may be, we can still reasonably hope that they will reflect God's image as they were intended to. Think here, again, of the hermeneutical circle: if I am watching a movie in which I know there is a Big Twist, I will assume that characters may not be what they seem, for the simple reason that they may turn out very differently once the twist has been revealed. We can do something similar when we encounter people in real life: if I know that someone is meant to bear the image of God, then irrespective of how awful they seem, I should hold off on making any final judgments about them, since I know that they may turn out very differently in the end. Negatively, then, looking for the image of God in others thus means that we should resist the urge to identify people with that which is worst about them.

21. Here I am tracing some of the steps in Schleiermacher's second *Speech*; for further elaboration, see Hector, *Theological Project of Modernism*, 75–125.

sees more of this richness and variety will thereby see more and more of God's infinite goodness, which is to say that they will see more and more of God's glory—and, by the logic just traced, be *filled* with more and more of God's glory, since the goodness one perceives in others opens up possibilities for one's own expression of that goodness. Here again, then, *kenosis* (in the form of attending to the image of God in others) leads to *exaltation* (as we are increasingly filled with God's glory and goodness).

***

In this epilogue, I have briefly considered one practical approach to the doctrine of kenosis, in the form of "attention." Such attention, I have argued, can train us to wonder at the world around us and, so, experience it as creation; it can likewise train us to attend more fully to God, even as it enables us to perceive more and more of God's beauty in the world around us. Attention can also train us to look for the image of God in others, which can help us see more and more of God's image and so, again, see more and more of God's glory. In all of these ways, accordingly, we empty ourselves before the reality of others in order to be filled with God's glory and thereby be exalted. Kenosis, in the form of attention, can thus be a spiritual practice.[22]

---

22. At the outset of this paper, I noted that Bruce McCormack's groundbreaking work on kenosis paved the way for this paper. In closing, I want to mention one further respect in which he paved the way. The sort of exacting attention to others that I discuss here is something that I learned from him more than from anyone else. Indeed, it was in his class on Schleiermacher that I first realized just how important it was to loosen up my preconceptions and attend to a figure in their own right. That is how he approached everyone we read together, and it is also how he approached students: he wanted to help us develop our own voices and our own insights, and he was constantly on the lookout for ways that he could encourage us to do so. There is a much deeper sense, then, in which Bruce McCormack paved the way for this essay, just as he paved the way for all of my work as a teacher and theologian. I am grateful, then, to have a friend and mentor who so beautifully embodied the sort of kenotic practice I have been talking about in this essay. I hope that this self-emptying on his part is met by the promised fullness and exaltation of God.

Contributors

John M. G. Barclay is the Lightfoot Professor of Divinity at Durham University.

Matthew J. Aragon Bruce taught most recently at Calvin University, Western Theological Seminary, and Wheaton College.

David Fergusson is Regius Professor of Divinity at the University of Cambridge.

Beverly Roberts Gaventa is Helen H. P. Manson Professor of New Testament Literature and Exegesis Emerita at Princeton Theological Seminary.

Kevin W. Hector is professor of theology and of the philosophy of religions at the University of Chicago.

Keith L. Johnson is professor of theology at Wheaton College.

Cambria Kaltwasser is assistant professor of biblical and theological studies at Northwestern College.

Han-luen Kantzer Komline is associate professor of church history and theology at Western Theological Seminary.

Grant Macaskill is Kirby Laing Chair of New Testament Exegesis at the University of Aberdeen.

John A. McGuckin is the Nielsen Professor Emeritus of Early Church History at Union Theological Seminary and Emeritus Professor of Byzantine Christian Studies at Columbia University; he is currently a member of the Faculty of Theology and Religion at Oxford University.

Paul T. Nimmo is King's Professor of Systematic Theology at the University of Aberdeen.

Georg Pfleiderer is professor of systematic theology/ethics at the University of Basel.

Rinse H. Reeling Brouwer was formerly the Miskotte/Breukelman Chair for Theological Hermeneutics of the Bible and senior lecturer in the history of Christian doctrine at the Protestant Theological University.

Hanna Reichel is associate professor of Reformed theology at Princeton Theological Seminary.

Christoph Schwöbel was, until his untimely passing in September 2021, professor of systematic theology at the University of St. Andrews.

Katherine Sonderegger is William Meade Chair in Systematic Theology at Virginia Theological Seminary.

Thomas Joseph White, OP, is rector of the Pontifical University of St. Thomas (Angelicum) in Rome.

Index of Names and Subjects

Index of Scripture

Jeremiah		18:9–14	165	1:26	32, 34
31:31–34	69	22:42	192	1:28	32, 34
				3:9	36
Daniel		**John**		3:9–18	33
4:9	297	1:1	84, 148, 273	3:21–26	33, 38
		1:3	145, 256	3:24	37
Joel		1:12	302	4:14	16
3:5	10	1:14	84, 94, 104, 109,	4:17	28
			145, 273, 297	4:20–21	28
Malachi		1:17	63	4:24	37
4:4–6	62	3:6	84	4:25	37
		5:17	148	5:1–11	38
NEW TESTAMENT		8:58	49	5:12	39
		13:23	82	5:12–21	13, 38, 302
Matthew		14:28	105, 112	5:14	36
1:18	85	14:30	89	5:17	36
2:8–9	89	15:15	244	6:4	29, 37
2:13	89	16:28	111	6:9	36
3:17	94	17:2	302	6:9–10	38
13:36	83	17:5	94, 156	6:12	36
16:27–28	91	19:36	64	6:14	36
17:1–8	90			6:18	36
17:14–15	91	**Acts**		6:23	36
18:14	89	2:3	149	7:12	38
19:14	89			7:12–14	36
27:46	192	**Romans**		7:24	38
		1:3	39, 302	8:2	38, 63
Mark		1:3–4	31	8:3	38–39
1:13	74	1:4	24, 27, 31, 40	8:7–8	29
9:1–8	90	1:7	37	8:9–11	35
12:29	65	1:15	40	8:15–17	282
13:32	117	1:16	31, 40	8:18	34
15:34	192	1:16–17	27, 33	8:19–23	10
		1:18	33, 38	8:21	12
Luke		1:20	28	8:29	39
1:38	84	1:21	28	8:31	31, 295
9:28–36	90	1:24	32, 34	8:31–32	15
12:49	149	1:25	28	8:31–39	35